Quantitative Global Bond Portfolio Management

Quantitative Global Bond Portfolio Management

Gueorgui S. Konstantinov
Finance Resolution, Germany

Frank J. Fabozzi
Johns Hopkins University, USA

Joseph S. Simonian
Autonomous Investment Technologies, USA

World Scientific

NEW JERSEY • LONDON • SINGAPORE • BEIJING • SHANGHAI • HONG KONG • TAIPEI • CHENNAI • TOKYO

Published by

World Scientific Publishing Co. Pte. Ltd.
5 Toh Tuck Link, Singapore 596224
USA office: 27 Warren Street, Suite 401-402, Hackensack, NJ 07601
UK office: 57 Shelton Street, Covent Garden, London WC2H 9HE

Library of Congress Cataloging-in-Publication Data
Names: Konstantinov, Gueorgui S., 1977– author. | Fabozzi, Frank J., 1948– author. |
Simonian, Joseph S., 1975– author.
Title: Quantitative global bond portfolio management / Gueorgui S Konstantinov,
Finance Resolution, Germany, Frank J Fabozzi, Johns Hopkins University, USA,
Joseph S Simonian, Autonomous Investment Technologies, USA.
Description: New Jersey : World Scientific, [2024] | Includes bibliographical references and index.
Identifiers: LCCN 2023008260 | ISBN 9789811272561 (hardcover) |
ISBN 9789811272578 (ebook) | ISBN 9789811272585 (ebook other)
Subjects: LCSH: Portfolio management. | Asset allocation. | Bonds.
Classification: LCC HG4529.5 .K66 2024 | DDC 332.6--dc23/eng/20230316
LC record available at https://lccn.loc.gov/2023008260

British Library Cataloguing-in-Publication Data
A catalogue record for this book is available from the British Library.

For any available supplementary material, please visit
https://www.worldscientific.com/worldscibooks/10.1142/13313#t=suppl

Desk Editors: Balasubramanian Shanmugam/Pui Yee Lum

Typeset by Stallion Press
Email: enquiries@stallionpress.com

To my son, Stefan

—Gueorgui Konstantinov

To the memory of my sister, Lucy

—Frank J. Fabozzi

To Karina, Joe, and Mike

—Joseph Simonian

Preface

Quantitative Global Bond Portfolio Management covers quantitative approaches to global bond and currency portfolio management and their applications to alpha generation and risk management. Drawing on practitioner and academic research, as well as the experience of the authors, the book provides a timely overview of cutting-edge tools that are applied to managing global bond portfolios. In addition to providing a solid theoretical foundation for global bond portfolio management, we focus on the practical implementation of yield curve and currency-driven approaches that can be successfully implemented in real-world global bond portfolios.

Covering a wide range of applications that are of interest to both practitioners and academics, we guide the reader by first developing a sound theoretical framework and then provide practical illustrations of how bonds and currencies are managed in actual portfolios. A major objective is to shed light on the problems faced by practitioners in portfolio optimization, bond trading, risk management, portfolio rebalancing, and performance measurement. Potential solutions to these problems are provided.

The target readership for this book includes portfolio managers, analysts, researchers, and academics who desire to expand their understanding of investment theory and gain knowledge of practical solutions to various problems in global bond portfolio management. In particular, in this work, we aim to provide institutional portfolio managers with an integrated framework to implement modern bond and currency investing concepts.

Central Themes

Quantitative Global Bond Portfolio Management contains 12 chapters divided into three parts. Part 1, Chapters 1–4, covers the global bond markets, benchmarks, and various approaches to yield curve and currency management. Coverage in Chapters 5–9, Part 2 of the book, includes portfolio and risk management. In Part 3, Chapters 10–12, we turn our attention to performance measurement and the performance evaluation of global bond portfolios.

Chapter 1 covers the role of quantitative management of global bond investing. Specifically, we provide a discussion of risk-and-return in global bond markets. The most important risk-and-return drivers in global bond markets are explained. Chapter 2 explains how global bond markets are structured and represented by various indices and factors. As we explain, currencies and currency exposure are important considerations when managing global bond portfolios. Chapter 3 is devoted to currency management. We show how expected currency returns and currency risk can be managed in a global bond portfolio using quantitative techniques. Yield curve management, the subject of Chapter 4, offers a broad view of how yield curves are estimated and how expected returns are derived. As we demonstrate, yield curve management is the cornerstone of managing global bond portfolios as yield curves can be used to gauge information about bond pricing determinants as they relate to country, sector, currency, and rating.

In Chapter 5, we show which factors are important for global bond portfolios and provide an explanation of how these factors can be derived and constructed using available data. Fundamental optimization models for top-down optimization for currencies and bonds are covered in Chapter 6 where we offer practical solutions and illustrations for asset class optimization. Chapter 7 provides a detailed explanation of bottom-up bond selection optimizations where we provide examples for emerging markets and global unconstrained bond portfolios. Tools for implementing bottom-up currency and country selection are provided. Chapter 8 presents an overview of portfolio rebalancing and trade execution. We also highlight the role of electronic exchanges. The objective of Chapter 9 is to describe and illustrate basic approaches to risk management as well as describing practical solutions that can help facilitate successful risk management in global bond portfolios. Specifically, we highlight currency and bond hedging and explain how currency and bond portfolio overlay strategies can be used.

Chapter 10 offers an overview of factor models, their economic meaning, and the issues associated with implementing them in global bond portfolios. Contemporary approaches to performance evaluation are the subject of Chapter 11. The aim of the chapter is to show how alpha and beta are measured and how to calculate the potential rate of return of a portfolio. In addition, we demonstrate how the time-varying exposure to factors is measured. The purpose of Chapter 12 is to provide a framework for and practical applications of currency and yield curve-based performance attribution. Real-world examples of global bond portfolios are used to illustrate the intuition behind return decomposition for bonds and currencies.

The Audience for this Book

The intended audience for this book includes portfolio managers, chief investment officers, consultants, researchers/analysts, investors (asset owners), sales managers, and academic researchers.

For portfolio managers, the book provides insights into a holistic approach to quantitative global bond portfolio management including risk analysis and control, portfolio optimization, and performance analysis. Specifically, we provide portfolio managers with a comprehensive guide that covers an array of quantitative techniques for yield curve and currency management.

Chief investment officers (CIOs) interested in expanding the role of global bond portfolios within their organizations and understanding the investment, legal, and operational risks of these portfolios and how portfolio managers can apply quantitative management will benefit from reading this book. The topics covered in this book go far beyond that of performance measurement and analysis and should be helpful for CIOs to better understand and evaluate their global bond portfolio management team.

Consultants need to be capable of analyzing and investigating the investment process of global bond portfolio managers. Consultants can use the information in this book for evaluating the merits of both quantitative and traditional (fundamental) bond portfolio managers. Moreover, consultants will find that this book can broaden their knowledge of portfolio management tools that are less well-known to investors and prospective clients.

Researchers/analysts seeking to expand their knowledge of the risks associated with global bond portfolios will find the coverage of this book useful. We believe researchers/analysts might especially benefit from our discussion of how factors can be constructed and implemented in portfolio management.

Investors (asset owners) should understand the process by which global bond portfolios are constructed and the risk attributes of portfolios for the purpose of fund selection. Investors will benefit by gaining an understanding of the drivers of return and risk and how portfolio managers apply various analytical tools to generate alpha.

A sales manager needs to be able to explain to existing and potential clients how their firm's asset management team performed and how the team added value. This requires a deep understanding of the risk–return profile of global bond portfolios, how global bonds portfolios are managed, and how investors might benefit from adding global bond portfolios to their fund line-up.

Finally, academic researchers need to understand how models are applied in practice, the various way that portfolio managers add value, and how practitioners deal with the challenges of theoretical models in actual portfolios. This book covers all of these topics, as well as providing practical examples that provide insightful information on factor models, bond trading, and optimization. We believe that the approach taken in this book presents a unique take on global bond portfolio management, blending academic rigor with practical utility in a manner that is not found in the majority of investment textbooks.

About the Authors

Gueorgui S. Konstantinov is an independent consultant. Over 17+ years, he held senior portfolio manager roles at several asset management companies, where he managed global bond portfolios and currencies for institutional investors and pension funds. He is an advisory board member of *The Journal of Portfolio Management* and an editorial board member of *The Journal of Alternative Investments*. He earned the designations of Chartered Alternative Investments Analyst (CAIA) and Financial Data Professional (FDP). He received his MA in economics in 2005 and received a doctoral degree in 2008 from Vienna University of Economics and Business Administration (WU).

Frank J. Fabozzi is Editor of *The Journal of Portfolio Management* and Co-Editor/Co-Founder of *The Journal of Financial Data Science*. He is a Professor of Practice at the Johns Hopkins Carey Business School. Over the past 45 years, he has held professorial positions at MIT, Yale, Princeton, EDHEC Business School, New York University, Carnegie Mellon, and Rutgers. He is a trustee of the BlackRock closed-end fund complex. Dr. Fabozzi is the CFA Institute's 2007 recipient of the C. Stewart Sheppard Award and the CFA Institute's 2015 recipient of the James R. Vertin Award. He was inducted into the Fixed Income Analysts Society Hall of Fame in November 2002. He earned the designations of Chartered Financial Analyst (CFA) and Certified Public Accountant (CPA). He received his B.A. and M.A. in economics in 1970 from the City College of New York where he was elected to Phi Beta Kappa. He received his Ph.D. in economics in 1972 from the City University of New York. In 1994, he was awarded an Honorary Doctorate of Humane Letters from Nova Southwestern University.

Joseph S. Simonian is Senior Investment Strategist at Scientific Beta and the Founder and CIO of Autonomous Investment Technologies. Over the course of an 18-year career in the investment industry, he has held senior portfolio management and research positions in several prominent asset management firms, including Acadian Asset Management, Natixis Investment Managers, Fidelity Investments, J.P. Morgan Asset Management, PIMCO, and Lehman Brothers. He is Co-Editor of *The Journal of Financial Data Science*, on the editorial board of *The Journal of Portfolio Management*, and an advisory board member for the Financial Data Professional Institute. Dr. Simonian has authored over 40 publications in leading investment journals. In addition to his portfolio management and research activities, he has extensive experience teaching in both academia and industry. He holds a Ph.D. from the University of California, Santa Barbara, an M.A. from Columbia University, and a B.A. from the University of California, Los Angeles.

Acknowledgments

The ideas and topics in this book are the result of our experience in asset management as well as our research in this area. We also benefited from discussions and feedback from colleagues, clients, and investment practitioners. In particular, we received invaluable feedback on several of the chapters from the following people:

- Mark Anson (Chief Executive Officer, President, and Chief Investment Officer for the Commonfund),
- Arik Ben Dor (Head of Quantitative Equity Research at Barclays Corporate & Investment Bank),
- Lev Dynkin (Managing Director at Barclays Corporate & Investment Bank),
- Brian Jacobsen (Senior Investment Strategist at Allspring Global Investments),
- Marielle de Jong (Associate Professor in Finance at the Grenoble École de management and Editor-in-Chief of the *Journal of Asset Management*),
- Adam Kobor (Managing Director of Investments at New York University),
- Wai Lee (Co-Head of Research in Systematic Edge at Allspring Global Investments),
- Richard Levich (Professor Emeritus of Finance at New York University Stern School of Business),

- Momtchil Pojarliev (Portfolio Manager at Wellington Management Company),
- Wesley Phoa (Senior Vice President, Investment Analyst, and Bond Portfolio Manager at the Capital Group Companies),
- Karthik Ramanathan (Senior Vice President, Global Clients Division at State Street Corporation).

Contents

Part 1

Framework for Global Bond Portfolios

Chapter 1

Quantifying Risks and the Role of Quantitative Management

Portfolio management involves the management of client funds. Clients can be institutional investors such as pension funds, sovereign or sub-government entities, or individual clients either via separate accounts or through collective investment vehicles. In managing funds, a portfolio manager must estimate risks and returns, and construct a portfolio that is expected to accomplish client-specified objectives. Portfolio construction, which involves the selection of the individual securities to be held in the portfolio, can be accomplished using optimization techniques. Once a portfolio is constructed, it is continuously monitored and performance is periodically evaluated. The cornerstone of the portfolio management process is identifying the risks associated with a portfolio strategy, quantifying the identified risks, estimating those risks, and then managing those risks.

Compared to managing a bond portfolio limited to only domestic bond issues, global bond portfolios deal with many more risks. The typical management tasks of global bond portfolio managers are the valuation and selection of global fixed-income securities and the allocation of funds to countries, currencies, bond market sectors, maturities, and credit ratings. While global markets provide very broad investment opportunities, these opportunities are embedded with major risks. Finding an optimal portfolio of global fixed-income assets is a challenging and critical task as it must incorporate a multitude of risks that may impact portfolio performance.

In this chapter, we describe the many risks associated with managing a global bond portfolio, and the cash and derivative market instruments which a portfolio manager can invest and/or use for controlling risks. In the last section of this chapter, the role of quantitative methods in managing a global bond portfolio is described.

1.1 The Risks in Global Bonds

Managers of global bond portfolios invest in heterogeneous fixed-income securities. Their focus is global, and compared to traditional bond funds, managers of global bond portfolios try to capture more market premiums. This means that the risks are broader for these funds compared to traditional bond portfolios such as a US corporate bond portfolio or a European government bond portfolio.

There are many possible ways to group the risks associated with bonds. The way we choose to group them is according to a portfolio's active risks. A broad overview of the important risks associated with fixed-income securities is provided by Fabozzi *et al.* (2021). The risks associated with global bond portfolios are:

- currency risk
- volatility risk
- model risk
- market risk
- political risk
- interest-rate risk
- macroeconomic risk
- liquidity risk
- equity market risk
- spread risk
- default risk
- rating risk

All these risks have an impact on the financial instruments comprising a portfolio. In the following, we provide a more detailed discussion of how each of these risks affects global bond portfolios.

1.1.1 *Currency risk*

Currency risk, also referred to as *foreign exchange risk*, represents one of the most important risks in global bond portfolios. However, as noted by Baz *et al.* (2001), expected currency returns are zero because currencies experience large volatility behavior which also impacts the performance of global bond portfolios. Currency risk is usually associated with the depreciation of a currency in which a bond is denominated. The impact of currency movements might be driven by factors like a country's monetary or fiscal policy, interest rates, inflation, gross domestic product (GDP) growth, financial market volatility, and market speculation to name a few. Importantly, currency risk often exceeds in magnitude the risk of other factors, which underscores that it is one of the most important risks to consider. Whereas currency appreciation of the bond exposure in a portfolio has a positive effect on portfolio performance, currency depreciation adversely impacts performance because it causes bond prices to decline.

1.1.2 *Volatility risk*

Controlling for portfolio risk measured by return volatility is a central part of global fixed-income portfolios and is referred to as *volatility risk*. Fixed-income volatility is driven primarily by the behavior of interest rates, spreads, and currencies, but can also be influenced by volatility in equity markets. An additional source of volatility stems from the implementation of derivative contracts and derivative strategies. The use of derivatives in a portfolio can be driven by the need to hedge certain risk exposures or by a desire to take speculative positions in an asset. For example, a global bond portfolio may establish short positions in emerging markets bonds to gain from imminent currency depreciation. In short, the sources of volatility impacting fixed-income investments are quite varied and portfolio managers must accordingly implement a risk management process that is attuned to the relevant drivers of volatility in their portfolios.

1.1.3 *Model risk*

Model risk encompasses the following four risks:

- factor sensitivity risk
- suitability risk

- estimation risk
- operational risk

Factor sensitivity risk pertains to the underlying exposures within asset classes that justify a return premium and drive the variation in asset class returns. One way to formalize risk factors is via the familiar statistical measure known as "beta" (denoted by β), which represents the sensitivity that an asset has to a given economic phenomenon. A beta of one represents average sensitivity to a risk factor and we would expect an asset with a beta of one to move in unison with that factor. A beta greater than one indicates above-average sensitivity to a risk factor and a beta of less than one indicates below-average sensitivity to a risk factor. In terms of model risk, the primary challenges are to select factors that properly explain a portfolio's performance and to ensure that the chosen risk factors are accurately measured.

Suitability risk pertains to the adequacy of a model in explaining the phenomenon that it is intended to explain. For example, a commonly used optimization model — minimum-variance-optimization — may be inappropriate for a portfolio manager who invests in assets with significant risks not captured by a variance–covariance matrix.

A somewhat related risk is *estimation risk*, which addresses the ability of models to properly estimate the risks and returns of heterogeneous bonds comprising a portfolio. Estimation risk often arises in quantitative investment contexts when managers develop capital market assumptions for their models. As capital market assumptions are often derived through a combination of historical data and forward-looking considerations, there is generally a risk that they are misspecified to a certain degree. In an optimization context, a misspecified model is likely to result in the generation of sub-optimal portfolios.

Finally, *operational risk* is the risk stemming from the active implementation of a portfolio, including trading and cash flows. It is the potential loss that can arise from either poor or failed internal processes, systems, and people, or from external events.

1.1.4 *Market risk*

Market risk is perhaps the primary risk in managing fixed-income portfolios. However, as de Jong and Fabozzi (2020) argued, the market risk for corporate bonds is very difficult to capture because bond markets are different from equity markets. Bond market risk is not easy to determine. Whereas market risk in equities is easily measured by the market portfolio, no specific market portfolio in bonds exists. It is rather specific; it is specialized because bond managers use observable measures such as spreads, yield changes, and credit changes to measure bond market risk. The level and change of interest rates and credit spreads are the primary market risks that impact global bond portfolios. As mentioned above, for global bond portfolios, currency risk is the major driver of portfolio risk and often exceeds other risks in magnitude. Indirect market risks, such as equity risk, may also impact certain kinds of fixed-income investments, such as corporate bonds. Liu and Xie (2019) showed that the equity risk inherent in the Cboe Volatility Index (VIX) futures contract is suitable for hedging the tail risks of emerging market bond portfolios. The reason for this can be traced back to the fact that credit risk is generally positively correlated with equity risk.

One aspect of market risk that merits noting is that due to the increase in the globalization of financial markets, the transmission of risks and information has increased the co-movement and connectedness of disparate bond markets. The latter development has made diversification an ever-increasing challenge for bond portfolio managers, including those managing global portfolios. However, broad diversification is not sufficient for bond portfolios. There are two reasons for this. The first reason is that global bond portfolios are managed against a benchmark and are therefore concentrated portfolios rather than diversified ones. This stems from the fact that global bond benchmark indexes like the Bloomberg Barclays Global Aggregate Treasury Bond Index or the J.P. Morgan Global Government Bond Index have concentrated exposure in three currencies — U.S. dollar, euro, and Japanese yen — and their corresponding local currency bonds exceed 70% of the total bond index exposure. As a result, a diversified bond portfolio will have excessive tracking error or deviation from the benchmark.

The second reason is U.S. Treasury, U.S. dollar, and corporate bond exposure in global bond portfolios. Leibowitz (2011) showed that there is equity risk in every bond portfolio. This equity risk is related to corporate bond exposure and in particular to high-yield corporate bonds that behave more like equity than fixed-income. As a result, corporate bond exposure — which Kinlaw *et al.* (2021) decompose into credit and duration (interest-rate) components — depends on the exposure to high-yield corporate bonds. More precisely, Leibowitz and Bova (2007) explained that a global bond portfolio with a large exposure to the high-yield bonds of issuers in developed markets would behave more like a balanced 60/40 portfolio with equity exposure than as a global bond portfolio with government bond exposure. However, diversification affects duration risk too. Specifically, emerging market hard currency bonds are strongly related to the U.S. dollar, thus large exposure to this segment could harm diversification.[1] For example, suppose market conditions are such that investors seek shelter in safe-haven assets — U.S. dollar, Japanese yen, U.S. Treasuries, and the Swiss franc. Emerging markets usually perform badly with rising bond yields and depreciating currencies. However, the U.S. dollar appreciation cannot compensate for losses attributable to increases in U.S. Treasury yields.

1.1.5 *Political risk*

Political risk is the risk that governments and other state institutions will act in ways that are detrimental to asset prices. While political risk is present in every country and domicile, it is especially a concern in emerging and frontier markets that tend to have less developed political institutions, courts of law, and financial regulators. Political risk is challenging to model as it does not naturally lend itself to quantitative analysis. Portfolio managers often depend on relatively primitive scoring models to assess political risk. That said, political risk is often connected to interest-rate, currency, and liquidity risks, through a country's monetary policy. For bond investors, political risk is also relevant for determining the probability of default measures for sovereign bonds and to a somewhat lesser extent, corporate bonds.

Various aspects of governance — from macroeconomic policies, to corruption, to the level of militarism that a government displays — impact

---

[1]Lian (2022) provides an extensive literature review on emerging market debt investing. De Jong and Fabozzi (2022) describe the development of emerging debt markets and de Jong and Swinkels (2022) discuss the portfolio advantages of inflation-linked bonds in emerging markets that aim at compensating for the losses to nominal bonds when inflation is rising.

the perceived creditworthiness of nations. Debt issued by countries with high levels of political risk will generally offer investors high-risk premia to compensate them for bearing that risk.

1.1.6 *Interest-rate risk*

Interest-rate risk is the risk to bond prices and a bond portfolio that results from changes in interest rates. There is no single interest rate in an economy. Rather, there is a structure of interest rates. Rates depend on the maturity of a bond which is graphically depicted by the yield curve for what is viewed as a default-free series of bonds. When one refers to interest-rate risk, it means the price sensitivity of a bond to shifts in the yield curve. The two most common types of shifts in the yield curve are a parallel shift and a change in the slope of the yield curve.

A parallel shift in the yield curve means that the yield for all maturities changes by roughly the same number of basis points. The most commonly used measure to quantify the impact of a parallel shift in the yield curve is *duration*. There are various measures of duration — modified, effective, and empirical — which will be discussed in Chapter 5. Regardless of the measure used, duration can be interpreted as the approximate percentage change in the value of a bond or a bond portfolio to a 100-basis point change in interest rates. So, this means that for a bond portfolio with a duration of 6, for a 100-basis point change in interest rates, the portfolio value will change by approximately 6%. The duration approximation is linear so for a 50-basis point change in interest rates, the portfolio value would change by approximately 3%.

The difficulties of using duration for a global bond portfolio are that the bonds comprising the portfolio are impacted by interest rates in different countries. What country's interest rates are assumed to change? The answer depends on the country and currency exposure of the benchmark index and on the total bond portfolio exposure. Benchmark indexes are more concentrated with exposure up to 70% in three main countries/regions (the US, Japan, and Eurozone). Diebold *et al.* (2008) showed that global interest-rate dynamics are closely interconnected and can be summarized by the three common factors that describe the yield curve: level, slope, and curvature. Following this, the overall duration of a broadly invested global bond portfolio can be related to a global bond yield only.

Alternatively, and most correctly, the overall bond portfolio duration should be decomposed into separate durations in corresponding country, currency, sector, and industry buckets, as the duration of the U.S. Treasury might be long, say, 7.5, while the duration of, say, South African exposure might be low, say, 3, and the overall duration of the bond portfolio might be 6. The various applications of duration and duration-based strategies are discussed in Chapter 5 where we discuss yield curve management.

Duration measures how a portfolio's value will change assuming a parallel shift in interest rates. A portfolio is also exposed to how the shape of the yield curve changes. In general, such measures are referred to as *yield curve duration*. However, in practice, yield curve duration is confined to the second most common type of shift after the parallel shift, a change in the slope of the yield curve. An interest-rate sensitivity measure that takes into account a change in the slope of the yield curve is referred to as *rate duration*. In theory, there is a rate duration for every maturity. For example, a five-year rate duration for a portfolio measures how sensitive the portfolio's value is to a change in the five-year spot rate holding the rate for all other maturities unchanged. Practitioners do not calculate a rate duration for every maturity. Instead, a rate duration is calculated for what are viewed as key interest rates on the yield curve and is accordingly referred to as *key-rate duration*.

1.1.7 *Macroeconomic risk*

Macroeconomic risks are important for bond markets, perhaps more important than they are for equity markets. This is due to the impact that countries' fiscal and monetary policies have on growth and inflation, two of the primary drivers of bond returns. Monetary policy is, of course, directly connected to interest rates, while fiscal policy is connected to the many drivers of a country's growth such as tax policy, public debt, and the expenditure and distribution of wealth and economic resources.

1.1.8 *Liquidity risk*

Liquidity risk is an important but sometimes elusive variable as it is hard to define, measure, and explain (Schwartz *et al.*, 2020). Liquidity risk can be associated with the adverse impact on prices when executing trades in the bond market. The reason for this is that in bond markets, liquidity is commonly measured by bid-ask spreads, which are only approximating solutions for measuring liquidity. Compared to equity pricing, bond pricing is the result of the notional amounts traded between counterparties, as there is no pre-determined observable (traded) price. Bonds are traded in the over-the-counter market and using electronic exchanges. Loistl and Konstantinov (2020) stressed that a comprehensive measure of liquidity would involve complete order book analysis. Liquidity, the ease at which market participants can transact, is fundamental to pricing risk in debt markets. Liquidity risk increases with maturity and is higher for lower-rated bonds. High-grade bonds, or bonds with a higher rating from major rating agencies, generally have better liquidity than lower-rated bonds. Another important issue related to liquidity risk is its positive relationship to a bond's issue size. The larger the issue size, the higher the liquidity of the bond. The stage in the development of a country's capital market also impacts liquidity, accounting for the higher illiquidity of bonds traded in emerging markets.

There are many measures of liquidity risk for bonds, with the bid-ask spread being perhaps the most commonly used. The various dimensions of bond liquidity will be discussed further in Part 2 where we describe trading in the bond market.

1.1.9 *Equity market risk*

Equity market risk is an indirect risk for bonds, especially corporate bonds whose returns are to an extent dependent on the performance of the companies that issue them. There is extensive research literature on equity risk originating from the Capital Asset Pricing Model (CAPM). Today, there are models that address equity market risk in a nuanced manner by considering different company characteristics/fundamentals (e.g., size, profitability, and value) as separate factors.

1.1.10 *Spread risk*

Spreads are one of the most important variables in bond management. Usually, spreads represent the risk premium for a bond relative to a reference yield curve. The spread risk is associated with the rise of the risk premium for a bond relative to a reference yield curve. The nominal spread of a bond is its yield premium relative to a reference security yield. The zero-volatility spread (or zero spread) is the spread that, when added to a U.S. Treasury spot curve, makes the present value of the cash flows equal to the price of the bond. Thus, the zero spread measures the spread to a U.S. Treasury curve. The option-adjusted spread (OAS) is the spread that incorporates option costs and is also added to the U.S. Treasury spot curve. Option costs are related to an embedded option in a bond. That is, the OAS is equal to the zero spread if no option costs exist.

Spread duration measures the sensitivity of a bond's price due to changes in the spread. The spread duration of a portfolio is a market-weighted sum of all bond spread durations.

1.1.11 *Default risk*

Default risk measures the probability that a country or company will not be able to pay off its debt obligations. Although default risk is a more prevalent measure in corporate bond space, it is also relevant to issuers of sovereign debt, especially emerging market issuers. The default of Argentinian government bonds in 2001–2002 and debt restructuring (Russia in 1998 and Greece in 2011) are some examples of sovereign-related default risk (see Papaioannou and Tsesekos, 2018).

Emerging markets are highly vulnerable to default risk. Despite the tremendous growth in emerging market investing and the global financial market integration of these markets as an important part of institutional portfolios, their dependencies on global growth and inflation are heightened (see Lian, 2022). Emerging market sovereign bonds remain riskier investment instruments overall compared to their developed market counterparts (see De Jong and Fabozzi, 2022).

1.1.12 *Rating risk*

Rating risk refers to the change in rating outlook or rating classification from one of the major credit rating agencies — Standard and Poor's, Fitch, or Moody's — or local credit rating agencies such as DBRS Morningstar for Germany, Canada, and the United Kingdom. Negative rating surprises often stem from changes in spreads and liquidity, often resulting from deterioration in the issuer's economic fundamentals. The credit risks often associated with rating risk deterioration are usually associated with changes in a rating outlook.

One of the reasons that rating risk is important in global bond portfolios is that different instruments (e.g., sovereign bonds and corporate bonds) may have the same rating but have different spreads. The bond issue size, market liquidity, and financial strength of issuers (whether corporate or sovereign) are typically additional factors that drive the level of spreads.

1.2 Instruments

In this section, we provide an overview of various fixed-income instruments. More detailed analyses of the instruments and the estimation of expected returns and risk metrics are presented in the chapters dedicated to those topics.

The instruments that are typical of global bond portfolios fall into three groups: bonds, derivatives, and currencies. Bond portfolio exposure can be long or short any of these instruments.

1.2.1 *Bonds*

Expectedly, bonds are the most important instrument in global bond portfolios. There are several bonds that typically populate global bond portfolios. The most important ones are as follows:

- bullet bonds
- callable and puttable bonds
- floating-rate bonds
- covered bonds
- inflation-linked bonds

1.2.1.1 *Bullet bonds*

Bullet bonds are the simplest type of fixed-income securities. A bullet bond is a sum of all coupons plus the principal repayment paid at the maturity date. Bullet bonds do not have embedded options or other embedded derivatives, and their coupons are determined in advance or at the day of issuance. That is, bullet bonds have a pre-specified coupon, which in general does not change according to market conditions. Bullet bonds are issued by governments and corporations.

The most commonly traded bonds by global bond portfolio managers are local currency and hard currency bonds. *Local currency bonds* are issued in the domestic currency of the respective country and most of their value reflects the macroeconomic risks of that country. *Hard currency bonds* are called *external debt* and are predominantly issued in U.S. dollars. External sovereign bonds represent disparities in economic and currency risk, as their cash flows are generated by domestic economic activities, but the currency risk is that of another country. In most cases, that currency is the U.S. dollar. However, several countries issue external debt denominated in euro or Japanese yen. According to Bisat (2010), the underlying currency and credit spread dynamics of these bonds are much more related to the U.S. Treasury market and the U.S. dollar in particular.

1.2.1.2 *Callable and puttable bonds*

The major difference between bullet bonds and callable bonds is that the latter have embedded options which represent the right of the issuer to call the issue. In contrast to callable bonds, which incorporate the right of the issuer to call, a bond that gives the bondholder the right to redeem the issue prior to the maturity date is called a puttable bond. Callable bonds are common instruments in global bond markets and are issued by both governments and corporations. To a large extent, embedded options impact the bond's projected cash flows. In general, callable bonds are very sensitive to falling interest rates, as the probability of option exercise increases.

1.2.1.3 *Floating-rate bonds*

Floating-rate securities are common instruments in global bond portfolios. With floating-rate bonds the coupon rate resets on designated dates based on a coupon-reset formula tied to a reference rate and a fixed quoted margin. Floating-rate bonds are issued in both hard currencies (U.S. dollar, euro, and Japanese yen) and in local currencies.

1.2.1.4 *Inflation-linked bonds*

Inflation-linked bonds base their performance on measures of inflation. As inflation is a major risk for the performance of nominal bonds, inflation-linked bonds are designed to provide a real rate of return to investors. For example, Treasury Inflation-Protected Securities (TIPS) issued by the U.S. Treasury have their principal adjusted according to the Consumer Price Index (CPI) measure of inflation. The principal value of inflation-linked bonds, or linkers, is adjusted periodically to compensate for the inflation rate. Usually, the difference between the nominal yield that simple government bonds yield and the yield of TIPS is a proxy for expected inflation. In the United States, linkers were first issued in 1997. Linkers are usually regarded as buy-and-hold instruments and bond managers trade them much less frequently than nominal government bonds (see Homer and Sylla (2005)). In general, linkers depend on the inflation expectations of investors because inflation-linked bonds compensate the investor for the adverse effects of rising inflation which is associated with purchasing power loss. De Jong and Swinkels (2022) showed that inflation-linked bonds outperform nominal bonds when inflation shocks hit the market. In other words, the difference between expected and realized inflation determines the performance of these bonds, resulting in higher yields than nominal government bonds when inflation is underestimated.

In comparison to the broad government bond market, inflation-linked bonds are a rather a small niche segment. That said, linkers are common instruments that are issued in developed bond markets, where much more liquidity is evident and investor demand for inflation-linked bonds exists. The most popular global inflation-linked bond index is the ICE BofA Global Inflation-Linked Government Index, which comprises roughly 150 bonds issued in U.S. dollars, euros, Australian dollars, Canadian dollars, British pounds, Japanese yen, New Zealand dollars, and Swedish krone. The highest weights in the index and the largest number of single securities are associated with the G3 currencies — U.S. dollar, euro, and Japanese yen. Note that inflation has not been an issue for the Eurozone in the period from 2000 to 2020, causing inflation-linked bonds to underperform nominal bonds. However, in the Eurozone, Spain, Italy, Germany, and France linkers outperformed the market post-COVID-19 and after the war in Ukraine drove commodity prices higher and disrupted global supply chains, causing massive both demand pull and cost-push inflation in the Eurozone. Moreover, similar negative inflation effects have been observed globally in emerging markets (see de Jong and Swinkels, 2022). In such an environment, inflation-linked bonds in emerging markets provide investors with a solution to neutralize the loss that nominal bonds usually experience. In an environment with low interest rates and rising inflation pressure globally, inflation-linked bonds represent a valuable add-on to bond portfolios. Inclusion of linkers in a global bond portfolio can thus provide a safe-haven exposure in periods of rising inflation.

1.2.2 *Foreign exchange*

Foreign exchange (FX) or currency exposure represents an important source of risk and return for global bond portfolios. Currencies are viewed as a financial asset. In this role, they enable the monetary expression and value determination of other assets like bonds, equities, and commodities, among others. Currencies are a natural instrument to gain exposure to foreign countries. Although many currencies are highly liquid, global trading volumes are dominated by the currencies of the 10 most traded currencies denoted as the G10: U.S. dollar, British pound, Canadian dollar, Australian dollar, Japanese yen, Swiss franc, Swedish krone, Norwegian krone, New Zealand dollar, and the euro. Currencies are directly related to the economic life of a country and impact not only government bonds but also corporate bonds and high-yield bonds (corporate and government) and drive equity and commodities markets. Monetary policy, fiscal policy, the balance of payments, interest rates, inflation, the unemployment rate, and economic growth have an immediate impact on FX.[2]

The dependency of a global bond portfolio on FX is significant. As such, some portfolio managers may try to avoid taking currency risk or hedge that risk. That said, currencies can also be a powerful tool in the bond manager's arsenal of sources of return.

Currencies are traded in pairs using conventions based on economic principles. For example, the EUR/USD currency pair comprises the euro and U.S. dollar. The most important currency convention and currency pair is the EUR/USD. This convention expresses the euro price of one U.S. dollar. For example, a EUR/USD of 1.083 indicates that the price of one euro is 1.083 U.S. dollars. Unfortunately, not all currency conventions exist. To better understand the mechanics behind currencies, it is important to note that a currency pair can be seen as a combination of

[2] We describe the relationship between foreign exchange and interest rates in Chapter 3.

foreign and domestic currency, or a long/short currency relationship. In a currency notation such as EUR/USD, the second term always denotes the domestic or base currency. The first term denotes the long exposure; in EUR/USD, this is the euro. In other words, the euro is the foreign currency from a U.S. dollar point of view and, therefore, the EUR/USD denotes the U.S. dollar price for 1 euro. For example, suppose that the EUR/USD moves from 1.10 to 1.15. This movement can be seen as a euro appreciation against the U.S. dollar, or as U.S. dollar deprecation against the euro.

The role of currencies in global bond portfolios is extensively explained in Chapter 4 where we describe currency management.

1.2.3 *Derivatives*

Derivative contracts, or simply *derivatives*, derive their value from the value of some underlying commodity, asset, currency, index, or reference rate. Derivatives include futures, forwards, options, and swaps. In this section, we briefly describe the role of derivatives in portfolio management and the classification of derivatives based on the type of payoffs that they provide.

1.2.3.1 *Role of derivatives*

Derivatives are often an efficient way to alter the exposure to a specific risk. Portfolio managers use derivatives to both control market risks and for alpha enhancement. For example, suppose that a global bond portfolio manager wants to eliminate the currency risk for its Mexican peso exposure. The portfolio manager might employ put options on the peso to accomplish this. Controlling risk, or managing risk to a specific target level, might also be desired. Suppose, for example, a bond portfolio has exposure to European bonds, but the investment guidelines mandate that currency exposure should not exceed a specific level, say, 15%. In this case, the bond portfolio might allocate, say, 30% to European bonds, but use a currency derivative to reduce the currency risk to euros to 15%.

The second purpose of derivative instruments in global bond portfolios is to enhance excess returns. There is a wide array of derivatives instruments which allow managers to express even the most nuanced market views.

1.2.3.2 *Risk sharing versus insurance derivatives*

Derivatives offer global bond portfolio managers two types of arrangements: risk sharing and insurance derivatives. The selection of the type of arrangement depends on the objective and the view of the portfolio manager. To understand these two types of derivative arrangements, consider a U.S. bond portfolio manager who has exposure to euros and is concerned that the currency will depreciate six months from now when euro-denominated cash flows are projected to be received. Assume that the EUR/USD is currently 1.10. That is, this portfolio manager faces currency risk and more specifically the risk that the EUR/USD will be less than 1.10 six months from now.

A straightforward way to manage this currency risk is for the portfolio manager to agree to exchange euros for US dollars six months from now at the current exchange rate (i.e., EUR/USD 1.10). Via the derivatives market, a counterparty willing to enter such an arrangement can be found for no upfront payment. Although this derivative arrangement allows the portfolio manager to eliminate currency risk six months from now, the portfolio manager forgoes the opportunity to benefit from a favorable movement in the exchange rate in the future (i.e., if the EUR/USD exceeds 1.10). The counterparty also foregoes the opportunity to benefit from a favorable movement in the euro six months from now (i.e., if the EUR/USD falls below 1.10). Basically, the portfolio manager and the counterparty are sharing the risk of an adverse movement in the exchange rate and willing to forgo a favorable exchange rate movement to do so. For that reason, this type of contract is referred to as a *risk-sharing arrangement*. Note that the portfolio manager does not pay the counterparty to enter into the agreement. Futures, forwards, and certain types of swaps (interest-rate swaps and currency swaps) are examples of *risk-sharing derivatives*.

Suppose instead that the portfolio manager wants to protect against a depreciation of the euro but still wants to benefit from an appreciation of the euro and is willing to pay another party a non-refundable sum of money to provide that protection. This derivative arrangement may call for the portfolio manager to pay USDX to the counterparty for the right to exchange one euro for USD 1.1 six months from now. If the portfolio manager elects to have the counterparty perform six months from now, the counterparty must perform. Obviously, the portfolio manager will elect to require the counterparty to perform if the euro depreciates, guaranteeing a EUR/USD of 1.10. However, the portfolio manager has the right to walk away from the agreement and will do so if the euro appreciates. That is, the portfolio manager is not required to perform and can realize the benefit of the euro appreciating. Regardless of what the portfolio manager decides to do six months from now, the fee paid to the counterparty is lost. Notice that in contrast to the risk-sharing arrangement where no payment was made to the counterparty at the outset of the contract, in this arrangement, the bond portfolio manager pays a fee to the counterparty because the only benefit that the counterparty can realize from this contract is the fee. Moreover, only one party (i.e., the counterparty) is required to perform. This type of derivative is referred to as an *insurance derivative*. Examples of insurance derivatives are options, options on swaps (swaptions), and certain types of swaps such as a credit default swaps.

1.3 The Role of Quantitative Portfolio Management

Thus far in this chapter, we have highlighted some important aspects of bond portfolio management. The quantitative nature of fixed-income instruments makes bond portfolio management a natural area of application for quantitative methods. Accordingly, the purpose of quantitative global bond portfolio management is to quantify and systematically invest in bonds, currencies, and other instruments and to capture the risks associated with global bond markets by maximizing expected returns. The major advantage of quantitative investment processes compared to more fundamentally based approaches is that portfolio managers can more precisely identify, quantify, and assess the possible sources of a portfolio's risk and return as well as objectively evaluate the models that are used to manage risks and generate returns.

Fabozzi and Fabozzi (2022) identified five important steps in investment management. Tailoring the steps to global bond portfolios, we specify the following phases of the investment management process:

1. setting investment objectives;
2. establishing investment policy;
3. selecting a portfolio strategy;

Figure 1.1: The Investment Process

4. asset allocation and selection;
5. performance measurement and attribution.

Rather than presenting these steps as a one-directional flow process, we characterize it as an interacting structure with feedback loops (see Figure 1.1). Specifically, the investment process should not be considered a static structure but a dynamic one that constantly adjusts to new feedback from investors and from the market; it is thus important to constantly monitor and revise long-term capital market expectations and to adjust and adapt one's investment process to changing market conditions.

In the following, we describe in detail the building blocks of the investment process.

1.3.1 *Investment objectives*

Setting investment objectives is the first component in an investment process. The process of setting objectives involves identifying and measuring risks, returns, and selecting client-appropriate investment vehicles.

To define strategic goals, investors and portfolio managers typically begin by defining a benchmark. A benchmark should represent the liability structure of an investor. To illustrate this, suppose an investor desires a stream of cash flows to cover long-term pension liabilities. In this case, a benchmark of long-dated bonds should be chosen to represent this desired level of cash flows.

The formulation of investment objectives also typically involves the definition of a *strategic asset allocation*. This entails the determination of an optimal asset mix that is likely to meet the long-term investment needs of a client. Strategic asset allocations are periodically revised, often on an annual basis.

1.3.2 *Investment policy*

The drafting of an investment policy statement in general refers to the written declaration of client constraints and restrictions relating to security types, asset allocation, portfolio turnover, and currency exposure, among others. Minimum and maximum restrictions on asset weights (countries, currencies, and sectors) are the most common types of restrictions. Bond investors might also specify restrictions on credit quality and duration. On a more granular level, bond investors might exclude specific issuers. Other common restrictions include limits on the use of derivatives and the short selling of assets.

Although setting investment restrictions and constraints within an investment policy statement is a common way for investors to meet their specific portfolio goals, care must be taken so that a portfolio is not "over-constrained" as that may raise additional operational and portfolio management challenges for managers related to benchmark selection, compliance, and alpha generation potential.

1.3.3 *Portfolio strategy*

Portfolio strategy involves making decisions regarding the structural features of a portfolio. Perhaps the most important decision is whether a primarily active or passive approach will be pursued by the portfolio manager. The decision whether to follow a passive or an active approach by necessity requires setting strategic goals regarding expected returns and costs (both fees and transaction costs).

Other questions relating to portfolio strategy include the geographic and sectoral tilt of a portfolio, if any, as well as decisions relating to trading frequency and trade sizing.

1.3.4 *Asset allocation and selection*

Strategic asset allocation sets the longer-term weights for assets in a portfolio. Portfolio rebalancing involves reallocation of a portfolio's asset weights to their strategic values after they have deviated due to price drift caused by tactical asset allocation decisions. In contrast to strategic asset allocation, *tactical asset allocation* aims at positioning and managing portfolios in a dynamic market environment, shifting a portfolio's exposures around its strategic weights according to perceived shorter-term changes in asset risk-and-return profiles. Portfolio optimization is commonly used to build tactical asset allocations in bond portfolios. The most important part of this process is to optimize and rebalance the portfolio according to changing return expectations and market conditions (Simonian, 2019).

Importantly, portfolio optimization for bond portfolios is much different than for equities (Deguest *et al.*, 2018). For example, Korn and Koziol (2006) used the minimum-variance optimization technique suggested by Markowitz (1952) to build government bond portfolios. This technique can be applied for broad allocation optimizations to derive sector, country, or currency asset allocation but not suitable to derive optimizations for tradable single bonds. Bond portfolio optimizations require a different setup that allows a portfolio manager to properly address bond-related constraints like duration, maturity, rating, and liquidity (Konstantinov and Fabozzi, 2021). We describe bond portfolio optimization in Chapter 6. Out-of-sample portfolio optimizations differ from in-sample during the research phase of investment process development, and specific market portfolio constraints also have a significant influence on the tradable portfolio. While broad country-specific or currency asset allocations for bond portfolios can be derived using minimum-variance optimization, it is important to remember that because significant types of bond risk such as default risk are not captured by the traditional optimization framework, the minimum-variance optimization may not be ideally suited to bond portfolio construction. In addition, bond portfolios comprise a large number of single bonds that are better optimized using alternative approaches.

We cover the foregoing topics in Part 2 where we discuss robust portfolio optimization and construction, which addresses model misspeficiation during the portfolio selection process (Fabozzi *et al.*, 2007).

1.3.5 *Performance measurement and attribution*

The purpose of performance measurement is to provide a numerical assessment of a portfolio manager's decisions over the measurement period. This includes the production of various risk-and-return metrics as well as performance attribution that seeks to identify the sources of a manager's performance against a benchmark. We provide an extensive performance attribution analysis for global bond portfolios in Chapter 12.

1.4 Key Takeaways

- Global bond portfolios are affected by currency risk, liquidity risk, interest-rate risk, political risk, spread risk, macroeconomic risk, equity market risk, default risk, model risk, and rating risk. The interaction of the various risks that global bond portfolios are exposed to is significant and bond managers need to be able to effectively manage these often correlated risks.
- The derivative instruments which are commonly used by global bond portfolio managers include swaps, futures, forwards, options, and swaps. Derivatives include risk-sharing-type instruments and insurance-type instruments. Derivative instruments exist for both bonds and foreign exchange.
- Quantitative global bond portfolio management consists of (1) setting investment objectives, (2) establishing investment policy, (3) selecting a portfolio strategy, (4) asset allocation and selection, and (5) performance measurement and attribution.

References

Baz, J., F. Breedon, V. Naik, and J. Peress. 2001. "Optimal Portfolios of Foreign Currencies." *Journal of Portfolio Management* 28(1): 102–111.

Bisat, A. 2010. "Sources of Return within an Emerging Markets Fixed-Income and Foreign Exchange Portfolio." *Journal of Alternative Investments* 13(1): 79–86.

De Jong, M. and F. J. Fabozzi. 2020. "The Market Risk of Corporate Bonds." *Journal of Portfolio Management* 46(2): 92–105.

De Jong, M. and F. J. Fabozzi. 2022. "Emerging Markets Debt Securities: A Literature Review." *Journal of Portfolio Management* 48(8): 109–112.

De Jong, M. and L. Swinkels. 2022. "The Capital-Protection Capacity of Emerging Markets Inflation-Linked Bonds." *Journal of Portfolio Management* 48(8): 109–112.

Deguest, R., F. Fabozzi, L. Martellini, and V. Milhau. 2018. "Bond Portfolio Optimization in the Presence of Duration Constraints." *Journal of Fixed Income* 28(1): 6–26.

Diebold, F. X., C. Li, and V. Z. Yue. 2008. "Global Yield Curve Dynamics and Interactions: A Dynamic Nelson–Siegel Approach." *Journal of Econometrics* 146(2): 351–363.

Homer, S. and R. Sylla. 2005. *A History of Interest Rates*. 4th Edition. Hoboken, New Jersey: John Wiley & Sons.

Fabozzi, F. J. and F. A. Fabozzi. 2022. *Bond Markets, Analysis, and Strategies.* 10thEdition. Cambridge, MA: MIT Press.

Fabozzi, F. J., A. Kobor, F. A. Fabozzi, and R. F. Dattatreya. 2021. "Risks Associated with Investing in Fixed Income Securities." Chapter 2 in F. J. Fabozzi (ed.), pp. 23–38, *The Handbook of Fixed Income Securities,* 9th Edition. New York, NY: McGraw Hill.

Fabozzi, F. J., P. N. Kolm., D. A. Pachamanova, and S. M. Focardi. 2007. "Robust Portfolio Optimization." *Journal of Portfolio Management* 33(3): 40–48.

Kinlaw, W., M. Kritzman, S. Page, and D. Turkington. 2021. "The Myth of Diversification Reconsidered." *Journal of Portfolio Management* 47(8): 124–137.

Konstantinov, G. S. and F. J. Fabozzi. 2021. "International Bond Portfolio Management." Chapter 57 in F. J. Fabozzi (ed.), *The Handbook of Fixed Income Securities.* 9th Edition. New York: McGraw Hill.

Leibowitz, M. L. 2011. "Alpha Orbits." *Financial Analysts Journal* 67(4): 6–7.

Leibowitz, M. L. and A. Bova. 2009. "Diversification Performance and Stress-Betas." *Journal of Portfolio Management* 35(3): 41–47.

Korn, O. and C. Koziol. 2006. "Bond Portfolio Optimization." *Journal of Fixed Income* 15(4): 48–60.

Lian, C. L. 2022. "Evolution of Emerging Markets Debt Investing." *Journal of Portfolio Management* 48(8): 109–112.

Liu, B. and H. Xie. 2019. "Hedging High-Yield and Emerging Market Bond Tail Risk with VIX Futures." *Journal of Alternative Investments* 22(2): 81–98.

Loistl, O. and G. S. Konstantinov. 2020. "Interactions and Interconnectedness Shape Financial Market Research." *Journal of Financial Data Scien*ce 2(2): 51–63.

Markowitz, H. 1952. "Portfolio Selection." *Journal of Finance* 7(1): 77–91.

Papaioannou, M. G. and G. Tsesekos. 2018. "Regaining Access to Capital Markets: An Overview of Issues and Strategies." *Journal of Investing* 27(3): 45–52.

Schwartz, R. A., R. Francioni, and P. Weber. 2020. "Market Liquidity: An Elusive Variable." *Journal of Portfolio Management* 46(8): 7–26.

Simonian, J. 2019. "Policy Portfolios and Portfolio Characteristics." *Journal of Portfolio Management* 46(1): 52–59.

Chapter 2

Global Markets and Bond Benchmarks

Global bond portfolios invest in different markets. The particular investment universe available to managers will depend on the type of strategy being run. Some managers are able to invest in both developed and emerging markets, the two primary ways that investments are categorized at the country level. Other managers will be dedicated developed or emerging market managers. Some of the latter managers will further narrow their focus on a select set of countries, sometimes even one country.

In this chapter, we discuss both emerging and developed bond markets within the context of global bond portfolio management. Our discussion covers each of the relevant dimensions of investing in developed and emerging bond markets including currency risk, benchmarking, liquidity risk, political risk, and macroeconomic risk. We conclude by touching upon asset allocation decisions at the country level.

2.1 Dimensions of Risk in Global Markets

Global markets present various risks to bond portfolio managers. While it is common to group countries as either developed or emerging, each country presents unique risks that must be considered by investors. These country-specific risks can be broadly categorized into three types: political risk, market risk, and contagion cross-asset risk.

2.1.1 *Country-specific risk*

Risks that are specific to a particular country or domicile relate to government institutions, macroeconomic stability, and international relations. *Country-specific risks* are often the primary type of risk associated with emerging market (EM) countries. This is understandable given that the macroeconomics of many EM countries are less mature than their developed market (DM) counterparts. As a result, high inflation rates, large current account deficits, and high unemployment rates make EM countries more vulnerable to exogenous shocks such as sudden changes in the terms of trade, as well endogenous shocks such as labor strikes. The relative underdevelopment of EM countries also generally constrains their governments' ability to enact countercyclical policies and enhanced liquidity measures during times of crisis. Expectedly, it also usually means that EM citizens have less household wealth, lower employment, and less education relative to DM country citizens. All of the foregoing characteristics of EM countries add to their macroeconomic fragility in tangible ways, and accordingly heighten their perceived risk among investors. Somewhat predictably, the risks associated with EM countries typically manifest themselves during times of economic and financial crisis, when investors are more likely to abruptly transfer capital from EM markets to "safe haven" DM markets. That action will in turn often induce a liquidity crisis in the countries affected by them.

Academic research supports the foregoing points. Rocha *et al.* (2007) identified that in EM bond markets, spreads are highly vulnerable to exogenous macroeconomic shocks. Such shocks might be, but are not limited to, equity market turmoil, commodity price shortages, demand-pulled or supply-pushed inflation, and cross-asset financial market contagion effects amplified by regional economic integration and globalization. Along the same lines, Uribe and Yue (2006) provide evidence showing how exogenous factors like shocks in U.S. Treasury rates and endogenous country-specific shocks jointly drive the movement in EM spreads.

Aside from macroeconomic risk, countries also present political and institutional risk to investors. Again, the latter risks are generally more significant in EM countries. For example, the judicial systems of many EM countries are not yet fully formed and often dispense justice in an unreliable and arbitrary way.[1] Moreover, the mechanisms of democracy,

[1] Lian (2022) discussed the problems and solutions that give rise to EM debt investing and De Jong and Fabozzi (2022) discussed the rise of EM bonds as an asset class, whose risks

such as elections and separation of powers, are also often ill-formed in EM countries. As a result, the organizational structure of EM countries is generally more fragile and prone to failure when compared to DM countries. Nevertheless, although institutional fragility is an important part of assessing the risk associated with EM markets, it is notoriously difficult to quantify. A common approach to quantifying country-level risk is the production of scores (or indexes) for individual countries. Scores are generally aggregations of values assigned to a country in various categories (e.g., political corruption,[2] legal system, regulatory regime). The individual scores for each category can be thought of as roughly analogous to the ratings that are assigned to corporate and sovereign bonds.[3] Such scoring systems are common among rating agencies like Fitch, Standard & Poor's, and Moody's.

Macroeconomic dynamics can often have a direct bearing on a country's market performance. For example, Balima *et al.* (2017) showed that EM countries that adopt inflation targeting improve their financial market integration which is associated with improved liquidity, investment rating, and financial market attractiveness for foreign investors like global bond portfolios. Current account deficits, GDP growth, unemployment rates, monetary policy, and fiscal policy are all important macroeconomics factors to consider. However, monetary policy is of special importance for bond investors given its direct relationship with interest rates.

2.1.2 *Market risk*

Market risks are those associated with the financial operations of countries. This includes the banking system as well as securities markets. This distinguishes market risks from country-level risks that are associated with the "real economy" factors such as growth, employment, and inflation, as well as the political and geopolitical risks impacting market factors. There are, of course, a multitude of interconnections between the financial market and real economies. Financial markets, however, represent unique sets of risks and so are treated separately for analytical purposes. The

---

and returns have changed with improving economic fundamentals, and market and financial integration.

[2]For example, the Corruption Perceptions Index (CPI) is an index which ranks countries "by their perceived levels of public sector corruption, as determined by expert assessments and opinion surveys."

[3]These points are further discussed in Paserman (2017) and Simonian (2021).

financial systems of developed markets differ from those of emerging markets in terms of their investability, global market integration, speed of information flow, and capitalization.

One reason developed markets are more investable than emerging markets is related to their regulatory institutions and property rights laws. Another reason is that developed markets are better capitalized than emerging markets, which makes them more liquid and transparent than the latter. As a result, developed markets are less susceptible to shocks stemming from large inflows and outflows of capital. This inherent stability is one of the reasons that the U.S., the European Union, and Japan have the largest weights in global bond indexes.[4] Their bonds are denominated in the three currencies — the U.S. dollar (USD), the euro (EUR), and Japanese yen (JPY) — that are characterized by high liquidity, which is reflected in low bid-ask spreads. Corporate bonds denominated in the latter three currencies are also among the most liquid credit instruments. Other well-capitalized markets with developed regulatory and property rights regimes, such as the United Kingdom and Australia, also have deep and liquid bond markets.

Like currencies, the interest-rate and spread dynamics in developed markets are different from the high-volatility interest rates, currencies, and spreads in emerging markets. These differences are important to understand and consider in bond portfolios. These differences stem from the fact that emerging markets suffer from capital controls, lack of transparency, illiquidity, operational difficulties like settlement and capital transfer, weak regulation, and underdeveloped financial markets. This justifies to some extent the liquidity premium associated with bonds issued in emerging markets. The liquidity premium might also be associated with long holding periods. Importantly, the premium is country specific and determined by country-specific macroeconomic issues.

Given the qualitative differences in risk between developed and emerging markets, it is unsurprising that developed markets typically make up a larger share of most global bond portfolios. In addition to the risks mentioned above, execution risk is also greater for EM bonds. This is due to the fact that emerging markets are generally smaller and less liquid relative to their DM counterparts. This reality makes trading in emerging markets relatively riskier from the standpoint of being able to fill large orders, get best execution, and minimize transaction costs.

---

[4] See Chapter 3.

Cash flows in and out of financial markets may also be restricted at times due to capital controls and other restrictive regulations. While capital controls and regulation measures are generally instituted by governments to provide stability to their financial systems, they nevertheless provide a challenge to investors who require the ability to move their capital in an unfettered manner. These trading risks also typically extend to the derivative instruments linked to EM debt.

2.1.3 *Contagion and coupling in global financial markets*

Over the years, in periods of market turmoil, most risky assets exhibit a high degree of correlation. For most investors, this means that there is usually "nowhere to hide" during times of financial crisis, aside from "safe haven" investments such as U.S. Treasuries or gold. Accordingly, one of the primary practical issues that investors have faced as markets have exhibited increasing correlation in times of market stress is that of diversification, and by extension, effective risk management has proven to be increasingly elusive.

The foregoing state of affairs was realized most recently during the Global Financial Crisis (GFC), where a dislocation in the mortgage market affected U.S. investment banks, which in turn affected emerging markets. From an asset allocation standpoint, we saw asset classes which are generally weakly correlated in "normal" markets, such as equity and investment-grade credit, move in tandem to the downside. Part of the reason that we have seen more global contagion over the years is due to the increased mutual dependence between national economies (including between developed and emerging economies), as well as heightened policy coordination among governments, in the realm of monetary policy, for example.[5]

The portfolio effects of financial contagion have been extensively investigated in the finance literature. Contagion effects result when risks arising in one market sector, asset class, or region are transmitted to other segments of the economy and/or market. All types of risk are subject to contagion including liquidity, political, and macroeconomic risks. Hamao *et al.* (1990) were among the first to investigate financial market

---

[5]For a review of topics related to contagion, globalization, and economic spillovers, see Cheung and Westermann (2013).

contagion effects across equity markets. Investigating the contagion effects of realized volatility within and across currency, fixed-income, equity, and commodity markets, Bollerslev *et al.* (2018) found that volatility is a source of contagion across a wide array of asset classes. Tiwari *et al.* (2018), who investigated global volatility contagions across equities, bonds, credit default swaps, and currencies found that FX is a significant risk transmission mechanism. As we shall see in Chapter 3, currencies are instruments for gaining exposure in different markets geographically, and next to interest rates, the most important driver of risk and return in global bond portfolios. Barunik *et al.* (2017) found significant currency volatility contagion. Currency volatility was also found to be marked by significant clustering, where large changes in asset prices are followed by further large changes (Mandelbrot, 1963). Wang (2010) found that volatility shocks in specific industries contribute most heavily to contagion effects. Bostanci and Yilmaz (2020) stressed that the level of connectivity among sovereign bonds and corporate bonds is particularly high among both developed and emerging market bonds. In a study dedicated to portfolio volatility contagion and to global bond portfolios, Konstantinov and Fabozzi (2022) found that global equity markets determine overall portfolio risk, but bond yields and currencies also play an important role. Much of the contagion and coupling among markets in times of stress has been a direct result of increasing globalization over the last several decades.

2.1.4 *Asset allocation and security selection*

One of the most important aspects of global bond investing is asset allocation. Deriving country allocations for bond portfolios is often accomplished using well-known optimization frameworks such as mean–variance optimization (MVO). In practice, however, deriving an optimal asset allocation and incorporating bond selection requires considering factors beyond those that are utilized within MVO.[6] Integrating security selection in the country or currency allocation is imperative for bond portfolios for liquidity and tradability reasons. Indeed, manager-imposed constraints must often be implemented during portfolio selection to ensure diversification to prevent concentration of the portfolio in one or more countries. Along

[6] See Chapter 7 for more information on the optimization techniques that can be used.

these same lines, constraints are also often imposed in order to guarantee a minimum allocation to one or more countries. Other common constraints include those that disallow shorting bonds and the use of leverage.

Although it is in theory possible to analyze portfolio holdings on a security-by-security basis, for large portfolios, such an exercise is usually impractical. A more common approach is to utilize factor models. Such models utilize parsimonious sets of explanatory variables to explain the behavior of a much larger set of securities. In equity investing, for example, the *Fama–French factors* identified by Fama and French (1992, 1993, and 2015) are used. The same factors have also been used to explain the behavior of corporate bond portfolios.[7] It is important to note that the effectiveness of a given factor as an explanatory variable often depends on the country and macroeconomic state in which they are applied.[8] In fixed-income research, perhaps the most well-known factor model is the application of principal component analysis (PCA) to analyze yield curve dynamics.[9] Factor models are discussed in more detail in Chapter 5.

In addition to concentration risk, additional risks in EM bonds include operational risks and investment costs (Masters, 2002). For example, the higher the rebalancing frequency, the higher the costs and thus the larger potential deviation of the final portfolio allocation from a desired tactical allocation. While operational risk is not unique to EM investing, it may be exacerbated due to the more illiquid nature of EM securities. Another risk we can mention in relation to EM investing is what we may call "strategy risk". Systematic approaches to investing in EMs, such as carry and momentum strategies, are commonplace among bond managers.[10] However, there are limitations on the ability of managers to implement systematic investment strategies with EM bonds due to their low trading volumes, illiquidity, and capacity constraints relative to their DM counterparts. Brooks *et al.* (2020) and Konstantinov (2022) proposed systematic strategies for hard currency EM portfolios. However, these systematic strategies work for highly liquid hard currency (U.S. dollar) denominated

---

[7]See, for example, Correia *et al.* (2012), Houweling and van Zundert (2017), Israel *et al.* (2018), and Heckel *et al.* (2020).

[8]Martirosyan and Simonian (2021) demonstrate this in the case of momentum in EM equities.

[9]Litterman and Scheinkman (1991) used PCA to identify the building blocks of interest-rate volatility.

[10]See Brooks *et al.* (2020) for a discussion of various investing styles.

bonds. Nevertheless, financial market turmoil, default events, and liquidity crises might impact these portfolios more heavily than DM portfolios.

Finally, we note that transaction costs are an important consideration when implementing asset allocation, especially when investing in bonds in EM countries. High transaction costs may impede a portfolio's liquidity and limit portfolio turnover, imposing opportunity costs on a portfolio manager in the form of missed alpha generation opportunities. A positive development over the last few decades has been the development of electronic securities exchanges which allow for a more transparent and cost-efficient way to trade corporate and government bonds. As a result, the improved liquidity of corporate and government bonds has allowed for the more efficient and dynamic management of bond portfolios.

Turning to security selection, we first note that the relatively high liquidity in developed markets allows for the utilization of a wider set of instruments and techniques relative to those available for EM securities. Security selection in bond portfolios generally encompasses two types of instruments — bonds and derivatives. Currency exposure is arguably the risk factor that is common to all fixed-income instruments (Ladekarl and Peters, 2013). In terms of currency allocation, at the most basic level, portfolios consisting of only local currency bond exposures represent an alignment of country and currency risks. Portfolios consisting of both hard and local currency bonds allow for more complex risk exposures. For example, bond portfolios might allocate to Japanese yen, but the exposure might be not only in Japanese yen local currency bonds, but also in Japanese yen-denominated sovereign, corporate, or quasi-sovereign bonds.

In terms of country selection, global bond portfolios are often anchored in European, Japanese, and U.S. corporate bonds as they are viewed as providing a sufficient level of diversification and attractive risk–return profile. The European, Japanese, and U.S. corporate and government bonds are also highly liquid and are tracked by a wide array of derivative instruments, allowing for complex portfolio solutions. Bond futures, swaps, currency derivatives, and other instruments are common instruments used to gain exposure to European, Japanese, and U.S. corporate and government bond markets.

2.2 Global Bond Benchmarks

The choice of a benchmark is generally among the first decisions made by bond portfolio managers. Global bond indexes present a multitude of risk exposures compared to traditional bond indexes. Investing in global bonds means taking currency, interest rate, spread, inflation, political, volatility, liquidity, and reinvestment risks. In their totality, the risks inherent in global bond indexes often exceed the risks associated with their domestic counterparts.

The major function of a benchmark is not only to represent the investment universe of instruments and markets in which the bond manager invests but also to provide reasonable information on market risk, investable instruments, and proper and reliable performance measurement and attribution. However, some portfolios might not be restricted to specific benchmarks, but can invest in a broad set of instruments and markets. Such global bond portfolios are special cases and are considered "unconstrained bond portfolios". In general, the configuration of a benchmark, measured as an index, for global bond portfolios is rather problematic except for dedicated EM bond portfolios. That is, an index might represent a broader or narrower universe than the bond portfolio might be currently invested in.

In this chapter, we highlight the role of the most important and widely used indexes in global bond portfolios and provide simple methods to quantify, analyze, and investigate the relationships within and across indexes used as benchmarks by global bond portfolio managers.

2.3 Bond Index Criteria for Investment Management

Bond indexes are not simple baskets of single securities but must fulfill certain criteria. Over the years, as transparency, flexibility, transaction velocity, and operational sophistication in the market have improved, we have observed that both practitioners and academics embrace the use of indexes as an essential part of investment management. As a result, the need for clear and objective criteria for indexes has also grown. Today, it is widely accepted that there are standard criteria that an index must fulfill in order to be used as an investment benchmark.

Lo (2016) states that an index allows for the separation of active management decisions from risk management decisions in a portfolio. That is, an index which proxies a given market provides direct information regarding market risk. But it also provides insight into the return enhancement opportunities available to a manager. For a benchmark to be appropriate, it must fulfill certain requirements. Sharpe (1992) suggested that a benchmark should possess the following characteristics:

- *Knowable*: The constituents must be identifiable and both portfolio managers and their clients must agree on the index to be used as a benchmark.
- *Investable and not easily beaten*: Portfolio managers must be able to hold the assets of an index and have the ability to hold these assets without limitations.
- *Low in cost*: The index must be possible to obtain, and portfolio managers should be able to estimate the daily index value and portfolio performance at low cost.
- *Diversified*: The index must properly reflect the investment universe and provide diversification to investors.

While the foregoing criteria are simply stated, in the realm of bond portfolio management, it is often the case that bond indexes have a high level of complexity, greatly exceeding that of equities. The multi-faceted risk exposure in fixed-income instruments (e.g., interest rate, credit, or prepayment) makes bond index construction a challenging task. The mechanics of some bonds (e.g., bonds with embedded options) also add to the complexity of benchmark construction. Because debt instruments have finite maturities, the individual bonds that comprise a benchmark country, sector, or currency exposure will eventually be replaced with new bonds.

Adding a bond to an index has an immediate impact on the liquidity and turnover of that bond, namely, that a bond's inclusion is usually a catalyst for improved market liquidity for that specific bond.

In the next section, we discuss the primary issues related to bond benchmark and index construction

2.4 Bond Index Description

In this section, we turn our attention to the specification of bond indexes. Reilly and Wright (2012) and Konstantinov and Osswald (2021) showed that among the most important descriptive components for bond indexes are the following:

- The number of issues — exceeding 20,000 for global aggregate indexes
- The overall maturity — usually greater than one year
- The weighting structure — market versus equal weighting schema

- Pricing sources and systematics — tradable security prices
- Reinvestment risk — reinvestment of cash flows
- Minimum issue size of single constituents — usually greater than USD 300 million for corporate bonds

Several criteria help to distinguish between domestic and global bond indexes. Here, we briefly discuss the most important criteria that are relevant to global bond indexes.

Global bond indexes comprise heterogeneous currency, country, sector, and credit ratings, as well as different types of fixed-income instruments. The bonds in an index can be bullet bonds, callable and/or puttable bonds, inflation-linked, and mortgage-backed securities, among other types of instruments. An index can include multiple bonds from the same issuer, denominated in different currencies, for example. Alternatively, corporate bonds from different issuers can be included in an index with different credit ratings and cash flow structures. One feature that distinguishes bonds from stocks is that fixed-income instruments have a termination date or maturity. This has a direct bearing on bond index construction because at a certain point in time, specific instruments will no longer be part of an index and must be replaced. On the other hand, if new bonds are issued, they can become part of an index and the number of instruments comprising the index will increase.

The evolving nature of bond markets and instruments depends on various factors including investor risk appetite, technological change, and the prevailing regulatory regime. This evolution impacts both the type of products that are made available to investors and the bond indexes that are used to benchmark the performance of fixed-income products. Over time, indexes have evolved from simple constructs containing a small number of constituents to complex portfolios with thousands of instruments.

Bond indexes are broad portfolios with risks related to currencies, interest rates, credit default, and (indirectly) equity markets. For this reason, the pricing of fixed-income securities can be a challenging task. For example, corporate bonds are priced in an over-the-counter (OTC) market where sources of liquidity and transparency can be difficult to evaluate. This poses a serious risk for index construction. However, with recent advances in electronic trading systems and platforms, some of the informational challenges inherent in the OTC market have been alleviated to some extent.

Many bond indexes are rebalanced monthly. Some bonds will be dropped from a given index (e.g., because the maturity falls below the minimum required maturity or if an issuer's rating was downgraded below the minimum requirement). Other bonds will be added to the index, newly issued bonds, for example. After the rebalancing date, some index metrics may change greatly. For instance, the average maturity or duration normally increases materially, with the effect that both passive and active portfolio managers will have to adjust their portfolios accordingly. Table 2.1 provides a simple overview of several indexes used in global bond portfolios.

Two of the most important indexes are the Bloomberg Barclays Global Aggregate Index and the Bloomberg Barclays Global Aggregate Treasuries Index. These indexes were launched in 1990 and 2000, respectively. Aside from these indexes, there are a number of other prominent indexes used in global bond portfolios, such as the ICE BofA Global Fixed Income Index and the J.P. Morgan Global Aggregate Bond Index.

Table 2.1: An Overview to Global Aggregate and Emerging Market Bond Indexes (January 2003–December 2020)

Index Name	Number of Index Constituent Members	Inception Date	Market Value ($bln.)
Bloomberg Barclays Global Aggregate Index	27,196	Mar. 1990	67,691
Bloomberg Barclays Global Aggregate Treasuries Index	1,727	Sep. 2000	35,882
Bloomberg Barclays Global Aggregate Credit Index	17,279	Sep. 2000	16,769
J.P. Morgan GBI-EM Global Composite Index	276	Dec. 2002	2,327
J.P. Morgan EMBI Global Composite Index	925	Dec. 1993	1,360
J.P. Morgan CEMBI Global Composite Index	784	Dec. 2001	666

Notes: For all bond indexes in this table, the market value weighting methodology is used, rebalancing is done monthly, and the reinvestment type is total return. Constructed using the data obtained from Bloomberg, LLC, as of June 2021.

All these indexes aim at representing the global bond market, which comprises more than 20,000 single corporate, government, quasi-sovereign, and covered bonds.

Bond indexes present the same analytical and implementation challenges as any bond portfolio such as the calculation of accrued interest on the bonds in the index and the reinvestment of bond cash flows. In general, there are a few possibilities in dealing with accrued interest and reinvestment:

- Immediate reinvestment of bond cash flows in the index.
- Investing the cash flows using a money market rate (LIBOR, EURIBOR, etc.) until the next rebalancing date (ICE BofA indexes are such examples).
- Simple reinvestment of the cash flows on the rebalancing date (JP Morgan indexes follow a similar approach).
- No reinvestment of cash flows (Bloomberg Barclays indexes are examples).

When selecting an index, it is necessary to consider an index's documentation because different index providers follow specific procedures which have a direct impact on index metrics such as index composition, weighting schemes, duration, yield to maturity, and convexity. The calculation of all these metrics is of obvious importance to the calculation of cash flows.

2.5 Common Bond Indexes Used as Benchmarks

In this section, we clarify the difference between DM and EM bond indexes following the framework for the global bond markets provided and highlight the role of bond indexes. We note that the developed/emerging market classification is but just one classification available to bond investors. Another commonly used classification framework is corporate versus government bond indexes. The differentiation between DMs and EMs is appropriate in the context of global bond portfolio management due to the often vast differences in liquidity and market risk that typically exist between these two markets. EMs are often burdened with challenges to capital mobility, capital controls, market transparency, and effective market regulations. All these factors play into both the availability of high-quality data in EMs, as well as investors' risk appetite for securities issued in developing countries.

Index providers use several levels of index decomposition to group index constituents. The first level is asset sub-class classification. This classification refers in general to the following asset classes: sovereign, corporate, securitized/collateralized, and quasi-sovereign exposure. The second classification level further distinguishes between collateralized, agencies, financial, industrial, utility, government, asset-backed, and quasi-sovereign bonds among others. Country, maturity, currency, and industry groups are further important categories that bear on global bond indexes.

In the following sections, we discuss EM indexes as they possess a number of unique characteristics that distinguish them from the DM bonds that make up the bulk of global bond portfolios.

2.5.1 *Emerging market bond indexes*

The development of global bond markets and the worldwide trading of fixed-income securities over the past three decades became a catalyst for the development of EM bond indexes. De Jong and Fabozzi (2022) explained the rise of EM bond investing and the differences between hard currency and local currency bonds. Whereas EMs were previously viewed as a niche market, the use of EMs in institutional portfolios is now mainstream because of its diversification and return capacity. Lian (2022) explained that the rise of EMs as an asset class in the late 1990s and the market boom of the new millennium was the most pronounced catalyst for EM bonds. As a result, over time, EM bonds have become integral components of well-known broad indexes such as the J.P. Morgan GBI-EM Global Composite Index, which is a widely used local currency bond index.

There are several important characteristics of EM bonds. First, they are issued in both local and hard currencies. Second, a majority of EMs are non-investment-grade bonds. Finally, as in the case of DM debt, both corporations and governments are issuers of EM debt.

Among broad-based EM bond indices, the J.P. Morgan indexes are some of the most popular among institutional investors. The indexes offer broad exposure to EMs. J.P. Morgan (2018) imposes several criteria for minimum turnover, maximum weight, liquidity, and notional size of an issue in order to make the indexes investable and transparent. Nevertheless, these indexes are associated with specific costs and subject to fees imposed by data providers such as J.P. Morgan who are providers of the J.P. Morgan EMBI Global Composite Index, J.P. Morgan GBI-EM Global Composite Index, and J.P. Morgan CEMBI Composite Index.[11]

Aside from broad aggregate indexes, more specialized EM indexes are also available. For example, the J.P. Morgan CEMBI Composite Index provides exposure in emerging market corporates in different sectors such as the financial, industrial, consumer, oil and gas, and real estate sectors (among others) across five regions — Europe, Latin America, Asia, Africa, and the Middle East. These bonds are denominated in hard currency — in most cases in U.S. dollars. There is a cap on country and single security exposure in the index. The minimum issue size of a bond in the index is USD 300 million. This requirement is designed to ensure sufficient liquidity for a given bond and therefore provides investors with a benchmark that satisfies the criteria for investability and representativeness.

Both local and hard currency bond indexes are also published by index providers. For example, the J.P. Morgan GBI-EM Composite Index has exposure to both investment- and non-investment-grade bonds in local currencies in five regions — Europe, Latin America, Asia, Africa, and the Middle East. The index is rebalanced monthly and includes only sovereign bonds with a minimum issue size of USD 1 billion. Usually, country exposure and single-bond exposure are capped in the indexes and should not exceed certain threshold levels.

Turning to hard currency indexes, the J.P. Morgan EMBI Global Composite Index is perhaps the most widely used hard currency EM bond index. The index comprises hard currency bonds denominated in U.S. dollars for both investment- and non-investment-grade bonds in five geographic regions — Europe, Latin America, Asia, Africa, and the Middle East. Over the years, the number of countries in the index has increased, now comprising more than 60 countries, with their corresponding hard currency bonds denominated in U.S. dollars. There is a cap on country and single security exposure in the index. The minimum issue size of a bond in the index is USD 500 million. The index includes both sovereign and quasi-sovereign bonds.

---

[11]A detailed explanation of the J.P. Morgan indexes is provided in the J.P. Morgan Index Product Guide. See J.P. Morgan (2015).

2.5.1.1 *Index statistics*

The attributes that are common for EM debt make EM portfolios or global bond portfolios with EM exposure highly complex. Table 2.2 provides an overview of the descriptive statistics for the monthly returns of the J.P. Morgan Emerging market indexes in the period from January 2003 to December 2020. To compute bond index returns, the logarithmic returns of the time series are used:

$$R_r = \ln(P_t) - \ln(P_{t-1}) \tag{2.1}$$

where P_t is the asset price or index level at time t and P_{t-1} is the asset price or index level at time t–1.

Table 2.2 provides an overview of the descriptive statistics for the three main J.P. Morgan emerging market indexes and their Sharpe ratios. The table also contains the Bloomberg Ticker for the three indexes. As the table shows, the local currency J.P. Morgan EMBI Global Composite Index has the highest mean return of 66 basis points per year while having the lowest risk with a standard deviation of returns of 2.52% per year. The Sharpe ratio of the J.P. Morgan GBI-EM Global Composite Index is 0.54 and is the lowest among all three EM bond indexes. EM corporate bonds, represented by the J.P. Morgan CEMBI Composite Index, have a Sharpe

Table 2.2: Descriptive Statistics for Monthly (Logarithmic) Returns on J.P. Morgan Emerging Market Indexes (January 2003–December 2020)

	J.P. Morgan CEMBI Composite	**J.P. Morgan GBI-EM Global Composite**	**J.P. Morgan EMBI Global Composite**
Mean	0.58%	0.54%	0.66%
Median	0.78%	0.96%	0.86%
Maximum	7.60%	9.38%	7.48%
Minimum	–22.56%	–15.17%	–16.12%
Std. Dev.	2.66%	3.46%	2.52%
Skewness	–3.5881	–0.8454	–2.3163
Kurtosis	31.0722	5.2273	15.6381
Sharpe Ratio	0.75	0.54	0.91
Bloomberg ticker	JPEGCOMP	JGENVUUG	JCBBCOMP

Note: Data obtained by the authors from Bloomberg, LLC.

Table 2.3: Monthly Return Correlations between the J.P. Morgan Emerging Market Indexes (January 2003–December 2020)

	J.P. Morgan CEMBI Global Composite	J.P. Morgan GBI-EM Global Composite	J.P. Morgan EMBI Global Composite
J.P. Morgan CEMBI Global Composite	1		
J.P. Morgan GBI-EM Global Composite	0.69	1	
J.P. Morgan EMBI Global Composite	0.91	0.77	1

Note: Data obtained by the authors from Bloomberg, LLC.

ratio of 0.75. Indeed, the J.P. Morgan CEMBI Composite Index has the largest observed monthly drawdown losses (–22.6%). However, this index exhibits a relatively low volatility per year (2.66%). Thus, depending on the metric used, different indexes may appear more or less risky than others.

Table 2.3 shows the monthly return correlation between the indexes for the period January 2003 to December 2020. As can be seen from the table, despite different index compositions as well as different levels of currency, interest-rate risk, and spread risk, the correlation between the three EM indexes is significant. That said, we note that the local J.P. Morgan GBI-EM Global Composite Index does provides a fair amount of diversification compared to the other indexes with a return correlation of 0.69 and 0.77 with the CEMBI and EMBI indexes, respectively.

2.5.2 *Global bond indexes*

Turning to global aggregate bond indexes, perhaps their most notable characteristic is the increase in the number of index constituents over the last 20 years. The expansion in the constituent universe has been primarily due to the increased popularity of global bond portfolios over the years. Global bond indexes offer a wider array of risk and return exposure relative to traditional bond indexes dedicated to a single asset class like U.S Treasuries, inflation-linked bonds, or European high-yield bonds. Traditional bond indexes might be, but are not necessarily limited to, only one currency — the U.S. dollar or euro. Investing in global bond indexes entails taking on currency, interest rate, spread, inflation, political, volatility, liquidity, and reinvestment risk to an extent that generally exceeds that associated with domestic bond indexes.

Major providers of global bond indexes include large financial institutions such as J.P. Morgan, Citibank, Barclays, and ICE BofA. Because the ICE BofA indexes are dedicated to the same investment universe, they have a significant number of similarities in terms of the type and number of securities that they are comprised of. As a consequence, similarly constituted indexes typically exhibit high correlations with one another and have similar risk–return profiles.

2.5.2.1 *Global government bond indexes*

Some investment mandates restrict the universe of investable securities to government bonds. Global bond indexes may be dedicated to a specific type such as government or corporate bonds, or may be aggregate indexes that include different types of securities. The number of index constituents in global indexes has risen over the years from 900 in the early 2000s to roughly 2,000 constituents in 2021 that span more than 40 currencies. In contrast, global aggregate indexes contain corporate and government bonds from multiple currencies and countries, totaling more than 20,000 constituents. Global sovereign indexes, which include local currency government bonds from more than 40 countries, are heavily tilted to DMs. The U.S. dollar, euro, and Japanese yen have historically comprised more than 60% of the currency exposure of global government bond indexes. The duration of the global government bond indexes is in general very long, ranging between 5.5 and 8.5 years.

Bolla (2017) analyzed the factor exposure of global government bond indexes and found that country exposure is highly relevant for the performance of these indexes. In fact, the country exposure is identical to currency exposure as country risk is equal to currency risks. For this reason, some global bond portfolios are dedicated hard currency portfolios that do not expose themselves to local currency risk. Levich and Thomas (1993) argued that the decision to hold currency risk might depend on the availability and cost structure of currency hedging instruments. The expectations of risk determine the portfolio exposures and the choice of the appropriate benchmark. As Huttman and Harris (2006) pointed out, it is essential to establish a framework that guides the manner in which FX exposure is addressed in a portfolio as currency fluctuations often affect portfolios and benchmarks differently depending on the exposure. For example, currency depreciation against a base currency negatively affects foreign bonds (both hard and local currency). The bonds will generally decrease in the respective base currency value. The contrary is also true: currency appreciation (against the base currency) has a positive impact on the bond benchmark.

To see how, suppose for example that we have a global bond portfolio with a benchmark which has 30% exposure to euro-denominated bonds. Consider first the EUR/USD exchange rate. For a euro-based investor, the move from 0.84 in September 2001 to 1.57 in June 2008 is positive for a U.S. dollar-based portfolio with exposure to euro-denominated bonds, but negative for euro-based investors with U.S dollar-denominated exposure because the bonds suffered from the U.S. dollar depreciation against the euro. Conversely, the EUR/USD moved from 1.40 in September 2008 to 1.07 in March 2015. This depreciation of euro against the U.S. dollar caused losses for U.S. dollar-based portfolios in euro-denominated bonds, but the same EUR/USD movement was positive for euro-denominated bond portfolios with EUR/USD exposure.

Properly managing currency risk relative to a benchmark therefore becomes among the highest priority components of an investment process. Given that currency volatility is also often quite high for bond portfolios, hard currency mandates offer investors a somewhat more stable investment experience relative to their local currency counterparts (Burger *et al.*, 2012).

2.5.2.2 *Global aggregate bond indexes*

Global aggregate bond indexes comprise multiple securities from different sectors, currencies, regions, industry groups, and fixed-income sub-asset categories. The number of single-bond constituents of global indexes rose from roughly 6,000 in the early 2000s to more than 25,000 at the beginning of 2021. The market value of the Bloomberg Barclays Global Aggregate Bond index (LEGATRUU) increased from USD 11,800 billion in 2000 to roughly USD 67,691 billion in 2021. Index constituents are classified into sovereign, corporate, securitized/collateralized, and quasi-sovereign categories. Sovereign bonds have the largest bond index exposure, usually higher than 50%, followed by corporate bonds with roughly 20% of index exposure.

DMs represent the majority of aggregate bond indexes. The currency decomposition is also tilted to DMs with U.S. dollar, euro, and Japanese yen exposure historically exceeding 70% of the index exposure. The duration of global aggregate indexes is in general slightly shorter than the duration of government bond indexes and has historically ranged between 4.5 and 7.5 years.

2.5.2.3 *Index statistics*

The most widely used indexes in global government bond portfolios are the FTSE World Government Bond Index, which is identical to the Bloomberg Barclays Global Aggregate Treasuries Total Return Index, and the ICE BofA Global Government Bond Index. According to Morningstar, the ICE BofA Global Government Bond Index is one of the most widely used benchmarks among global bond portfolio managers. Overall, the Bloomberg Barclays Global Aggregate Index is the broadest globally invested index, comprising more than 20,000 individual government, corporate, and quasi-sovereign bonds.

Table 2.4 shows the descriptive statistics for four of the most widely used indexes in the period spanning January 2003 to December 2020. Note that the Bloomberg Barclays Global Aggregate Index has the largest

Table 2.4: Descriptive Statistics for Global Aggregate Bond Indexes (January 2003–December 2020)

	Bloomberg Barclays Global Aggregate Bond Index	**J.P. Morgan GBI Global Unhedged Index**	**Bloomberg Barclays Global Aggregate Credit Index**	**Bloomberg Barclays Global Aggregate Treasuries Index**
Mean	0.29%	0.35%	0.41%	0.33%
Median	0.29%	0.45%	0.54%	0.33%
Maximum	3.03%	6.02%	5.78%	6.97%
Minimum	–2.01%	–4.05%	–8.17%	–05.10%
Std. Dev.	0.89%	1.57%	1.80%	1.84%
Skewness	0.1463	–0.1730	–0.8601	–0.1238
Kurtosis	3.1295	3.8287	6.8992	3.9548
Sharpe Ratio	1.15	0.77	0.79	0.64
Bloomberg Ticker	LEGATRUU	JPMGGLTR	LGDRTRUU	LGTRTRUU

Notes: The table displays annualized data based on monthly logarithmic returns. Data obtained by the authors from Bloomberg, LLC.

Sharpe ratio (1.15). The Barclays Global Aggregate Credit Index has the largest mean return of 41 basis points per year, while the Barclays Global Aggregate Treasuries Index has the lowest (33 basis points per year).

Table 2.5 provides an overview of the monthly return correlations between the global aggregate bond indexes in the period spanning January 2003 to December 2020. Computing historical return correlations for different indexes and/or from different index providers helps us in two ways. First, it offers information on the statistical differences between index products. Second, it helps to see the correlations and potential statistical diversification advantages between indexes of the same provider.

As we see in the table, the monthly returns of the indexes are highly correlated with a correlation of 0.97 between the J.P. Morgan GBI Global Unhedged Index and the Bloomberg Barclays Global Aggregate Treasuries Index. This is not altogether surprising as different index providers use similar bonds in their index construction. Data availability depends on the costs associated to obtain index constituents. This is a critical point as both for portfolio and risk management access to the index constituents is

Table 2.5: Return Correlation between Global Aggregate Indexes (January 2003–December 2020)

	Bloomberg Barclays Global Aggregate Index	**J.P. Morgan GBI Global Unhedged**	**Bloomberg Barclays Global Aggregate Credit Index**	**Bloomberg Barclays Global Aggregate Treasuries Index**
Bloomberg Barclays Global Aggregate Index	1			
J.P. Morgan GBI Global Unhedged	0.54	1		
Bloomberg Barclays Global Aggregate Credit Index	0.37	0.9	1	
Bloomberg Barclays Global Aggregate Treasuries Index	0.58	0.98	0.79	1

Note: Data obtained by the authors from Bloomberg, LLC.

important. Moreover, the correlation between the Bloomberg Barclays Global Aggregate Treasuries Index and the Bloomberg Barclays Global Aggregate Index is 0.58, which is an indication that there is some, albeit limited, diversification advantage.

2.6 Bond Benchmarks: A Deeper Dive into Risk and Return

In this section, we provide more detail into the contours of global bond benchmark risk and return. We begin with Figure 2.1, where we plot the risk–return relationship between the six important indexes discussed in this chapter. First, we see that the risk and return relationship between bond indexes is positive. The J.P Morgan GBI-EM Global Composite Index is

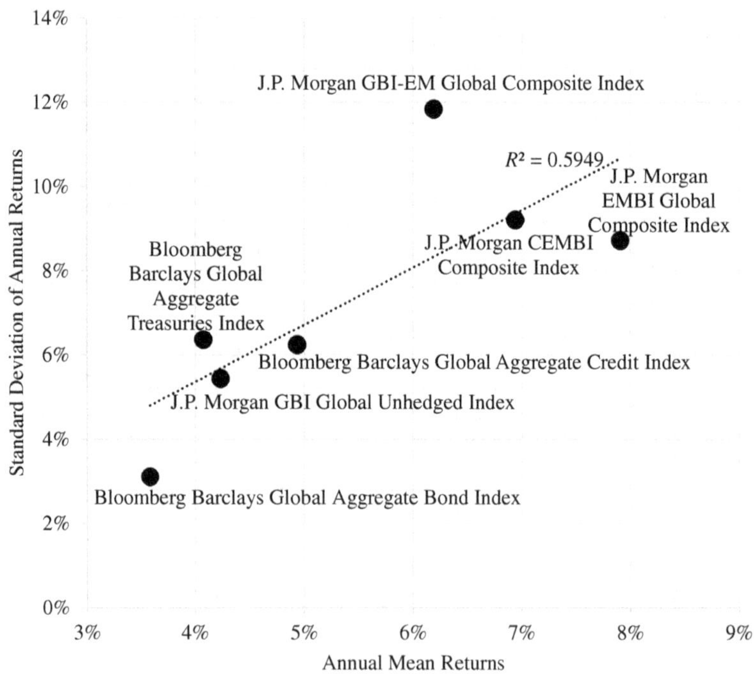

Figure 2.1: Risk–Return Characteristics of Global Bond Indexes (January 2003–December 2020)

Note: The figure displays annualized data based on monthly logarithmic returns. Data obtained by the authors from Bloomberg, LLC.

on the far right with the largest annualized standard deviation and return. The Bloomberg Barclays Global Aggregate Index is on the bottom left part of the figure, indicating a low risk–return profile. We apply a simple linear trend line to highlight the positive relationship between risk and return for the bond indexes shown. As we see, the positive risk–return relationship increases as the credit rating of the index and the ratings of the index constituents decrease. Thus, the J.P. Morgan CEMBI Global Composite Index which includes high-yield bonds has high returns but also presents higher risk exposure as measured by the standard deviation. That said, we see that contrary to intuition, the Bloomberg Barclays Global Aggregate Treasuries Index and the Bloomberg Barclays Global Aggregate Credit Index exhibit a similar standard deviation of annual returns of roughly 6%. However, their annual mean returns are different with an annual return of roughly 5% for the Bloomberg Barclays Global Aggregate Credit Index compared to a return of around 4% for the Bloomberg Barclays Global Aggregate Treasuries Index.

2.6.1 *Currency impact on benchmarks*

The currency denomination of an index is a major driver of its performance. Indexes are often denominated in a specific hard currency — U.S. dollar, euro, British pound, or Japanese yen. These indexes are typically called "hedged indexes". However, they can also comprise "local currency" bonds, which are bonds issued in their domestic currencies. Both DM and EM local currency bonds are available. Bonds issued in local currencies are exposed to the volatility of the currency in which they are denominated; hence, they may present more volatile investments relative to their hard currency counterparts. In the following sections, we provide an overview of both local and hedged currency index performance.

2.6.1.1 *Local vs. hedged currency indexes*

Ladekarl and Peters (2013) showed that currency is an important driver of returns in EMs. Currency risks are more significant for local currency benchmarks than for hard currency benchmark indexes. Specifically, hard currency bond indexes generally have exposure to a single "base" currency (e.g., U.S. dollar). In contrast, multi-currency bond indexes have no specific base currency, but are specified as "local currency indexes". Thus, for a global multi-currency index, the currency conversion in a specific base currency requires careful treatment to avoid possible miscalculations. More precisely, an index might be reported in terms of the U.S. dollar, which reflects the overall index valuation, while its individual constituents are still in local currency terms. As might be expected, currency adjustments of multi-currency indexes are more important than for hard currency indexes as benchmarks and indexes reported in different currencies result in different risk and return metrics.

When conducting performance measurement, index and portfolio performance should be computed in the same currency. Glück *et al.* (2021) also demonstrated that the same currency conversion convention should apply to factors. This is relevant for performance measurement because the currency denomination of factors should be aligned with the base currency of the global bond portfolio. That is, the performance of a bond portfolio with the U.S. dollar as a base currency should be measured against U.S. dollar-denominated factors. Similarly, the performance of a euro-based bond portfolio should be computed using euro-denominated factors.

A good way to provide an overview of the different indexes in terms of their respective currency exposures is to examine the statistical characteristics of various hedged and unhedged indexes. Summary statistics of the monthly logarithmic returns provided in Table 2.6 indicate that the

Table 2.6: Local Currency, Hedged and Unhedged Indexes (January 2003–December 2020)

	J.P. Morgan GBI-EM Global Composite Hedged USD	**J.P. Morgan GBI-EM Global Composite Local Currency**	**J.P. Morgan GBI-EM Global Composite Unhedged USD**
Mean	0.36%	0.69%	0.51%
Median	0.52%	0.82%	1.02%
Maximum	5.95%	6.01%	9.11%
Minimum	–3.55%	–3.22%	–15.01%
Std. Dev.	1.16%	1.13%	3.6%
Skewness	–0.0461	–0.0631	–0.8883
Kurtosis	5.6455	5.5877	4.9087
Sharpe Ratio	1.07	2.11	0.49

Notes: The figure displays annualized data based on monthly logarithmic returns. Data obtained by the authors from Bloomberg, LLC.

lowest mean and median returns per year are exhibited by the J.P. Morgan GBI-EM Global Composite Hedged USD while the J.P. Morgan GBI-EM Global Composite Unhedged USD Index posts the largest downside performance (–15%).

It is important to note that a global bond portfolio in U.S. dollars should be managed against a corresponding index that has the same underlying currency. Although hedged indexes have higher Sharpe ratios than their unhedged counterparts, using a hedged index as a benchmark implies that the portfolio being managed should be hedged in the same currency as the index. For example, a U.S. dollar hedged global EM bond portfolio should be managed against an appropriate benchmark such as the J.P. Morgan GBI-EM Global Composite Hedged USD Index. Similarly, a U.S. dollar unhedged bond portfolio should have a benchmark in the same currency such as the J.P. Morgan GBI-EM Global Composite Unhedged USD Index.

2.7 Quantitative Index Analysis

The mathematics of matrix algebra is essential for quantitative bond portfolio management where the investment universe may encompass a broad set of return drivers and risk exposures such as geography, currency, duration, and credit rating, among others. In this section, we provide an overview of matrix algebra as it pertains to global bond portfolio benchmarks. The advantage of this approach is that it provides mathematical representation of the most important index weight components. Both clients and portfolio managers often use such data representations in tabular form to provide an overview of complex index data.

2.7.1 *Matrix decomposition of indexes*

While examination of descriptive statistics is useful for understanding the differences between various indexes, in this section we provide a more in-depth analysis of index structure through matrix decomposition, which is carried out using the basic linear algebra operations of vector and matrix multiplication.

The matrix approach to index representation is perhaps best introduced with an example. Suppose that we would like to compute the weights of an index by considering currency and maturity characteristics of the index's constituent bonds. We begin by building binary matrices in which we assign 1 if the specific variable meets pre-specified criteria and 0 if not. Each dummy index consists of n bonds and m currencies.

Importantly, a bond $bond_n$ must appear only once with 1 in the matrix. That is, every single bond $bond_n$ is assigned only one position in the matrix. The currency matrix of a benchmark or index then has the following form for an allocation with binary variables:

$$\begin{pmatrix} & FX_1 & FX_2 & \cdots & FX_m \\ bond_1 & 1 & 0 & \cdots & 0 \\ bond_2 & 0 & 1 & & \vdots \\ \vdots & & & \ddots & \\ bond_n & 0 & \cdots & & 1 \end{pmatrix}$$

Similarly, we may define l maturity buckets M_l with bonds falling into the categories of 1–3-years to maturity, 3–5 years to maturity, 5–7 years to maturity, 7–10 years to maturity, and 10+ years to maturity. We assign 1 if a bond is in the first maturity bucket l and 0 if not. Importantly, a bond B_n must appear only once with 1 in the maturity matrix.

The matrix then has the following form for a maturity allocation with binary variables:

$$\begin{pmatrix} & M_1 & M_2 & \cdots & M_l \\ bond_1 & 1 & 0 & \cdots & 0 \\ bond_2 & 0 & 1 & & \vdots \\ \vdots & & & \ddots & \\ bond_n & 0 & \cdots & & 1 \end{pmatrix}$$

To compute the currency–maturity matrix, we can multiply the $n \times m$ matrix with the $n \times 1$ vector of index weights and multiply the $n \times l$ matrix with the $n \times 1$ vector of index weights. The index weights of the n single bonds in the index w_{bond_n} sum up to 100%. That is,

$$\begin{pmatrix} w_{bond_1} \\ w_{bond2} \\ \vdots \\ w_{bond_n} \\ \Sigma = 100\% \end{pmatrix}$$

Multiplying the $m \times 1$ vector of currency exposures with the transpose of the $l \times 1$ vector of maturity exposures shows the currency–maturity matrix of the index as an $m \times l$ matrix. The matrix contains the weights corresponding to the matrix definition. In other words, the currency–maturity matrix contains the currency–maturity weights $w_{FX_m M_l}$:

$$\begin{pmatrix} & M_1 & M_2 & \cdots & M_l \\ FX_1 & w_{FX_1 M_1} & w_{FX_2 M_2} & \cdots & w_{FX_1 M_l} \\ FX_2 & w_{FX_2 M_1} & w_{FX_2 M_2} & & \vdots \\ & \vdots & & \ddots & \\ FX_m & w_{FX_m M_1} & \cdots & & w_{FX_m M_l} \end{pmatrix}$$

Note that the total elements in the matrix sum up to 100%. The matrices will thus allow allocation comparisons between indexes and between an index and a portfolio.

Matrix decomposition of a benchmark reveals further details about its structure. The currency–maturity pair is but one way to analyze benchmarks via matrix decomposition. In the following, we list different characteristic combinations that can also be used to understand the structure of different types of benchmarks:

- *Currency–Maturity* — for multi-currency bond indexes like the Bloomberg Barclays Global Aggregate Treasuries Index.
- *Country–Maturity* — for geographically broad indexes like the J.P. Morgan EMBI Global Diversified Index.
- *Sector–Maturity* — for broad indexes comprising many sectors and maturity buckets like the Bloomberg Barclays Global Aggregate Credit Index.
- *Sector–Currency* — for multi-currency broad and corporate indexes like the Bloomberg Barclays Global Aggregate Index.
- *Sector–Rating* — for broad corporate indexes comprising many issues like the J.P. Morgan CEMBI Global Diversified Index.
- *Rating–Region* — for geographically diverse indexes like the J.P. Morgan EMBI Global Diversified Index.
- *Duration–Maturity Type* — for corporate bond indexes comprising different maturity types like bullet bonds, callable, puttable, sinkable, and perpetual bonds (e.g., the J.P. Morgan EMBI Global Diversified Index).

- *Currency–Rating* — matrices are used for multi-currency indexes and provide valuable information for yield curve positioning in rating buckets.

Figures 2.2–2.4 provide examples of possible matrix decompositions and visualizations. Figure 2.2 contains the region–maturity weights of the J.P. Morgan EMBI Global Composite Index, in which the bonds with the longest maturities are concentrated in Europe, the Middle East, and Latin America. Figure 2.3 contains the rating–maturity weights of the J.P. Morgan EMBI Global Composite Index in which the largest weights are concentrated in the ratings B+, BB−, and BBB to BBB+. The bonds are grouped by maturity buckets (<1Y, 1Y–3Y, 3Y–5Y, 5Y–7Y, 7Y–10Y, and <10Y). Figure 2.4 contains the rating–region matrix weights of the J.P. Morgan EMBI Global Composite Index.

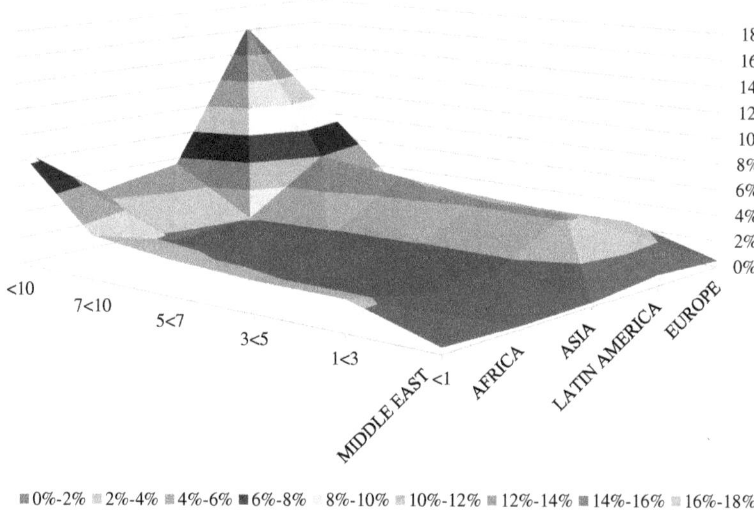

	EUROPE (%)	LATIN AMERICA (%)	ASIA (%)	AFRICA (%)	MIDDLE EAST (%)
<1Y	0.48	0.84	0.29	0.23	0.47
1Y<3Y	2.44	4.30	1.47	1.19	2.40
3Y<5Y	2.44	4.29	1.47	1.19	2.40
5Y<7Y	2.74	4.84	1.66	1.34	2.71
7Y<10Y	3.39	5.98	2.04	1.65	3.34
<10Y	9.18	16.19	5.54	4.47	9.06

Figure 2.2: Region–Maturity Weights — J.P. Morgan EMBI Global Composite Index

Note: Data obtained by the authors from Bloomberg, LLC.

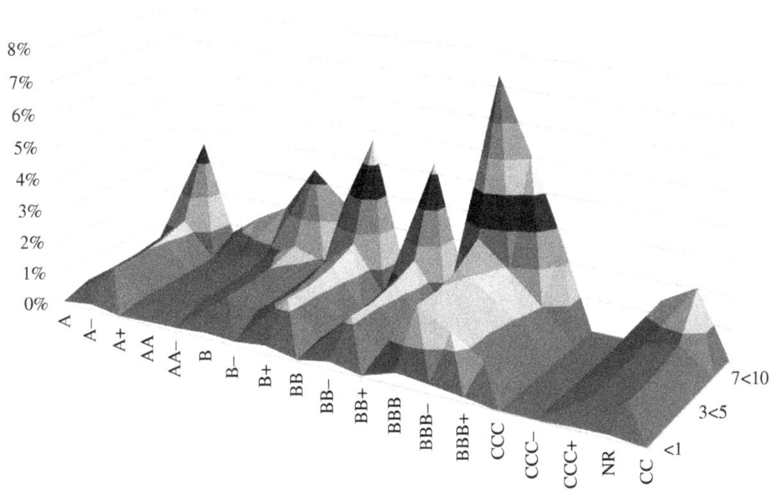

	<1Y (%)	1Y<3Y (%)	3Y<5Y (%)	5Y<7Y (%)	7Y<10Y (%)	<10Y (%)
A	0.07	0.36	0.36	0.40	0.50	1.35
A–	0.19	0.95	0.95	1.07	1.33	3.60
A+	0.04	0.20	0.20	0.22	0.27	0.74
AA	0.07	0.38	0.38	0.43	0.53	1.44
AA–	0.10	0.52	0.52	0.59	0.73	1.98
B	0.18	0.91	0.91	1.02	1.26	3.42
B–	0.13	0.67	0.67	0.75	0.9	2.52
B+	0.25	1.26	1.26	1.42	1.75	4.74
BB	0.05	0.23	0.23	0.26	0.32	0.88
BB–	0.23	1.16	1.16	1.30	1.61	4.36
BB+	0.04	0.19	0.19	0.22	0.27	0.73
BBB	0.38	1.95	1.95	2.19	2.71	7.34
BBB-	0.27	1.37	1.37	1.54	1.91	5.17
BBB+	0.14	0.72	0.72	0.81	1.00	2.71
CCC	0.00	0.00	0.00	0.00	0.00	0.00
CCC–	0.00	0.00	0.00	0.00	0.00	0.00
CCC+	0.07	0.38	0.38	0.43	0.52	1.42
NR	0.11	0.54	0.54	0.61	0.75	2.04
CC	0.00	0.00	0.00	0.00	0.01	0.02

Figure 2.3: Rating–Maturity Weights — J.P. Morgan EMBI Global Composite Index

Note: Data obtained by the authors from Bloomberg, LLC.

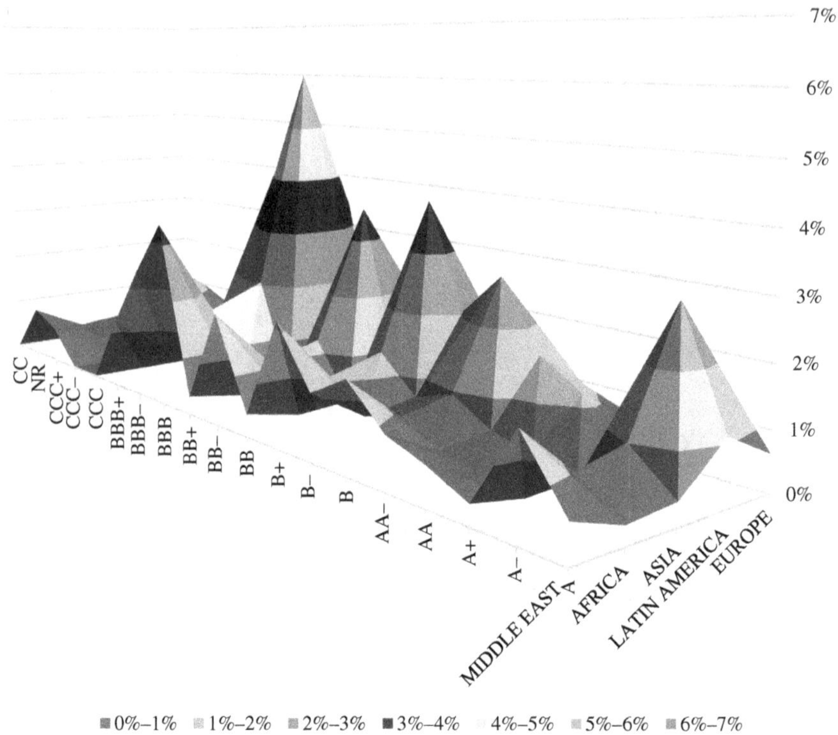

Figure 2.4: Rating–Region Weights — J.P. Morgan EMBI Global Composite Index
Note: Data obtained by the authors from Bloomberg, LLC.

Visual inspection of Figure 2.2 and the corresponding matrix shows that the maturity buckets with bonds that have a maturity of more than 10 years have the highest weights in the benchmark. This is an indication of long duration. Additionally, the allocation in the index is weighted towards Latin America and Europe. There is a lower index allocation in the maturity–country representation to Africa and Asia.

In Figure 2.3, we show the rating–maturity representation of the J.P. Morgan EMBI Global Composite Index. Representing the index as a rating–maturity matrix is perhaps one of the most informative ways to see the index tilts and gain information about possible index risks. Because maturities and ratings are highly related to liquidity risk, the index weights in the longer maturity buckets (>10Y) in lower rated bonds might be the first source of information about potential liquidity issues in case of financial market turmoil.

In Figure 2.4, the rating–region matrix and visualization provide information about the index geographical risk in relation to the ratings. This figure, which is a graphical representation of an underlying geographical region–rating matrix, provides information regarding the geographical–rating index decomposition. Interestingly, the lower rating buckets are heavily weighted in the index. Again, Europe and Latin America are the most heavily weighted in the benchmark and the index is tilted to the lower rating buckets in all markets except Europe.

Again, we note that matrix analysis allows benchmark decomposition through the consideration of durations, spreads, yields, and other variables in addition to those described above. Finally, we mention that matrix analysis provides not only insight into benchmark composition and allocation but often serves as a tool in portfolio optimizations, which we show in Chapter 6.

2.7.2 *Correlation analysis*

There are different ways to look at bond index relationships. One traditional method is to consider the pairwise Pearson correlations between index returns.[12] In Table 2.7, we show the monthly return correlation coefficients for some of the most important global bond index returns for the period January 2003 to December 2020. Again, the correlation coefficients between indexes provide initial information about diversification potential. In addition, correlation analysis helps in making return performance comparisons among index providers.

A natural question that arises is if there is any common factor that explains the variance of bond index returns. To answer this question, it is often helpful to use a technique known as *principal component analysis* (PCA) which is used to reduce large sets of correlated assets into a small number of unrelated factors. Figure 2.5 shows that the cumulative proportion of the bond index variance explained by three factors (level, slope, and curvature) in the period spanning January 2003 to December 2020 is 95%.

To demonstrate the practical meaning of the three factors for global bond indexes, we provide a simple estimation using PCA and three

---

[12]The most common way to do this is to consider the logarithmic price returns of the index time series.

Table 2.7: Return Correlation of Global Bond Indexes (January 2003–December 2020)

	Bloomberg Barclays Global Aggregate Index	Bloomberg Barclays Global Aggregate Credit Index	Bloomberg Barclays Global Aggregate Treasuries Index	J.P. Morgan GBI-EM Global Composite Index	J.P. Morgan CEMBI Composite Index	J.P. Morgan EMBI Global Composite Index	J.P. Morgan GBI Global Unhedged Index
Bloomberg Barclays Global Aggregate Index	1.00						
Bloomberg Barclays Global Aggregate Credit Index	0.90	1.00					
Bloomberg Barclays Global Aggregate Treasuries Index	0.98	0.79	1.00				
J.P. Morgan GBI-EM Global Composite Index	0.67	0.77	0.57	1.00			
J.P. Morgan CEMBI Composite Index	0.56	0.80	0.41	0.71	1.00		
J.P. Morgan EMBI Global Composite Index	0.64	0.82	0.50	0.80	0.91	1.00	
J.P. Morgan GBI Global Unhedged Index	0.54	0.37	0.58	0.09	0.17	0.26	1.00

Note: Data obtained by the authors from Bloomberg, LLC.

factors. In other words, we explain the variance of bond index returns and plot the values of the factors. We show this in Figure 2.5.

The solid line in the figure shows the cumulative proportion of the explained variance with the clear circles representing the variance by factor, which are the three principal components in this case. The dashed line is a reference line. The variance explained should stay above the reference line. As we see in the figure, the first factor explains roughly 68% of the bond index's return variance. The second and third factors, respectively, explain roughly 18% and 8% of the index's return variance. Notably, the first and the second factors together explain roughly 87% of the index's return variance.

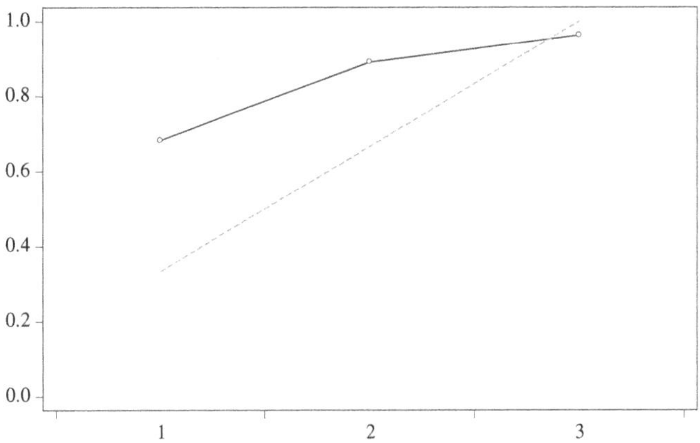

Factor Number	Value	Difference	Proportion	Cumulative Value	Cumulative Proportion
1	4.78	3.48	0.68	4.78	0.68
2	1.29	0.73	0.18	6.07	0.87
3	0.56	0.32	0.08	6.63	0.95

Figure 2.5: Principal Component Analysis of Bond Market Indexes (January 2003–December 2020)

While informative, statistical techniques such as PCA often provide limited answers related to the analysis of risk. Some are limited to analyzing linear relationships and/or ignore important interactions among risk factors, or they may only provide marginal insight into the return behavior of certain assets given their limited ability to detect patterns in time series data. Finally, in a portfolio management context, many traditional statistical frameworks often perform poorly as predictive tools, which is of obvious importance to any quantitative manager engaged in building trading models. The need for more sophisticated analytical tools has been stressed by Lopez de Prado and Fabozzi (2017), Simonian *et al.* (2018), and Simonian and Fabozzi (2019) who highlight that the complexity of financial data demands embracing analytical methods beyond linear models and calculus-based frameworks, the traditional tools of quantitative investors. Here, we describe one such approach and its potential utility for analyzing benchmark structure. It is based on a consideration of index relationships in a graph structure. Graphs allow us to classify data into clusters based on the proximity of observations to one another.

In applying clustering to index analysis, we begin by stipulating the Pearson correlation of returns as our basic similarity metric. Correlation among different bonds is measured for individual characteristics such as duration and credit quality. Correlations are then transformed into distance metrics using the following formula:

$$d_{ij} = \sqrt{2(1-\rho_{ij})}, \quad \text{with } i \neq j \tag{2.2}$$

where the pairwise correlation coefficients between the indexes i and j are denoted by ρ_{ij} and d_{ij} is the distance metric computed from the pairwise correlation coefficients. In Table 2.8, we show the distance metric for the indexes discussed in this chapter based on the correlations shown in Table 2.7.

Table 2.8: Distance Metrics for Global Bond Indexes (January 2003–December 2020)

	Bloomberg Barclays Global Aggregate Index	**Bloomberg Barclays Global Aggregate Credit Index**	**Bloomberg Barclays Global Aggregate Treasuries Index**	**J.P. Morgan GBI-EM Global Composite Index**	**J.P. Morgan CEMBI Composite Index**	**J.P. Morgan EMBI Global Composite Index**	**J.P. Morgan GBI Global Unhedged Index**
Bloomberg Barclays Global Aggregate Index	0.00	0.46	0.21	0.81	0.93	0.85	0.96
Bloomberg Barclays Global Aggregate Credit Index	0.46	0.00	0.65	0.69	0.63	0.61	1.12
Bloomberg Barclays Global Aggregate Treasuries Index	0.21	0.65	0.00	0.93	1.09	1.00	0.92
J.P. Morgan GBI-EM Global Composite Index	0.81	0.69	0.93	0.00	0.76	0.63	1.35
J.P. Morgan CEMBI Composite Index	0.93	0.63	1.09	0.76	0.00	0.42	1.29
J.P. Morgan EMBI Global Composite Index	0.85	0.61	1.00	0.63	0.42	0.00	1.22
J.P. Morgan GBI Global Unhedged Index	0.96	1.12	0.92	1.35	1.29	1.22	0.00

Notes: The monthly return correlation coefficients are converted to distance metrics using Equation (2.2). Data obtained by the authors from Bloomberg, LLC.

Note that the distance metrics in Table 2.8 reveal that the distance of an index to itself is zero. The larger the correlation coefficient, the lower the distance metric and thus the lower the diversification advantage. Conversely, the lower the correlation coefficient, the larger the distance of the index to the other indexes and thus the greater the diversification that an index might provide. Computing a graphical representation of the distance matrix allows a portfolio manager to visualize and easily detect the clusters in the index data.

Figure 2.6 shows hierarchical clustering[13] using equation (2.2) based on the distance metrics shown in Table 2.8, which show the global bond

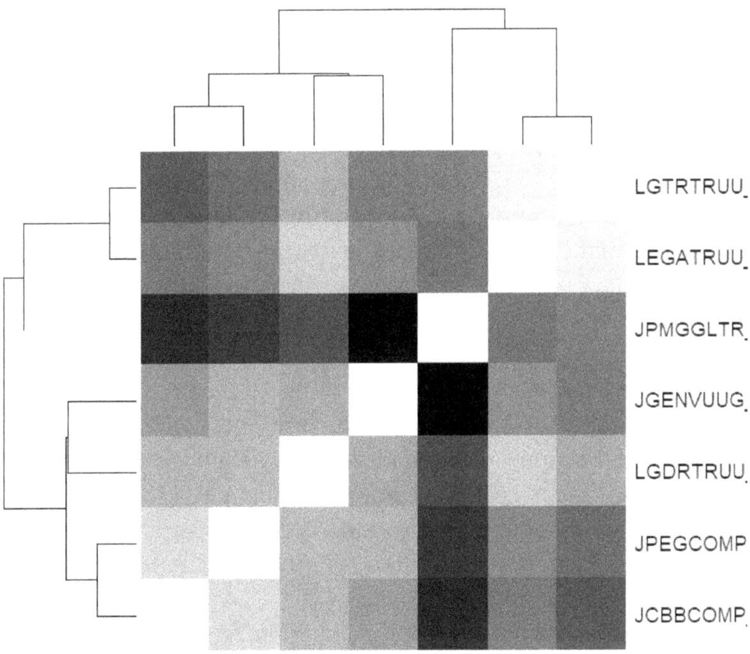

Figure 2.6: Global Bond Index Clusters and Relationships (January 2003–December 2020)

Notes: LEGATRUU is the Bloomberg Barclays Global Aggregate Index, JPMGGLTR is the J.P. Morgan GBI Global Unhedged Index, LGDRTRUU is the Bloomberg Barclays Global Aggregate Credit Index, LGTRTRUU is Bloomberg Barclays Global Aggregate Treasuries Index, JPEGCOMP is the J.P. Morgan EMBI Global Composite Index, JGENGVUUG is J.P. Morgan GBI-EM Global Composite Index, and JCBBCOMP is J.P. Morgan CEMBI Global Composite Index. Data obtained by the authors from Bloomberg, LLC.

---

[13] For a formal description of hierarchical clustering see James *et al.* (2013).

index relationships. To identify clusters, we can make a cutoff in the connecting lines. These clusters comprise indexes that have similar properties, which might be interest rate and/or spread dynamics, similarity in index construction and constituents, currency exposure, and ratings, among other features. For example, the Bloomberg Barclays Global Aggregate Treasuries Index, the Bloomberg Barclays Global Aggregate Index, and the J.P. Morgan GBI Global Bond Index are included in the same cluster, whose exposure to U.S. Treasuries and interest rates might be similar. The other indexes comprise a second cluster with properties different from the first cluster. The return drivers might be similar credit and country exposures.

2.8 Key Takeaways

- Global bond portfolios have a broad investment universe which encompasses both DM and EM countries. Global bonds may be issued as local currency bonds denominated in a country's domestic currency or hard currency bonds denominated in a major global currency like the USD. It is often possible for countries to issue cross-currency bonds in both their home currencies and major foreign currencies.
- Quantitative models can be used to model both DMs and EMs. However, due to their differing structure and dynamic, the models applied to DMs may differ considerably from the models used to model EMs. Matrix analysis can provide insight into index structure and allows index comparisons along several dimensions — ratings, currencies, countries, regions, sectors, and maturities, among others.
- Global markets are more complex than domestic markets in terms of the variety of risks and returns that bond portfolios might have exposure to. Contagion effects during episodes of financial market stress are a major risk. Common contagion effects include deterioration of the macroeconomic environment and financial market stress. Transaction costs and bond market liquidity are among the most important determinants in the quantitative investment process as these costs might harm portfolio rebalancing and quantitative strategies.

- Global bond indexes offer multiple risk and return sources compared to traditional bond indexes that comprise only one currency and one asset class like U.S. Treasuries or European high-yield bonds. Investing in global bond indexes entails taking on exposure to currency, interest rate, spread, inflation, political, volatility, liquidity, and reinvestment risks, which often exceed the risks associated with domestic bond indexes. Bond indexes are important sources of information for both portfolio managers and investors with regard to performance measurement, active portfolio management, and risk management.
- Hard currency and local currency bonds are two major categories of global bond indexes. Hard currency bond portfolios are denominated in a single major currency, while local currency bond portfolios comprise bonds denominated in the currency of their issuing country.
- Benchmark analysis is one of the most important aspects of a quantitative investment process. Matrix analysis and dimension reduction have become part of the standard toolkit for the majority of sophisticated quantitative investors.

References

Balima, W. H., J.-L. Combes, and A. Minea. 2017. "Sovereign Debt Risk in Emerging Market Economies: Does Inflation Targeting Adoption Make Any Difference? *Journal of International Money and Finance* 70: 360–377.

Barunik, J., E. Kocenda, and L. Vacha. 2017. "Asymmetric Volatility Connectedness on the Forex Market." *Journal of International Money and Finance* 77: 39–56.

Bolla, L. 2017. "Fundamental Indexing in Global Bond Markets: The Risk Exposure Explains It All." *Financial Analysts Journal* 73(1): 101–120.

Bollerslev, T., B. Hood, J. Huss, and L. H. Pedersen. 2018. "Risk Everywhere: Modeling and Managing Volatility." *Review of Financial Studies* 31(7): 2729–2773.

Bostanci, G. and K. Yilmaz. 2020. "How Connected is the Global Sovereign Credit Risk." *Journal of Banking and Finance* 113: 105761.

Brooks, J., S. Richardson, and Z. Xu. 2020. "(Systematic) Investing in Emerging Market Debt." *Journal of Fixed Income* 30(2): 44–61.

Burger, J. D., F. E. Warnock, and V. C. Warnock. 2012. "Emerging Local Currency Bond Markets." *Financial Analysts Journal* 68(4): 73–93.

Cheung, Y.-W. and F. Westermann (ed.), 2013. *Global Interdependence, Decoupling and Recoupling.* Cambridge, Massachusetts: The MIT Press.

Correia, M., S. Richerdson, and I. Tuna. 2012. "Value Investing in the Corporate Bond Market." *Review of Accounting Studies* 17(3): 572–609.

De Jong, M. and F. J. Fabozzi. 2022. "Emerging Markets Debt Securities: A Literature Review." *Journal of Portfolio Management* 48(8): 113–126.

Fama, E. F. and K. R. French. 1992. "The Cross-Section of Expected Stock Returns." *The Journal of Finance* 47(2): 427–465.

Glück, M., B. Hüberl, and H. Scholz. 2021. "Currency Conversion of Fama–French Factors: Ho wand Why?" *Journal of Portfolio Management* 47(2): 157–175.

Hamao, Y., R. W. Masulis, and V. Ng. 1990. "Correlations in Price Changes and Volatility across International Stock Markets." *Review of Financial Studies* 3(2): 281–307.

Heckel, T., Z. Amghar, I. Haik, O. Laplenie, and R. Leote de Carvalho. 2020. "Factor Investing in Corporate Bond Markets: Enhancing Efficacy Through Diversification and Purification." *Journal of Fixed Income* 29(3): 6–21.

Houweling, P. and J. van Zundert. 2017. "Factor Investing in the Corporate Bond Market." *Financial Analysts Journal* 73(2): 100–115.

Huttman, M. and L. Harris. 2006. "Generating Alpha from Currency Programs." *Journal of Alternative Investments* 8(4): 48–54.

Israel, R., D. Palhares, and S. Richardson. 2018. "Common Factors in Corporate Bond Returns." *Journal of Investment Management* 16(2): 17–46.

J. P. Morgan. 2015. "J. P. Morgan Index Product Guide." J. P. Morgan Global Index Research, January 2015.

J. P. Morgan. 2018. "Introducing the J.P. Morgan ESG Index Suite (JESG)." J.P. Morgan Global Index Research, April 18 2018.

Konstantinov, G. S. 2022. "Emerging Market Bonds: Expected Returns and Currency Impact." *Journal of Portfolio Management* 48(8): 139–158.

Konstantinov, G. S. and F. J. Fabozzi. 2022. "Portfolio Volatility Contagion." *International Journal of Theoretical and Applied Finance* 26(4): 2250019.

Konstantinov, G. S. and F. Osswald. 2021. "Bond Indexes and Bond Portfolio Management." Chapter 45 in F. J. Fabozzi (ed.), *The Handbook of Fixed Income Securities*. 9th Edition. New York: McGraw-Hill.

Ladekarl, J. and E. E. Peters. 2013. "Emerging Market Currency: The Common Risk Factor in Emerging Markets." *Journal of Investing* 22(3): 135–143.

Levich, R. M. and L. R. Thomas. 1993. "The Merits of Active Currency Risk Management: Evidence from International Bond Portfolios." *Financial Analysts Journal* 49(5): 63–70.

Lian, C. L. 2022. "Evolution of Emerging Markets Debt Investing." *Journal of Portfolio Management* 48(8): 109–118.

Litterman, R. and J. Scheinkman. 1991. "Common Factors Affecting Bond Returns." *Journal of Fixed Income* 1(1): 54–61.

Lo, A. 2016. "What is an Index?" *Journal of Portfolio Management* 42(2): 21–36.

Lopez de Prado, M. and F. J. Fabozzi. 2017. "Who Needs a Newtonian Finance?" *Journal of Portfolio Management* 44(1): 1–4.

Mandelbrot, B. B. 1963. "The Variation of Certain Speculative Prices." *Journal of Business* 36(4): 394–419.

Mantegna, R. N. 1999. "Hierarchical Structure in Financial Markets." *The European Physical Journal B: Condensed Matter and Complex Systems* 11(1): 60–70.

Martirosyan, A. and J. Simonian. 2021. "Emerging Market Stock Momentum Returns during US Economic Regimes." *Journal of Portfolio Management* 47(7): 27–45.

Masters, S. J. 2002. "Emerging Markets." *Journal of Portfolio Management* 28(3): 96–101.

Markowitz, H. 1952. "Portfolio Selection." *Journal of Finance* 7(1): 77–91.

Paserman, M. 2017. "Comovement or Safe Haven? The Effect of Corruption on The Market Risk of Sovereign Bonds of Emerging Economies During Financial Crises." *Journal of International Money and Finance* 76: 106–132.

Reilly, F. K. and D. J. Wright. 2012. "Bond Market Indexes." Chapter 3 in Frank J. Fabozzi (ed.) *The Handbook of Fixed Income Securities*. 8th Edition. New York: McGraw-Hill.

Rocha, K., R. Siqueira, and F. Pinheiro. 2007. "Vulnerability of Emerging Markets to Global Shocks: The Role of Debt and Governance on Sovereign Spreads." *Journal of Fixed Income* 17(2): 77–91.

Sharpe, W. 1992. "Asset Allocation: Management Style and Performance Measurement." *Journal of Portfolio Management* 18(2): 7–19.

Simonian, J. 2021. "Geopolitical Risk in Investment Research: Allies, Adversaries, and Algorithms." *Journal of Portfolio Management* 47(9): 92–109.

Simonian, J., M. López de Prado, and F. J. Fabozzi. 2018. "Order from Chaos: How Data Science is Revolutionizing Investment Practice." *Journal of Portfolio Management* 45(1): 1–4.

Simonian, J. and F. Fabozzi. 2019. "Triumph of the Empiricists: The Birth of Financial Data Science." *Journal of Financial Data Science* 1(1): 10–13.

Simonian, J. and C. Wu. 2019. "Minsky vs. Machine: New Foundations for Quant-Macro Investing." *Journal of Financial Data Science* 1(2): 94–110.

Tiwari, A. K., J. Cunado, R. Gupta, and M. Wohar. 2018. "Volatility Contagions across Global Asset Classes: Evidence from Time and Frequency Domains." *Quarterly Review of Economics and Finance* 70: 194–202.
Wang, Z. 2010. "Dynamics and Causality in Industry-Specific Volatility." *Journal of Banking and Finance* 34(7): 1688–1699.
Uribe, M. and V. Z. Yue. 2006. "Country Spreads and Emerging Countries: Who Drives Whom?" *Journal of International Economics* 69(1): 6–36.

Chapter 3

Currency Management

Currencies play an important role in global bond portfolios because they constitute one of the major risks for fixed-income instruments. *Currency risk* appears via two channels. First, through the *passive currency exposure* that is present in bond portfolios simply as a result of holding bonds in foreign currencies. Second, currency risk may appear through *active currency management* where currency overlays are implemented in a portfolio with the objective of enhancing returns and minimizing risks. In this chapter, we provide a comprehensive overview of currency risk and active currency management. Included in our discussion are detailed formal accounts of various metrics for measuring currency risk and performance, as well as an overview of various active currency strategies.

3.1 The Role of Currency Markets

Let's begin by highlighting the important role of currency markets in global bond portfolio management. The growing need for diversified products, investment solutions, and management skill has driven the development and trading of more currency market products.

3.1.1 *Development of currency markets*

Foreign exchange is an asset class with large volumes and numerous interacting market participants. Pojarliev and Levich (2012) explained that in the late 1980s the view that currencies represented a separate asset class was adopted by some market participants. Galati and Melvin (2004) documented that the internationalization in financial markets and the growth in equity and bond portfolios helped the development of currency overlay programs dedicated to separately managed currency exposure. King *et al.* (2013) and Su and Zhao (2017) showed that international financialization and globalization in financial markets have positively impacted the currency market, resulting in a market with a high degree of liquidity, with numerous participants, large transaction volumes, and low transaction costs. The growth in currencies as an asset class can be traced back to the demand for international diversification and the rise in globally oriented products, which in turn has driven the development of electronic platforms and electronic exchanges, and has further increased market liquidity and participation.[1]

The BIS Triennial Central Bank Survey (2019, 2022) has documented the way trades are executed in the foreign exchange (FX) market. FX trade execution is executed predominately electronically, replacing traditional "voice" execution. The 2019 Triennial Survey showed that the share of FX trading executed electronically is close to 60%. The market segment with the highest growth rates is dealer-to-customer (D2C) transactions. Spot market transactions remain the instrument with the highest electronic trading share, accounting for 75% of D2C transactions. Interestingly, in contrast to the rise in D2C markets, electronic spot trading in inter-dealer markets has declined over time. As a consequence, inter-dealer trading accounted for less than a third of the total electronic spot market trades in 2019. This decline in electronic inter-dealer trading is driven principally by "internalization".

Internalization refers to a type of currency management that is a consequence of the growing financial need for investment products and the global focus of many equity, bond, and multi-asset portfolios. Diversification is crucial for investors and investing in global markets requires currency exposure. Currency exposure requires distinctive currency management, which can take two forms. The first is overlay management where currency exposure is managed passively or actively by specialized currency managers. The second type of currency management, resulting from internalization, is the need for excess returns as

[1] Konstantinov and Pojarliev (2021) provide information on the development of electronic exchanges in currency markets.

portfolio managers and investors try to exploit inefficiencies in currency markets.

In contrast to the FX cash market, FX derivative instruments are still driven by traditional trading. Both the 2019 and 2022 Triennial Survey show that inter-dealer trading of FX swaps has remained heavily voice reliant (although D2C trading is mainly executed by electronic execution methods). There are two main reasons for this. First, swap trades involve particularly large notional amounts. FX swaps are among the most widely used instruments for managing currency risk. Indeed, FX swaps accounted for more than 50% of total global foreign exchange market turnover in 2022. The market share of FX spot transactions has decreased in recent years. In the 2022 survey, it accounted for 28% compared to 30% in 2019 and 37% in 2010. We note however, that the foregoing trades are those executed via OTC contracts, and their trading depends on the parties' acceptance of counterparty risk.

Overall, spot and swap transaction volumes remain dominated by a few developed market currency pairs, namely, EUR/USD, USD/JPY, and GBP/USD. These are the most liquid currencies and are centered on the so-called "G3" currency group that includes the largest developed economies in the world — the United States, the European Union, and Japan. Following the G3, the G10 currencies include the currencies with the largest demand and supply volumes. Emerging market currencies still lag behind but are gaining pace in trading and settlement.

We show the most liquid and widely used currencies and their trading symbols in Table 3.1. Note however that not all "liquid" currencies are created equal. For example, according to the Triennial Survey released in 2022, the NZD has a reported turnover of only 2% versus USD of 88% and EUR of 31%. Notable is the turnover development of the G3 currencies (USD, EUR, and JPY) and the rising international importance of the Chinese renminbi (CNY). It is interesting to note the increase in turnover

Table 3.1: Countries, Currencies, and Currency Symbols

G10 Countries	**Currency**	**Symbol**
United States	U.S. dollar	USD
European Monetary Union	Euro	EUR
Japan	Japanese yen	JPY
United Kingdom	British pound	GBP
Australia	Australian dollar	AUD

(*Continued*)

Table 3.1: (*Continued*)

G10 Countries	**Currency**	**Symbol**
Switzerland	Swiss franc	CHF
Canada	Canadian dollar	CAD
Sweden	Sweden krone	SEK
Norway	Norwegian krone	NOK
New Zealand	New Zealand dollar	NZD
Non-G10 and EM Countries	**Currency**	**Symbol**
Brazil	Brazilian Real	BRL
The Philippines	Philippine peso	PHP
Mexico	Mexican peso	MXN
South Africa	South African rand	ZAR
Poland	Polish zloty	PLN
Hungary	Hungarian forint	HUF
Russia	Russian ruble	RUB
Turkey	Turkish lira	TRY
Malaysia	Malaysian ringgit	MYR
Indonesia	Indonesian rupiah	IDR
Thailand	Thai baht	THB
Korea	Korean won	KRW
China	Chinese renminbi	CNY
China (Offshore)	Chinese renminbi	CNH
Hong Kong	Hong Kong dollar	HKD
Singapore	Singapore dollar	SGD
Taiwan	Taiwanese dollar	TWD
Argentina	Argentine peso	ARS
Chile	Chilean peso	CLP
Romania	Romanian Leu	RON
India	Indian rupee	INR
Columbia	Colombian peso	COP
Peru	Peruvian sol	PEN
Denmark	Danish krone	DKK

Note: This table provides an overview of countries, their currencies, and currency symbols.

in CNY over the last 10 years, perhaps at the expense of major G10 currencies (EUR and JPY). Reported turnover in CNY was only 1% in 2010 and increased to 7% in 2022, while combined turnover in EUR and JPY decreased by 10% over the same period. The rise in turnover volume can be explained not only by the role of China in international trade, monetary transactions, and portfolio investments but also by the rise of FX transactions and central bank policies to keep monetary reserves in CNY.

3.1.2 *Drivers of FX market structure*

The supply and demand dynamics and liquidity of FX markets are primarily determined by three important drivers: (1) market-maker activities, (2) policymakers (central banks, government institutions, and regulators), and (3) portfolio flows.

3.1.2.1 *Market-maker activities*

Financial markets can be largely described by a lower supply versus a higher demand for liquidity and investment instruments. This supply–demand imbalance applies to all types of asset classes from cash to equities. Exacerbating the situation has been the changing scope of market makers in financial markets. As investment banks have been cutting back on market making for regulatory and capital-saving reasons, there has been even more pressure on market liquidity while demand has continued unabated. The growth of the asset management industry has also been a driver of liquidity demand. With an ever-increasing array of products and assets under management, the operational need for liquidity is greater today than ever before. The growth in the asset management industry has not been limited to bond strategies of course, but has also been driven by fund flows into equity, multi-asset, commodity, and alternative products. Strategies that serve as liquidity providers for the market (e.g., developed market sovereign bond funds) are therefore potentially well positioned to fill a structural niche in the current market environment.

3.1.2.2 *Central banks, government institutions, and regulators*

Monetary policy has evolved considerably in recent years. Today, central banks provide direct liquidity support to market participants to a greater degree than any time in their histories. The European Central Bank (ECB), the Federal Reserve (Fed), and the Bank of Japan (BoJ) are examples of monetary institutions engaged in conducting market activities in the form of monetary operations such as asset purchases. Such central bank activity has the potential to change the structure of the currency market, influence bid-ask spreads and market risk, and as a result potentially shift bond portfolio allocations to longer duration bonds, with biased maturity structures and risk–return profiles. In a sense, perennial central bank purchasing mechanisms have transformed the market. Because of the significant balance sheet expansion of central banks and the large number of transactions executed in the market with bond purchases, central banks have become influential market players.

The role of regulators in fostering liquid markets is also significant, especially in the aftermath of the 2007–2008 Global Financial Crisis (GFC), where the regulation of financial flow has intensified. The impact of algorithmic trading has been a special focus given the amount of volatility that automated trades can inject into the market. Of course, currency markets have been a central concern of regulators, as the role of FX as a medium of exchange is critical to the functioning of capital markets. The net result of post-GFC regulatory activity has been that the most liquid segments of the bond market such as the spot FX and sovereign debt markets have increased in liquidity even further with market depth increasing and bid-ask spreads narrowing.

3.1.2.3 *Portfolio allocation*

Bond managers must constantly adjust their views and expectations in accordance with changing market conditions. Accordingly, portfolios must be rebalanced as the interest-rate environment, credit conditions, and market liquidity evolve. In addition, portfolio rebalancing of global bond portfolios must also account for currency exposure.

Since the GFC, bond portfolio managers have also had to contend with a low interest-rate environment, heightening the reinvestment risk inherent in rebalancing. For example, the bond yield of the Bloomberg Barclays Global Aggregate Bond Index declined from 9.5% in April 1990 to 0.8% in April 2020. During the same period, the 10-year U.S. Treasury bond yield declined from 8.6% to 0.65%. During this period, the relative attractiveness of investment-grade bonds denominated in low-yielding currencies diminished considerably. Portfolio managers and other investors understandably had to consider alternative sources of income, including higher-yielding corporate and emerging market debt. The search for higher-yielding assets has thus been an important catalyst for the development of the FX market, as more and more types of international debt markets became "mainstream" (see de Jong and Fabozzi, 2022). The large amount of fixed-income assets under management and investor demand for internationally diversified portfolios, has been an important driver for the positive trend in the appetite for local and hard currency debt.

Now that we have a basic understanding of the mechanics of FX markets and the market players, we next provide an overview of the major metrics and calculations used to estimate currency expected returns and relative value.

3.1.3 *Expected returns of currencies*

Calculating expected returns for foreign exchange instruments is more challenging than estimating expected returns for stocks and bonds. For example, the Gordon growth model allows the derivation of the expected return of a company's stock based on readily available information such as dividend growth rates.[2] Alternatively, one may simply use a company's earnings yield as an estimate for its expected return, among other methods.

Similarly, the expected return of bonds can be estimated using simple metrics like yield-to-maturity or carry. Incorporating additional metrics like default rates into expected returns for bonds is also relatively simple. For both stocks and bonds, an expected total return value is a function of an income component (dividends in the case of equities, interest in the case of bonds) and the price change in the security. In contrast, calculating expected returns for currencies is not as straightforward as in the case of stocks and bonds. FX is a rate of exchange. To buy dollars, for example, one must sell another currency. It is thus unlike stocks and bonds in that it is not an instrument that represents a claim on some underlying asset. The explanation that currencies have expected return of zero can be traced back to the works of Meese and Rogoff (1983) and Rogoff (2001) who argued that short-term currency movements follow a random-walk

---

[2]See Gordon and Shapiro (1956).

process with no drift and are impossible to model and predict. Moreover, the value and expected returns of currencies have only relative meaning. This refers also to the currency strategies that we will discuss in this chapter.

Economic theory provides the theoretical framework for currency valuation. From a macroeconomic perspective, the most relevant variables in pricing currencies include interest rates, money supply, inflation rates, and current account balances. These are the inputs to calculate a currency's *fair value* based on forward rate estimation as discussed in the sections that follow.

3.2 Foreign Exchange Exposure for Global Bond Portfolios

In this section, we provide an overview of how currency and bond exposure are related. Notably, to determine the currency and bond exposure in global bond portfolios, the prices, notional amount, and portfolio exposure are considered. We provide examples as to how different portfolio management views can be integrated and related to bond and currency investing.

3.2.1 *Currency notation and cross-currency rates*

As mentioned above, FX transactions involve two currencies, buying one and selling the other. Thus, a currency's value is always relative and depends on a country's interest and inflation rates relative to the other country in the currency pair. FX returns should always reflect the base currency of a portfolio.

The first step in deriving FX returns is to convert all unit notations into prices. This is necessary because conventions used in the FX market are not uniform. For example, the EUR/USD means the U.S. dollar price of one euro. The USD/JPY represents the Japanese yen price of one U.S. dollar. This notation may differ from the base currency of the portfolio or the currency in which the portfolio's net asset value (NAV) is denominated. Note that the NAV of a portfolio is computed in a single reference or base currency. For example, a global bond portfolio with the euro as the base currency has to convert the unit notation into a price notation with the euro as the base.

Table 3.2: Currency Notations Depending on the Base Currency

FX/Base	U.S. Dollar	Euro	British Pound	Swiss Franc	Canadian Dollar	Australian Dollar
U.S. dollar		USD/EUR	USD/GBP	USD/CHF	USD/CAD	USD/AUD
Euro	EUR/USD		EUR/GBP	EUR/CHF	EUR/CAD	EUR/AUD
British pound	GBP/USD	GBP/EUR		GBP/CHF	GBP/CAD	GBP/AUD
Swiss franc	CHF/USD	CHF/EUR	CHF/GBP		CHF/CAD	CHF/AUD
Canadian dollar	CAD/USD	CAD/EUR	CAD/GBP	CAD/CHF		CAD/AUD
Australian dollar	AUD/USD	AUD/EUR	AUD/GBP	AUD/CHF	AUD/CAD	

Table 3.2 shows the most important currency pairs in different base currency notations.

Let's consider a simple example to illustrate how to read and interpret currency pairs. Consider the currency pair EUR/USD which expresses the U.S. dollar price of one euro. The convention is that the first currency in the pair (EUR in our example) denotes the reference or base currency, and the second term refers to the "foreign" currency.

If an investor's domestic currency is the euro, then the investor's U.S. dollar exposure at time t is estimated by taking the reciprocal value of the EUR/USD rate, for example,

$$\text{USD/EUR} = \frac{1}{1.083} = 0.9233$$

which tells us that the price of one U.S. dollar for a euro-based investor is 0.9233. The price of one euro for a U.S. dollar investor, or portfolio with U.S. dollar as a base currency, is 1.083. Using the price notations, we can always compute the returns in base currency using the prices in the local currency. In general, this is the mechanism to convert unit to price notations. Importantly, the latter currency conversion is not mandatory. The notation using the base currency of the portfolio assures that every amount or exposure would be calculated using the right currency notation.

A serious drawback in currency investing is that cross rates for all currency pairs do not exist. The reason for this is that the necessary economic relations and capital flows between some countries are not present. Consider, for example, the currency pair involving a cross rate between the South African rand (ZAR) and the Hungarian forint (HUF). This cross-currency rate would be ZAR/HUF. Unfortunately, a currency rate to satisfy this trade does not exist. Investors wishing to trade ZAR/HUF could nevertheless create a *synthetic* trade by executing two trades involving USD/ZAR and USD/HUF.

3.2.2 *Foreign exchange returns and exposure estimation*

To compute a currency return over a given period, we must convert the second term in a currency pair to the base currency. Again, a rise in the EUR/USD from 1.20 to 1.30 is an appreciation of the EUR against the USD, or depreciation of the USD against the EUR depending on the point of view or base currency. To estimate the currency returns using a base currency, the conversion of the exchange rate is necessary so that the base currency is the second currency in the pair. For example, for a EUR-based portfolio, the returns in USD exposure are USD/EUR. The following equation captures the relationship:

$$R_t^{fx/\mathrm{BC}} = \ln(qx/\mathrm{BC})_t - \ln\left(\frac{qx}{\mathrm{BC}}\right)_{t-1} \tag{3.1}$$

where BC is the base currency, qx is the "foreign" or quoted currency, and $R_t^{fx/\mathrm{BC}}$ is the currency return expressed in domestic currency or the reference base currency of the portfolio.

For example, the normal convention for the U.S. dollar and the South African rand is USD/ZAR. To calculate the currency return in a portfolio of investments in South African rand for a portfolio with U.S. dollar base currency $R_t^{qx/\mathrm{BC}}$, we use equation (3.1) and use the reciprocal values of the USD/ZAR, because ZAR/USD

$$R_t^{\mathrm{ZAR/USD}} = \ln(\mathrm{ZAR/USD})_t - \ln\left(\frac{\mathrm{ZAR}}{\mathrm{USD}}\right)_{t-1} \tag{3.2}$$

This approach helps to reveal one of the most important issues for global multi-currency or hard currency bond portfolios. Specifically, the return decomposition shows that the local currency bond effects are equal for all investors holding the same portfolio, and it is the base currency of the fund that makes the difference.[3] To understand the role of the base currency of a portfolio, we consider the case of a global bond portfolio with one currency. Recall that to show the separate currency effects as a total sum, it is necessary to determine the single bond currency impact using price notation and multiply by the portfolio weight. The sum is the total bond portfolio currency impact. For a continuous[4] return estimation with long holding periods, it is convenient to use the following notation provided by Paape (2003):

$$R_t^{\mathrm{BC}} = (1 + R_t^{\mathrm{LC}})(1 + R_t^{qx/\mathrm{BC}}) - 1 \tag{3.3}$$

where the bond return in the base currency is R_t^{LC}, and the product of the local currency return R_{lc}, and $R_t^{qx/\mathrm{BC}}$ is the currency return in the corresponding base (or domestic) currency at time *t*.

Decomposing the currency returns of bond portfolios in this way might additionally provide information to bond portfolio managers regarding which styles determine currency returns, especially if the bond portfolio manager follows a specific currency strategy. In other words, bond portfolio managers might follow a specific investing style when investing in currencies. The style might be carry, value, or momentum. This is particularly relevant for unconstrained, or opportunistic, bond portfolios. We provide insights regarding currency return decomposition in Chapter 12 where we discuss performance attribution.

3.2.3 *Bond exposure and foreign exchange*

Bond exposure and FX are inevitably connected in a global bond portfolio. To illustrate this, we compare two types of bond portfolios each respectively managed by a quantitative and discretionary investment management process.

---

[3] Konstantinov (2022) used four different portfolio base currencies (USD, EUR, CHF, and JPY) for emerging market bond portfolios and showed different expected returns and portfolio allocations that are impacted by the base currency.

[4] It is possible to use a discrete or continuous notation when estimating a currency's impact on a bond.

3.2.3.1 *Simple bond trading and foreign exchange*

We begin this section by describing the primary ways that FX exposure is gained in a portfolio. When trading multi-currency bonds, there are three widely used methods for gaining currency exposure:

Method 1: Automatic conversion of the FX amount in the base currency of the portfolio.

Method 2: Separate FX and bond transactions using the specific notional amount of the bonds in the respective currency.

Method 3: Bond exposure in specific currencies to determine the amount of overlay required to cover that exposure.

The first method, automatic conversion, is best explained with an example. Consider a U.S.-based investor who buys a German government bond and a French corporate bond with notional size of 20 million and 10 million euros, at the price of 105.00 and 109.50, respectively. Note that these quotes mean the bonds are trading at a premium to par value of 105% and 109.5%, respectively. Assume that the current EUR/USD rate is 1.083 (bid price is 1.082 and ask price is 1.084, so we are using the midpoint). The amounts in euro are converted to U.S. dollars since the USD is the portfolio's base currency. If we choose the midpoint price between the bid and ask price (1.083), this results in amounts of 22,743,000 (105% × 20,000,000 × 1.083) and 11,858,850 (109.5% × 10,000,000 × 1.083) U.S. dollars. Note that from the perspective of a portfolio manager, choosing the midpoint price for spot FX transactions is often unfavorable. The portfolio manager might be able to get a better FX quote than to receive the middle price. The larger the bid-ask spread, the higher the potential costs and unfavorable effects of automatic conversion.

The second method involves a bond portfolio manager placing FX orders separately and using electronic trading platforms for FX spot transactions. This method often results in narrower bid-ask spreads and lower costs. Consider a portfolio manager who wishes to express a view on the EUR/USD exchange rate. If the manager expects the euro to depreciate in the next few days, then they could express that view by selling euros short today and then buying in a few days at a cheaper rate.

The third method for a portfolio manager to gain FX exposure in a portfolio is by utilizing an overlay strategy. In an FX overlay strategy, bond exposure is first calculated, and then the weights are applied to trade FX. The portfolio manager can place an FX order in the spot market or use currency forwards to allocate capital for the bond for a future settlement day. This trade is a potential alpha source for bond portfolio managers, particularly in highly volatile currency market environments.

In general, a portfolio manager's process determines which exposures should be prioritized. For example, suppose that a bond portfolio manager decides to buy a long-term Italian government bond based on relative value analysis that shows that an overweight of Italian government bonds versus Italian corporates is currently preferable. As a consequence, the portfolio manager might increase the portfolio's exposure to EUR/USD, and thus emphasize carry returns based on a large interest rate differential versus the portfolio manager's base currency (i.e., the U.S. dollar).

3.2.3.2 *Estimating bond exposure in local currency*

Let us extend our analysis and include FX and bond portfolio exposure in local currency debt instruments. Again, we use a simple hypothetical example to illustrate the relevant relationships. Suppose that a U.S. dollar-based global bond portfolio invests in two bonds — an Australian local currency bond in Australian dollars and an Italian government bond in euros. Our task is to estimate the notional amount of the bonds given the amount of capital to be invested.

We do this by first multiplying the portfolio weight of an asset (w_i) by the amount of capital available for investing which we denote by V_{PF}. Then, by dividing the product $V_{\text{PF}} w_i$ by the bond's ask price, denoted by P_i^{ASK}, we calculate the notional amount that the portfolio manager must buy. The following equation shows how to estimate the notional amount of the bond (q_i):

$$q_i = \frac{\text{Portfolio Exposure}_{\text{BC}}}{P_i^{\text{ASK}}} = \frac{V_{\text{PF}} \times w_i}{P_i^{\text{ASK}}} \tag{3.4}$$

However, the estimated notional amount given by equation (3.4) is still not the correct one because the bonds are in specific local currencies — euros and Australian dollars. The amount $V_{PF} w_i$ will only estimate the capital allocated in the two bonds in euros and in Australian dollars in their local currencies, but not in the portfolio base currency (e.g., the U.S.

dollar). However, multiplying the product by the current FX ask price in the corresponding base currency of the portfolio $FX_i^{qx/\text{BC}}$, in this case, the AUD/USD and EUR/USD, would adjust the notional amount to reflect base currency exposure. The formula is as follows:

$$q_i = \frac{\text{Portfolio Exposure}_{\text{BC}}}{P_i^{\text{ASK}}} = \frac{V_{PF} * w_i}{P_i^{\text{ASK}}} FX_i^{qx/\text{BC}} \tag{3.5}$$

where $FX_i^{qx/\text{BC}}$ is the FX ask price in the corresponding price notation using equation (3.1).

Table 3.3 summarizes the example using two global bond portfolios — one with the U.S. dollar as the base currency and one with the euro. To better understand the relationships, we provide more detailed information about the portfolio. The example is estimated assuming a portfolio with 500 million in capital, in U.S. dollars and euros. Let us assume that the bond portfolio manager follows a quantitative investment process and the weights of the bonds are the result of a portfolio optimization.

Table 3.3: Bond and Currency Exposure Estimation

U.S. Dollar Portfolio	**Weight (%)**	**FX**	**FX Ask**	**Bond Ask**	**Notional (*q*)**	**Exposure in BC (USD)**	**Exposure in LC**
T 1 1/2 08/15/22	6.00	USD		101.59	29,530,000	29,999,481	30,000,000
BTPS 1.2 04/01/22	3.00	EUR	1.189	101.28	12,450,000	14,997,129	12,611,401
ACGB 1 11/21/31	5.00	NZD	0.699	94.92	37,700,000	24,998,762	35,785,857
Euro Portfolio	**Weight (%)**	**FX**	**FX Ask**	**Bond Ask**	**Notional (*q*)**	**Exposure in BC (EUR)**	**Exposure in LC**
T 1 1/2 08/15/22	6.00	USD	0.841	101.59	35,110,000	29,982,684	35,688,794
BTPS 1.2 04/01/22	3.00	EUR		101.28	14,810,000	14,999,124	15,000,000
ACGB 1 11/21/31	5.00	NZD	0.588	94.92	44,830,000	24,999,147	42,553,191

Note: To compute the proper amounts in the example we use actual values as of September 2021. Data obtained by the authors from Bloomberg, LLC.

Specifically, the portfolio has a 6% weight in a U.S.-dollar denominated Treasury bond (T 1 1/2 08/15/22), which is a 1.5% bond with maturity on August 15, 2022, a 3% weight in a euro-denominated Italian 1.2% coupon government bond with maturity in 2022, and a 3% weight in a 1% coupon Australian government bond in Australian dollars with maturity in 2031. Note that the bonds are in local currencies, but as we shall see, the local currency denomination corresponds to different portfolio exposures of the same notional amounts (shown in column Notional (q)) that changes according to the changes in the currency rates, the portfolio base currency, and the current bond prices.

In Table 3.3, we use the corresponding price notations for the currency pairs in the case of the euro-based bond portfolio (AUD/EUR and USD/EUR). The values in the columns "Exposure in BC" and "Exposure in LC" give the corresponding values in base currency and in local currencies by multiplying and dividing by the correct price notation ("FX Ask"), respectively.

It is important to note that currency conversion is not mandatory. Estimates of bond exposure in a given portfolio currency can be made using the normal currency conventions; however, some care must be taken to compute the amount correctly. For example, in the above example in the euro-based portfolio, it is not mandatory to convert the price notation using the reciprocal value (1/1.189 = 0.841), but it would then be necessary to divide the bond exposure by 1.189, instead of multiplying by the reciprocal value of 0.841.

It is easy to see that the nominal bond prices (quotes obtained from Bloomberg) are the same for every investor and are unrelated to the portfolio base currency. However, the notional amounts on which the bond portfolio manager places orders depend on the base currency; thus, the demanded notional amount given a portfolio weight of say 6% is effectively adjusted by the FX ask price. An analogous rule applies to bid prices when selling fixed-income securities. Therefore, rebalancing portfolios is directly affected by bid-ask spreads, which in turn affect notional amounts.

The most important takeaway from our discussion is that a bond's performance is directly linked to the currency it is denominated in. We now turn our attention to the mechanics of currency management as a distinctive building block in global bond portfolios. When we cover portfolio construction in Part 2 of this book, we will combine currency management and bond management in a holistic quantitative process.

3.3 Currency Management

In this section, we describe currency management from the point of view of a global bond portfolio manager. The task for global bond investors is challenging because it involves the management of both bond and currency exposure. As we show in this section, bond portfolio managers can employ various strategies to manage their currency risk as well as potentially generate excess returns through their currency exposure and currency management.

3.3.1 *Currency investment strategies*

In analyzing currency managers and their benchmarks, Pojarliev and Levich (2008) report that currency returns can be decomposed into four currency management strategies: carry, value, momentum, and volatility. Pojarliev and Levich (2011a) also found that currency managers are to some extent equal in their exposure to these strategies. However, these strategies are not restricted to currency managers. Konstantinov (2017) showed that these strategies are found in global bond portfolios as well. The results of these findings are important as they show that currency carry, value, momentum, and volatility strategies may complement or serve as counterpoints to the same strategies employed in the bond holdings of portfolios.

Again, recall that currency investment strategies always involve two currencies, and it is critical to express the value of one currency in terms of the other. In other words, we always have a domestic or base currency (BC) and a quote currency (*qx*). For example, in the EUR/USD exchange rate, we express the relationship between a portfolio facing a domestic or base currency return of the USD and a foreign currency denominated return of EUR.

3.3.2 *Currency value*

The intuition behind the currency value strategy is to buy undervalued currencies and to sell overvalued currencies over specific time horizons. For a single currency pair, say, EUR/USD, the strategy would be to identify the over- and undervalued currencies. If the euro is overvalued and the U.S. dollar is undervalued, a portfolio manager will buy the undervalued U.S. dollar and sell the euro. Of course, determining the fair value of a currency is the cornerstone of this strategy. Fortunately, economic theory provides several frameworks to help us determine a currency's fair value. The most widely used currency value estimation method, and the one described below, is based on the theory of purchasing power parity. We discuss this theory next.

3.3.2.1 *Purchasing power parity*

The theory of *Purchasing Power Parity* (PPP) has two forms — relative and absolute. Our main focus is on the relative PPP, which states that the economic relationship between two currencies is governed by the relationship between the inflation rates of their home countries. In other words, if there is a difference in the inflation rates between two countries over a specific time period, the currency of the country with the higher inflation rate should depreciate against the currency with the lower inflation rate. Mathematically,

$$\frac{S_{\text{PPP}}}{S_t} = \frac{1+\inf_{\text{BC}}}{1+\inf_{qx}} \tag{3.6}$$

where the equilibrium spot currency price is denoted by S_{PPP}, $\inf_{\text{BC}}$ is the base currency inflation rate, the foreign inflation rate is denoted by $\inf_{qx}$, and the current spot price is S_t.[5]

While PPP provides a simple framework for understanding currency mechanics, as noted by Pojarliev and Levich (2012), there are two primary reasons to question the validity of this PPP framework despite its popularity. The first reason is that because inflation rates generally change more slowly and over longer periods relative to significant changes in currency rates, it is not altogether clear whether we can use a longer-term measure like inflation to seriously justify the short-term fair value of a currency. This is a major reason why short-term currency price movements always depart from the currency fair value. Fortunately, PPP is mean reverting in the long term, which means that the fair value is a long-term phenomenon, a fact which can be used to justify short-term trading strategies based on disparities in the actual and fair value of a currency. The second reason is that it is challenging to apply PPP to specific calculation methodologies used to estimate the fair value of a currency pair. For example, the currency exchange rate between the euro and

[5]Here, we follow the notation format found in Kazemi *et al.* (2016).

U.S. dollar (EUR/USD) can deviate substantially based on the different methods applied to calculate PPP and fair value. Driver and Westaway (2004) and Loretan (2005) provide details on currency fair value estimations.

Currency Value Returns: To measure the currency value return, it is necessarily to compute the fair value (S_{FV}) of a currency pair as follows[6]:

$$R_t^{\text{FX Value}} = \ln(S_{t+1}/S_{\mathrm{PPP}}) \quad \text{if } S_{\mathrm{PPP}} > S_t \quad \text{and} \quad \ln(S_{\mathrm{PPP}}/S_{t+1}) \quad \text{if } S_{\mathrm{PPP}} > S_t \tag{3.7}$$

where S_{t+1} is the spot rate at time $t + 1$, S_t is the spot rate at time t, S_{PPP} is the fair value of the currency at time t, and $R_t^{\text{FX Value}}$ is the currency value return.

In Table 3.4, we demonstrate how equation (3.7) is calculated by means of a simple example. Note that the inflation numbers need to be forward looking. Backward-looking inflation numbers may be used to explain how exchange rates changed in the past, which is useful in performance attribution analysis. When we are thinking about "value", then it is about where inflation (and, ergo, exchange rates) is going. Suppose the expected inflation rates for the Eurozone and the United States are 0.50% and 1%, respectively. Using the spot rate of 1.083, the PPP EUR/USD exchange rate is 1.088. Because the Eurozone has lower inflation than the United States, we can expect the euro to appreciate against the U.S. dollar. Similarly, the value of the USD/JPY exchange rate is determined using PPP inflation rates of 1% in the United States and 0% in Japan. Again, according to PPP, we can expect the U.S. dollar to depreciate against the Japanese yen. The PPP fair value of USD/JPY is 105.22.

Currency value estimation assumes the existence of equilibrium among exchange rates. However, empirical results show that deviations

Table 3.4: Estimating Currency Fair Value

	$\mathbf{inf}_{qx}$	$\mathbf{inf}_{\mathrm{BC}}$	S_t	S_{PPP}
EUR/USD	0.50	1.00	1.083	1.088
USD/JPY	1.00	0.00	106.28	105.22
GBP/USD	1.00	1.00	1.236	1.23

Note: The values used in this table are hypothetical.

[6] See Kazemi *et al.* (2016) and Pojarliev and Levich (2012).

from the theoretical equilibrium are the norm rather than the exception, at least in the short run. Pojarliev and Levich (2008, 2011), Konstantinov (2017), and Konstantinov and Rebmann (2019) found that both currency and bond managers have negative beta exposure to the currency value factor. Note that when a majority of portfolio managers follow the crowd on a factor — as expressed by the beta exposure to that factor — practitioners and academics define the positions as *protrarian*. However, not all portfolio managers might necessarily agree on the expected factor returns. In this case, portfolio managers build *contrarian* positions, having negative beta exposure to that factor. In other words, in both currency and bond portfolios, the real value of currencies often departs from their estimated value. This is a demonstration of the fact that currency value is time varying and difficult to estimate.

An additional challenge with estimating currency fair values stems from the inputs used to compute them, which contain a great deal of imprecision. Inflation rates, forward rates, and interest rates are either announced with a time lag or the information flow in the markets does not allow their values to be measured precisely. Consider inflation data, which are proxied by the Consumer Price Index (CPI). To construct the CPI, different countries use basket prices of goods and services in past periods to determine current inflation, or the CPI's value. However, past values (say six months) are used to determine the inflation index today. In other words, the fair value of a currency is hard to determine as the data used in inflation and PPP estimation may deviate from country to country and the inflation value calculated today uses the inflation numbers with backward-looking data. The CPI basket in the United States might be different from the CPI basket in Hungary, South Africa, or in the Eurozone. This compounds the challenges presented by the specific calculation methodologies used to derive the fair value used in different countries. Some fair value metrics consider all the relevant trade parties of a country and goods to measure inflation, and are weighted and rebalanced according to changing trade conditions. Others deviate from this template, sometimes significantly. There is thus an issue of consistency between country-specific fair value metrics.

3.3.3 *Currency carry*

Currency carry is perhaps the most intuitive currency management strategy. The intuition behind carry trades is to buy currencies with high interest rates and to sell currencies with low interest rates. The low-yielding currencies are referred to as "funding currencies" because their low interest-rate levels provide low financing cost with which to purchase high interest-rate currencies. For example, a portfolio manager can borrow in the low-yielding Japanese yen and buy high-yielding South Africa rand. To illustrate the intuition behind currency carry in a bond portfolio, consider that a bond portfolio might be short the low-yielding Japanese yen and the euro while going long the high-yielding Australian dollar, South African rand, Mexican peso, Polish zloty, and Hungarian forint.

Two important concepts when considering currency carry are covered interest-rate parity and uncovered interest-rate parity. The two topics are covered next as they provide a sound theoretical background for explaining the mechanics of currencies.

3.3.3.1 *Covered interest parity*

The phenomenon of the "forward rate puzzle" is central to understanding the currency carry management strategy known as *covered interest parity* (CIP). The forward currency premium is the premium when trading currencies with forward contracts. The intuition behind this currency trade is provided by Kazemi *et al.* (2016):

- If the forward rate is higher than the spot rate of a currency, one should sell the foreign currency forward rate and buy the domestic currency forward. This represents a forward rate premium.
- If the FX rate forward is lower than the spot rate, one should buy the foreign currency forward and sell the domestic currency forward rate. This represents a forward rate discount.

The intuition behind CIP is to find the relationship between the current spot rate and the forward rate of a currency using the corresponding interest rates given by

$$\frac{F_t}{S_t} = \frac{1 + i_{\mathrm{BC}}}{1 + i_{qx}} \tag{3.8}$$

CIP estimates the forward price of a currency F_t using the relationship between the base currency interest rate i_{BC}, the foreign interest rate i_{qx}, and the current spot price S_t.

Research on the CIP strategy is provided by Pojarliev (2009) and Konstantinov and Fabozzi (2021).

3.3.3.2 *Uncovered interest parity*

The intuition behind *uncovered interest parity* strategy (UIP) is found in the relationship between the current spot rate and the unknown expected future spot rate of a currency using the corresponding interest rates given by

$$\frac{E(S_{t+1})}{S_t} = \frac{1+i_{\text{BC}}}{1+i_{qx}} \tag{3.9}$$

UIP estimates the expected spot future price of a currency $E(S_{t+1})$ using the relationship between the base currency interest rate i_{BC}, the foreign interest rate i_{qx}, and the current spot price S_t.

Note that the difference between the UIP and CIP lies in economic intuition. Specifically, in the case of the CIP, the forward rate is an unbiased estimator of the exchange rate. The CIP uses the forward rates F_t determined with the forward curve instead of the $E(S_{t+1})$ that is computed using the domestic and foreign interest rates. Pojarliev and Levich (2012) stressed that CIP relies on the intuition that two currency investments exposed to the same underlying risks must have the same expected returns. In other words, in equilibrium, markets should bring about the parity between exchange rates and interest rates. UIP does not hold in the short-term as the value of a currency is not known with certainty, the FX rate exhibits nonlinearity, and equilibrium (at least in the short term) does not exist.[7] Nevertheless, CIP, UIP, and the PPP are among the primary building blocks that are used to build currency investment strategies.

One of the early investigations regarding UIP in currency investing goes back to the work of Froot and Thaler (1990). Notably, the authors found that contrary to the expectations of the UIP, currencies with higher interest rates were observed to appreciate against currencies with lower interest rates. As a consequence, borrowing in low interest-rate currencies and investing in high interest-rate currencies can be a profitable, but risky strategy. The dynamics of crash risk in carry trades is discussed in Jurek (2007) and in Melvin and Shand (2017).

Because carry strategies can be applied to both currencies and bonds, there has been research that has investigated the interaction between the two. For example, Nucera and Valente (2013) and Konstantinov (2014)

[7] Taylor and Peel (2000) and Norman (2010) studied USD/GBP and USD/DEM using long-term data and documented significant short-term nonlinearity in their value estimation.

investigated the use of bonds and yield curve positioning to match the currency and bond exposure. Applying a similar approach, Martens *et al.* (2019) showed that a global carry strategy for developed markets based on yield curve estimations generates significant profits. That said, Melvin and Shand (2017) and Czasonis *et al.* (2019) showed that the success of carry trades is likely time varying, so managers need to be attuned to background conditions in the economy and market when considering them.

3.3.3.3 *Measuring currency carry returns*

To measure the FX carry profit-and-loss (P&L) of a strategy, we use the following formula, adapted from Pojarliev (2009) and Kazemi *et al.* (2016):

$$R_t^{\text{FX Carry}} = \ln(E(S_{t+1})/S_{t+1}) \quad \text{if } E(S_{t+1}) > S_t \quad \text{and} \quad \ln(S_{t+1}/E(S_{t+1})) \quad \text{if } E(S_{t+1}) < S_t \tag{3.10}$$

where S_{t+1} is the spot rate at time $t + 1$, S_t is the spot rate at time t, $E(S_{t+1})$ is the forward rate at time t, and $R_t^{\text{FX Carry}}$ is the currency carry return. We can calculate the carry return using the forward rates as soon as we exchange the expected spot rate $E(S_{t+1})$ with the forward rate F_t.

Again, we can illustrate the currency carry returns using CIP and UIP. For this purpose, we compute the expected future spot rate at time $t + 1$. Using UIP, the expected spot rate $E(S_{t+1})$ of the EUR/USD is 1.09 and using the forward rate F_t according to the CIP, the EUR/USD rate is 1.084. Based on both CIP and UIP, the GBP/USD is priced. We provide a simple example for this currency carry derivation in Table 3.5.

3.3.4 *Currency momentum*

Currency momentum or *trend-following strategies* are the most commonly implemented strategies in currency investing. Whereas the motivation

Table 3.5: Estimating Currency Carry

	i_{qx}	i_{BC}	S_t	**Forward Points**	F_t	$E(S_{t+1})$
EUR/USD	–0.445	0.198	1.083	6.44	1.084	1.09
USD/JPY	0.198	–0.061	106.28	–4.7	106.279	106
GBP/USD	0.159	0.198	1.236	1.56	1.236	1.236

Note: Data obtained by the authors from Bloomberg, LLC.

behind carry and value strategies is based on economic fundamentals, the nature of momentum strategies lies in the observation of return pattern persistence. That is, there is evidence that past returns are persistent and can be used to predict future returns.

There has been extensive research on momentum strategies over the last several decades. Trend-following investment strategies were being developed and applied by professional investors such as William Dunnigan and Richard Donchian for many years before they aroused academic interest (Kolanovic and Wei, 2015). In terms of academic research, in a well-known study, Jegadeesh and Titman (1993) found that the strategy of buying stocks that have performed well in the past and selling stocks that have performed poorly generated significant positive returns over 3- to 12-month investment horizons. Asness *et al.* (2013) looked beyond equities and found evidence in other major asset classes (e.g., commodities, bonds, and currencies). Specific to currencies, a comprehensive study of currency momentum is provided by Menkhoff *et al.* (2012b). Other studies on currency momentum include Binny (2005) and Pojarliev and Levich (2008).

Evidence on the success of currency momentum on a standalone basis is mixed. Levich and Thomas (1993) and Olson (2004) found evidence for currency momentum profits. However, Pukthuanthong-Le *et al.* (2007) and Abbey and Doukas (2012) found that currency momentum strategies using developed market currencies and that rely on technical indicators generated losses over the longer term. Studies analyzing emerging market currency returns such as Kuang *et al.* (2014) and Poti *et al.* (2020) found little evidence of currency return predictability. However, Hsu *et al.* (2016) found patterns to predict currency returns and thus evidence for currency momentum. As in the case of currency carry strategies, currency momentum strategies have also been found to be time varying (see Binny, 2005) and Menkhof *et al.* (2012a).

3.3.4.1 *Momentum trading rules*

There are two major alternative rules that are typically applied in currency momentum strategies. The first is to use lagged values over specific previous periods of 1, 2, 3, 6, 9, or 12 months when computing currency momentum returns or entry and exit currency price levels. This approach was investigated by Menkhof *et al.* (2012b).

Alternatively, Abbey and Doukas (2012) use well-known indicators from technical analysis to drive momentum trading currency strategies.

They investigated the efficacy of moving averages, Bollinger bands, moving average convergence divergence indicators, and relative strength indexes. We describe each of these metrics below.

Moving average (MA): This metric is a simple indicator that bases its buy–sell signals on an asset's price deviations from its average price over a given measurement period. Buy signals are generated as soon as the price moves above the MA threshold value. The MA is simply calculated using the average prices over h periods:

$$\mathrm{MA} = \frac{\sum_i FX_i^{qx/\mathrm{BC}}}{h} \tag{3.11}$$

where $\mathrm{FX}_i^{qx/\mathrm{BC}}$ denotes the currency price.

Bollinger bands (BB): These bands are indicators based on volatility. They produce buy signals for an asset when its price moves below two standard deviations from the current trend. Similarly, sell signals for assets will be generated when the price moves higher than two standard deviations from the current trend. Obviously, there are two indicators that mark the lower and upper levels for the BB. The computation of BB incorporates the MA estimator as follows:

$$\begin{aligned} \mathrm{BB}_{\mathrm{Upper}} &= \mathrm{MA} + \sqrt{\frac{(\mathrm{FX}_i^{qx/\mathrm{BC}} - \mathrm{MA})^2}{h}} \quad \text{and} \\ \mathrm{BB}_{\mathrm{Lower}} &= \mathrm{MA} - \sqrt{\frac{\left(\mathrm{FX}_i^{\frac{qx}{\mathrm{BC}}} - \mathrm{MA}\right)^2}{h}} \end{aligned} \tag{3.12}$$

Moving average convergence divergence (MACD): This is an indicator that uses exponential moving averages for asset prices and indicates long and short signals as soon as differences in the short-term and long-term thresholds arise.

$$\mathrm{MACD}(9) = \mathrm{EMA}(12) - \mathrm{EMA}(26)$$
$$\text{with } \mathrm{EMA}_t = P_t\mathrm{SF} + (1 - \mathrm{SF})\,\mathrm{EMA}_{t-1}, \quad \text{and} \quad \mathrm{SF} = 2/(n+1) \tag{3.13}$$

In equation (3.13), the MACD(9) is a 9-period indicator using 12-period and 26-period exponentially weighted moving average (EMA) values. The EMA indicator depends on the smoothing factor, the price at time t, and the number of periods n.

Relative strength index (RSI): This index is an indicator that includes specific prices and computes the strength or magnitude of recent price developments. The RSI indicates oversold or overbought positions. It is formally expressed as

$$\mathrm{RSI} = 100 - \left[\frac{100}{1 - \frac{\sum_i U}{\sum_i D}} \right] \tag{3.14}$$

where U is the average of all price changes over a specific period i with positive changes, and D is the average of all price changes over the same period i with negative price changes. The RSI's value ranges from 0, which indicates a market low, to 100, which indicates a market high. Usually, thresholds are used to determine whether an asset is currently oversold or overbought. The most commonly used thresholds are 30 and 70. An RSI below 30 indicates that the market is oversold, and an RSI above 70 means that the market is overbought.

3.3.4.2 *Measuring currency momentum returns*

The following formula is used to compute the profit and loss from FX momentum trades:

$$R_t^{\text{FX Momentum}} = \begin{array}{ll} \ln(S_{t+1}/S_{t-\mathrm{h}}) & \text{if } S_{t-h} - S_t > 0 \quad \text{and} \\ \ln(S_{t-h}/S_{t+1}) & \text{if } S_{t-h} - S_t < 0 \end{array} \tag{3.15}$$

where S_{t+1} is the spot rate at time t + 1, S_t is the spot rate at time t, S_{t-h} is the spot rate at time t based on h lagged values, and $R_t^{\text{FX Carry}}$ is the currency momentum return. In Table 3.6, we provide a simple example for currency momentum estimation using the moving average price.

Table 3.6: Estimating Currency Momentum

	S_{t-1}	S_t	S_{MA}
EUR/USD	1.0858	1.0834	1.0892
USD/JPY	108.83	106.28	107.58
GBP/USD	1.2383	1.2362	1.2420

Note: Data obtained by the authors from Bloomberg, LLC.

3.3.4.3 *Currency volatility*

In contrast to the return profile of other currency strategies returns, the return profile of currency volatility strategies is non-directional (Binny, 2005). Specifically, this strategy is not designed to profit from the up or down movement of a security's price, but on price movement in general.[8] Sun *et al.* (2011) showed that volatility is a serious source of risk in currencies for even the most liquid currency pairs such as EUR/USD, JPY/USD, and GBP/USD, and that volatility clustering — the tendency for large changes in price to be followed by further large changes in price of either sign — is especially prevalent in currency markets.

Currency options like plain-vanilla puts and calls and options strategies like straddles and strangles, and also volatility-based derivatives such as variance swaps, are widely used to express views on currency volatility in global bond portfolios. The following example can help understand the intuition behind their use. Suppose that the historical volatility of the EUR/USD at time t is 8.18% and the implied volatility at time t is 7.15%. A long straddle — comprising two long options, one put option, and one call option, with the same strike and expiration date — can be implemented to potentially profit from large swings in EUR/USD exposure. If the realized volatility at time $t + 1$ is higher than the implied volatility at time t, the long currency option on the exchange rate will generate a positive payoff for a portfolio.

There are several volatility models available to portfolio managers. Perhaps the most popular model is the Autoregressive Conditional Heteroscedasticity (ARCH) class of models developed by Engle (1982) and its extension Generalized ARCH (GARCH) by Bollerslev (1986). The most important structural property of GARCH models is the assumption that volatility changes rather than remaining constant. This property is referred to as *heteroscedasticity*.[9]

The basic GARCH model comprises a constant term, a "volatility surprise" parameter, and an autoregressive term representing past volatility. The most commonly used variant of GARCH is the GARCH (1,1) model, which uses a one-period lag value for past volatility realizations:

$$\sigma_t^2 = \alpha_0 + \beta_t \epsilon_{t-1}^2 + \gamma_t \sigma_{t-1}^2 \tag{3.16}$$

[8]A broad overview of currency volatility strategies is provided by Taleb (1997).

[9]Although important for understanding volatility, the presence of heteroscedasticity is ignored in some prominent financial models such as the Black–Scholes option pricing model.

where α_0 is a non-negative normal constant term and is often assumed to be the value of an asset's long-term variance, β_t represents the volatility surprise effect of past squared return realizations ϵ_{t-1}^2, and γ_t is the constant volatility term. It is assumed that α_0, β_t, and γ_t are ≥ 0 and $\beta_t + \gamma_t = 1$. A high value for β_t means that volatility is "spiky", while a high value for γ_t means that volatility is "persistent".

While useful, the basic GARCH model has some notable drawbacks. For one, option-derived implied volatility for the underlying asset often overestimates the estimated volatility from the GARCH (1,1). According to Taleb (1997), one of the reasons for this is that implied volatility contains information not incorporated in previous prices, a key input to GARCH models. An additional drawback is the normality assumption for asset returns, which is not the case for currency returns. In one study, for example, 10,000 synthetic datasets were produced (each spanning approximately one century), using the GARCH (1,1). In approximately one million years of simulated trading, not once in a single GARCH century was a market drop identified that approached the magnitude of the three largest drops observed in the Dow Jones Industrial Average during the 20th century (Johansen and Sornette, 1998). Finally, the basic GARCH models only consider the magnitude of returns, ignoring information regarding the direction of returns. This feature of the model is inconsistent with a number of empirical studies for both equities and fixed-income assets that find that the occurrence of market declines is generally a better predictor of higher volatility when compared to instances of market advances. As a response to this shortcoming in the original GARCH model, there are now several so-called "asymmetric" GARCH models including exponential GARCH (EGARCH) (Nelson, 1991), threshold GARCH (TARCH) (Rabemananjara and Zakoian, 1993), and Glosten–Jagannathan–Runkle GARCH (GJR GARCH) (Glosten, Jagannathan, and Runkle, 1993).

3.3.5 *Relativity of currency returns*

The examples and currency strategy return decomposition we provided in previous sections show that there are many methods for measuring the fair value of a currency using UIP and PPP. The most important point is that bond portfolio holdings determine the direction of a currency trade to a large extent. This is the main difference between pure currency management and currency management for bond portfolios.

3.3.5.1 *Value*

In our discussion of the limitations of the PPP theory, we explained that the time period used to specify the PPP and the lags associated with inflation rate estimations are serious concerns when deriving currency value. Additionally, the PPP and the UIP result in different value estimations. Which one is the correct value estimation is not easy to determine and is still debated in the academic literature.

Finally, PPP and UIP provide mid- and long-term currency value estimations. Therefore, short-term currency value regularly departs from its fair value, which both currency and global bond portfolios reflect in their positioning (as shown in the studies of Pojarliev and Levich (2011b), Konstantinov (2017), and Konstantinov and Rebmann (2019)). In general, the high-frequency velocity of FX transactions results in an immediate market adjustment that departs from the fair, equilibrium value. In short, currency markets are never in equilibrium.

3.3.5.2 *Momentum*

The relative view on currency momentum is twofold. The first refers to the time period applied to measure currency momentum and the second refers to positioning and bond portfolio exposure.

First, there are many ways to measure currency momentum — like MA, or the RSI over specific time periods. The definition of a currency momentum period is not uniform in the literature and much less in the practitioner community. Momentum returns are short-lived and often become overcrowded when many investors follow the same strategies. Therefore, momentum strategies depend on the models applied to capture information and the signals used to enter and exit the market. Portfolio managers often use momentum to trade well-known currency pairs — EUR/USD, GBP/USD, and the JPY/USD. The holding period of assets and currency exposure in the portfolio depends on the information and models applied. Performance attribution models show, *ex post*, the success of these models and the exposures in a portfolio.

The second issue related to the relative nature of currency momentum strategies is even more problematic than the first. Currency momentum strategies for bond portfolios, or in general for portfolios with local currency exposure, are relative in their direction and depend on the base currency of the portfolio, or the currency in which the trade is denominated. More precisely, suppose there is "positive" momentum in EUR/USD. For example, an appreciation of the euro against the U.S. dollar where the EUR/USD moves from 1.20 to 1.25. However, this positive momentum is also a depreciation of the USD against the EUR for a euro-based investor. The reciprocal value of the EUR/USD is 0.83 (= 1/1.2) and the reciprocal value of 1.25 is 0.8. The change from 0.83 to 0.8 (USD/EUR) is a depreciation of the USD against the EUR. In this case, the momentum is "negative" for a bond portfolio with base currency euro and U.S. dollar bond exposure. The momentum is negative from the euro-based portfolio and the currency depreciation contributes negatively to the bond exposure. Therefore, currency momentum depends on the base currency and the local currency bond exposure of the portfolio. Obviously, the momentum trade can be positive or negative, and a negative momentum (depreciation of one currency against the portfolio base currency) can be used to hedge the bond exposure using derivative instruments (e.g., currency forwards or futures). Because they are highly related to hedging and overlay activities, we discuss them in Chapter 9.

3.3.5.3 *Volatility*

The volatility return is always relative because the rate of change between implied volatility and realized volatility does not indicate a directional trade. The change in volatility might be used for long or short currency options. Implied volatility is used to estimate the expected future volatility of the underlying currencies. Therefore, currency option strategies are profitable when the implied volatilities are underestimated, but the direction, long or short, depends on the portfolio exposure and the purpose of the options used — hedging or return enhancing.

If the realized volatility at time $t + 1$ is lower than the implied volatility at time t, a short currency option might generate a positive payoff for a portfolio. Otherwise, higher realized volatility at time $t + 1$ relative to implied volatility at time t would be positive for a long currency option as it would be exercised. This example makes clear that the positioning in a bond portfolio on volatility and currency options might depend on tactical views, the currency exposure in the portfolio, and the portfolio manager's aim — hedging or alpha enhancement.

3.3.6 *Benchmarking*

Performance measurement and attribution in fixed-income portfolios can be challenging when bond portfolios implement the currency strategies discussed in this chapter. One tool that has been developed to deal with this challenge is currency-strategy-specific benchmarks. For example, several data providers (e.g., Citi, Barclays, J.P. Morgan, Royal Bank of Scotland, and UBS) offer custom carry indexes that replicate styles. In general, indexes for currency value, currency momentum, and currency carry as well as for currency volatility strategies are offered to customers.

In addition, there are several indexes that are designed to track the overall performance of professional currency managers. One example is the Deutsche Bank Currency Return Index. However, the most important and widely used indexes have been discontinued and are no longer available. For example, one widely used index in the literature on momentum strategies was the AFX Index developed by Lequeux and Acar (1998). This index tracked the performance of seven currencies — EUR/USD, USD/JPY, USD/CHF, GBP/USD, EUR/JPY, EUR/GBP, and EUR/CHF — weighted by their turnover volume in the spot market.

Although benchmark alternatives to measure success and performance in currency value investing are more limited, several do exist. The most common way is to use fair-value indexes such as the J.P. Morgan Tradable Currency Indexes that represent tradable fair value indexes in corresponding base currencies — U.S. dollar, euro, British pound, and Japanese yen. Another option is the Bank of International Settlement Effective Exchange Rate Indexes that reflect their estimation of the fair value of currencies.

Aside from commercially available indexes, portfolio managers have the option of building customized benchmarks to capture their currency exposures. A reasonable approach that reflects the investment universe and management of global bond portfolios is to use the currency weights of global bond benchmarks (e.g., the currency/country weights of a local currency bond benchmark index such as the ICE BofA World Sovereign Bond Index or the Bloomberg Barclays Global Aggregate Treasuries Index). The currency weights of a bond index — e.g., 35% in U.S. dollar, 25% in Japanese yen, 30% in euro — can be used to measure the currency management success relative to that benchmark exposure. In other words, currency returns would be separately considered from bond returns. This intuition would be in line with the approach suggested by Paape (2003). While convenient, this approach bears considerable bias toward three currencies — U.S. dollar, euro, and the Japanese yen. The reason is that most global government bond indexes have at least 70% exposure to these currencies. As a result, such benchmarks might be very liquid, but biased in their exposure, which might present a challenge to performance evaluation if the portfolio allocates aggressively in local currencies and bonds and does not follow a benchmark that does the same. Unconstrained bond portfolios are examples of strategies that are likely to face the foregoing difficulty.

Another approach to currency benchmark construction (suggested by Konstantinov, 2020) is to construct a currency spot return index using the weights of the Deutsche Bank FX Volatility Indicator (CVIX Index and CVIX1I Index in Bloomberg). The Deutsche Bank FX Volatility Index is similar to the Cboe Volatility Index, except that it measures the volatility of currency markets. The index is based on the following currency pairs: EUR/USD, USD/JPY, GBP/USD, AUD/USD, USD/CAD, USD/CHF, EUR/JPY, EUR/GBP, and EUR/CHF.

Since global bond portfolios invest in multiple currencies, using U.S. dollar spot as a benchmark is only appropriate for hard currency bond portfolios. It is unsuitable for portfolios with multiple currency exposures as it would not reflect the multiple existing risks. Therefore, currency benchmarks are useful not only for global bond portfolios but also for other strategies where currency exposure is a significant driver of portfolio returns.

3.4 Key Takeaways

- Currencies represent a distinct asset class. Currency markets are among the most liquid and transparent. Exposure to foreign exchange using derivatives or spot transactions may be used for hedging or alpha enhancement.
- Currencies are traded in pairs. The first currency in a pair is the domestic currency and is known as the "base" currency. Currency trades always involve buying one currency and selling another. The base currency is the currency in which the portfolio net asset value is computed. The base currency is the reference currency when estimating bond exposure and currency return estimation.

- There are four commonly employed currency strategies: carry, value, momentum, and volatility. Carry strategies exploit currency mispricing based on interest-rate differentials using the covered interest parity and uncovered interest parity frameworks. Value strategies attempt to capitalize on undervalued currencies that have deviated from their long-term equilibrium market value as determined by the purchasing power parity metric. Momentum strategies capture short- and long-term trends in currency pricing. Volatility is a non-directional strategy that is implemented using options.
- Currency-specific benchmarks are sometimes needed to measure the performance of a portfolio's currency exposure. A convenient way to do so is to use the country/currency exposure of major bond benchmarks and to track the currency performance on an individual basis.

References

Abbey, B. S. and J. A. Doukas. 2012. "Is Technical Analysis Profitable for Individual Currency Traders?" *Journal of Portfolio Management* 39(1): 142–150.

Asness, C., T. J. Moskowitz, and L. H. Pedersen. 2013. "Value and Momentum Everywhere". *Journal of Finance* 68(3): 929–985.

Baku, E., R. Fortes, K. Herve, E. Lezmi, H. Malongo, T. Roncalli, and J. Xu. 2020. "Factor Investing in Currency Markets: Does it Make Sense?" *Journal of Portfolio Management* 46(2): 141–155.

Bank for International Settlements. 2019. "Triennial Central Bank Survey: Report on Global Foreign Exchange Market Activity in 2019". Monetary and Economic Department, Bank of International Settlements.

Bank for International Settlements. 2022. "Triennial Central Bank Survey: Report on Global Foreign Exchange Market Activity in 2022". Monetary and Economic Department, Bank of International Settlements.

Binny, J. 2005. "Currency Management Style through the Ages". *Journal of Alternative Investments* 8(3): 52–59.

Bollerslev, T. 1986. "Generalized Autoregressive Conditional Heteroscedasticity". *Journal of Econometrics* 31: 307–327.

Chambers, D. R., M. J.P. Anson, K. H. Black, and H. Kazemi. 2015. *Alternative Investments: CAIA Level*. 3rd Edition. Hoboken, New Jersey: John Wiley & Sons.

Czasonis, M., B. Pamir, and D. Turkington. 2019. "Carry On". *Journal of Alternative Investments* 22(2): 100–111.

Driver, R. L. and P. F. Westaway. 2004. "Concepts of Equilibrium Exchange Rates". Working Paper no. 248, Bank of England.

Engle, R. F. 1982. "Autoregressive Conditional Heteroscedasticity with Estimates of the Variance of U. K. Inflation". *Econometrica* 50: 987–1008.

Froot, K. A. and R. H. Thaler. 1990. "Anomalies: Foreign Exchange". *Journal of Economic Perspectives* 4(3): 179–192.

Galati, G. and M. Melvin. 2004. "Why Has FX Trading Surged? Explaining the 2004 Triennial Survey". *BIS Quarterly Review* 12: 67–74.

Gordon, M. and E. Shapiro. 1956. "Capital Equipment Analysis: The Required Rate of Profit". *Management Science* 3(1): 102–110.

Glosten, L. R., R. Jagannathan, and D. E. Runkle. 1993. "On the Relation between the Expected Value and the Volatility of the Nominal Excess Returns on Stocks". *Journal of Finance* 48(5): 1779–1801.

Hsu, P.-H., M. P. Taylor., and Z. Wang. 2016. "Technical Trading: Is It Still Beating the Foreign Exchange Market?" *Journal of International Economics* 102: 188–208.

Jagadeesh, N. and S. Titman. 1993. "Returns to Buying Winners and Selling Losers: Implications for Stock Market Efficiency." *Journal of Finance* 48(1): 65–91.

Johansen, A. and D. Sornette. 1998. "Stock Market Crashes Are Outliers". *The European Physical Journal B-Condensed Matter and Complex Systems* 1(2): 141–143.

Jurek, J. W. 2007. "Crash-Neutral Currency Carry Trades". *Journal of Financial Economics* 113(3): 325–347.

Kazemi, H., K. H. Black, and R. D. Chambers. 2016. *Alternative Investments: CAIA Level II*. 3rd Edition. Hoboken, New Jersey: John Wiley & Sons.

King, M. R., C. Osler, and D. Rime. 2013. "The Market Microstructure Approach to Foreign Exchange: Looking Back and Looking Forward". *Journal of International Money and Finance* 38(C): 95–119.

Kolanovic, M. and Z. Wei. 2015. "Momentum Strategies across Asset Classes: Risk Factor Approach to Trend Following". Quantitative and Derivatives Strategy, J.P. Morgan.

Konstantinov, G. S. 2014. "Active Currency Management of International Bond Portfolios". *Financial Markets and Portfolio Management* 28(1): 63–94.

Konstantinov, G. S. 2017. "Currency Crowdedness Generated by Global Bond Funds". *Journal of Portfolio Management* 43(2): 123–135.

Konstantinov, G. S. and F. J. Fabozzi. 2021. "Carry Strategies and the US Dollar Risk of US and Global Bonds". *Journal of Fixed Income* 30(3): 26–46.

Konstantinov, G. S. and J. Rebmann. 2019. "From Risk Factors to Networks: A Case Study on Interconnectedness Using Currency Funds". *Journal of Financial Data Science* 3(1): 108–123.

Konstantinov, G. S. 2020. "Who Needs a Currency Benchmark?" Working Paper, Frankfurt.

Konstantinov, G. S. and M. Pojarliev. 2021. "International Bond Portfolio Management [Chapter 44]." In F. J. Fabozzi (ed.), *The Handbook of Fixed Income Securities*, 9th Edition. New York: McGraw Hill.

Kuang, P., M. Schröder, and Q. Wang. 2014. "Illusory Profitability of Technical Analysis in Emerging Foreign Exchange Markets". *International Journal of Forecasting* 30(2): 192–205.

Lequeux, P. and E. Acar. 1998. "A Dynamic Benchmark for Managed Currencies Funds". *European Journal of Finance* 4(4): 311–330.

Levich, R. M. and L. R. Thomas III. 1993. "The Significance of Technical Trading Rules in the Foreign Exchange Markets: A Bootstrap Approach". *Journal of International Money and Finance* 12: 451–474.

Loretan, M. 2005. "Indexes of the Foreign Exchange Value of the Dollar". *Federal Reserve Bulletin* 91: 1–8.

Martens, M., P. Beekhuizen, J. Duyvesteyn, and C. Zomerdijk. 2019. "Carry Investing on the Yield Curve." *Financial Analysts Journal* 75(4): 51–63.

Meese, R. A. and K. Rogoff. 1983. "Empirical Exchange Rate Models of the Seventies: Do They Fit Out of Sample?" *Journal of International Economics* 14(1): 3–24.

Melvin, M. and D. Shand. 2017. "When Carry Goes Bad: The Magnitude, Causes and Duration of Currency Carry Unwinds". *Financial Analysts Journal* 73(1): 121–144.

Menkhoff, L., L. Sarno, M. Schmeling, and A. Schrimpf. 2012a. "Carry Trades and Global Foreign Exchange Volatility". *Journal of Finance* 67(2): 681–718.

Menkhoff, L., L. Sarno, M. Schmeling, and A. Schrimpf. 2012b. "Currency Momentum Strategies". *Journal of Financial Economics* 106(3): 660–684.

Nelson, D. B. 1991. "Conditional Heteroscedasticity in Asset Returns: A New Approach". *Econometrica* 59(2): 347–370.

Norman, S. 2010. "How Well Does Nonlinear Mean Reversion Solve the PPP Puzzle?" *Journal of International Money and Finance* 29(5): 919–937.

Nucera, F. and G. Valente. 2013. "Carry Trades and the Performance of Currency Hedge Funds". *Journal of International Money and Finance* 33: 407–425.

Olson, D. 2004. "Have Trading Rule Profits in the Currency Market Declined Over Time?" *Journal of Banking & Finance* 28: 85–105.

Paape, C. 2003. "Currency Overlay in Performance Evaluation". *Financial Analyst Journal* 59(2): 55–68.

Pojarliev, M. 2009. "Trading the Forward Rate Puzzle". *Journal of Alternative Investments* 11(3): 26–36.

Pojarliev, M. 2018. *Some Like It Hedged.* New York, NY: CFA Institute Research Foundation.

Pojarliev, M. and R. M. Levich. 2008. "Do Professional Currency Managers Beat the Benchmark?" *Financial Analysts Journal* 64(5): 18–32.

Pojarliev, M. and R. M. Levich. 2011a. "Are All Currency Managers Equal?" *Journal of Portfolio Management* 37(4): 42–53.

Pojarliev, M. and R. M. Levich. 2011b. "Detecting Crowded Trades in Currency Funds". *Financial Analysts Journal* 67(1): 26–39.

Pojarliev, M. and R. M. Levich. 2012. *A New Look at Currency Investing*. Charlottesville, VA: CFA Institute.

Poti, V., R. M. Levich, and T. Conlon. 2020. "Predictability and Pricing Efficiency in Forward and Spot, Developed and Emerging Currency Markets". *Journal of International Money and Finance* 107: 102223.

Pukthuanthong-Le, K., R. M. Levich, and L. R. Thomas III. 2007. "Do Foreign Exchange Markets Still Trend?" *Journal of Portfolio Management* 34(1): 114–118.

Rabemananjara, R. and J. M. Zakoian. 1993. "Threshold ARCH Models and Asymmetries in Volatility". *Journal of Applied Econometrics* 8(1): 31–49.

Rogoff, K. 2001. "The Failure of Empirical Exchange Rate Models: No Longer New, but Still True". *Economic Policy Web Essay* 1(1).

Su, F. and J. Zhao. 2017. "Foreign Exchange Market: Institutional Structure, Regulation, and Policy Implications". *Journal of Finance and Economics* 5(5): 195–203.

Sun, E. W., O. Rezania, S. T. Rachev, and F. J. Fabozzi. 2011. "Analysis of the Intraday Effects of Economic Releases on the Currency Market". *Journal of International Money and Finance* 30(4): 692–707.

Taleb, N. N. 1997. *Dynamic Hedging*. Hoboken, New Jersey: John Wiley & Sons.

Taylor, M. P. and D. A. Peel. 2000. "Nonlinear Adjustment, Long-Run Equilibrium and Exchange Rate Fundamentals". *Journal of International Money and Finance* 19(1): 33–53.

Chapter 4

Yield Curve Management

Bond pricing is the essence of bond portfolio management. The most important determinant of bond pricing is the yield curve, or alternatively, the term structure of interest rates. In this chapter, we highlight the role of yield curve management in global bond portfolios, provide an overview of how to estimate bond prices and spot curves, and develop yield and spot curve strategies that are the cornerstone of a quantitative investment process. Importantly, spot curves, bond expected returns, and option-adjusted spreads are input parameters for the optimization processes applied to allocation and security selection which we cover in Chapters 6 and 7. Further applications of bond pricing and expected risk-and-return estimations are the fundamentals of yield curve strategies.

4.1 Fundamentals of Bond Pricing

In this section, we explain basic bond pricing fundamentals that are the backbone of yield curve strategies.

4.1.1 *Theoretical prices and price sensitivity*

In contrast to stocks, which represent a stakeholder's rights and represent equity capital, bonds represent debt. A bond's price is the sum of its discounted cash flows (coupons and principal payment made at maturity).

Bonds have a finite life and their prices are the sum of all discounted cash flows during the lifetime of the bond.

The formula for the price of an annual-pay, option-free bond at time t, denoted by $P(t)$, is equal to

$$P(t) = \sum_{t=1}^{T} \frac{\text{CF}}{(1+y_t)^t} \tag{4.1}$$

where T is the maturity of the bond, CF is the annual coupon interest, and y_t the yield at time t for discounting the coupons. For a semiannual-pay bond, C and y_t are reduced by one half and T is doubled.

Decomposing bond prices provides valuable information for understanding both bond price dynamics and how variables like yields impact bond prices. Therefore, the risk of a bond is mainly associated with the change of interest rates or yields as these changes immediately impact the price of the bond. The two primary measures of interest-rate risk are duration and convexity.

Duration is a measure of the bond price elasticity to changes in the yield. It is estimated as follows:

$$\text{Duration} = \frac{P_{-} - P_{+}}{2(P_0)(\Delta y)} \tag{4.2}$$

where P_0 is the initial price, P_- and P_+ represent the bond prices resulting from a decrease or increase in the yield, respectively, and Δy is the change in yield used to calculate the new prices (in decimal form).

Duration as computed using equation (4.2) has a different name depending on what is assumed when computing the new prices in the numerator of equation (4.2). The term *modified duration* is used to describe duration when it is assumed that when yields change, the cash flows do not change. For bonds with embedded options, the cash flows may change when yields change based on some valuation model. When a valuation model that allows for the changing of cash flows when yield changes is used to compute the two prices in the numerator of equation (4.2), the computed duration is referred to as *effective duration.*

As we will see, understanding bond yields and their behavior is critical for bond pricing, estimating bond expected returns, and quantitative bond portfolio management. Therefore, we start with the most fundamental part of bond price estimation — the yield curve — which is an expression of interest rates in a country, sector, asset class, or bond market segment.

4.1.2 *The yield curve*

The yield curve is the most fundamental source of information for valuation in bond portfolio management. The yield curve represents the relationship of various bonds with maturities plotted on the horizontal axis and yields plotted on the vertical axis.

4.1.2.1 *Theoretical background*

Plotting yields of different bonds according to their maturities produces the yield curve. The yield curve then represents, for example, all Treasury security yields according to their maturities (the 1, 2, 3 years to maturity, etc.) that correspond to the bonds with these maturities. However, yields used to create the yield curve are not true measures of the potential return from holding a bond to maturity for two reasons. First, yield-to-maturity measures not only assume that the bond will be held to maturity but also assume that the coupon received can be reinvested at the yield to maturity. Second, it assumes that all interim cash flows from the bond should be discounted at the yield to maturity. From a bond portfolio manager's perspective, the foregoing assumptions are a serious enough issue to make yield to maturity a practically inadequate proxy for bond returns and for the purposes of bond valuation.

Because of the questionable information contained in yield-to-maturity measures, an alternative yield measure is needed. The appropriate rate to discount cash flows is that obtained from the spot rate curve, not the yield curve. The spot rate curve is different from the yield curve. The yield curve is directly observable in the market as it captures the yields of tradable bonds. The spot rate curve, also referred to as the *term structure of interest rates*, captures the hypothetical yields of zero-coupon bonds. In the case of the U.S. Treasury market, there are zero-coupon Treasuries issued under the Treasury STRIPS (Separate Trading of Registered Interest and Principal Securities) program. However, there are technical reasons why the yield on zero-coupon Treasuries created from the STRIPS program are biased yield measures.[1]

[1] The reasons are explained in Fabozzi and Fabozzi (2021, p. 140).

Given the theoretical spot rates (denoted by s_t's), the theoretical price of a bond at time t using the spot curve s for an annual-pay, option-free bond is as follows:

$$P(t) = \sum_{t=1}^{T} \frac{\text{CF}}{(1+s_t)^t} \tag{4.3}$$

Now, we can use the spot rates based on the corresponding yield curve instead of yield-to-maturity measures to discount the bond's cash flows.

4.1.2.2 *Yield curve models*

There are several practical models for estimating spot curves based on an assumed interest-rate model. Interest rates are typically modeled using a branch of mathematics known as *stochastic differential equations* (SDEs) Steele (2001). There are two approaches for implementing the same SDE: equilibrium and no arbitrage. While these two approaches begin with a given SDE, they differ as to how each approach applies the SDE to bonds with embedded options and contingent claims (i.e., options, caps, and swaptions). Equilibrium models begin with an SDE model and develop pricing mechanisms for bonds under an equilibrium framework. *No-arbitrage models*, also referred to as *arbitrage-free models*, start with the same or similar SDE frameworks as *equilibrium models*. However, no arbitrage models use observed market prices to generate an interest-rate lattice. The interest-rate lattice represents the short-term interest rate in such a way as to ensure that there is a no-arbitrage relationship between the observed market price and the value derived from the model.

No-arbitrage models to value options in bonds with embedded options and contingent claims are preferred by practitioners because such models minimally ensure that the prices observed in the market for underlying bonds match the current term structure of interest rates. As a result, bonds and interest-rate derivatives will be valued in a consistent framework. Equilibrium models, in contrast, are not parameterized to produce bond prices that are consistent with the term structure and, therefore, there is no consistent framework for valuing options on bonds and the underlying bonds.

There is an extensive literature that proposes no-arbitrage and equilibrium models of the term structure of interest rates, but we will not discuss them here.[2] The reason is that these approaches are less frequently used in global bond portfolio management than the approaches suggested in Nelson and Siegel (1987) and Svennson (1995). Theoretically, finding a perfect fit that matches observed bond prices to the estimated theoretical prices satisfies the assumptions of no-arbitrage models. The most serious problem when applying yield curve models to estimate theoretical bond prices is the definition of an observable market price of a bond. In fact, observable bond market prices do not exist because bond prices are quoted. That is, the quoted price is not the one executed or traded. The observed market prices are ones at which a trade is executed, and these prices depend on notional amounts. The quoted prices are used in yield curve models, but as we shall see in Chapter 8, the observed bond market prices depend on notional amounts traded in the bond markets or in electronic exchanges. There exist parsimonious approaches (discussed in the next section) which allow a portfolio manager to use quoted prices to fit the yield curve using ordinary least squares regression. Proprietary bond market data that gauge the trading volumes and prices represent the most reliable way to estimate no-arbitrage models.

An important reason for using the Nelson-Siegel and the Svensson models is that no-arbitrage and equilibrium approaches are not compatible with the three factors identified by Litterman and Scheinkman (1991) — level, slope, and curvature. These factors are widely used by bond managers because they represent an efficient way to capture bond portfolio interest-rate risk. The approach suggested by Nelson and Siegel (1987) and Svennson (1995) are referred to as *parsimonious approaches*. The economic reasoning behind the three factors makes them reliable inputs for yield curve models and factors used in portfolio management. A further advantage of the parsimonious approaches is that they are straightforward to estimate and implement. We describe parsimonious approaches to yield curve management for bond portfolios in the next section.

---

[2] See Chapter 19 in Fabozzi and Fabozzi (2023).

4.1.2.2.1 Parsimonious approaches

A parsimonious model for yield curves uses a handful of parameters to explain interest-rate dynamics. As noted above, Litterman and Scheinkman (1991) identified three yield curve parameters that are intuitive and economically and statistically sound. Although there are several approaches to yield curve modeling that can be used, from a practitioner perspective, parsimonious yield curve models are often more efficient to implement. Two important features of parsimonious models are that they do not make any assumption about the interest-rate distribution or the behavior of interest-rate variance. The parsimonious approach to analyzing the spot curve is not computationally challenging and is less time consuming compared to other complex yield curve models.

There are two commonly used parsimonious models to fit a yield curve from observed bond prices: the Nelson and Siegel (1987) and the Svensson (1995) models. We discuss them in turn.

4.1.2.2.2 The Nelson–Siegel approach

Nelson and Siegel (1987) showed that spot rates are the average of the forward rates with settlement between time 0 and maturity m. The forward rates are a function of the time t, maturity m, and parameter β_i. The Nelson-Siegel polynomial is an integrated function of the forward rates comprising Laguerre terms that are solutions of differential equations:

$$s_t(\beta_i, m, \tau) = \beta_0 + \beta_1 \left[\frac{1 - e^{-\frac{m}{\tau}}}{\frac{m}{\tau}} \right] + \beta_2 \left[\frac{1 - e^{-\frac{m}{\tau}}}{\frac{m}{\tau}} - e^{-\frac{m}{\tau}} \right] \tag{4.4}$$

where β_0, β_1, and β_2 are the parameters that need to be varied to fit the shape of the underlying spot curve, τ is a scale length parameter that reflects the curvature of the yield curve, and m is the maturity.

Usually, the parameter β_0 is associated with the level of interest rates. The parameter β_1 is the parameter used to model the slope of the yield curve, and β_2 is used to gauge curvature. The interpretation of the β_i

parameter is derived by finding the limits of the polynomial. Computing the maturity limit to zero $m \to 0$ reveals that as the maturity approaches zero, interest rates are explained by $\beta_0 + \beta_1$. This means that both the curve level and the slope help to explain the dynamics of the spot curve as maturity approaches zero. Computing the infinite maturity limit $m \to \infty$ suggests that long-term maturity spot rates are explained by the curve level parameter, or β_0. That is, the interest-rate level determines the long-term behavior in equation (4.4).

The Nelson-Siegel approach allows one to compute the discount factors needed to discount a bond's cash flows. The discount factors are time specific and depend on the beta components defined in equation (4.4). Note that obtaining the beta parameters using an ordinary least squares regression is critical for the computation of the discount factors which are computed as follows:

$$df_t(\beta_i, m, \tau) = e^{-s_t(\beta_i, m, \tau), m} \tag{4.5}$$

where s_t is the spot rate at time t and all other variables are as defined previously.

The Nelson-Siegel approach is suitable for sectors, countries, and asset classes when there are a small number of outstanding traded bonds available to estimate the model. The local currency spot curves derived from government bonds in Hungary, Poland, the Czech Republic, New Zealand, Norway, Sweden, South Africa, and Mexico are good candidates for this model because the number of bond issues is not large, and the problem of overfitting is not present.[3]

In Figure 4.1, we provide an overview of the possible realizations for market yield curves according to the specific parameterization in the Nelson-Siegel approach. In this figure, we change only the parameters responsible for the slope and the curvature of the yield curve, but keep the level constant.

---

[3]Bank of International Settlements (2005) (BIS Papers No. 25) provides an extensive report as to which countries Nelson–Siegel applies and for which countries the Svensson approach is suitable.

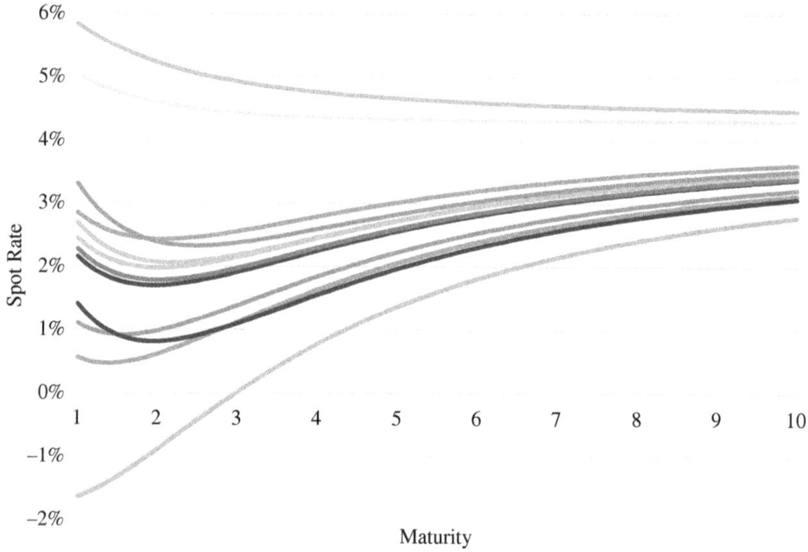

Figure 4.1: Nelson-Siegel Polynomial for Various β_1 and β_2 Parameters

Note: For illustrative purposes, the β_0 parameter is held constant at 0.042 and the parameter τ is held constant with a value of 1. Bond yields are on the vertical axis, and time to maturity is on the horizontal axis.

In reality, the level does change. Figure 4.1 shows that by changing one or two parameters of the yield curve, the third changes too. This means that there is a relationship between the parameters for the level, slope, and curvature and that the spot curves react to the changes in the variables.

4.1.2.2.3 The Svensson approach

The Svensson model is an extension of the Nelson–Siegel approach. The difference is in an additional curvature component and a decay parameter in the Svensson model that are useful for explaining short-term bond yields. This model is preferred for countries, industry segments, and sectors with a large number of traded bonds. The primary utility of providing an extension of the Nelson–Siegel model is that the Svensson model provides a better fit for the short-term maturities in bond markets with a large number of outstanding short-term bonds. Because the curvature explains a large part of short-term bond yield dynamics, the additional expansion helps for a better fit to the large amount of outstanding and tradable bonds.

The Svensson approach is widely applied to the spot curve estimation of European government bonds, U.S. Treasuries, and Japanese government bonds. The Svensson approach better models the short-term maturities with additional curvature impact, where the liquidity is sufficient. Formally, the Svensson model is like the Nelson–Siegel model given by equation (4.5) but contains additional β_i components that gauge the short-term behavior of the spot curve. The Svensson model has the following form:

$$\begin{aligned} S_t(\beta_i, m, \tau_1, \tau_2) &= \beta_0 + \beta_1 \left[\frac{1 - e^{-\frac{m}{\tau_1}}}{\frac{m}{\tau_1}} \right] + \beta_2 \left[\frac{1 - e^{-\frac{m}{\tau_1}}}{\frac{m}{\tau_1}} - e^{-\frac{m}{\tau_1}} \right] \\ &+ \beta_3 \left[\frac{1 - e^{-\frac{m}{\tau_2}}}{\frac{m}{\tau_2}} - e^{-\frac{m}{\tau_2}} \right] \end{aligned} \tag{4.6}$$

where $\beta_0, \beta_1, \beta_2$, and β_3 are the parameters that need to be varied to fit the shape of the underlying spot curve, τ_1 and τ_2 are scale length parameters that reflect the curvature of the yield curve, and m is the maturity. Computing the maturity limit to zero $m \to 0$ reveals that as the maturity approaches zero, interest rates are explained by the level parameter and the additional curvature parameter designed to better fit the short-term maturity bucket.

The shape of a local currency spot curve varies substantially depending on the asset class (e.g., different countries, economic sectors, and industries). Nelson–Siegel and Svensson polynomials are a good choice for modeling local currency spot curves that behave like real curves and are also a good choice to use for performance attribution analysis. Figure 4.2 shows possible spot curves generated using the Svensson approach.

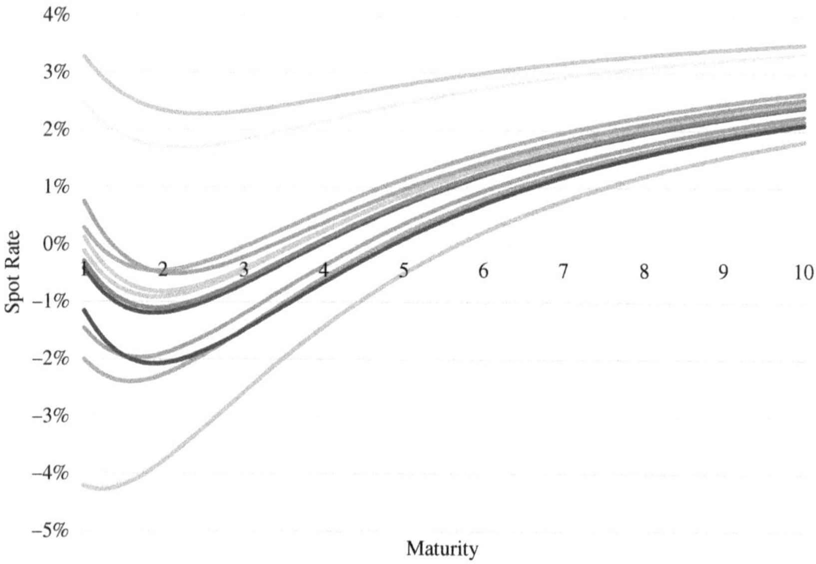

Figure 4.2: Svensson Polynomial for Various β_1 and β_2 Parameters

Note: The β_0-parameter is held constant at 0.042 and the parameter τ_1 and τ_2 are held constant with a value of 1. The parameter β_2 is also held constant with a value of 1. Bond yields are on the vertical axis and time to maturity is on the horizontal axis.

Note that compared to the Nelson–Siegel approach, the additional curvature parameter (β_3) results in more dynamics being exhibited by the short end of the spot curve. In markets with a large number of bonds with a short-term maturity, the Svensson approach allows better model fit and thus explains the behavior of interest rates much better than the Nelson–Siegel polynomial.

Armed with two powerful approaches to explain the term structure of interest rates, we can now discuss the practical application of yield curve models. For simplicity, we use only the Nelson–Siegel model, but the implementation of the Svensson model is similar. Note that both approaches provide reliable solutions to the type of spot rate estimation needed by bond managers.

4.1.2.3 *Fitting the yield curve*

In this section, we use the Nelson–Siegel approach for different types of curves and illustrate how spot curve fitting is implemented. To estimate a spot curve, we use bond prices and fit a regression to the time-specific rates that make the theoretical bond prices given by equation (4.3) estimated at time t with the spot curve s from equation (4.4). The bond price estimated with the spot curve from equation (4.4) should be equal to the observed bond price at the market.

The objective function that aims to minimize the sum of squared errors (SSE) that represents the difference between the observed and theoretical bond prices is as follows:

$$Arg \min_{\beta_i, \tau} \sum_{t=1}^{n} (P(t) - T(s,t))^2 \tag{4.7}$$

where $P(t)$ is the quoted market price of a bond and the $T(s, t)$ is the theoretical bond price estimated using the spot curve. Note that the yield curve fitting applies to all types of curves and no separation between currencies is made.

Table 4.1 displays the steps and intuition behind using a sample spot curve estimation for Polish government bonds and explains the steps used in the spot curve fitting process.

Table 4.1: Steps in Local Currency Spot Curve Estimation

Panel A: Maturity Decomposition										
Bond	t	$t+1$	$t+2$	$t+3$	$t+4$	$t+5$	$t+6$	$t+7$	$t+8$	$t+9$
POLGB 2 1/2 01/25/23	1.6	0.6								
POLGB 2 1/2 04/25/24	2.8	1.8	0.8							
POLGB 2 3/4 10/25/29	8.4	7.4	6.4	5.4	4.4	3.4	2.4	1.4	0.4	
POLGB 0 3/4 04/25/25	3.9	2.9	1.9	0.9						
POLGB 1 1/4 10/25/30	9.4	8.4	7.4	6.4	5.4	4.4	3.4	2.4	1.4	0.4
POLGB 0 04/25/23	1.8	0.8								
POLGB 0 1/4 10/25/26	5.4	4.4	3.4	2.4	1.4	0.4				
POLGB 5 3/4 09/23/22	1.2	0.2								
POLGB 5 3/4 04/25/29	7.9	6.9	5.9	4.9	3.9	2.9	1.9	0.9		
POLGB 4 10/25/23	2.3	1.3	0.3							
POLGB 2 3/4 04/25/28	6.9	5.9	4.9	3.9	2.9	1.9	0.9			
POLGB 3 1/4 07/25/25	4.1	3.1	2.1	1.1						
POLGB 2 1/2 07/25/27	6.1	5.1	4.1	3.1	2.1	1.1				
POLGB 2 1/2 07/25/26	5.1	4.1	3.1	2.1	1.1	0.1				
POLGB 0 07/25/22	1.1	0.1								
POLGB 2 1/4 10/25/24	3.4	2.4	1.4	0.4						

(Continued)

Table 4.1: (*Continued*)

Panel B: Spot Rate Decomposition

Bond	t	$t+1$	$t+2$	$t+3$	$t+4$	$t+5$	$t+6$	$t+7$	$t+8$	$t+9$
POLGB 2 1/2 01/25/23	0.9%	4.1%								
POLGB 2 1/2 04/25/24	0.6%	0.7%	2.7%							
POLGB 2 3/4 10/25/29	1.7%	1.6%	1.4%	1.3%	1.0%	0.7%	0.5%	1.2%	6.2%	
POLGB 0 3/4 04/25/25	0.9%	0.6%	0.7%							
POLGB 1 1/4 10/25/30	1.8%	1.7%	1.6%	1.4%	1.3%	1.0%	0.7%	0.5%	1.2%	6.2%
POLGB 0 04/25/23	0.7%	2.7%								
POLGB 0 1/4 10/25/26	1.3%	1.0%	0.7%	0.5%	1.2%	6.2%				
POLGB 5 3/4 09/23/22	1.4%	7.2%								
POLGB 5 3/4 04/25/29	1.6%	1.5%	1.4%	1.1%	0.9%	0.6%	0.7%	2.7%		
POLGB 4 10/25/23	0.5%	1.2%	6.2%							
POLGB 2 3/4 04/25/28	1.5%	1.4%	1.1%	0.9%	0.6%	0.7%	2.7%			
POLGB 3 1/4 07/25/25	0.9%	0.7%	0.6%	1.8%						
POLGB 2 1/2 07/25/27	1.4%	1.2%	0.9%	0.7%	0.6%	1.8%	9.3%			
POLGB 2 1/2 07/25/26	1.2%	0.9%	0.7%	0.6%	1.8%					
POLGB 0 07/25/22	1.8%									
POLGB 2 1/4 10/25/24	0.7%	0.5%	1.2%							

Panel C: Discount Rate Decomposition

Bond	t	$t+1$	$t+2$	$t+3$	$t+4$	$t+5$	$t+6$	$t+7$	$t+8$	$t+9$
POLGB 2 1/2 01/25/23	0.99	0.98								
POLGB 2 1/2 04/25/24	0.98	0.99	0.98							
POLGB 2 3/4 10/25/29	0.87	0.89	0.91	0.93	0.96	0.98	0.99	0.98	0.98	
POLGB 0 3/4 04/25/25	0.97	0.98	0.99							
POLGB 1 1/4 10/25/30	0.85	0.87	0.89	0.91	0.93	0.96	0.98	0.99	0.98	0.97
POLGB 0 04/25/23	0.99	0.98								
POLGB 0 1/4 10/25/26	0.94	0.96	0.98	0.99	0.98	0.98				
POLGB 5 3/4 09/23/22	0.98	0.98								
POLGB 5 3/4 04/25/29	0.88	0.90	0.92	0.95	0.97	0.98	0.99	0.98		
POLGB 4 10/25/23	0.99	0.98	0.98							
POLGB 2 3/4 04/25/28	0.90	0.92	0.95	0.97	0.98	0.99	0.98			
POLGB 3 1/4 07/25/25	0.96	0.98	0.99	0.98						
POLGB 2 1/2 07/25/27	0.92	0.94	0.96	0.98	0.99	0.98				
POLGB 2 1/2 07/25/26	0.94	0.96	0.98	0.99	0.98					
POLGB 0 07/25/22	0.98									
POLGB 2 1/4 10/25/24	0.98	0.99	0.98							

Table 4.1: (*Continued*)

Panel D: Discounted Principal and Cash Flow Decomposition

Bond	**T(*t*,*s*)**	**Principal**	**CF *t***	**CF *t* + 1**	**CF *t* + 2**	**CF *t* + 3**	**CF *t* + 4**	**CF *t* + 5**	**CF *t* + 6**	**CF *t* + 7**	**CF *t* + 8**
POLGB 2 1/2 01/25/23	103.5	101.1	2.4								
POLGB 2 1/2 04/25/24	105.7	100.8	2.5	2.4							
POLGB 2 3/4 10/25/29	110.2	89.3	2.4	2.5	2.6	2.6	2.7	2.7	2.7	2.7	
POLGB 0 3/4 04/25/25	98.9	97.4	0.7	0.7							
POLGB 1 1/4 10/25/30	96.4	85.8	1.1	1.1	1.1	1.2	1.2	1.2	1.2	1.2	1.2
POLGB 0 04/25/23	98.8	98.8									
POLGB 0 1/4 10/25/26	95.0	93.7	0.2	0.2	0.2	0.2	0.2				
POLGB 5 3/4 09/23/22	109.6	103.9	5.7								
POLGB 5 3/4 04/25/29	131.5	93.0	5.2	5.3	5.4	5.6	5.7	5.7	5.6		
POLGB 4 10/25/23	110.6	102.7	3.9	3.9							
POLGB 2 3/4 04/25/28	108.5	92.6	2.5	2.6	2.7	2.7	2.7	2.7			
POLGB 3 1/4 07/25/25	108.9	99.3	3.2	3.2	3.2						
POLGB 2 1/2 07/25/27	106.3	94.1	2.4	2.4	2.4	2.5	2.4				
POLGB 2 1/2 07/25/26	106.2	96.4	2.4	2.4	2.5	2.4					
POLGB 0 07/25/22	98.1	98.1									
POLGB 2 1/4 10/25/24	104.2	99.8	2.2	2.2							

Panel E: Observed and Theoretical Price and the Vector of Sum of Squared Errors (SSE)

Bond	***P*(*t*)**	***T*(*t*,*s*)**	**SSE**
POLGB 2 1/2 01/25/23	104.03	103.55	0.23
POLGB 2 1/2 04/25/24	106.35	105.69	0.44
POLGB 2 3/4 10/25/29	109.39	110.23	0.70
POLGB 0 3/4 04/25/25	100.37	98.90	2.14
POLGB 1 1/4 10/25/30	96.04	96.45	0.17
POLGB 0 04/25/23	99.68	98.79	0.80
POLGB 0 1/4 10/25/26	95.82	94.96	0.74
POLGB 5 3/4 09/23/22	107.77	109.60	3.35
POLGB 5 3/4 04/25/29	132.35	131.46	0.79
POLGB 4 10/25/23	109.38	110.56	1.39
POLGB 2 3/4 04/25/28	109.54	108.54	0.99
POLGB 3 1/4 07/25/25	110.36	108.91	2.11
POLGB 2 1/2 07/25/27	107.76	106.26	2.27
POLGB 2 1/2 07/25/26	107.72	106.19	2.35
POLGB 0 07/25/22	99.89	98.09	3.26
POLGB 2 1/4 10/25/24	106.03	104.23	3.24

Note: Data obtained by the authors from Bloomberg, LLC.

Yield curve fitting follows six steps identified by Bolder and Streliski (1999):

Step 1: Set the initial parameters for the yield curve required to generate meaningful bond price values and decomposition. For example, the long-term bond yields are used to set the β_0 parameter, β_1 is the difference between 10-year and 1-year bond yields, and τ is set to 1. Build a matrix according to the specific dates for coupon and principal payments (see panel A of Table 4.1).

Step 2: Build a matrix of spot rates and discount rates (see panels B and C of Table 4.1).

Step 3: Build a discounted cash flow matrix comprising all discounted coupons and principal repayments (see panel D of Table 4.1).

Step 4: Estimate a vector of theoretical bond prices and an error vector comprising the squared differences between theoretical and observable bond prices (see panel E of Table 4.1).

Step 5: Using numerical optimization, minimize the objective function comprising the sum of squared price errors subject to parameter values

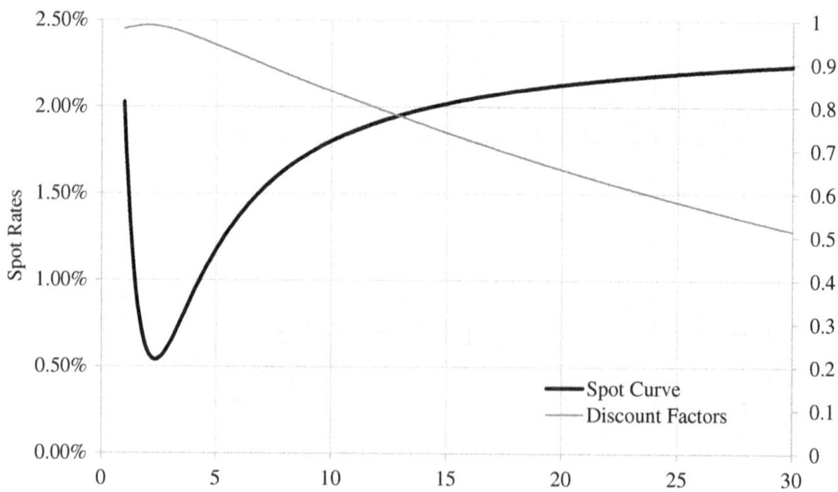

Figure 4.3: Spot Curve Example: Polish Government Bond Term Structure

Note: Spot rates are plotted on the left-hand side, whereas the discount factors are plotted on the right-hand side. Bond yields are on the vertical axis and time to maturity is on the horizontal axis.

and constraints. For example, both β_0 and the sum of β_0 and β_1 should be non-negative (see panel A of Table 4.1 and equation (4.7)). Figure 4.3 shows the spot curve and discount factors for the Polish government bonds.

Remember that the spot curves represent the starting point for bond portfolio management and yield curve strategies. However, before demonstrating how yield curve strategies are implemented, we need to understand bond valuation based on the estimated spot curves.

4.2 Yield Curve Valuation

Yield curve analysis is perhaps the most important part of bond portfolio management. In this section, we explain the role of yield curves in deriving expected bond returns which are used in portfolio optimization.

4.2.1 *Bond expected returns*

While bond yields are important for determining bond returns, yields and returns are not the same for the reasons we identified previously, namely re-investment risk and the hold-to-maturity problem. Bond return derivations must account for coupon effects, accrued interest, and price effects due to changes in yields. Importantly, until now, we have used a price notation of a bond that is called a clean price. The *clean price* is usually the theoretical price of a bond. However, bond returns should also include coupon payments. Adding accrued interest to the clean price changes it into a *dirty price*. Thus, bond return is the sum of the following components:

$$\text{Bond Return} = \text{Coupon Effects} + \text{Change in Price} + \text{Accrued Interest}$$

4.2.1.1 *Accrued interest*

Accrued interest is a component of bond returns and is related to the coupons paid by the bond. The accrued interest of a bond is due when trading the bond between the coupon payment dates. The accrued interest is the amount that the buyer has to pay to the seller for a bond not trading flat because the seller earned that amount. The issuer will in turn make the full coupon payment to the buyer.

The computation of accrued interest is straightforward using a 30/360 daycount convention. For this convention, every month is assumed to have 30 days and 360 days in a year. The formula for accrued interest is

$$\text{Accrued Interest} = \frac{CF}{\text{freq}}\left(1 - \frac{\text{freq} \times CF(t)_{t+1}}{360}\right) \tag{4.8}$$

where CF is the annual coupon of the bond, *freq* is the coupon frequency, and $CF(t)_{t+1}$ are the number of days from trading day (t) till the next coupon payment date. An example will illustrate the calculation of equation (4.8).

Consider a Polish government bond (POLGB 2 1/2 01/25/23) with a coupon rate of 2.5% that makes a coupon payment once per year (i.e., annual-pay bond). In this case, *freq* is 1 and CF is 2.5% of the notional value (100). Let us assume that t is July 26, 2021. Then, the number of days until the next coupon payment date, which is on January 25, 2022, is 183. The accrued interest following equation (4.8) would be 0.0123, or 1.23%. Adding the latter value to the clean bond price results in the dirty price.

4.2.1.2 *Bond price changes*

Once the spot curve is estimated, we can focus on valuation t and derive the bond expected returns that are due to price dynamics. Again, bond yields are not equal to expected returns. To illustrate this, we begin with simple return estimation using bond prices.

Considering the discrete price change of a bond with respect to a small change in time to maturity shows the relationship between changes in yield and time. To understand the latter relationship, it is necessary to decompose the total return of a bond into a price change due to the passage of time and a price change due to a change in yield. Note that the yield component does not differentiate between yield and spreads. The formula for the return attributable to the passage of time and yield change (R_t) is

$$R_t = \frac{P_t - P_{t-1}}{P_{t-1}} = \frac{\Delta P(t,y)}{P} = \underbrace{\frac{\partial P}{\partial t}\frac{1}{P}\Delta t}_{\text{time impact}} + \underbrace{\frac{\partial P}{\partial y}\frac{1}{P}\Delta y}_{\text{yield impact}} \tag{4.9}$$

where ΔP is the price change due to changes in time Δt and the price effect due to changes in yield Δy, assuming P is a differentiable function of t and y in real space, and it does not have stochastic components.

The first part of equation (4.9) shows the price change due to changes in time Δt which is labeled in the equation as the *time impact*. The second part shows the price effect due to changes in yield Δy, labeled the *yield impact*. Note that the uncertainty is substantial for both the time and the yield. To derive bond expected returns using the change in yields, it is crucial to have a process for predicting interest-rate dynamics using econometric, parametric, or Bayesian models, to name a few tools for doing so.

Litterman and Scheinkman (1991) showed that the volatility of U.S. Treasury bond returns is explained by three factors: the parallel shift of the yield curve, changes in the slope of the yield curve, and changes in the curvature of the yield curve. Empirical research has shown that predictive models exist that can be used to provide return enhancement. Indeed, Dolan (1999) showed that it is possible to forecast yield curve changes using the three factors mentioned above. Fabozzi *et al.* (2005) suggested an alternative approach for estimating the U.S spot curve structure. Instead of focusing on level, slope, and curvature, the estimation model should consider default spreads, equity volatility, and short-term interest rates.

Of course, applying any factor framework can be a challenging task for broadly invested global bond portfolios, in particular if the bond portfolio universe comprises, for example, 40 different countries and/or currencies. Predicting all three factors or spreads and short-term rates for different sectors and countries would bear some risks, as the interaction effects of interest rate changes within countries and sectors might be highly correlated, or there might exist evidence of co-movement, for example.

To reduce this complexity, we can derive expected returns by means of the time impact component.[4] The passage of time expected return, or roll down return, is the sum of a vertical term (as explained below) that

[4] Zimmerer (2003) and Konstantinov (2022) showed how expected returns are estimated and used in bond portfolios using the time impact component.

captures yield curve volatility ($D\Delta y$) and an initial yield adjusted by the change in time ($y\Delta t$). That is,

$$\text{Roll Down Return} = D\Delta y + y\Delta t \tag{4.10}$$

where duration (D) is the measure of the interest sensitivity of a bond price to interest rate changes multiplied by the yield change Δy. As we can see from the graphical expression in Figure 4.4, ($D\Delta y$) is a vertical term in the roll down and the term ($y\Delta t$) represents a horizon effect.

The vertical and horizon terms represent two parts of the yield curve that have an important role for global bond portfolios. Konstantinov (2014, 2022) showed that equation (4.10) captures the impact of both bond and currency effects that impact the expected bond returns. Below we explain how the two components impact global bond portfolios.

Suppose the change in time is equal for all bonds. The horizon return and the change in time $y\Delta t$ would be less for shorter time periods. In other words, the initial yield of a bond in local currency terms depends on the specific yield curve. If a global bond portfolio has exposure to say, four different bonds (e.g., a U.S. Treasury, an Australian government bond, a European corporate bond, and an emerging market high-yield bond) with

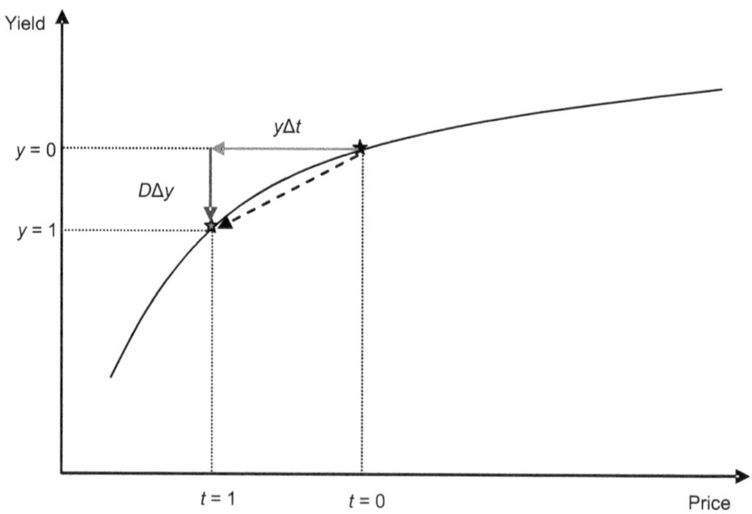

Figure 4.4: Roll Down over Yield to Maturity and Duration

different durations, the horizon effect would capture bond carry weighted by the change in time. Carry (horizon term) is in local currency terms.

The vertical term of equation (4.10) is more interesting from the perspective of global bond portfolio management. The vertical term of the roll down return of a bond is responsible for the largest volatility and is responsible for the risk and dynamics in the roll downs. Despite that, we assume that the yield curve remains constant and that the vertical term reacts to changes in yields, as the duration is responsible for capturing the volatility of interest rates. That is, duration is the source of interest-rate risk as it gauges the changes in interest rates which might be caused by currency volatility, among other risks. Recall that the Uncovered Interest Parity (UIP) does not hold in the short term and that the causality between currency and interest-rate movements is not one directional. That is, interest rate changes might cause the currency to move, but the opposite effect is also true. Suppose, for example, that a country depreciates its currency when its balance of payments changes. Then its interest rates will likely adjust with respect to capital flows.

If the Δy and duration remain constant, then the realized roll downs will be affected by changes in the yield and the volatility of currencies and interest rates. However, because of the negative trade-off between yield and duration, the longer the maturity of the bond, the higher the impact of the vertical term will be. Hence, the higher the interest-rate level is, the shorter the duration. As a result, roll downs in local currency terms capture both bond and foreign exchange dynamics. Put differently, if the yield curve changes and shifts upward, the roll down returns will decrease, but the disadvantage that the roll down returns experience might be comensated by possible currency appreciation as UIP does not hold in the short run (Chinn and Meredith (2004)). This bond–currency relationship has been studied in currency returns by Binny (2005) who identified that interest-rate dynamics and currency returns are closely related in portfolio management styles, with a nevertheless ambiguous causal relationship.

The vertical and horizontal terms depend on the duration and coupons as there is an inverse relationship between coupon and duration. Because the change in yields has a smaller impact on high-coupon bonds than lower-coupon bonds, the larger the coupon is, the lower the duration impact will be. Therefore, the reliability of roll downs as expected returns in global bonds depends on the holding period. A common approach is to estimate roll downs for 30 days for liquid bonds like sovereigns or high-grade corporate bonds, and slightly longer holding periods for illiquid securities.

From equation (4.10), we see that the expected return of a bond within a reasonable, short-time period can be considered the same as the roll down and depends on the yields, time, and duration, whose determinants are coupons, time to maturity, and yields. In the case of the four local currency bonds cited in the example above, the roll downs would immediately capture relations in the bond and currency risks that are incorporated into the expected returns. Obviously, keeping the time period short is essential in estimating expected bond returns based on the passage-of-time convention. Moreover, this notation is in discrete time and refers to changes in yields, but no further yield specification is made. Therefore, it is critical to integrate the yield curve into the analysis.

The spot curve is used to compute the bond price, or its fair, theoretical value. The expected roll down return $E(R)_t$ is the difference between the theoretical price measured at time t_1 and t_0 using the same underlying spot curve s_0:

$$E(R)_t = T(t_1, s_t) - T(t_0, s_t) \tag{4.11}$$

where $T(t_1, s_t)$ is the estimated bond price at time t_1 with spot curve s_0 and $T(t_0, s_t)$ is the estimated bond price at time t_0 with spot curve s_0.

Critical for this expected return estimation is that if the curve remains constant for a given time period, a bond rolling down the spot curve and approaching maturity would gain in price. That is, a holding period of three months for example, would be too long. Using roll downs as a proxy for expected returns under the assumptions of a constant yield curve for a three-month period and assuming a constant option-adjusted spread (OAS) for the bonds thus holds significant estimation risk.

4.2.2 *Bond fair value, expected bond returns, and the option-adjusted spread*

Fitting the relevant spot curves that apply to the markets in which a global bond portfolio invests is an important step which allows for bond pricing and estimation of expected returns. A quantitative bond portfolio management approach will generally derive expected returns using continuous price notation.

The spot curve is used to compute the bond price, or its fair, theoretical value. Until now, we only referred to the theoretical price that uses the yield curve. However, bond yields do not refer to pure spot rates, because there is a spread to add to or subtract from the rate that makes the bond trade slightly below or above the yield curve.

The (observable) bond price (P) at time t is equal to the theoretical price (T) at time t using the underlying spot curve s and the OAS:

$$P(t) = \sum_{t=1}^{n} \frac{\text{CF}}{(1 + s_t + \text{OAS}_t)^t} = \sum_{t=1}^{n} \text{CF} \cdot e^{-t(s_t + \text{OAS}_t)} \tag{4.12}$$

where the OAS is the spread of a bond that is added to the underlying spot curve in order to estimate the observable price of a bond, and all other variables have been already defined.

The OAS is a sum of the zero-volatility spread (z-spread), or the spread to the spot-rate curve (ZS) and the option component (OC) of a bond with an embedded option. Thus, for bonds without embedded options, the OAS is equal to the ZS, which is true for most government bonds; that is,

$$\text{OAS}_t = \text{ZS}_t + \text{OC}_t \tag{4.13}$$

where ZS is the zero-volatility spread, or the z spread added to the underlying spot curve, and OC are the option costs.

If a bond has an embedded call option, the option costs are positive; that is, this is a short call option. Here is why. Consider a callable bond, a bond with an embedded call option. The callable bond allows the bond issuer the right to redeem the bond before maturity. Therefore, the call option is held by the issuer and the issuer compensates the bond buyer with a premium in the form of a higher yield at issuance for this right that the issuer retains. The issuer will exercise the option when rates fall below certain threshold levels. The economic reason is that the issuer (a corporation, government, or agency) can “refinance” the debt at a lower interest rate. Lower interest rates constitute a lower cost of capital for the issuer.

What does it mean for the spread? The ZS is less than the OAS because the issuer pays a premium to the investor for the right to redeem the bond. Therefore, the OC is said to be positive. If a bond includes a put option, the investor pays the option premium, or the right to redeem the bond prior to the maturity date, and the option costs are negative. The option is a long put and in this case the OAS is less than the ZS.

Thus, the expected return of a bond under the assumption of a constant yield curve and constant OAS is estimated using the spot curve at the beginning of the period and the OAS is added. Mathematically,

$$E(R)_t = T(t_1, s_t + \text{OAS}_t) - T(t_0, s_t + \text{OAS}_t) \tag{4.14}$$

Furthermore, the assumption holds that OAS_t is held constant when estimating bond prices. As spreads and interest rates change over time, choosing an appropriate holding period becomes an important issue.

The expected roll down applies to all fixed-income securities in a global bond portfolio and is the building block for portfolio construction and optimization, and for spot curve-based performance attribution. A simple example illustrates the intuition behind the foregoing. In Table 4.2, we apply the analysis using a corporate sector spot curve and estimation of the 90-day roll down returns using equation (4.14). The corporate bonds have different maturities and coupons and we provide the current price as quoted from Bloomberg, with the theoretical price $T(t,s)$ estimated using equation (4.3) and equation (4.12). A positive OAS means the bond is undervalued relative to the underlying spot curve used for valuation and the negative spread indicates that the bond is overvalued relative to that spot curve.

Importantly, fair-valued bonds lie on the yield curve. Comparing the $P(t)$ and the theoretical prices $T(t,s)$, we obtain a first impression about the

Table 4.2: Observed and Theoretical Prices, 90-Day Roll Downs and OAS for Corporate Bonds

Bond	***P*(*t*)**	***T*(*t*,*s*)**	**Roll Down (%)**	**OAS (%)**
GE 2 5/8 03/15/23	104.79	104.62	0.03	–0.11
CKHH 1 1/4 04/06/23	102.27	101.87	0.03	–0.23
EMR 0 3/8 05/22/24	101.43	100.41	0.03	0.08
MMM 1 1/2 11/09/26	108.30	107.39	0.14	–0.17
SUFP 0 7/8 12/13/26	105.18	103.60	0.15	0.66
GE 4 5/8 02/22/27	124.38	125.77	0.15	0.22
SUFP 1 3/8 06/21/27	108.17	106.19	0.18	0.64
MMM 1 1/2 06/02/31	111.836	107.585	0.41	0.54

Note: Data obtained by the authors from Bloomberg, LLC.

price differences. If the $P(t)> T(t,s)$, the bond is overvalued and vice versa. The OAS is the metric that indicates if the bond is over- or undervalued and by how much. A negative OAS means that the bond price is trading below the yield curve and is overvalued. Note again that the OAS comprises the zero-volatility spread (z spread, or ZS) and option costs. The zero-spread indicates how much the underlying spot curve must be shifted upward by the amount of the OAS including the option costs of the bond, which are independent of the underlying yield curve.

Let us consider a single bond to explain the economic intuition behind the foregoing. The GE 2 5/8 03/15/23 bond has an OAS of 11bps as of July 2021. That is, the spot curve for the corporate bond sector is estimated as of July 2021 and the bond valuation is the result of the yield curve estimated at that point. To assure proper valuation, bond portfolio managers update the spot curves and evaluate the expected roll down returns and OAS. There are undervalued (trading with a positive spread above the spot curve) and overvalued bonds (showing a negative spread and trading under the spot curve). The GE 4 5/8 02/22/27 is trading 22bps above the spot curve. This means that the bond is undervalued, and the term structure must change by 22bps for the price to be fair.

To visualize the relationship between over- and undervalued bonds and roll down returns, it is often convenient to plot the roll down return curves, which are derived from the spot curve and the OAS. We show these relationships in Figure 4.5. Because OASs are negative or positive values, they are easily plotted above or under the zero line. The roll down curve is an effective way to show the attractiveness (as measured by expected returns) of bonds in a specific sector, asset class, or country.

The roll down curve suggests that short maturities have negative expected returns. A portfolio manager might wish to select bonds with maturities longer than seven years because these bonds have positive roll downs. Both expected bond returns and OAS are taken into account when selecting bonds. Specifically, a bond might have an attractive roll down, but at the same time it might have a negative OAS. The reason is that the roll downs are estimated without any spread, but the OAS provides the rich/cheapness information unrelated to the expected bond return.

Next we compare the OAS and roll downs of a bond sector. Figure 4.5 provides an example of observed prices $P(t)$, the theoretical prices $T(t,s)$

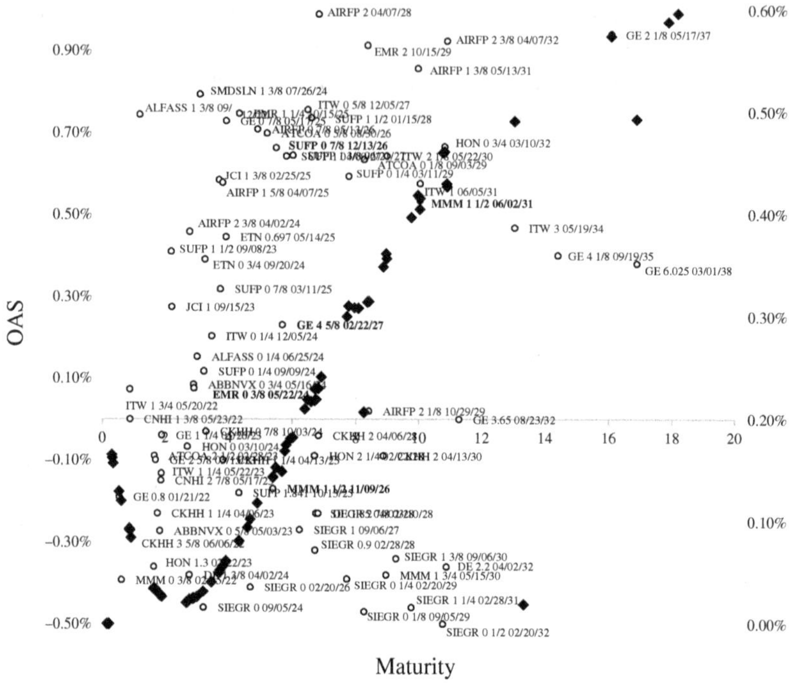

Figure 4.5: 90-Day Roll Down Curve and OAS for a Corporate Sector

Note: The OAS of the bonds from Table 4.2 is in bold text. Constructed by the authors from data obtained from Bloomberg, LLC.

expected returns (roll downs), and OAS for a sample of fixed-income securities computed with the corresponding spot curve. Visual inspection of the figure reveals that the steepest part of the curve with long maturities over 10 years offers the highest roll downs. However, expected bond returns are only one part of the strategy. These bonds have the highest interest-rate risk as measured by duration, and their spreads are widely distributed. Roll downs are, as expected returns, important, but the OAS is also a critical indicator to consider. In other words, comparing the roll down returns to OAS is an indication of the cost of expected returns, as a bond might have favorable roll down returns, but a negative OAS which would indicate that the attractiveness comes at a specific cost — the rising yields that would evaporate the roll downs.

The information provided in Figure 4.5 is very useful for visualizing and understanding expected returns (roll downs) and spreads (OAS). The bonds below the zero line (left-hand side) in the figure are overvalued. The bonds above the zero line are undervalued. Note that the figure captures the roll downs and OAS of a specific sector, but it is common for global bond portfolios to make similar comparisons and estimations for the sectors in the relevant investment universe.

In the context of bond portfolio management, a quantitative optimization strategy would be to assign high portfolio weights to the bonds with high roll downs and to avoid the ones with low expected returns. One of the possible bond portfolio strategies to implement is a relative value strategy, which is suitable for sectors, specific countries, and industry groups. Relative value strategies are explained in Section 4.3.4.

4.2.3 *Duration-times-spread*

Thus far, we have gained an understanding of yield curve dynamics and risk metrics that measure the change in bond prices in case of percentage changes of yields or spot rates. There is a similar metric that measures the impact on bond prices in the case of a change in spreads. This metric, coined by Leibowitz *et al.* (1990), as *spread duration* measures not only the single bond spread risk but the risk at the portfolio level.

A more recent modification of the spread duration metric provides even more insights into a bond's spread risk. A widely used metric to estimate the risk of bonds is to apply the Duration-times-Spread (DTS) metric developed by Ben Dor *et al.* (2007). In this measure, the spread duration of a bond is used and multiplied by the spread change. It is first worth pointing out the differences between spread duration and other duration metrics.

Spread duration holds the yield curve constant and measures the changes in the bond price by changes in OAS. In terms of spread duration, we hold the spot curve constant and estimate the spread impact by changes in the OAS. The extension provided by Ben Dor *et al.* (2007) is to multiply spread duration by changes in the spread and thus gain a dynamic picture of the bond risk changes. DTS is calculated as follows:

$$\mathrm{DTS}_k = -\mathrm{SD}_k \Delta \mathrm{OAS}_k \tag{4.15}$$

where the DTS_k of bond k is a product of the spread duration (SD_k) and the change in the spread of the bond (ΔOAS_k).

The DTS is a good indicator for positive and negative spread effects. Positive values for DTS are associated with favorable bond price effects of decreasing spreads while negative values for the DTS indicates spread widening, which has a negative price impact.

To visualize the risk that the DTS measures, we provide a simple illustration in Figure 4.6 comprising the DTS between the Broad U.S. market and the ICE BofA Emerging Market External Sovereign Bond Index. To compare the DTS among markets, the second plot illustrates the DTS between the ICE BofA EMU Broad Market Index and the ICE BofA US Broad Market Index. Visual inspection of Figure 4.6 shows that DTS for emerging markets has a much higher volatility and impact than the DTS between developed markets. Using factor models and correlations, Duyvesteyn and Martens (2014) documented that emerging market local currency sovereign bonds behave more like developed markets sovereign bonds and less like credit. However, the DTS of emerging market bonds as represented by the ICE BofA Emerging Market External Sovereign Bond Index behaves like lower-rated bonds, whose spreads have much larger volatility than investment-grade bonds, proxied by the ICE EMU Sovereign Bond Index. Therefore, bond portfolio spread risk across global bond markets, segments, and assets can be easily estimated and monitored using the DTS metric.

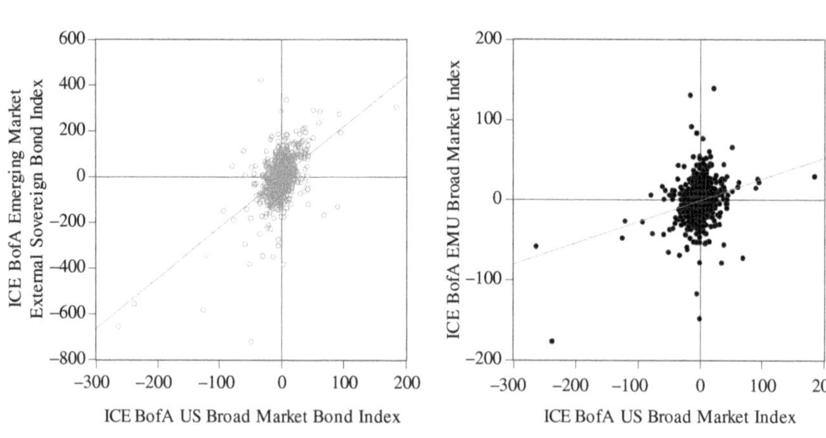

Figure 4.6: DTS for Emerging and Developed Market Indexes

Note: Data obtained by the authors from Bloomberg, LLC.

We can measure the portfolio DTS spread, which is the weighted sum of all individual bonds' DTS_k. It is also meaningful to compute the DTS for sub-portfolios or portfolio segments as follows:

$$\mathrm{DTS}_p = \sum_{k=1}^{K} w_k \, \mathrm{DTS}_k \tag{4.16}$$

where w_k is the weight of an individual bond holding in the portfolio and DTS is the individual bond-specific DTS.

Let's illustrate the meaning of the DTS for the single bonds shown in Table 4.2. An inspection of Table 4.3 reveals that the OAS change of the SUFP 0 7/8 12/13/26 has the largest negative impact. On the other hand, the OAS changes have a positive impact on the MMM 1 1/2 11/09/26 bond. Obviously, spread changes and term structure changes are different and their dynamics provide broad possibilities for yield curve strategies. From this illustration, a possible strategy would be to select bonds with a positive OAS. As we shall see, there are different yield curve strategies that seek to capture spread and yield curve movements.

Of critical importance is that the DTS applies to all bond market segments — from developed markets to emerging markets and from higher investment-grade rating to lower non-investment grade bonds. The spread duration and the DTS combined with other duration metrics offer a good estimator for both interest rate and spread risk of single bonds and a portfolio.

Table 4.3: Duration-Times-Spread

Bond	**OAS (t – 1) (%)**	**OAS (t) (%)**	**Spread Duration**	**DTS (%)**
GE 2 5/8 03/15/23	–0.04	–0.11	1.64	0.11
CKHH 1 1/4 04/06/23	–0.22	–0.23	1.71	0.02
EMR 0 3/8 05/22/24	0.08	0.08	2.75	0.00
MMM 1 1/2 11/09/26	0.14	–0.17	5.10	1.58
SUFP 0 7/8 12/13/26	0.15	0.66	5.05	–2.58
GE 4 5/8 02/22/27	0.23	0.22	5.03	0.05
SUFP 1 3/8 06/21/27	0.65	0.64	5.50	–0.44
MMM 1 1/2 06/02/31	0.55	0.54	9.01	0.90

Note: Bond data obtained by the authors from Bloomberg, LLC. Estimation as of July 2021.

4.3 Yield Curve Strategies

Several strategies can be identified for yield curve management. The purpose of yield curve strategies is to manage the risk and return of yield curves in a bond portfolio. We have already made a distinction between yield curves and spot curves. Therefore, in our discussion of yield curve strategies, we use the two curves interchangeably but actually refer to spot curves. Global bond markets provide broad opportunities for estimating yield curves — ratings, sectors, asset classes, currencies, and countries among others. This broad investment universe allows for great variability and even the possibility of using cross-curves like sector ratings or currency sectors. In general, the decision as to which spot curves to use in global bond portfolios stems from the investment process and the benchmark universe.

In traditional or simple bond portfolios dedicated to domestic markets, the yield curve choice is simple. A portfolio dedicated to U.S. Treasuries would obviously be focused on the U.S. Treasury spot curve. However, the choices for global bond portfolios are much more heterogeneous and a portfolio manager's choice depends on risk criteria, which we discuss next.

Note that yield curve strategies seek to measure and manage the risk of changes in slope, level, and curvature of the yield curve. The types of strategies include duration and maturity strategies, rating and credit strategies, and relative value strategies. Importantly, these three groups might be highly integrated within a global bond portfolio investment process.

4.3.1 *The choice of the yield curve*

The yield curve choices in global bond portfolios are not trivial. Several possibilities exist and the most convenient way is to choose the yield curves that match the policy portfolio and portfolio strategy. An additional advantage of using benchmarks like the Bloomberg Barclays Global Aggregate Bond Index for spot curve estimation is that indexes comprise liquid bonds that are tradable in the market.

The benchmark index defined in the policy portfolio and investment policy statement should represent the investment universe that is the most suitable. The most convenient sources of information are the benchmark composition and its allocation to currencies, countries, sectors, industries, and ratings. Benchmarks often comprise the following structure:

- *Geographical*: Europe, Asia, Latin America, Africa, North America, Middle East.
- *Currency*: multiple or single currency.
- *Asset class level*: sovereign, quasi-sovereign, corporate, asset-backed.
- *Industry groups*: financial, industrials, utility, sovereign, securitized.
- *Sub-industry groups*: banking, healthcare, real estate, retail, etc.
- *Countries*: single countries when different than currency exposure.
- *Rating categories*: Moody's, Standard & Poor's, Fitch, Bloomberg Composite.

Obviously, some of this information might be more macro- or microscopic depending on the index. For example, the J.P. Morgan EMBI Global Composite Index which has more than 700 bonds comprises only U.S. dollar-denominated emerging market bonds, but includes five geographic regions, more than 60 countries, two sectors (sovereign and quasi-sovereigns), and multiple rating categories. The Bloomberg Barclays Global Aggregate Treasuries Index comprises more than 40 local currencies, five geographic clusters, and multiple rating categories, but the country and currency risks are identical and the number of single securities exceeds 1,500.

In general, the most informative solution is to show the risk-and-return decomposition of a benchmark and to analyze the most common sources of risk and return. Several examples illustrate this. The choice of the yield curve should not be too narrow because the spot curves would not be representative and economically and statistically meaningful. Alternatively, the spot curves should not be estimated too broadly. Although sometimes it may be practical to build bond clusters from cross exposure, these clusters should comprise economically representative indexes. For example, it would be convenient for a broad index to group clusters in countries and sectors, or to combine sectors and ratings.

Cluster estimation is important for another reason. Cluster decomposition or segmentation is a helpful approach to break down the portfolio to sub-portfolios that would be representative and economically meaningful for bond portfolio optimization. This clustering might find its roots in the investment process, as investors might desire specific maturity buckets or pose constraints on specific exposures, or even cross-asset exposure (e.g., foreign exchange allocation with minimum weights on specific currencies and countries). Such restrictions might force breaking down the portfolio into specific buckets and segments that are representative and suitable to use in the bond optimization approach. The segmentation helps to adjust risks and restrictions easily into a quantitative process. We shall see the advantages of this segmentation in the next section and explain it further in Chapter 6.

Hybrid curves are mostly used for aggregate and broad indexes comprising multiple sectors, industries, and groups (e.g., the Bloomberg Barclays Global Aggregate Bond Index). The hybrid spot curves are usually combined using three of the four sector levels specified by Merrill Lynch indexes. In addition, the corresponding currencies, ratings, and countries in an index help to determine hybrid yield curves. The levels and the possible selection groups are summarized in Table 4.4.

In general, the selection should be made by considering the relevant sources of risk (e.g., currencies, ratings, countries, and sectors). Hybrid spot curves estimated from bonds comprising, for example, heterogeneous

Table 4.4: The Important Selection Criteria for Spot Curve Estimations

Country	**Currencies**	**Rating**	**Asset Class (Level 1)**	**Industry Group (Level 2)**	**Sub-Group (Level 3)**
USA	USD	Standard & Poor's	Corporate	Financial	Healthcare
Australia	CAD	Moody's	Securitized	Industrials	Basic Industry
China	AUD	Fitch	Quasi & Foreign Government	Covered	Retail
Germany	GBP		Sovereign	Securitized	Real Estate
Japan	EUR			Utility	Sovereigns
Brazil	JPY			Sovereign	Banking
Poland	SEK				…
France	NOK				
Russia	MXN				
…	…				

Note: Data obtained by the authors from Bloomberg, LLC.

country and currency exposure provide meaningful and practical solutions with good results.

The economic rationale behind such curves has been documented by Van Landschoot (2008), who found evidence of the importance of U.S. interest-rate dynamics for other markets and for cross-market dynamics associated with the level and slope factors between the U.S. and European corporate bond markets. Other examples are industry-country groups for broad indexes like the ICE BofA US Broad Market Index. Further examples suitable for aggregate indexes like the Bloomberg Barclays Global Aggregate Bond Index are industry group-rating spot curves. Table 4.5 provides examples that offer meaningful possibilities for broad aggregate indexes. In general, the currency exposure of an index

Table 4.5: Examples of Spot Curves for Emerging Market or Aggregate Indexes

Country-Currency	Industry-Currency	Rating Level	Sector-Rating	Sector-Country
South Africa-USD	Financial-USD	AAA	FinancialAAA	Sovereign-France
South Africa-EUR	Industrial-USD	AA+	FinancialAA+	Sovereign-Germany
China-USD	Utilities-USD	AA	FinancialAA	Sovereign-Spain
China-EUR	Consumer-USD	AA−	...	Sovereign-Italy
Indonesia-USD	Securitized-USD	A+		Sovereign-US
Indonesia-EUR	....	A		Sovereign-Australia
Mexico-USD	Financial-EUR	A−		Sovereign-Poland
Mexico-EUR	Industrial-EUR	BBB+		Industrials-Germany
...	Utilities-EUR	BBB	IndustrialsA+	Industrials-France
	Consumer-EUR	BBB−	IndustrialsA	Industrials-Italy
	Securitized-EUR	BB+	IndustrialsA−	Industrials-UK
		BB	IndustrialsBBB+	Financials-US
	...	BB−	IndustrialsBBB	Financials-France
		B+	IndustrialsBBB−	...
		B	IndustrialsBB+	
		B−	IndustrialsBB	
		CCC+	IndustrialsBB−	
		CCC	IndustrialsB+	
		...	...	

Notes: For ratings, the Standard and Poor's rating notation is used. Data obtained by the authors from Bloomberg, LLC.

determines to a large extent the first choice of hybrid spot curves that might be implemented. The country-level spot curves are highly suitable for hard currency emerging market bond indexes comprising different countries and bonds in the same currency (U.S. dollar) like the J.P. Morgan EMBI Global Composite Index.

Rating and industry spot curves are a good choice for specific indexes dedicated to large markets — like the United States, European, or other developed markets. Economically, such spot curves make sense as Chen *et al.* (2011) found evidence of a close relation between spread dynamics determined by liquidity risk and corporate credit risk. Perraudin and Taylor (2004) found that ratings and bond yields are closely related and react consistently in different market environments. From this point of view, sector-rating spot curves might reflect market dynamics associated with credit, rating, and liquidity issues that impact bond prices. This segmentation for spot curves is less meaningful for emerging markets.

Local currency spot curves are the most prominent choice for global aggregate bond indexes comprising a large number of currencies and local currency bonds like the J.P. Morgan GBI Broad Index or the Bloomberg Barclays Global Aggregate Treasuries Index. For example, hybrid curves like the sector-rating curves are suitable for segments without currency risk. Sector-country hybrid curves offer a good solution for capturing the interest-rate risk for segments of broad benchmarks like the ICE BofA U.S. Broad Market Index or the ICE BofA EMU Broad Market Index. Obviously, the broader a global bond portfolio is, the more options there are for spot curve definitions.

Note that the yield curve specification must be aligned with the portfolio objectives and investment process. Not surprisingly, unconstrained or opportunistic bond portfolios that try to capture excess returns in different markets, segments, and niches try to extract alpha from different cross segments and often implement different yield curve scenario analysis and yield curve management techniques. The reason is that different spot curves will generate different pricing and spreads for the same bonds. The cross-clusters are usually preferred for heterogeneous bond exposures because they allow mispricing and allow for possible interactions between different types of risks. Specifically, a cross-cluster (e.g., country-sector) might be made with the purpose of evaluating mispriced bonds that might gain or lose in value from interactions between rating changes, country-specific interest-rate and spread dynamics, and sectoral developments.

4.3.2 *Duration and maturity allocation strategies*

In Chapter 1, we explained the importance of duration as a measure of interest-rate risk on a single bond and for global bond portfolios. In this section, we focus on the management of a global bond portfolio comprising different durations and duration segments, and their interactions.

First, we discuss the duration of bond portfolios. In general, duration strategies depend on the slope and level of multiple maturity positionings on different country yield curves. Again, the changes of level and slope are two of the most important risk factors for bonds and bond portfolios.

Figure 4.7 captures typical yield curve changes. The two general shifts we see are the *bear parallel shift* and the *bull parallel shift*, in which the yield curves move upward or downward, respectively. Bear parallel shifts have an adverse impact on the portfolio as a rising yield curve and interest rates reduce bond prices. Bull parallel shifts have a positive impact on bond prices due to a decline in interest rates. More interesting curve changes are those we call *bear steepeners* and *bear flatteners*. The reason is that for both of these, the yield curve changes are associated with changes of all three of the factors identified by Litterman and Scheinkman (1991): level, slope, and curvature.

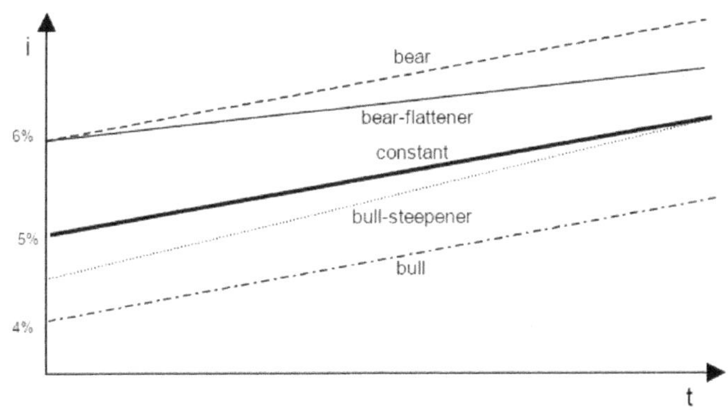

Figure 4.7: Simplified Yield Curve Changes

Note: This plot captures the sterilized yield curve changes expressed as changes in interest rates (*i*) on the vertical axis and time to maturity on the horizontal axis. This is a simplified visualization of yield curve changes. The neutral or constant scenario for the yield curve is assumed to be 5%, which is only for illustrative purposes.

The two most widely known maturity allocation strategies in bond portfolio management are bullet-and-barbell structures. Bullet allocation is associated with a concentration of the portfolio weights in the middle maturity buckets. For a barbell allocation, both the short and the long maturity buckets will have large weights in the portfolio, but the middle maturity bucket will have much less weight. Note that the maturity buckets are not defined *a priori*. Figure 4.8 provides a simple illustration of the strategies using maturity buckets.

The ladder strategy is a special case in which the maturity buckets are spread like a ladder. A ladder strategy is a commonly used strategy because the broad maturity allocations of some indexes are tilted to very long maturities. Examples of indexes with a tilt toward long maturity bonds are the J.P. Morgan EMBI Global Composite Index and the J.P. Morgan GBI Broad Index. These indexes have a historically strong allocation to bonds with more than 10-year maturities and have long durations exceeding seven years.

Tactical maturity allocation allows the greatest flexibility for allocating to different maturity buckets according to estimated expected bond

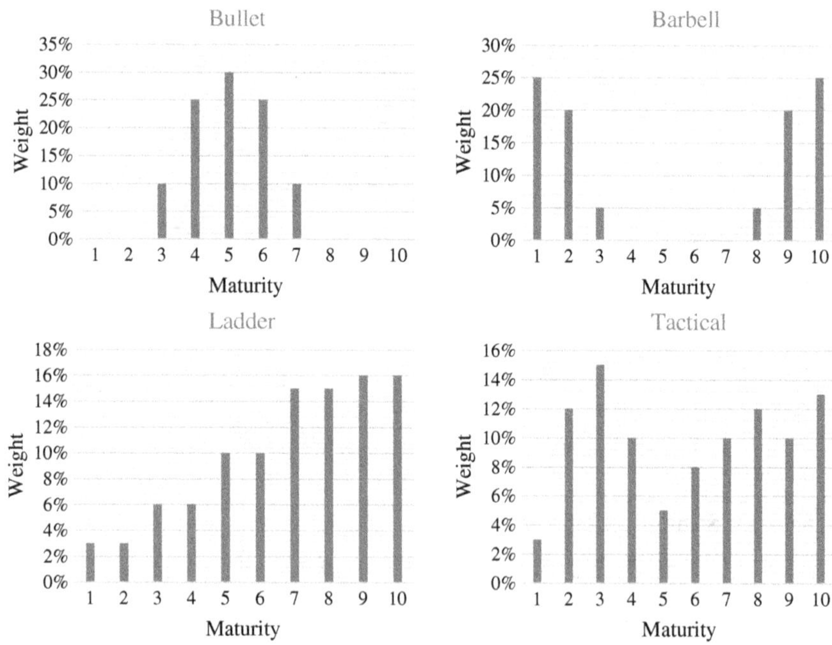

Figure 4.8: Examples of Maturity-Related Portfolio Allocations

returns and risks. Tactical positioning is mostly used on an overall portfolio basis because in a broadly invested bond portfolio with exposure to several countries, sectors, and industries, it is difficult to determine a target maturity allocation. We use an example to illustrate the complex duration and maturity allocation decision that is often associated with global bond portfolio allocations.

Suppose the portfolio manager of a global bond portfolio allocates to several countries. For example, the exposure in the U.S. Treasury market and Polish government bond market might be a barbell structure, with only short-term bonds in Italy and South Africa, a bullet structure in Hungarian bonds, and an allocation to high-yield emerging market bonds in hard currencies. The overall duration of the portfolio might be, say, 4.8. What does it mean for the portfolio? In general, the question is simple, but the answer is not trivial. Specifically, every segment has its own duration contribution and maturity allocation that in fact might be deemed "strategic" for the overall portfolio, but highly specific and tactical with respect to the different asset classes and segments.

To understand the foregoing problem more clearly let's consider a simple case study. We will use the barbell and bullet allocation to provide a numerical example that helps to understand the issue at hand. An active management approach requires estimating the portfolio weights of bullet or barbell strategies. To estimate and compare the strategies it is necessary to consider the overall durations and convexities of the bonds. We use three bonds with their corresponding durations, convexities, yields to maturity (YTM), and weights to show the intuition of the approach in Table 4.6.

Note that the portfolio duration and portfolio convexities are weighted sums of the individual bond durations k and convexities, respectively. Specifically, the portfolio duration and the portfolio convexity are

Table 4.6: Bullet–Barbell Duration-Neutral Portfolio Allocation

Bond	**Duration**	**Convexity**	**YTM**	**Weights**	**Weighted Duration**	**Weighted Convexity**
POLGB 2 1/2 01/25/23	1.50	0.04	0.27	0.53	0.80	0.02
POLGB 1 1/4 10/25/30	8.58	0.85	1.70	0.47	4.02	0.40
HGB 1 1/2 08/26/26	4.83	0.29	2.07	1.00	4.82	0.29

Note: Data obtained by the authors from Bloomberg, LLC.

weighted sums of the individual bond durations and convexities as follows:

$$D_p = \sum_{k=1}^{K} w_k D_k \quad \text{and} \quad C_p = \sum_{k=1}^{K} w_k C_k \tag{4.17}$$

where w_k is the individual bond weight in a portfolio and D_k and C_k are the single bond durations and convexities, respectively.

To solve the problem with the Polish and the Hungarian duration-neutral bullet-and-barbell strategies, we set the duration of the bullet $D^{\text{Bullet}}_{\text{Hungary}} = D^{\text{Barbell}}_{\text{Poland}}$ equal to that of the barbell exposure, that is, 4.8 in our example. Then, we search for the weights for the Polish bond exposure w_{Poland} that satisfies the duration neutrality requirement. Note that the Hungarian bond comprises 100% of the bullet portfolio and the barbell portfolio comprises two Polish bonds whose sum is also 100%. The weight of one Polish bond is w_k and the weight of the second bond is then $1 - w_k$.

To build a duration-neutral bond portfolio between bullet-and-barbell strategies, we must set the duration of the barbell equal to the duration of the bullet bond. Note that the bullet portfolio comprises 100% of one bond with known duration. Obviously, the bullet duration and weight are known in advance, but the weights of the barbell strategy must be determined so that the portfolio duration of the barbell equals the portfolio duration of the bullet. Therefore, the weights of the barbell portfolio are optimized to produce a duration-neutral portfolio. The following expression summarizes the calculations:

$$w_{\text{Hungary}} D^{\text{Bullet}}_{\text{Hungary}} = w_{\text{Poland Bond 1}} D^{\text{Barbell}}_{\text{Poland Bond 1}} + (1 - w_{\text{Poland Bond 1}}) D^{\text{Barbell}}_{\text{Poland Bond 2}}$$

We can now determine the weights of the duration-neutral Polish government bond exposure that is equal to the bullet allocation for the Hungarian government bond. The convexity of the Polish portfolio (0.42) is higher than that for the Hungarian portfolio convexity (0.29). Going forward for the other bonds, we could determine duration-neutral segments for the other exposures — high-yield emerging markets, U.S. Treasuries, Italian bonds, and South African bonds.

Note that the above allocation is duration neutral. That is, the interest-rate risk as captured by the durations is similar in the portfolio, but completely different in economic terms. More precisely, the interest-rate risk for the Polish government bond is different from the one for U.S. and South African government bonds. Moreover, the currency risk is also completely different. In this example, we have Hungarian forint and Polish zloty currency risk. Obviously, maturity allocation with duration-neutral portfolios helps to define strategies, but the risk associated with spreads, currencies, and other risk factors remains open.

In Chapter 7, we provide a comprehensive approach to dealing with complex bond portfolios comprising many heterogeneous single bonds and many possible constraints. Again, portfolio segmentation and cluster affiliation are important approaches to quantitatively manage exposure, risks, and constraints. Data analytical approaches provide valuable solutions as to how to decompose portfolios based on the underlying information from indexes, benchmarks, and portfolio investment universes.

Of course, if the portfolio is managed against a benchmark, the maturity allocation strategies can be implemented against the benchmark allocation. In such cases, the bullet-and-barbell strategies are actively managed strategies against a benchmark. In Chapter 12, we discuss the implications of these strategies in an active management context and highlight the differences again.

It is worth mentioning the specific implications of yield curve dynamics for the yield curve maturity allocation in bullet-and-barbell strategies. Both bull steepening and bear flattening usually have mixed effects across the yield curve; therefore, careful positioning is essential because much depends on the magnitude of these two effects. If the changes caused by bull steepening and bear flattening are around the middle maturity points, bullet maturity allocation is usually preferred as the convexity impact is still small. However, large swings in bull steepening and bear flattening are better captured by barbell strategies with large exposure in the long and short maturities, because the convexity adjustment is for higher-yield volatility which is much higher than the duration effect might indicate.

In general, duration and maturity strategies should not only focus on duration but consider the convexity effects on a portfolio. To mitigate the shortcomings of the strictly dedicated bullet-and-barbell strategies, a tactical positioning in yield curves is often considered more effective. However, tactical positioning depends on the variables considered in the portfolio investment process and on the quantitative models applied.

These inputs require high conviction views on all underlying yield curves, and, in the case of quantitative bond portfolio management, an optimization approach capable of capturing such positioning and risks. As we shall see in Chapter 6, the minimum-variance approach or similar optimization approaches are not capable of dealing with complex solutions for tactical bond portfolio optimizations.

4.3.3 *Rating and credit strategies*

The major intuition behind rating and credit strategies is based on the different ratings and credit risks associated with the term structure of credit risk. The underlying assumption is that credit ratings of, say, AAA rating sectors are to a large extent independent of the development of, say, BBB+ rating sectors. However, the reverse is not true. The credit curves with lower ratings (BBB+) depend on the dynamics of AAA credit sectors. Note that credit sectors also might be government bonds, corporate bonds, financials, covered bonds, etc., and credit yield curve strategies are related to the yield curve management of credit term structure risk.

The mechanics of credit and rating curve management are directly related to duration neutrality. Leibowitz *et al.* (1995) showed that curve positioning is to a large extent spread and interest-rate differential positioning using different types of credit risk relative to the U.S. Treasury curve. However, this positioning is not restricted to the three major factors (level, slope, and curvature). Howell (2019) indicated that there might exist other risk premiums that justify such positioning. This is the motivation for credit and rating curve management as a different yield curve strategy. Figure 4.9 provides possible spot curves relative to the U.S. Treasury spot curve. Note that such positioning is associated with bond carry. The different credit curves provide different yield premiums, which are not linear. That is, the premium for the BB+ spot curve over the U.S. Treasury spot curve is not proportional to the AA− premium.

Importantly, credit and rating strategies do not exclude specific duration and maturity positioning. Duration is a linear approximation while convexity is not. For example, the slope of the USD non-investment-grade yield curve is steeper than the slope of the U.S. Treasury curve. Analysis of curve flattening and curve steepening might reveal important

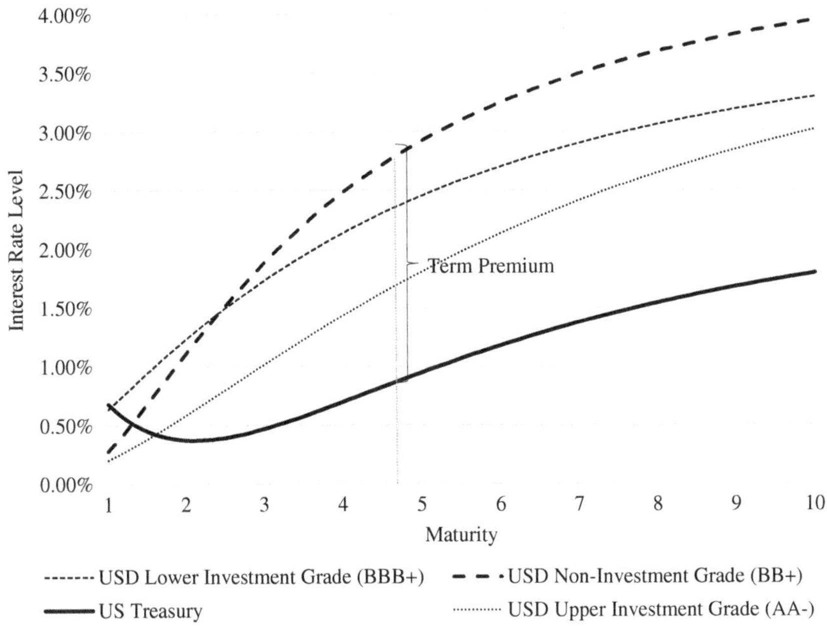

Figure 4.9: Relative Spot Curves

information regarding specific duration positioning. Hodges and Parekh (2006) and Ilmanen and Iwanovski (2007) explained that convexity, market risk changes, and the required risk premiums are decisive for positioning. Flattening expectations make yield curves more concave and steepening expectations change the shape to an inverted yield curve.

Parallel shifts in the yield curves of the USD non-investment-Grade curve might be more severe than the parallel shifts of the U.S. Treasury curve. Volatility is greater when interest rates are low, but the spreads for lower investment-grade bonds are more volatile. In addition, the magnitude (spikes) of changes of lower-rated yield curves (e.g., yield curves with a BB− rating) is larger than the changes of yield curves comprising higher-rated bonds. The same applies to spreads. The magnitude of credit curve dynamics is therefore larger for bond portfolios with lower overall ratings. For the latter types of portfolios, a barbell yield curve would be a better choice when large parallel shifts in both directions of the yield curves are expected. The intuition is that for duration-neutral exposure in, say, all four rating curves, the curve positioning with the higher convexity will adjust to the changes in yield curve dynamics more efficiently. In general, in the case of lower curve volatility in parallel shifts, bullet structures would be a better choice.

Alternatively, steepening yield curve changes are better captured by bullet maturity structures. Again, in a bullet duration-neutral positioning in all four curves, the bonds with shorter maturities roll down the steep curves more aggressively than longer-term bonds on the same curves. However, if flattening is expected, then a barbell structure would be a better choice (given duration neutrality), because the higher convexity of the barbell structure better adjusts bond prices to changing yields.

The most challenging aspect of implementing credit strategies in global bond portfolios is due to the different rating curve dynamics associated with lower- and higher-rated bonds. Suppose a parallel shift occurs in all four curves. The lower-rated curves would react with greater intensity than the credit curves with AAA ratings. In other words, lower-rated yield curves for emerging markets and high-yield bonds require more aggressive management that in turn also requires more intense risk control.

4.3.4 *Relative value strategies*

Relative value strategies might comprise several strategies that are integrated into a bond portfolio. These strategies might be, but are not limited to, intra-curve strategies and inter-curve strategies.

4.3.4.1 *Inter-curve positioning*

Inter-curve strategies involve positioning across many yield curves. Examples might be positioning in specific emerging market bonds in U.S. dollars versus euros, or exposure in a specific corporate bond from the same issuer in different currencies. These strategies represent a form of carry strategy in different yield curve regimes, but similar rating exposure. Alternatively, the currency risk might be identical, but mispricing sources might be of particular interest. Importantly, some of the inter-curve strategies involving currency risk might involve high-risk positions and as a consequence are often currency hedged. That is, the currency risk might be eliminated using currency derivative instruments such as forwards.

In Figure 4.10, we show inter-curve strategies based on corporate sector spot curves for European and U.S. corporate bonds. For example, the U.S. financial spot curve (USFinancial) is roughly flat, but the European Financial spot curve (EURFinancial) is downward sloping, which means favorable roll down positioning. However, the yield level for the U.S. financial sector is higher. A currency-neutral positioning might be favorable if the U.S. Financial curve is expected to realize a bull steepening and the European Financial corporate bond curve is expected to remain relatively constant. The euro-denominated curves are downward sloping, with lower average yields.

The following example using hard currency bonds in emerging markets reveals how challenging it is to manage global bond portfolios. The example is slightly more complex than the previous one, but reveals several important facets related to yield curve positioning, duration, and relative value strategies. The important information to consider when implementing inter-curve trades includes currency exposure, economic exposure, relative yield curve positioning, maturity and duration positioning, yield curve expectations, and cross-relations. Inter-curve positioning also requires analysis of market liquidity. For example, corporate bonds

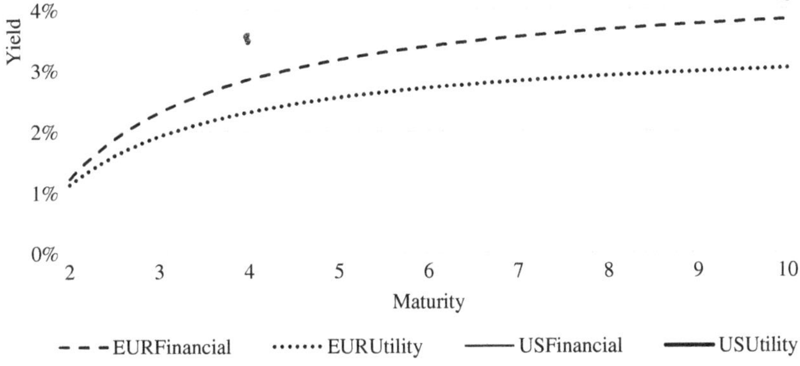

Figure 4.10: Inter-Curve Strategy for Corporate Sector and Currencies

issued by manufacturers of capital goods (e.g., bonds from General Electric, 3M, Airbus, and Rolls-Royce) have different liquidity than say financials. The liquidity in the maturity buckets might be completely different and tradability might come at the cost of expected returns and unattractive spreads. Additionally, inter-curve trades in different currencies require strong risk management. For example, trading a Chinese government bond in US dollars has different risks and liquidity than EUR-denominated Chinese government bonds. Yield curve attractiveness as measured by the term spreads is not enough to properly estimate risks. This is a critical point when investigating inter-curve strategies for currencies and countries.

Figure 4.11 plots eight spot curves estimated using the Nelson-Siegel model for four different currency regimes. Specifically, there is a spot curve for China in U.S. dollars (USDCN) and in euros (EURCN). Similarly, there is a spot curve for Mexico in both euro (EURMX) and U.S. dollar (USDMX). In addition, there are euro- and U.S. dollar-denominated

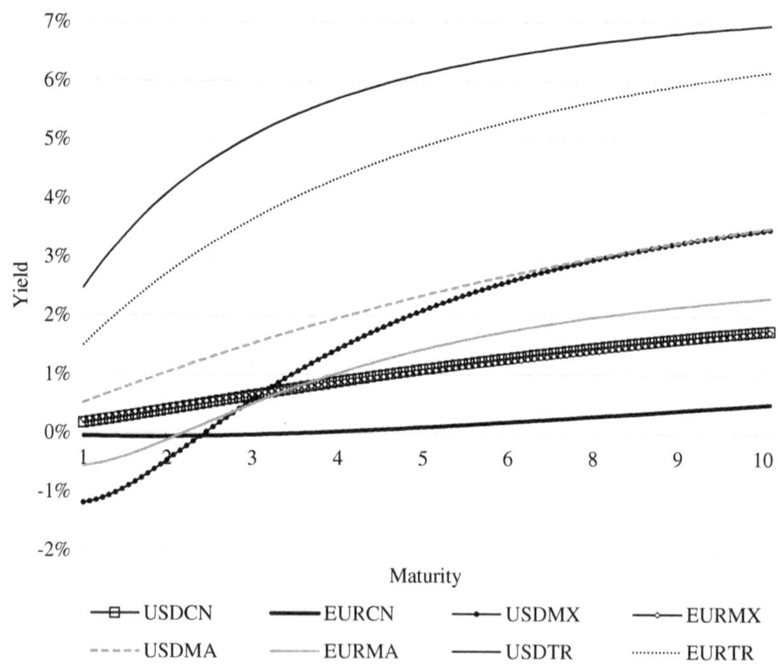

Figure 4.11: Inter-Curve Strategy for Countries and Currencies

spot curves for Turkey and Malaysia with EURTR and USDTR, and EURMA and USDMA, respectively. Let us discuss some important dimensions of a portfolio comprised of bonds that correspond to the latter spot curves.

First, our currency risk is twofold: U.S. dollar and euro. A global bond portfolio manager can select the curves on a standalone basis depending on the expected foreign exchange dynamics and the expectation regarding appreciation or depreciation. However, as these are hard currency bonds, their underlying currency exposure is detached from the economic exposure of the underlying bonds. The economic exposure is determined by the macroeconomic development and fiscal and monetary policies in Mexico, Turkey, China, and Malaysia. However, the currency exposure depends on U.S. Treasuries and the U.S. economic policy that impacts the value of the U.S. dollar. Whereas the choice between bond portfolio duration exposure in all country-specific spot curves (e.g., China, Turkey, Malaysia, and Mexico) might be easily determined from a bond carry perspective, the choice between the U.S. dollar- and euro-denominated bonds in Turkey or Malaysia might require a broader quantitative toolset comprising curve shift models, bond fair value and OAS estimations, and cross-currency risk estimations.

If currency risk is neutral, the economic rationale can be a decisive instrument. The U.S. dollar-denominated spot curves of Malaysia and Mexico are overlapping in long maturity buckets. In this case, a portfolio optimization technique might help to select the bonds with higher roll downs and attractive OAS if the economic rationale between the two countries is neutral.

Cross-country and currency allocation decisions typically have many layers. For example, the Mexico spot curve in euros is identical to the U.S. dollar-denominated China hard currency bond curve. The positioning depends on the economic rationale, currency exposure, relative bond pricing, and OAS associated with the underlying bonds.

From this example, we see that the possibilities that bond portfolios have is virtually endless. Nevertheless, possible solutions to highlight are those that build strategies based on the following:

- *currency exposure* — decide U.S. dollar versus euro currency risk.
- *economic or country exposure* — decide analytically which country to select given the economic risk–return profile (e.g., Mexico versus China in U.S. dollars).

- *spot curve positioning* — steeper versus flat curves reflecting the economic development and expectations (e.g., China in U.S. dollars versus Mexico in euros).

Machine learning frameworks might provide effective analytical solutions as the complexity of such portfolios is often sizable. Such a solution for countries and sector regimes is provided by Garvey and Madhavan (2019) using hierarchical clustering. A similar solution for index choice is provided in Chapter 2.

4.3.4.2 *Intra-curve positioning*

The purpose of intra-curve strategies is to gain exposure on the same yield curve. It is important to note that relative value strategies are not only limited to estimating yield curve factor movements but can also consider spread estimations and identification of cheap/rich bonds and even entire segments. Consequently, the OAS becomes a vital part in positioning and strategy implementation. The mechanics behind such strategies would involve the evaluation of both expected bond returns and the OAS.

Note that relative value strategies usually have much shorter holding periods than other strategies. This is because disparities and arbitrage possibilities might disappear more quickly. Such relative value strategies are not implementable on fixed timeframes. For example, relative value strategies open as opportunities arise and close as the attractiveness of these strategies disappears or are no longer statistically and economically justified. Econometric analysis of co-moving time series is often applied to statistically evaluate such trades. Suppose for example, that a mispricing of a government bond, say, a South African government bond, is trading with too large a spread over the relevant yield curve. A trade might be implemented immediately, and the holding period will depend on the relative cheapness of the bond to the curve as measured by the spread. The trade does not depend on a pre-specified monthly, weekly, or any fixed holding period as signals and information arrive not at pre-determined periods, but sporadically.

The most prominent examples of such relative value or opportunistic strategies are debt-restructuring trades. Another example would be the trades we highlighted with South African bonds which we referred to as an example of an over- or undervaluation intra-sectoral opportunity. Other examples include the over- and undervaluation of bonds from the same issuer and mispricings in the U.S. Treasury market. Country-focused examples of this type of trade are relative value strategies on sovereign debt — Greece in 2011, Argentina in 1993 and 2005, Russia in 2000, Ecuador in 1995, 2000, and 2009, and Cote d'Ivoire in 1998 and in 2010. In these cases, bond portfolios have exposure to credit default swap spreads and/or implement currency positions (usually shorting the foreign currency with forwards).

4.4 Key Takeaways

- Bond pricing, expected returns, and estimating spreads are important in global bond portfolio management. Therefore, spot curve estimation and applications are vital in a quantitative investment process. Bond indexes and markets provide a broad spectrum for analysis and spot curve choice that can match portfolio management objectives and investment approaches.
- Based on spot curves, there are three groups of strategies — duration, credit, and relative value — that interact and are closely related. These strategies are not isolated from each other, and their foundations are bond returns, spot curves, and bond valuation. Currencies, countries, asset classes, industry groups, and sectors are among the information sources for spot curves and strategies. Cross-asset curves might be required depending on the portfolio exposure and risk.
- Spot curve estimation and strategies are the cornerstone of the quantitative process based on expected returns and risks. Spot curves are input parameters for currency and fixed-income allocation as well as for bond selection optimizations that may form an important part of the investment process.
- The choice of yield curves depends on portfolio risks and the portfolio manager's investment process. Yield curve estimation depends on bond data. Benchmark indexes are widely used to estimate spot curves. The choice as to whether currency risk, rating risk, country risk, or sector risk prevails is the first principle in spot curve choice. Often, currency risk is the most important for global government bond portfolios. In this case, estimating local currency spot curves is necessary. However, country-rating or sector-rating curves might be more preferred for global aggregate bond portfolios that invest in several asset classes.

- The Nelson-Siegel and Svensson models for yield curve estimation are among the most commonly used choices for practitioners because of their easy implementation, interpretability, and sound economic foundation. Because these approaches use the three most important factors for explaining interest-rate volatility (level, steepness, and curvature), bond portfolio managers are able to gauge not only portfolio returns but are also capable of monitoring the risks of their exposures. The two approaches allow one to model bond markets with both large and small numbers of tradable bonds. The spot curves allow a portfolio manager to model negative rates and dynamically adjust to changing bond market data.
- The spot curves allow a portfolio manager to implement relative value strategies based on intra-curve and inter-curve analysis. Intra-curve analysis is focused on the term premium within the same yield curve and tries to exploit strategies based on the level, steepness, and curvature within the same curves. Inter-curve strategies require strong risk management because different spot curves are driven by different fundamental, liquidity, timing, and tradability dynamics. Risks might be significant and include currency, liquidity, credit, country, rating, sector, and political risk.

References

Bank for International Settlements. 2005. “Zero-coupon Yield Curves: Technical Documentation”, BIS Papers N25, Monetary and Economic Department, October 2005.

Ben Dor, A., L. Dynkin, J. Hyman, P. Houweling, E. van Leeuwen, and O. Penninga. 2007. “DTS (Duration Times Spread)”. *Journal of Portfolio Management* 33(2): 77–100.

Binny, J. 2005. “Currency Management Style through the Ages”. *Journal of Alternative Investments* 8(3): 52–59.

Bolder, D. J. and D. Streliski. 1999. “Yield Curve Modelling at the Bank of Canada”. Bank of Canada Technical Report No.84.

Chen T-K., H-H. Liao, and P-L. Tsai. 2011. “Internal Liquidity Risk in Corporate Bond Yield Spreads”. *Journal of Banking and Finance* 35(4): 978–987.

Chinn, M. D. and G. Meredith. 2004. “Monetary Policy and Long-Horizon Uncovered Interest Parity”. *IMF Staff Papers* 51(3): 409–430.

Dolan, C. P. 1999. “Forecasting the Yield Curve Shape”. *Journal of Fixed Income* 9(1): 92–99.

Duyvesteyn, J. and M. Martens. 2014. "Emerging Government Bond Market Timing". *Journal of Fixed Income* 23(3): 36–49.

Fabozzi, F. J. and F. A. Fabozzi. 2023. *Fixed Income Mathematics*. 5th Edition. New York: McGraw-Hill.

Fabozzi, F. J., L. Martellini, and P. Priaulet. 2005. "Predictability in the Shape of the Term Structure of Interest Rates". *Journal of Fixed Income* 15(1): 40–53.

Garvey, G. and A. Madhavan. 2019. "Reconstructing Emerging and Developed Markets Using Hierarchical Clustering". *Journal of Financial Data Science* 1(4): 84–102.

Hodges, S. D. and N. Parekh. 2006. "Term Structure Slope Risk." *Journal of Fixed Income* 16(3): 54–59.

Howell, M. J. 2019. "Measuring Bond Investors' Risk Appetite Using the Interest Rate Term Structure". *Journal of Investing* 28(6): 115–127.

Ilmanen, A. and R. Iwanowski. 1997. "Dynamics of the Shape of the Yield Curve". *Journal of Fixed Income* 7(2): 47–60.

Kazemi, H., Black, K. H., and R. D. Chambers. 2016. *Alternative Investments: CAIA Level II*. 3rd Edition. Hoboken, NJ: John Wiley & Sons.

Konstantinov, G. 2014. "Active Currency Management of International Bond Portfolios". *Financial Markets and Portfolio Management* 28(1): 63–94.

Konstantinov, G. S. 2022. "Emerging Market Bonds and Currencies". *Journal of Portfolio Management* 48(8): 139–158.

Leibowitz, M. L., S. Kogelman, and L. N. Bader. 1995. "Spread Immunization". *Journal of Investing* 4(3): 49–56.

Leibowitz, M. L., W. S. Krasker, and A. Nozari. 1990. "Spread Duration: A New Tool for Bond Portfolio Management". *Journal of Portfolio Management* 16(3): 46–53.

Li, Y., D. Turkington, and A. Yazdani. 2020. "Beyond the Black Box: An Intuitive Approach to Investment Prediction with Machine Learning". *Journal of Financial Data Science* 2(1): 61–75.

Litterman, R. B. and J. Scheinkman. 1991. "Common Factors Affecting Bond Returns". *Journal of Fixed Income* 1(1): 54–61.

Martens, M., P. Beekhuizen, J. Duyvesteyn, and C. Zomerdijk. 2019. "Carry Investing on the Yield Curve". *Financial Analysts Journal* 75(4): 51–63.

Nelson, C. R. and A. F. Siegel. 1987. "Parsimonious Modeling of Yield Curves". *Journal of Business* 60(4): 473–489.

Nucera, F. and G. Valente. 2013. "Carry Trades and the Performance of Currency Hedge Funds". *Journal of International Money and Finance* 33: 407–425.

Parikh, H. and F. J. Fabozzi. 2018. "The Impact of Market Conditions on Bond Fund Managers". *Journal of Fixed Income* 27(3): 6–22.

Perraudin, W. and A. P. Taylor. 2004. "On the Consistency of Ratings and Bond Market Yields". *Journal of Banking and Finance* 28(11): 2769–2788.

Steele, J. M. 2001. *Stochastic Calculus and Financial Applications*. New York: Springer Verlag.

Svensson, L. E. O. 1995. "Estimating Forward Interest Rates with the Extended Nelson and Siegel Method". *Sveriges Riksbank Quarterly Review* 3: 13–26.

Van Landschoot, A. 2008. "Determinants of Yield Spread Dynamics: Euro versus US dollar Corporate Bonds". *Journal of Banking and Finance* 32(12): 2597–2605.

Zimmerer, T. 2003. "Der Roll Down im Bond Management: Theoretisches Phänomen und praktische Implementierung." *Finanz Betrieb* 4: 234–252.

Part 2

Portfolio Management

Chapter 5

Factors in Global Bond Portfolios

Factor models are now pervasive in investment management.[1] The primary attraction of factor models is that they help explain asset return behavior using a parsimonious set of return drivers, hence simplifying the construction and analysis of portfolios consisting of many assets. Because factor models provide a transparent view of the systematic risks to which a portfolio is exposed, they can be used for both risk management and alpha generation. Indeed, portfolio managers will often try to control the amount of their active risk deriving from systematic risk (beta) versus idiosyncratic risk (alpha). Alternatively, other portfolio managers may want to stray from the factor profile of their benchmarks in order to generate incremental alpha based on systematic bets. Although some factors have a purely statistical nature, other factors are derived from economic variables or fundamental variables, thereby directly related to asset return behavior.

Explaining the underlying building blocks of portfolios and asset classes in terms of factors is the main topic of this chapter. Our aim is to provide practical insights on the wide range of applications of factor models to global bond portfolios.[2] We discuss and provide information on

---

[1]For a description of the different types of factor models, see Connor (1995). Kritzman (2021) provides an overview of factor strategies and their properties.

[2]A clarification is in order here. The term "factor model" has two meanings. In statistics, a factor model (or factor analysis) is a statistical tool for modeling the behavior of a large set of observed variables and their covariance structure in terms of a smaller set of unobservable underlying "factors". The factors derived from a statistical factor model are

common (systematic) factors applied to a wide range of asset classes and give special attention to the most important factors for bond portfolio managers. In Chapter 10, we focus on factor models in performance analysis, highlighting the role of linear regression models — both traditional regression models and more sophisticated statistical techniques. The practical problems and issues associated with factor investing in global bond portfolios are highlighted as they pertain to performance measurement, risk assessment, and asset pricing.

5.1 Overview of Factor Models and their Purpose

Probably the most well-known factor model in equity space is the Fama–French–Carhart model.[3] The latter model is a multifactor extension of the capital asset pricing model (CAPM), where the market represents the sole source of systematic risk.[4] The Fama–French–Carhart model extends the CAPM framework by[5] introducing three additional factors to the market factor: the size factor (small-cap stock returns minus large-cap stock returns), value (high book-to-price stock returns minus low book-to-price stock returns), and momentum (high-returning stocks minus low-returning stocks). Both the CAPM and the Fama–French–Carhart model are typically estimated using linear regressions. Both academic research and practitioner research have embraced the idea of testing the Fama–French factors in bond portfolios. For example, Bektic *et al.* (2019), Konstantinov and Rusev (2020), Gava *et al.* (2020), and Konstantinov and Fabozzi (2021b), among others, have tested the prevalence of these factors in explaining bond returns. Houweling and van Zundert (2017), Bektic (2018), and Kaufmann and Messow (2020) presented empirical evidence that equity factor momentum is a driver of corporate bond returns. Fischer and Wermers (2013) argued that the Fama–French model (Fama and

referred to as "latent factors". In finance, a factor is a variable that has been determined to drive the returns of an asset class. The factors can be observed variables or can use the statistical tool of factor models to obtain latent factors. Factors are then used to construct portfolios and assess return performance.

[3]See Fama and French (1992, 1993) and Carhart (1997). For a machine learning based analysis of the Fama–French–Carhart model, see Simonian *et al.* (2019).

[4]The CAPM was formulated by several economists such as Sharpe (1964).

[5]See, for example, Fama and French (1993), Blake *et al.* (1993), Asness *et al.* (2013), Jostova *et al.* (2013), and Asness and Frazzini (2013).

French, 1993) can be an appropriate tool for investigating the return behavior of bond funds but note that few factor-based style analyses have been conducted for bond funds, at least in the academic literature.

While factors across all asset classes have an explanatory role, the drivers of the performance of each asset class have their own underlying structure, a fact which necessitates a nuanced approach to factor construction. For example, Martellini and Milhau (2015) and Rebonato *et al.* (2019) stressed that the identification of statistically significant and economically meaningful sources of risk specific to the bond market is important. De Jong and Fabozzi (2020) showed that the bond market exhibits very different dynamics compared to those implied by the Fama–French equity factors. They explained time-varying bond returns using factors derived from observable bond market data — duration-times-spread, liquidity, and a term factor — and showed that these factors successfully explain the dynamic nature of bond prices. Bender *et al.* (2019) describe the methodology of how to implement the Fama–French factors using market data, which can then be applied to bond market data. However, there are certain challenges when using these factors for bonds, which have been highlighted in several studies (see Konstantinov, 2023).

De Jong and Fabozzi also point out the non-trivial question of how to define the market risk for corporate bonds. One of the reasons is the non-linearity of the bond return–risk profile. Therefore, it is almost impossible to provide a comprehensive explanation for bond market risk by simply applying equity factors to bond space. The reason lies in the time-varying risk premiums of bonds and the challenges arising when determining bond market risk compared to equity market risk. In fact, a considerable amount of financial research has demonstrated that so-called "style premiums" such as carry, which captures the differential between short-term and long-term interest rates, explain a significant amount of bond risk.[6]

In a similar line of research, Pospisil and Zhang (2010) found that bond-specific momentum is a significant driver of bond performance. L'Hoir and Boulhabel (2010) and Correia *et al.* (2012) investigated a bond-specific value factor in the corporate bond market, translating the value concept to bond markets by comparing credit spreads to fundamental risk metrics. Bond momentum on the other hand could be linked to changes in the steepness of the yield curve. Specifically, bond momentum might be associated with trends in steepness according to which long-term

[6] See, for example, Brooks *et al.* (2018) and Mladina and Germani (2019).

bonds generate positive returns compared to short-term bonds. The greater the steepness of the yield curve, the larger the premium associated with holding long-term bonds.

Although the bond market possesses many unique characteristics as an asset class, it is nevertheless possible to apply equity risk factors to the study of bond return behavior. Several studies, for example, have applied the Fama and French (1993, 2015) factors to explain corporate bond returns.[7] Applying the Fama–French factors to a broad set of global and US bond indexes, Konstantinov and Fabozzi (2021a) report that the Fama–French factors have explanatory power when explaining the returns of high-yield and broad indexes, but are less suitable for global bond market indexes, where other factors that reflect currency risk are needed. Broad indexes (including indexes with credit and government exposure) require modified carry strategies to mitigate the impact on the U.S. dollar. These results show that the exposure to the equity-based profitability factor — one of the factors in the Fama–French five-factor model — is to some extent a natural hedge against the U.S. dollar risk of high-yield and corporate bond market indexes. The results suggest that investors should consider currency carry. The authors also provide a framework that can be used to diversify the impact of individual equity-based factors and currency style factors on bond benchmarks.

5.2 Factors and Factor Selection: Overview of Major Factor Categories

There are a large number of factors used in bond research. Whereas some of them are market-based factors, others are based on macroeconomic data or purely statistical constructs (i.e., latent variables) as estimated from principal component analysis (PCA) or other techniques. To be effective, factors need to sufficiently explain the target variable in question (i.e., returns).

In a multi-asset portfolio that invests in passive indexes, factors could be related to the broad features of asset classes such as equity beta, bond beta, and commodity beta. The bond and equity factor exposures are often proxied by publicly available indexes. For example, global bond portfolios investing in global corporate bonds might include the returns of a corporate bond index as representative of "credit beta". Similarly, investigating the non-U.S. developed market currency exposure of a

[7] See Asness *et al.* (2013), Houweling and van Zundert (2017), and Bektic *et al.* (2019).

global bond portfolio might take into account the US Dollar Basket Currency Index (DXY Index), which comprises several currencies against the U.S. dollar.

Factors can also be derived from macroeconomic variables such as changes in GDP and inflation. We refer to these broad categories of factors as *macro factors*. Alternatively, an active manager doing security selection may need to select more granular factors such as yield curve steepness or equity value. These factors are used to model more specific exposures within asset classes and are referred to as *micro factors*. Such factors are generally constructed from more than one observable market instrument like bonds, equities, or other derivatives.[8]

The difference in the choice of factors is largely a matter of preference, depending on the portfolio exposure and investable universe. That is, a global bond manager might choose government bonds in multiple currencies rather than U.S. high-yield bonds. For example, a bond portfolio manager might need to consider equity factors if the global bond portfolio or the investment universe comprises more equity-like instruments such as high-yield bonds or emerging market bonds. In general, the lower the investment grade of the bond portfolio and the greater the exposure to corporate high-yield bonds, the more relevant equity factors are in investment analysis. Below, we provide more detail on several important micro factors in the bond and equity space, including descriptions of how they are measured and/or constructed. Table 5.1 provides a listing of the most common factors in each group.

Table 5.1: Factor Classification

Market Yield and Currency Factors	**Asset-based Factors**	**Equity Market Factors**	**Strategy (Style) Factors**
Level	Term	Fama–French–Carhart	Bond Carry
Steepness	Default	Liquidity	Bond Trend
Curvature Spread	DTS	Betting-Against-Beta	Currency Carry
			Currency Value
Yield Volatility			Currency Momentum
Currency Volatility			FX (Implied) Volatility

Note: Authors' own factor clustering based on economic intuition and market data.

[8] Statistical factors such as principal components can be derived from either macro or micro factors.

5.2.1 *Market yield and currency factors*

The first detailed quantitative investigations into fixed income factors were provided by Merton (1974) and Litterman and Scheinkman (1991). Since the introduction of quantitative bond models, there has been extensive research on fixed-income factors, and today, portfolio managers can access factors that describe almost every aspect of bond return behavior. Here, we describe a selection of the most prominent market yield and currency factors currently used in practice.

5.2.1.1 *Level factor*

The *level factor* is simply the change of the long-term bond yield level. Because the 10-year bond yield is widely used as proxy for the long-term yield level, in this chapter we will denote the level factor by ($\Delta 10Y$). The reference instrument can be a government, corporate, or covered bond.

Within this setup, the factor gauges the daily changes for the long-term government yields that we will denote by $-\Delta y_\tau^n$, on each day τ.[9] It is convenient to adjust the values with a negative sign based on the assumption that a positive unit premium would automatically be associated with decreasing bond yields. Then, the daily data are averaged over all long-term bond yields available on any given day and average daily values are summed up to the weekly frequency T. The same procedure can be applied to weekly data, summed up to monthly data. A portfolio manager can construct the level factor using the following formula and the changes in the long-term government yields $-\Delta y_\tau^n : q$:

$$\text{Level factor} = \frac{1}{T_t} \sum_{T_t} \left[\sum_{N_\tau} \left(\frac{-\Delta y_\tau^n}{N_\tau} \right) \right] \tag{5.1}$$

where n denotes the level changes, N denotes the number of level values available on day τ, and T denotes the total number of trading days in week t. The level changes are equally weighted.

5.2.1.2 *Steepness factor*

The *steepness factor* refers to the slope of the yield curve as measured by the rate of change of the differences in the corresponding long-term and

[9]Depending on the investment universe, long-term corporate bond yields with specific market liquidity can be used to represent the level factor.

short-term bond yields. The long-term yield is proxied by the 10-year bond yield ($10Y$) and the short-term bond yield is proxied by the two-year bond yield, denoted by $2Y$. Then, $\Delta(10Y - 2Y)$ denotes the steepness factor which is calculated in a straightforward way.

The specific yield curve steepness is first calculated as the difference between the 10- and two-year bond yields n and measures the daily changes for steepness on each day τ. Then, these values are averaged over all bond-curve steepness values N available on any given day τ. Finally, the average daily values are summed up to the weekly frequency T. The same procedure applies to weekly data, summed up to monthly data. The following mathematical expression can be used to calculate the steepness factor:

$$\text{Steepness factor} = \frac{1}{T_t} \sum_{T_t} \left[\sum_{N_\tau} \left(\frac{\Delta(10Y_\tau^n - 2Y_\tau^n)}{N_\tau} \right) \right] \tag{5.2}$$

where n denotes the available steepness changes, N denotes the number of steepness values available on day τ, and T denotes the total number of trading days in week t. The steepness changes are equally weighted.

5.2.1.3 *Curvature factor*

As described by Litterman and Scheinkman (1991), the *curvature factor* captures the residual curve movements in excess of the level and steepness factors. It is usually measured by doubling the difference of the five-year bond yield less the 10-year and the two-year bond yields; that is, $(2\Delta 5Y - \Delta(10Y - 2Y))/2$. It is convenient to derive the curvature factor using highly reliable and liquid instruments. The government bond yields of U.S. Treasuries, European, and Japanese government bonds provide good source data for measuring the curvature factor.

5.2.1.4 *Spread factor*

The *spread factor* is derived from the absolute daily log return for each asset-swap spread.[10] Absolute values for the spread factor, denoted by

---

[10] Asset-swap spread is the difference between the yields on a fixed-rate bond and a floating rate bond of similar maturity. Specifically, the asset-swap spread is an indication of the credit risk of a bond over an underlying yield curve. For example, an asset-swap spread is the difference between the yield on a 10-year US Treasury bond and the yield on 10-year corporate bond.

$|spreads_{\tau}^{n}|$, are used in order to minimize the impact of outlier spreads. It is important to note that because it is assumed that spreads should converge in the long run, spreads should have a mean value of zero. This assumption indicates that spreads are mean reverting, with under- or overvalued bonds eventually converging to their fair value. More precisely, a spread constitutes a risk premium which has to be added/subtracted in the case of a negative sign to spot rates when determining a bond's price.

A spread of zero means that a bond is fairly valued based on an underlying yield curve. Because the swap curve is assumed to be risk-free when used as an underlying valuation tool, asset swap spreads usually have positive values. This assumption does not always hold in practice. Nevertheless, the assumption gives bond portfolio managers the ability to efficiently measure how much the spread of bonds departs from fair value. Once this is done, the average over all spreads, $|spreads_{\tau}^{n}|$, available on any given day τ are computed, and the average daily values up to the weekly frequency T are calculated. Thus, the spread factor proxy in week t is given by

$$\text{Spread factor} = \frac{1}{T_t}\sum_{T_t}\left[\sum_{N_\tau}\left(\frac{|spreads_{\tau}^{n}|}{N_\tau}\right)\right] \tag{5.3}$$

where n denotes the available spread changes, N denotes the number of spread values available on day τ, and T denotes the total number of trading days in week t. The spread changes are equally weighted.

5.2.1.5 *Yield volatility factor*

Yield volatility is an important factor in global bond portfolios for both alpha generation and risk management. This factor can be customized to the specific needs of a portfolio manager using government bond yields, corporate bond yields, or covered bond yields. The *yield volatility factor* is derived from observed market bond yields and can be further broken down to capture different bond yield volatilities. Thus, a portfolio manager might separately estimate government and corporate bond yield volatility factors.

The global 10-year ($10Y$) yield volatility factor that gauges the absolute daily changes for the 10-year government bond yield, denoted by $|\Delta 10Y_{\tau}^{q}|$, is given by the following expression:

$$\text{Yield volatility factor} = \frac{1}{T_t}\sum_{T_t}\left[\sum_{N_\tau}\left(\frac{|\Delta 10Y_\tau^n|}{N_\tau}\right)\right] \tag{5.4}$$

where n denotes the available 10-year government bond yield changes, N denotes the number of 10-year government bond yield changes available on day τ, and T denotes the total number of trading days in week t. The 10-year government bond yield changes are equally weighted.

We note that a number of investment banks provide data on interest-rate volatilities in the form of specific indexes. Notable examples are the Credit Suisse Interest Rate Volatility Estimate (Bloomberg ticker CIRVE Index) and Nomura Interest Rate Volatility Risk Premium Index (Bloomberg ticker NMIVRU Index).

5.2.1.6 *Currency volatility factor*

Currency volatility is derived in a manner like that for the yield volatility factor.[11] Also, just as in the case of yield volatility, it is possible to calculate volatility factors for different currency pairs or currency baskets. We derive the currency volatility factor using the formal description found in Menkhoff *et al.* (2012):

$$\text{Currency volatility factor} = \frac{1}{T_t}\sum_{T_t}\left[\sum_{N_\tau}\left(\frac{|\Delta FX_\tau^q|}{N_\tau}\right)\right] \tag{5.5}$$

where n denotes the currency return changes, N denotes the number of absolute currency return changes available on day τ, and T denotes the total number of trading days in week t. The currencies in the factor are equally weighted.

5.2.2 *Asset-based factors*

The group of *asset-based factors* refers to the term, default, and the duration-times-spread factors. Importantly, these factors are directly observable and represented by bond indexes. The major advantage of these factors is that financial research has defined them as assets, and underlying

[11] Konstantinov and Fabozzi (2022) measure the absolute changes for a set of currencies using the same methodology.

economic variables drive their risk and return profile (e.g., Fama and French, 1993, and Ben Dor *et al.*, 2007). As a result, their practical implementation is readily found in bond portfolio management and research.[12]

5.2.2.1 *Term factor*

The *term factor* is a proxy for bearing maturity-type risks. The original version of the factor was proposed for the U.S. market by Fama and French (1993). The simplest way to quantify the term factor is by taking the difference between a government bond index return (e.g., the Bloomberg Barclays US Government Bond Index) and the risk-free rate. Different versions of the factor can be computed for different maturities to reflect the relationship between risk and the assumed holding period for the bond.[13]

5.2.2.2 *Default factor*

The *default factor* captures the risk that corporate bond issuers will fail to honor their commitments to bond holders. For global bond portfolios, the default factor can be measured as the difference between the return on the Bloomberg Barclays Euro High Yield Index and the Bloomberg Barclays US Government Bond index.

A related measure is the *default risk premium* which is a widely accepted proxy for the corporate bond risk premium. It is measured as the spread between the Baa bond yield and the 10-year US Treasury yield.

5.2.2.3 *Duration-times-spread factor*

As mentioned earlier in Chapter 4, Ben Dor *et al.* (2007) derived a duration-times-spread (DTS) measure using the durations and spreads of single bonds and demonstrated that DTS can be applied successfully to both emerging and developed bond market instruments. As duration is the sensitivity of a bond price to absolute changes in interest rates, the spread duration, denoted by D_{Spread}, is the absolute sensitivity of a bond to

---

[12] See Mladina and Germani (2019) and Konstantinov and Fabozzi (2021b).

[13] It is generally assumed that there is a positive relationship between holding period and risk, such that there is more risk associated with longer maturity bonds.

changes in the yield spread. If the return of a bond is driven solely by changes in spread (denoted by Δs), then the DTS (Ds) is

$$R_{\text{Spread}} = -D_{\text{Spread}} \Delta S = -D_{\text{Spread}} S \frac{\Delta S}{S} \tag{5.6}$$

where R_{Spread} is the bond return due to a change in spread, s is the spread, and Δs is the change in the spread. From equation (5.6), we can see that DTS is the sensitivity to a relative change in spreads.

5.2.3 *Strategy (style) factors*

The *strategy (style) factors* comprise a set of factors often used in investment research to identify investment style and are provided by investment and brokerage houses. The application of such factors in the investment process might be associated with additional costs because brokerage houses charge fees. Important properties of these factors are that they are structured as long-short strategies that implement long and short views on certain assets. The underlying assumptions behind index and style factors are that they are rules based, back tested, based on economic rationale and fundamentals, implement long-short views, and provided to customers or portfolio managers that can passively invest in them. Therefore, these indexes are often not synthetic, but highly sophisticated with a live track record. These features make strategy factors the proper choice if researchers want to replicate trading strategies and different management styles.[14]

5.2.3.1 *Bond carry factor*

Carry can be defined as the return accruing to an investor from holding a higher-yielding security over a lower-yielding security, assuming prices remain constant. The *bond carry factor* is intended to measure the term premium and differences in interest rates and bond yields. In the European bond market, for example, we may construct a bond carry factor by going long the 10-year European bond futures contract and short the two-year Schatz futures contract.

---

[14] See Pojarliev and Levich (2008), Konstantinov (2017), Brooks *et al.* (2018), and Maeso *et al.* (2020).

5.2.3.2 *Bond trend factor*

The *bond trend factor* seeks to capture the steepening trend behavior in the bond market resulting from central bank monetary policy, changes in economic conditions, and changes in investor preferences (including risk appetite). The most common measure of steepness is (10*Y*–2*Y*). The yield curve steepness factor, which reflects changing economic conditions, captures economic trends: inverted yield curves which have negative steepness signal recession, while normal or positive steepness signals a healthy economic environment. The bond trend factor thus expresses a combination of macroeconomic and market sentiment.

5.2.3.3 *Currency carry factor*

The *currency carry factor* represents the difference between borrowing in low-yielding currencies and investing in high-yielding currencies. As in the case of the bond carry factor, there are several index providers for currency carry strategies. Some of the strategies incorporate the entire yield curve in different currencies, while others focus on short-term interest-rate differentials. In general, carry index strategies are long-short products that follow simple rules-based investment processes. These indices are generally constructed by taking long positions in several high-yielding currencies and short positions in three to five low-yielding currencies. For example, a widely used carry style index is the Deutsche Bank Currency Harvest Index.

Currency carry is an important factor for both bond and currency managers trying to exploit global interest rate differentials. The specification of a given currency carry factor might be based on the entire yield curve or on specific interest-rate differentials — three-month, two-year, or even 10-year bond yields. They can be based on both developed and emerging market currencies.[15]

5.2.3.4 *Currency value factor*

As its name implies, the *currency value factor* is designed to capture the relative richness or cheapness of currencies. Currency value is typically

[15] See Chapter 3 for a detailed explanation of the styles and strategies in foreign-exchange management and the corresponding country and currency symbols.

based on the concept of purchasing power parity (PPP), which in turn derives from the law of one price (i.e., the idea that identical goods in different markets should have the same price when translated from one currency to another). A belief in PPP implies that price differences between countries should narrow over time through exchange rate movements. Like several of the other factors described, there are a number of notable providers for currency value indices. These indices typically consist of a long position in the three most undervalued currencies and short positions in the three most overvalued currencies. A popular index is the Deutsche Bank Currency Value Index.[16]

It is important to note that the rebalancing of the strategy, and its success to some extent, depends on the process and methodology used to determine PPP by the index provider.

5.2.3.5 *Currency momentum factor*

The *currency momentum factor* describes the short-/mid-term behavior in price movements based on market technicals. The Deutsche Bank Trend Index is an example of an index that tracks this factor.[17] Alternative indexes are provided by Barclays, Citibank, and Deutsche Bank.[18] Currency momentum is often implemented as an overlay strategy to generate incremental alpha over shorter-term horizons. The basic way the currency momentum factor is constructed is to buy currencies that have exhibited positive returns during the recent past and sell currencies that have exhibited negative returns over the same period.

5.2.3.5.1 Foreign exchange (implied) volatility factor

In our discussion of market yield and currency factors, we showed a specific currency volatility factor, which can be computed using historical currency volatilities. An alternative is a foreign exchange (FX) volatility index that is constructed using implied currency volatilities. Of course, implied volatilities are not directly observable, but derived from option prices. Information on implied currency volatilities is an important source

---

[16]The Bloomberg Ticker for the Deutsche Bank Value Index is DBPPPUSF Index.

[17]The Bloomberg Ticker for the Deutsche Bank Trend Index is DBMOMUSF Index.

[18]Technical analysis is to some extent problematic for currency returns as Abbey and Doukas (2012) demonstrate.

for derivative strategies using currency options. The implied volatility index is usually compared to realized historical currency volatility. It is important to note that the FX volatility factor is not a directional trade. That is, implied historical volatility can be used for short and long strategies, but the direction of currency movement is not directly observable because depreciation or appreciation of currencies might not be directly evident from the factor. A widely used index that captures risk in foreign exchange is the Deutsche Bank FX Volatility Index.[19] Like the Chicago Board Options Exchange (Cboe) Volatility Index (VIX Index), the Deutsche Bank FX Volatility Index measures the implied volatility of the FX market. Thus, the index gauges expected future FX volatility. The Deutsche Bank FX Volatility Index captures implied volatilities which are informative for trading.

5.2.4 *Equity market factors*

Bonds are generally considered diversifiers against equity risk; therefore, bond portfolio managers need to control for indirect equity risk in their portfolios, especially from corporate bonds. Global bond portfolio managers must also be concerned with the occasional coupling that occurs between global markets during financial market dislocations. Indeed, it may very well be the case that in a global market sell-off, the equity movements in one country may impact bond prices in another. For this reason, equity factors must be considered by bond portfolio managers.

The pursuit of more specific equity factors began in earnest with the work of Fama and French (1992, 1993). According to their research, equity returns can be explained by the variability of returns tied to specific variables beyond the CAPM market factor, namely, size and value. Fama and French (1993) expanded their initial set of equity factors to explain bond returns using the factors term and default. In a subsequent empirical study, Fama and French (2015) added two more factors — profitability and investment — to explain equity returns.

[19]The Bloomberg ticker is the CVIX Index.

5.2.4.1 *Fama–French–Carhart (FFC) factors*

The Fama–French–Carhart model is a multifactor extension of the CAPM. Whereas in CAPM the market represents the sole source of systematic risk, the Fama–French–Carhart model introduces three new factors in addition to the market factor: the size factor (small-cap stock returns minus large-cap stock returns), value (high book-to-price stock returns minus low book-to-price stock returns), and momentum (high-returning stocks minus low-returning stocks). Konstantinov and Fabozzi (2021) investigated the explanatory power of the Fama–French–Carhart factors in relation to U.S. and global bond indexes and found that some of these factors have explanatory power for global bond benchmark indexes.[20]

5.2.4.2 *Liquidity factor*

Liquidity is an important characteristic for any asset.[21] In bond investing, many popular measures of liquidity are based on bid-ask spreads. While Pastor and Stambaugh (2003) and Sadka (2006) used bid-ask spreads to identify liquidity, there are in fact various ways to approach bond liquidity risk. For example, Bolla (2017) used the changes in the Cboe VIX to capture the liquidity risk of global bond market indices.[22]

A common way to express bid-ask spreads is to compute them as returns using bid P^{Bid} and ask prices P^{Ask}:

$$\text{Liquidity factor}_{\text{Bid–Ask Spreads}} = \ln(P^{\text{Ask}}/P^{\text{Bid}}) - 1 \tag{5.7}$$

where P^{Ask} is the quoted bond ask price and P^{Bid} is the quoted bond bid price.

It is important to note that while popular, measuring bond market liquidity using bid-ask spreads provides only approximate measures for the most liquid and heavily traded government bonds of the G3 countries (US Treasuries, German bunds, and Japanese bonds).

---

[20] We provide a detailed explanation of the use of factor models in Chapter 10.

[21] Notable studies on liquidity are Brunnermeier *et al.* (2009), Adrian and Shin (2010), and Nagel (2012).

[22] A description of the different measures for bond liquidity is provided in Chapter 18 in Fabozzi and Fabozzi (2021).

The bid-ask spread is not a reliable metric for corporate bonds (even less for high-yield bonds) as corporate bonds are traded in the over-the-counter market.[23] We further note that measuring liquidity as bid-ask spreads derived from quoted prices in bond markets is highly problematic and not a reliable source of information. Konstantinov and Pojarliev (2021) and Loistl and Konstantinov (2020) highlight that bond market prices are the result of notional amounts exchanged and not quotes. A bond's price depends on the executed order size only and not on the quoted prices. If liquidity affects bond prices, then it should always be possible to determine a bond's price. However, as bond prices depend on notional exchange, the liquidity premium, and thus yield, for the same bond might be different according to the notional exchanged (e.g., whether the order size of a corporate bond is 500,000 or 10 million will determine the bond's price and thus a different liquidity premium).

Other challenges in measuring bond liquidity risk are that it is not stationary. Liquidity is also not directly observable, but a market-wide factor determined through bond trading. In contrast to equity markets, directly derived bid-ask spreads are not available. For practical purposes, it is necessary to use volume-weighted bid-ask spreads. For all these reasons, the bid-ask spreads for government bonds from developed markets are the most logical choice as approximating factors for liquidity, as government bonds from the G10 countries are exchanged even in times of financial market stress.

Betting-Against-Beta Factor: Betting-against-beta (BAB) is a strategy that involves going long low-beta assets and going short high-beta assets. The intuition behind this factor is that leveraging less risky (low-beta) assets will generate greater risk-adjusted returns than leveraging riskier (high-beta) assets. Frazzini and Pedersen (2013) found empirical evidence that the BAB factor helps explains the *low volatility anomaly* in several markets — the tendency for low-volatility stocks to generate higher returns than high-volatility stocks.

Although this factor is defined for equity markets, Durham (2016) found evidence that the BAB factor can play an explanatory role in

[23] See Chapters 2 and 8 for further information about bond trading.

analyzing government bonds. The "bond BAB factor" used by Durham is constructed by going long the short-term and short the long-term end of the yield curve. An important attribute of the bond version of the BAB factor is that it nets out the exposure to the level factor. Thus, BAB might be positively related to the level factor, but exhibit different risk to the steepness and curvature factors.

5.3 Takeaways

- The factors that find application in global bond portfolios might be summarized in four clusters: market yield and currency factors, equity market factors, strategy (style) factors, and asset-based factors. All four clusters have different properties and reflect different underlying economic rationales.
- Market yield and currency factors play an important role in global bond portfolios as these portfolios have large exposure to currency risk, and foreign-exchange management is a distinctive part of portfolio management. These factors are among the most central when investigating bond portfolio returns because they focus on the yield curve dynamics and return drivers associated with yield curves and interest rates.
- Equity market factors for size, value, and the broad equity market are applied to global bond portfolios when portfolio exposure is tilted toward global high-yield and corporate bonds.
- Factors are the building blocks of factor models which are aimed at explaining the variance of returns. Therefore, having identified both statistically and economically relevant factors is central for understanding the dynamics of global bond portfolios.
- The asset-based factors have a sound economic foundation in investment management because they are represented by indexes comprised of liquid instruments that are widely traded.
- The strategy (style) factors are among the most popular factors in investment management because they represent statistically and economically sound strategies implemented as long-short portfolios that are designed to replicate different management styles like carry, value, and momentum among others.

References

Abbey, B. S. and J. A. Doukas. 2012. "Is Technical Analysis Profitable for Individual Currency Traders?" *Journal of Portfolio Management* 39(1): 142–150.

Adrian, T. and H. S. Shin. 2010. "Liquidity and Leverage". *Journal of Financial Intermediation* 19(3): 418–437.

Asness, C. and A. Frazzini. 2013. "The Devil in HML's Details". *Journal of Portfolio Management* 39(4): 49–68.

Asness, C., T. J. Moskowitz, and L. H. Pedersen. 2013. "Value and Momentum Everywhere". *Journal of Finance* 68(3): 929–985.

Bektić, D. 2019. "Residual Equity Momentum Spillover in Global Corporate Bond Markets". *Journal of Fixed Income* 28(3): 46–54.

Bektić, D., J. S. Wenzler, M. Wegener, D. Schiereck, and T. Spielmann. 2019. "Extending Fama–French-Factors to Corporate Bond Markets". *Journal of Portfolio Management* 45(3): 141–158.

Ben Dor, A., L. Dynkin, J. Hyman, P. Houweling, E. van Leeuwen, and O. Penninga. 2007. "DTS (Duration Times Spread)". *Journal of Portfolio Management* 33(2): 77–100.

Ben Dor, A., L. Dynkin, J. Hyman, and B. D. Phelps. 2012. *Quantitative Credit Portfolio Management: Practical Innovations for Measuring and Controlling Liquidity, Spread and Issuer Concentration Risk*. Hoboken, NJ: John Wiley & Sons.

Bender, J., J. L. Sun, and R. Thomas. 2019. "Asset allocation vs. Factor Allocation — Can We Build a Unified Method?" *Journal of Portfolio Management* 45(2): 9–22.

Blake, C. R., E. Elton, and M. Gruber. 1993. "The Performance of Bond Mutual Funds". *Journal of Business* 66(3): 370–403.

Bolla, L. 2017. "Fundamental Indexing in Global Bond Markets: The Risk Exposure Explains It All". *Financial Analysts Journal* 73(1): 101–120.

Brooks, J., D. Palhares, and S. Richardson. 2018."Style Investing in Fixed Income". *Journal of Portfolio Management* 44(4): 127–139.

Brunnermeier, M., S. Nagel, and L. H. Pedersen. 2009a. "Carry Trades and Currency Crashes". *NBER Macroeconomic Annual* 23(1): 313–348.

Brunnermeier, M., S. Nagel, and L. H. Pedersen. 2009b. "Market Liquidity and Funding Liquidity". *Review of Financial Studies* 22(6): 2201–2238.

Carhart, M. 1997. "On Persistence in Mutual Fund Performance". *Journal of Finance* 52(1): 57–82.

Connor, G. 1995. "Three Types of Factor Models: A Comparison of Their Explanatory Power". *Financial Analysts Journal* 51: 42–46.

Correia, M., S. Richardson, and I. Tuna. 2012. "Value Investing in Credit Markets". *Review of Accounting Studies* 17(3): 572–609.

De Jong, M. and F. J. Fabozzi. 2020. "The Market Risk of Corporate Bonds". *Journal of Portfolio Management* 46(2): 92–105.

Durham, J. B. 2016. "Betting against Beta with Bonds: Worry or Love the Steepener? *Financial Analysts Journal* 72(6): 57–85.

Fabozzi, F. J. and F. A. Fabozzi. 2021. *Bond Markets, Analysis and Strategies.* Cambridge, MA: MIT Press.

Fama, E. F. and K. R. French. 1992. "The Cross-Section of Expected Stock Returns". *Journal of Finance* 47(2): 427–465.

Fama, E. F. and K. R. French. 1993. "Common Risk Factors in the Returns on Stocks and Bonds". *Journal of Financial Economics* 33(1): 3–56.

Fama, E. F. and K. R. French. 2015. "A Five-Factor Asset Pricing Model". *Journal of Financial Economics* 116: 1–22.

Fischer, B. and R. Wermers. 2013. *Performance Evaluation and Attribution of Security Portfolios*. Oxford: AP Elsevier.

Frazzini, A. and L. Pedersen. 2014. "Betting Against Beta". *Journal of Financial Economics* 111(1): 1–25.

Gava, J., W. Lefebvre, and J. Turc. 2020. "Beyond Carry and Momentum in Government Bonds". *Journal Fixed Income* 29(4): 48–74.

Houweling, P. and J. van Zundert. 2017. "Factor Investing in the Corporate Bond Market". *Financial Analysts Journal* 73(2): 100–115.

Jostova, G., S. Nikolova, A. Philipov, and C. W. Stahel. 2013. "Momentum in Corporate Bond Returns". *Review of Financial Studies* 26(7): 1649–1693.

Kaufmann, H. and P. Messow. 2020. "Equity Momentum in European Credits". *Journal of Fixed Income* 30(1): 29–44.

Konstantinov, G. 2017. "Currency Crowdedness Generated by Global Bond Funds". *Journal of Portfolio Management* 43(2): 123–135.

Konstantinov, G. S. and F. J. Fabozzi. 2021a. "Carry Strategies and the U.S. Dollar Risk of U.S. and Global Bonds". *Journal of Fixed Income* 30(3): 26–46.

Konstantinov, G. S. and F. J. Fabozzi. 2021b. "Towards a Dead End? EMU Bond Market Exposure and Manager Performance". *Journal of International Money and Finance* 116: 102433.

Konstantinov, G. S. 2023. "Errors and Challenges Associated with Investing in EMU Government Bonds". *Journal of Portfolio Management* 49(6): 132–143.

Konstantinov, G. S. and F. J. Fabozzi. 2022. "The Geometry of the World of Currency Volatility". *Computational Economics* 60(1): 125–145.

Konstantinov, G. S. and M. Pojarliev. 2021. "Trading in the Bond Market", Chapter 44 in Frank J. Fabozzi (ed.), *The Handbook of Fixed Income Securities*. 9th Edition. New York: McGraw-Hill.

Konstantinov, G., and M. Rusev. 2020. "The Bond-Equity Fund Relation Using the Fama–French–Carhart Factors: A Practical Network Approach". *Journal of Financial Data Science* 2(1): 24–44.

Kritzman, M. 2021. "The Role of Factors in Asset allocation". *Journal of Portfolio Management* 47(5): 58–64.

L'Hoir, M. and M. Boulhabel. 2010. "A Bond-Picking Model for Corporate Bond Allocation". *The Journal of Portfolio Management* 36(3): 131–139.

Litterman, R. and J. Scheinkman. 1991. "Common Factors Affecting Bond Returns". *Journal of Fixed Income* 1(1): 54–61.

Loistl, O. and G. S. Konstantinov. 2020. "Interactions and Interconnectedness Shape Financial Market Research". *Journal of Financial Data Science* 2(2): 51–63.

Maeso, J. M., L. Martellini, and R. Rebonato. 2020. "Factor Investing in US Sovereign Bond Markets: A New Generation of Conditional Carry Strategies with Applications in Asset-Only and Asset-Liability Management". *Journal of Portfolio Management* 46(2): 121–140.

Martellini, L. and V. Milhau. 2015. "Factor Investing: A Welfare-Improving New Investment Paradigm or Yet another Marketing Fad?", EDHEC-Risk Institute Publication.

Menkhoff, L., L. Sarno, M. Schmeling, and A. Schrimpf. 2012. "Carry Trades and Global Foreign Exchange Volatility". *Journal of Finance* 67(2): 681–718.

Merton, R. C. 1974. "On the Pricing of Corporate Debt: The Risk Structure of Interest Rates". *Journal of Finance* 29(2): 449–470.

Mladina, P. and S. Germani. 2019. "Bond-Market Risk Factors and Manager Performance". *Journal of Portfolio Management* 45(6): 75–85.

Nagel, S. 2012. "Evaporating Liquidity". *Review of Financial Studies* 25(7): 2005–2039.

Pastor, L. and R. F. Stambaugh. 2003. "Liquidity Risk and Expected Stock Returns". *Journal of Political Economy* 111(3): 642–685.

Pojarliev, M. and R. M. Levich. 2008. "Do Professional Currency Managers Beat the Benchmark?" *Financial Analysts Journal* 64(5): 18–32.

Pospisil, L. and J. Zhang. 2010. "Momentum and Reversal Effects in Corporate Bond Prices and Credit Cycles". *Journal of Fixed Income* 20(2): 101–115.

Rebonato, R., J. M. Maeso, and L. Martellini. 2019. "Factor Investing in Sovereign Bond Markets: Cross-Sectional and Time Series Momentum in US Sovereign Bond Market". EDHEC-Risk Institute Working Paper.

Sadka, R. 2006. "Momentum and Post-Earnings-Announcement Drift Anomalies: The Role of Liquidity Risk". *Journal of Financial Economics* 80(2): 309–349.

Sharpe, W. F. 1964. "Capital Asset Prices: A Theory of Market Equilibrium under Conditions of Risk". *Journal of Finance* 19(3): 425–442.

Simonian, J., C. Wu, D. Itano, and V. Narayanam. 2019. "A Machine Learning Approach to Risk Factors: A Case Study Using the Fama–French–Carhart Model". *Journal of Financial Data Science* 1(1): 32–44.

Chapter 6

Top-Down Portfolio Allocation

Top-down portfolio allocation pertains to the allocation of capital across different countries, sectors, factors, currencies, and other assets. This stands in contrast to bottom-up security selection (discussed in Chapter 7), which is concerned with the allocation of capital to individual securities within an asset class. We frame this chapter using well-known theoretical frameworks from the financial literature. Specifically, we identify several practical and theoretically sound techniques that can assist in portfolio allocation. The main task of portfolio allocation is determining the allocation to asset classes — countries, currencies, or industry sectors. In contrast to portfolio allocation, portfolio selection is the selection of the actual bonds to include in the portfolio once the weight of the asset class in the portfolio is determined via the portfolio allocation process. Following a bottom-up investment approach, portfolio selection has the highest priority, and asset allocation is determined once the individual securities are evaluated.

However, integrated approaches exist, which allow the portfolio manager to combine top-down intuition and portfolio construction with the bottom-up approach.[1] Allocation to broad categories can be driven by portfolio allocation. Bond selections within sub-asset classes can be derived using individual bond risk–return attractiveness. Suppose that the allocation to currencies is derived using a top-down approach and the choice between corporate and government bond exposure within the allocation is determined using a bottom-up process. For example, the

[1] See Kazemi *et al.* (2016).

allocation to 20% euros might be the result of an optimization. Importantly, the bottom-up approach might help to select the optimal exposure to government and corporate bonds. The result is a systematic approach to global bond portfolios that might be more complex than standard top-down procedures.

To highlight the different role of portfolio allocation and portfolio selection, Chapter 7 provides an integrated example. In this chapter, however, we focus on the top-down process. In particular, we provide information about how the optimization techniques fit into the global bond portfolio management framework and identify the main advantages and challenges when implementing portfolio allocation models.

6.1 The Importance of Investment Objectives

As we highlighted in Chapter 1, the formulation of investment objectives is part of the investment process and guides the implementation of a portfolio strategy. Portfolio construction begins with selecting a universe of assets, then proceeds to the formulation of inputs, determination of constraints, and is finalized with portfolio selection, the latter often accomplished using a mathematical optimization procedure.

An optimization framework should capture all relevant information of a portfolio that satisfies three important criteria: (1) a set of decision variables, (2) an objective function, and (3) a set of constraints. Discussions of portfolio optimization typically begin with the model formulated by Markowitz (1952), commonly referred to as the mean-variance optimization (MVO) model. We discuss the theoretical framework of MVO that is used to derive portfolio allocation, focusing on the important sources of risk and return influencing portfolio allocation. For this purpose, we focus not on individual securities within an asset class, but on the asset classes themselves — currencies, countries, sectors, and factors.

6.1.1 *The objective function and determinants of portfolio allocation*

Here we provide details of the major determinants of portfolio allocation and how quantitative investment processes deal with portfolio objectives. Before doing so, let's define the top-down and the bottom-up structure in the portfolio investment process and its impact on portfolio allocation. The top-down approach emphasizes the quantitative attractiveness of asset classes using risk premiums or macro fundamentals. The asset classes can be very broad or granular. In general, the asset classes that are relevant for global bond portfolios are currencies, countries, and sectors. The prioritization of the asset classes is closely related to the investment objectives of the portfolio and the underlying investment universe. Once the portfolio allocation is determined, the top-down approach focuses on the selection of individual securities. In the bottom-up approach, the asset class weights are the result of the evaluation of the individual bond risk and expected returns.

6.1.1.1 *Portfolio objectives and measures of risk and return*

The formulation of an optimization process requires a proper identification of investment objectives. For example, a portfolio objective might be to maximize expected portfolio return, or to minimize expected portfolio risk. Once basic portfolio objectives are defined, they need to be formally defined through the selection of specific measures of return and risk.

An asset's return is its price change over a specified period. In portfolio allocation, it is often common to use an asset's observed mean return over some time period. Statistically, the historical mean of a variable is treated as its expected value. The most common measure of risk in investment applications is standard deviation (the positive square root of the variance) which measures the deviations from the variable's expected value. In finance, standard deviation is often referred to as *volatility*. A large volatility for an asset's return is viewed negatively by investors because it represents greater risk.

A portfolio comprises many assets whose returns generally exhibit some degree of co-movement, both positive and negative. As a result, portfolio variance is not derived solely by summing the variances or volatilities of the assets in the portfolio, but by also accounting for asset covariances or correlations. This is done formally by means of what is known as a *variance–covariance matrix*, or alternatively, a *correlation matrix*. As a practical matter, correlation matrices are more commonly used by investors as they are invariant to scale, and thus are generally considered more intuitive than covariance matrices which are not invariant to scale.

In the original formulation of MVO, Markowitz (1952) expressed his framework using a variance–covariance matrix, as it allows a more mathematically compact way to derive portfolio variance. We show this formulation as follows:

$$\sigma_{\mathrm{PF}}^2 = \sum_{i=1}^{n}\sum_{j=1}^{n} w_i w_i \sigma_{i,j} \tag{6.1}$$

where w is an n-dimensional vector of portfolio weights, $\sigma_{i,j}$ is n-variance–covariance between asset i and asset j, and σ_{PF}^2 is the portfolio variance. To derive portfolio volatility (standard deviation), we would simply take the square root of the derived portfolio variance.

6.1.1.2 *Maximization or minimization of an objective function*

Portfolio allocation in its most basic form either minimizes risk for a given target return or maximizes return for a given target risk. For example, for a minimization of portfolio risk given a target return, the mathematical algorithm searches for all possible weights w that minimize the portfolio risk captured by the portfolio variance σ_{PF}^2, which is a weighted product of the individual weights and the variance–covariance matrix Ω:

$$\begin{aligned} &\min_{w} w'\Omega w \\ &\text{s.t. } x \geq L \end{aligned}$$

where w is a transposed n-dimensional vector of portfolio weights and Ω is the n-dimensional variance–covariance matrix of the portfolio assets. The variable x represents the portfolio return, while L represents the minimum return value that the portfolio must satisfy.

The formulation given by (6.1) is an unconstrained optimization. In general, there will be several types of constraints applied at the portfolio and asset level. We discuss these constraints in the following sections.

When maximizing an objective function, the optimization searches for weights that maximize the value of $w'E(r)$ over all possible values of w to achieve the highest expected return. Formally, the maximization is expressed as follows:

$$\max_{w} w'E(r)$$

where w is a transposed n-dimensional vector of portfolio weights and $E(r)$ is an n-dimensional vector of portfolio expected returns.

Following Jorion (1994), the mean–variance framework for portfolio allocation can be defined as maximizing the expected utility (objective function) U that is positively related to portfolio expected returns denoted by $E(r)_{\text{PF}}$ and inversely related to expected portfolio risks denoted by σ^2_{PF}. In this case, the portfolio optimization is centered on $U(E(r)_{\text{PF}}, \sigma^2_{\text{PF}})$. As in the minimization case, a host of constraints can be added to the maximization case.

6.1.2 *Constraints*

The number and type of constraints in portfolio optimization span a wide spectrum. The most widely used constraint in portfolios is that the individual portfolio asset weights be non-negative. This is known as the "no shorting" constraint. Another often used constraint is that the sum of all portfolio weights must sum up to 1. This is known as the "no leverage" constraint. For example, if the sum of all weights is 110%, then the portfolio allocates more to assets than the funds available to invest, implying that the portfolio manager may have to borrow funds (i.e., use leverage) to get the desired portfolio exposure. Adding leverage exposes the portfolio to additional risks.

Minimum and maximum weights are another important category of constraints. Maximum weights cap an asset's weight at a specific ceiling. Maximum weight constraints are used to manage a portfolio's concentration risk, while minimum weight constraints are used to ensure that there is sufficient diversification in a portfolio by requiring that each asset be

Table 6.1: Minimum and Maximum Weights of a Portfolio

Asset Class	Minimum Weight (%)	Maximum Weight (%)
US Treasuries	5	10
Emerging Market Sovereign Bonds	20	60
Emerging Market Corporate Bonds	10	30
Emerging Market High Yield Bonds	10	30
Local Currency Exposure	10	30

allocated a non-zero weight above some minimum threshold. Table 6.1 provides an example of constraints for a hypothetical bond portfolio dedicated to emerging markets.

Note that it is common practice for global emerging market bond portfolios to use benchmarks. One of the most widely used benchmarks for emerging market bonds is the J.P. Morgan EMBI Global Diversified Index. However, investors may choose to construct emerging market bond portfolios that are not run against a benchmark. In both cases, the portfolio allocation framework applies, and the constraints govern the exposures of the portfolio, perhaps using tracking error as a measure of active risk against benchmark allocation weights.

In addition to constraints on asset weights, additional restrictions may be imposed on a portfolio related to turnover or transaction costs. The portfolio turnover constraint is typically imposed when changes are being made to an existing portfolio, such as during portfolio rebalancing.

6.2 Quantitative Frameworks for Portfolio Allocation

There are several quantitative approaches to constructing portfolios. The two major optimization models most commonly used in global portfolio allocation are the MVO framework and the Black–Litterman framework.

6.2.1 *Mean–variance optimization*

Portfolio allocation models often try to integrate decisions relating to both the generation of active excess returns (alpha) and risk. Moreover, considerations of return and risk must generally be weighed simultaneously when analyzing any given asset. Formally, we integrate the consideration of risk and return by maximizing expected utility by means of an objective function that takes expected returns and expected portfolio risks as its basic inputs using the utility function U:

$$\operatorname{Arg} \max_{w_{\mathrm{FX}}, w_{\mathrm{Bond}}} U\left(E(r)_{\mathrm{PF}}, \sigma_{\mathrm{PF}}^{2}\right) \tag{6.2}$$

where σ_{PF}^{2} is the global bond portfolio risk, $E(r)_{\mathrm{PF}}$ is the global bond portfolio expected return, and w_{FX} and w_{Bond} are the currency and bond weights, respectively.

The formulation given by the expression (6.2) captures risk in the variance–covariance matrix which encapsulates both the individual risk (variance) of each asset as well the co-movement (covariance) of asset returns with one another.

The standard MVO framework involves one objective function (maximizing return or minimizing risk) and uses the investor's other goals as constraints. However, some optimization models can deal with several objective functions. This class of optimization procedures is collectively known as *multi-objective optimization*.[2] The defining feature of this type of optimization technique is that it is designed to facilitate the prioritization of different objectives, some of which may be conflicting, in accordance with the importance assigned to them by investors. Accordingly, the output of a multi-objective optimization technique tends to produce compromise, "satisficing" solutions.[3]

Multi-objective optimization has been applied in several investment contexts.[4] Here, we apply one type of multi-objective optimization, *sequential optimization*. As the name implies, sequential optimization proceeds by solving a series of optimizations, with each taking a specific goal for its objective function. The defining feature of sequential optimization is that each optimization is constrained by the outcome of the optimization that directly precedes it. For example, we may choose to first minimize expected currency risks in a global bond portfolio. Given the already estimated weights that minimize the expected currency risk, we may run a second optimization to maximize portfolio return. The second optimization will determine the optimal bond portfolio that maximizes the expected bond returns given the universe of portfolios that minimize currency risk. We state this procedure formally in the following:

$$\text{First optimization: } \operatorname{Arg}\min_{w_{\text{FX}}} U\left(\sigma_{\text{FX}}^2\right) \tag{6.3}$$

$$\text{Second optimization: } \operatorname{Arg}\max_{w_{\text{Bond}}} U\left(E(r)_{\text{Bond}}, \sigma_{\text{Bond}}^2 \middle| w_{\text{FX}}\right) \tag{6.4}$$

[2] For details about goal-programming based multi-objective optimization, see Tamiz *et al.* (1998) and Jones and Tamiz (2010).

[3] Such solutions are in the spirit of Simon (1956) and are well suited to the type of customization that portfolio managers generally need.

[4] See Simonian and Barschdorff (2013) and Konstantinov (2014).

where σ^2_{FX} is the currency portfolio risk, σ^2_{Bond} is the bond portfolio risk, $E(r)_{\text{Bond}}$ is the bond portfolio expected returns, and w_{FX} and w_{Bond} are the currency and bond weights, respectively.

Of course, the objective functions given by (6.3) and (6.4) are not the only ones that can be chosen. Any number of maximizations and minimizations can be solved in sequence. That said, we note that after each optimization, the number of portfolios satisfying each objective and set of constraints narrows considerably.

In addition to the sequential approach to multi-objective optimization, we can utilize what is known as *weighted multi-objective optimization*. This approach produces a compromise solution satisfying disparate objective functions consistent with their relative importance. When applying this optimization approach, goals are assigned weights according to their relative importance. In the following, we show how to formally construct a factor-tracking portfolio, using the latter framework:

$$\min z = \sum_{i=1}^{k} \left(u_i n_i + v_i p_i\right)$$
$$\text{s.t. } f_i\left(x\right) + n_i - p_i = b_i,\; i = 1,\ldots,Q, x \in C_s \tag{6.5}$$

where $f_i(x)$ is a linear objective function of x, b_i is the target value for that function, n_i and p_i signify the negative and positive deviations from the target value, and u_i and v_i represent the positive weights attached to these deviations in the objective function z. Finally, C_s is an optional set of hard constraints that are common to quadratic programming. Typical examples of hard constraints in global bond portfolios are the limits on country or currency risk.

6.2.2 *The Black–Litterman allocation model*

The most basic approach to asset allocation utilizes the MVO framework. The objective function of the mean–variance investor is expressed by the following:

$$\max_{w} w'\mu - \frac{\gamma}{2} w' \Sigma w \tag{6.6}$$

with the optimal weights w satisfying

$$w = \frac{1}{\gamma} \Sigma^{-1} \mu \tag{6.7}$$

where μ represents asset returns, Σ is the covariance matrix of assets, w represents the portfolio weights to each asset, and γ is the risk aversion parameter.

Another popular portfolio allocation optimization framework is the one proposed by Black and Litterman (1992), referred to accordingly as the Black–Litterman (BL) model. The BL approach was introduced for multi-asset portfolios. This model provides a simple and transparent Bayesian framework for portfolio allocation, building on the familiar MVO framework.[5] The defining feature of the BL model is that it gives portfolio managers the ability to incorporate their forward-looking market views into the portfolio allocation process. For that reason, it presents an advantage over the MVO framework as it provides the means to free portfolio managers from total reliance on historical return information, while also providing a way to generate portfolios based on views on the assets comprising the portfolio. For example, if the portfolio allocation has the goal of estimating the global country allocation, BL allows the portfolio manager to include specific views on specific countries in the portfolio. In this respect, the BL approach is very suitable for global bond portfolios without currency risk. A good example is an emerging market bond portfolio or a bond portfolio dedicated to developed market countries in hard currency denominated bonds (e.g., US dollar or euro). In the case of emerging market portfolios in hard currencies, the BL approach might provide successful country allocation by incorporating country views.

We can also apply the BL approach to global bond portfolios using local currencies. In this case, it is imperative to apply analytical tools and to identify the carry (yield + roll down) contribution, what comes from spread and default, as well as quantify the FX impact. This would be the case of a global bond portfolio managed versus a global aggregate benchmark like the Bloomberg Barclays Global Aggregate Bond Index, or the

[5]For a comprehensive overview of the BL model, see Kolm *et al.* (2021).

World Government Bond Index (WGBI). In this case, the largest uncertainty comes from the application of hedged or unhedged (local currency) returns. Konstantinov (2022) showed that for a hard currency bond portfolio with a different portfolio base currency, it is most convenient to estimate local currency returns and use them in the optimization model. In Chapter 3, we showed how currency management might help bond portfolio managers and, in this respect, the inputs might be used in the BL framework. Specifically, the views incorporated in the BL model might be the result of other quantitative models employed in the investment process. Examples of such models are ones used to forecast interest rates, spreads, or currency returns, or macroeconomic variables like inflation and GDP growth, and industrial production.

In the BL model, the portfolio manager reverse engineers the mean excess returns μ_0 by plugging in the relative weights of the assets in the benchmark portfolio w_0, as well as the values of the risk-aversion parameter γ and the covariance matrix Σ:

$$\mu_0 = \gamma \Sigma w_0 \tag{6.8}$$

The variance of the prior[6] on the mean[7] is then assumed to be proportional to the covariance matrix using a hyperparameter[8] τ, which in the context of active management applications of the BL model can be considered a measure of the confidence in the benchmark portfolio or an expression of the portfolio manager's desired degree of active management. The reverse engineering process results in a prior that takes the form of a normal distribution with mean μ_0 and variance $\tau\Sigma$. The absence of views of the

---

[6]In Bayesian terminology, a prior is the probability distribution that represents an agent's beliefs about an uncertain parameter before consideration of any evidence.

[7]The underlying assumption of the model is that the returns are normally distributed and so are the expected returns (see Lee, 2000).

[8]The hyperparameter captures the difference between the variance–covariance matrix of historical and expected returns. A lower value for τ means that the variance of historical returns is higher than the variance of the expected returns and vice versa. In other words, the higher the confidence in the benchmark returns is, the lower the hyperparameter. Because the variance of historical returns is usually higher than the variance of expected returns, the parameter typically gets small values.

portfolio manager results in the replication of the benchmark portfolio; as a portfolio manager introduces views on asset returns, the portfolio risk characteristics deviate from the benchmark in a manner consistent with mean–variance optimality.

The views of the portfolio manager employing the BL model are specified by building the matrices C and M such that the expected returns on each asset, here given by the vector μ_1, can be represented as follows:

$$C'\mu_1 = M \tag{6.9}$$

Additionally, the portfolio manager must specify the variance of the views, which is given in the matrix. He and Litterman (1999) assume that the variance of the views is proportional to the variance of the asset returns, as in the case of the variance of the prior, thus setting $\Omega = \tau * \text{diag}(C'\Sigma C)$. The resulting mean and covariance of the posterior distribution[9] of asset returns can be represented as follows:

$$\tilde{\mu} = \mu_0 + \tau \Sigma C\left[\tau\left(C'\Sigma C\right) + \Omega\right]^{-1}\left[M - C'\mu_0\right] \tag{6.10}$$

There are several challenges when implementing the BL approach in global bond portfolios. While the estimation of subjective expected returns is not problematic, the expected returns of global bonds and currencies are not normally distributed. Second, the covariance matrix might not be a proper metric for bond market risks. In this respect, the input variables in the covariance matrix should reflect the major risks in the portfolio. Specifically, for emerging-market hard currency bond portfolios, country indexes are the optimal choice, but for local currency bond portfolios, the choice between local currency country indexes and currency-hedged indexes might result in a large misestimation of risk.

---

[9]The intuition behind the Bayesian statistic is the *a priori* distribution of the expected returns. As soon as new information arrives, the Bayesian statistic helps to update the return distribution using the newly arrived information (called a *posterior distribution*). The advantage of the BL approach is that it incorporates newly arrived information about return expectations. See Satchell and Scowcroft (2000) for a detailed analysis of the volatility of expected returns.

While it is not necessary to include a risk-aversion parameter, it is often useful in aligning the portfolio allocation with the portfolio manager's risk aversion (or alternatively, risk tolerance). A higher value of λ expresses a higher level of risk aversion. In other words, the degree of risk aversion λ is an indicator of the risk that the portfolio manager is willing to take in the pursuit of returns and serves as a penalty factor in the objective function. The formal derivation of λ is given by the following:

$$\lambda = \frac{E\left(R_{\text{Index}}\right) - R_f}{\sigma^2_{\text{Index}}} \tag{6.11}$$

where $E(R_{\text{Index}})$ are the historical returns of the index being used as the benchmark, R_f is the risk-free rate, and σ^2_{Index} is the index variance.

Note that the σ^2_{Index} is not the standard deviation of the index or benchmark historical returns, but their squared term (i.e., their variance). The value of the risk-aversion parameter λ can be computed using the underlying benchmark or index which then represents the investment universe of the bond portfolio.

6.3 Practical Portfolio Allocation and Model Estimation

In previous sections, we highlighted the theoretical background and economic intuition of two of the most widely applied optimization models for portfolio allocation. In this section, we specify some specific examples of portfolio allocation in global bond portfolios, using two of the most important risks for such portfolios — currency and country risks. For this purpose, we consider the MVO model and show how the portfolio manager can specify and estimate their portfolio allocation. Moreover, we discuss some practical considerations during the allocation process like derivation of portfolio risk and expected returns, transaction costs, and portfolio net asset value.

Sometimes, it is reasonable to modify equation (6.1) such as when explicit expected return estimates exist. The portfolio optimization process would then have an objective function minimizing the matrix product of the transposed vector of portfolio weights, multiplied by the product of the $(k \times k)$ variance–covariance matrix and the vector of portfolios weights. This is equivalent to minimizing portfolio risk:

$$\operatorname*{Arg\,min}_{w} = \left(w_1^k, \ldots, w_k^k\right) \begin{pmatrix} \sigma_1^2 & \cdots & \rho_{1k}\sigma_1\sigma_k \\ \vdots & \ddots & \vdots \\ \rho_{k1}\sigma_k\sigma_1 & \cdots & \sigma_k^2 \end{pmatrix} \begin{pmatrix} w_1^k \\ \vdots \\ w_k^k \end{pmatrix},$$

$$\text{with } \left(w_1, \ldots, w_k\right) \begin{pmatrix} 1 \\ \vdots \\ 1 \end{pmatrix} = 1 \tag{6.12}$$

where the w_k's are the asset weights, ρ's are the pairwise correlation coefficients between input variables, and σ's are the variances of the input parameters.

The MVO framework only considers one source of risk — asset variance. However, with many types of assets, including bonds, other types of risk are often the primary drivers of portfolio risk. Among the primary risks in bond portfolios is liquidity risk. To account for this risk, we can add a penalty function to the basic MVO framework that penalizes assets for liquidity-related risks such as higher transaction costs relative to other assets. This type of adjustment for global bond portfolios has been demonstrated for individual securities within portfolio optimizations by Konstantinov and Fabozzi (2021a), and Kazemi *et al.* (2016). To illustrate, in the following, we show an example of a liquidity-adjusted optimization:

$$\operatorname*{Arg\,max}_{w} = \left(w_1, \ldots, w_k, tc_1, \ldots, tc_k\right) \begin{pmatrix} E(r)_1 \\ \vdots \\ E(r)_k \\ tc_1 \\ \vdots \\ tc_k \end{pmatrix}$$

$$-\lambda\left(w_1^k, \ldots, w_k^k\right) \begin{pmatrix} \sigma_1^2 & \cdots & \rho_{1k}\sigma_1\sigma_k \\ \vdots & \ddots & \vdots \\ \rho_{k1}\sigma_k\sigma_1 & \cdots & \sigma_k^2 \end{pmatrix} \begin{pmatrix} w_1^k \\ \vdots \\ w_k^k \end{pmatrix},$$

$$\text{with } \left(w_1, \ldots, w_k\right) \begin{pmatrix} 1 \\ \vdots \\ 1 \end{pmatrix} = 1 \tag{6.13}$$

where w' is the transposed vector of portfolio weights including transaction costs and $E(r)$ is the vector of expected returns, including an asset-class-specific transaction cost penalty parameter tc.

Note that the penalty parameter for transaction cost is added only to the first term of equation (6.13). This is attributable to the fact that expected returns have the largest impact on the estimation of the objective function in MVO.[10] The optimization only considers so-called explicit transaction costs (e.g., bid-ask spreads, brokerage fees, and trade and custodian commissions) which are relatively easy to measure. In practice, portfolio managers must also consider implicit transaction costs such as market impact and price movement costs. While these costs are less easily measurable relative to explicit transaction costs, they must nevertheless be considered during the portfolio management process.

Whatever set of risks portfolio managers consider in their process, they must also contend with the fact that investment risks are not temporally stable, but time-varying. Because there is constant information flow into the world's financial markets, portfolio managers need to periodically update their market views.[11] Rather than constantly re-optimizing portfolios to address time-varying asset price behavior, many portfolio managers rebalance their portfolios to rectify imbalances that have caused their portfolio weights to drift from their strategic allocation over time.

As Kazemi *et al.* (2016) and Rattray *et al.* (2020) have emphasized, portfolio rebalancing can be an effective way to improve diversification and drawdowns. Portfolio drawdowns are one of the most problematic issues for portfolio managers and of course for clients. Drawdowns represent the drop in the NAV of the portfolio from the recent peak NAV to the all-time-low NAV since the peak of the NAV was reached. Drawdowns are informative as they provide information on the losses sustained by portfolio managers.

Positive performance is always desired, but portfolios exhibit losses. Drawdowns are a useful measure to explain the negative periods in a portfolio. The drawdown duration captures the period between the two peaks in the NAV of the portfolio. That is, it measures the time, typically in months, between when the portfolio moves from one peak to another. A short timeframe means that the portfolio recovers quickly from losses.

[10] See, for example, Chopra and Ziemba (1993).

[11] See Lee and Liu (2021) for a detailed discussion of this point.

A longer period means that portfolios cannot recover from losses and can be interpreted as inconsistencies in risk management and lack of ability of the portfolio to respond to changing market conditions. Often, portfolio allocation models, trading algorithms, and portfolio manager skill are challenged as to whether they work properly in the current market environment.

Rebalancing is in particular relevant during periods of financial market stress when it can lead to smaller drawdowns. Drawdown durations in quantitatively managed portfolios supply information on possible model reevaluations and the possible adjustments to the quantitative approaches, portfolio trading systems, and risk management that are employed in a portfolio manager's investment process.

The time-varying nature of asset price behavior is related to another set of criticisms of the standard MVO framework. For example, Duarte and Rajagopal (1999) show that MVO is not capable of optimizing with respect to different market scenarios as its inputs are only point-in-time estimates. Moreover, regime shifts and time-varying premiums often require more sophisticated rebalancing that is not fixed to a predefined frequency (e.g., monthly, quarterly, or weekly), but based on market thresholds that may be achieved at intermittent points in time.

6.3.1 *Asset class expected returns*

Asset class-based portfolio allocation is the basis of traditional portfolio management. Although factor research has become popular over the years, some research suggests that portfolio allocation based on asset classes may in fact produce superior results.[12]

Generating asset class level return expectations is part of many if not most portfolio managers' investment process. A common starting point in generating capital market assumptions for various asset classes is to draw on the indexes that broadly track them. Index data must be handled with care for several reasons. First, it is challenging because there may be a mismatch between the currency of the index and the base currency of the portfolio, something which has an impact on portfolio performance. For example, Konstantinov (2022) shows that for emerging market bond portfolios, it is more beneficial to use local currency returns instead of

[12] See, for example, Kritzman (2021).

currency adjusted, or hedged expected bond returns. Hedging costs for developed markets and local currencies of the G10 group are much lower than emerging market hedging costs. Furthermore, the hedging costs for emerging markets differ substantially. The cost for hedging South African rand (ZAR) or Mexican peso (MXN) is different from the hedging cost for Nigerian naira (NGN) local currency returns. Aside from currency-related issues, there are additional operational reasons why using indexes as a source for expected returns can be challenging. First, global bond portfolios do not have large positions in less liquid emerging market countries that are often included in major indexes. Second, it may be impossible to replicate broad global bond indexes due to liquidity, investability, and tradability reasons. Third, while index data can be used as a basis for expected return generation, it needs to be modified before being used in most practical applications.

Two studies demonstrate how bond returns can be derived directly from index data — Koijen *et al.* (2018) and Martens *et al.* (2019). Both studies use index data (and the risk-free rate) to derive bond and currency returns using forward contracts. Koijen *et al.* (2018) use forward rates while Martens *et al.* (2019) use index data of different maturity bucket indexes to show the relevance of yield curve positioning. A major drawback of the two approaches is that they do not explicitly highlight the difference between local and base currency for portfolios and the relevance of the different portfolio base currencies when estimating expected bond returns. In addition, the two studies do not show how bond expected returns are derived, which is critical for global bond portfolios.

Consequently, there are two major issues when using index data denominated in a given currency, namely, to derive local currency bond returns and to estimate bond returns adjusted for a portfolio's base currency. These have been investigated by Konstantinov (2022). The estimation of the foregoing types of expected bond returns is exposed to estimation risk because local currency and domestic currency each impact portfolio selection in different ways.

In this section, we present both types of expected return estimation and highlight their differences. As shown by Konstantinov (2014, 2022), expected bond returns can be derived using yield curves, whose estimation was shown in Chapter 4. Alternatively, the expected bond returns for portfolio allocation optimization can be based on directly observable market data — duration, duration-times-spread, and yield to maturity. The following approach differs from that used in the studies of Koijen *et al.*

(2018) and Martens *et al*. (2019) as it adds maturity and drops the risk-free rate from its return estimation formula:

$$E(R)_t^{\text{LC Index}} = \text{MD}_t^{\text{LC Index}} \Delta y_t^{\text{LC Index}} + y_t^{\text{LC Index}} \Delta t \tag{6.14}$$

where $\text{MD}_t^{\text{LC Index}}$ is the index duration, $y_t^{\text{LC Index}}$ is the index yield to maturity, and $E(R)_t^{\text{LC Index}}$ is the local currency expected return on a bond index level. Again, note that in equation (6.14), all terms are in local currency.

An alternative approach for estimating expected bond returns that considers bond yields and foreign exchange (FX) is based on forward rates or expected spot rates. This approach has been advocated by Thornton and Valente (2012) and Nucera and Valente (2013). We can formalize their approach as follows:

$$E(R)_t^{\text{BC Index}} \equiv y_t^{\text{BC Index}} = \left(1 + y_t^{\text{LC Index}}\right)\frac{E(S_{t+1})}{S_t} - 1 \tag{6.15}$$

where $y_t^{\text{LC Index}}$ is the bond yield of the foreign currency bond index, $E(S_{t+1})$ is the expected spot rate at time $t + 1$, S_t is the current FX rate, and $E(R)_t^{\text{BC Index}}$ is the expected bond index return in domestic currency.

Note that while the expected returns in equation (6.14) denote local currency returns, the bond yield expression in equation (6.15) converts local currency bond yields into domestic yields using the current and expected spot FX rate. An important formal difference between equations (6.14) and (6.15) is that (6.14) is more yield curve driven, in contrast to (6.15), which is structured around currency and bond yield returns. It is important to keep in mind that, as previously mentioned in Chapter 3, expected spot rates are only to some extent a reliable predictor of future realized spot rates.

Another challenge in estimating expected returns from equation (6.15) stems from the fact that bond excess returns are not equal to expected bond yields as the term structure of interest rates changes with time, while equation (6.15) assumes that bonds are held to maturity with a static flat yield curve. A possible way to address the foregoing challenge is to use the domestic currency estimates from equation (6.14) as input parameters in equation (6.15) to jointly determine excess bond returns.[13]

[13] Note that the expected return estimates in equation (6.14) can be applied to determine country, sector, asset, and currency expected returns at the index level.

6.3.2 *Expected portfolio risks*

Portfolio level returns are a function of their primary drivers. As in the case of asset classes, we may formally derive portfolio level risk. For example, Dym (1991) and Jorion (1994), among others, represent the risk of global bond investments in the following manner:

$$\sigma_{\text{PF}}^2 = \sigma_{\text{Bond}}^2 + \sigma_{\text{FX}}^2 + 2\rho_{\text{Bond,FX}}\sigma_{\text{Bond}}\sigma_{\text{FX}} \tag{6.16}$$

where σ_{PF}^2 is the portfolio variance in the global bond portfolio's base currency, σ_{Bond}^2 is the bond variance of returns, and σ_{FX}^2 is the variance of currency returns. The term $2\rho_{\text{Bond,FX}}\sigma_{\text{Bond}}\sigma_{\text{FX}}$ represents the covariance of bond and currency returns.

Note that here local currency variance is used and not the hedged currency returns. The third term on the right-hand side of equation (6.16) represents the interaction between bond and currency variance. The interaction can be very small depending on the covariance between bond risk and currency risk. However, the correlation between currency risk and bond risk might have a strong impact on the interaction term and on portfolio risk. This might be the case when there is a strong positive or negative correlation between bond and currency returns. Note that in the case of negative correlation between bond and currency risks, the interaction term might be large, in which case it would decrease portfolio risk. However, strong positive correlation between currency and bond risks might add additional stress to global bond portfolios during market dislocations.

As we see in (6.16), risk management in global bond portfolios can be challenging as portfolio managers need to account for the risk associated with both domestic (local) currency bond returns given by σ_{Bond}^2, and the risk of FX investments given by σ_{FX}^2.

It is important to remember that the risk, returns, and correlations of currency and local bonds are time-varying which necessitates the periodic reestimation of the input parameters. As with other elements of portfolio management, portfolio optimization is a dynamic process which requires constant attention on the part of investment teams.

6.4 Currency and Country Considerations

In this section, we touch on a selection important considerations in portfolio construction with respect to countries and currencies.

6.4.1 *Currencies*

When constructing global bond portfolios, the focus is often on optimal currency choice since currency volatility is perhaps the largest driver of risk in global bond portfolios.[14] As an illustration of the risk that currency exposure poses relative to other risk factors, in Figure 6.1, we show the Deutsche Bank Currency Implied Volatility Index (CVIX Index) and the Credit Swiss Interest Rate Volatility Estimate Index. We see that currency volatility exceeds interest-rate volatility. Nevertheless, there also appears to be a strong correlation between the two indexes' time series, implying that interest-rate volatility is not independent from currency volatility.

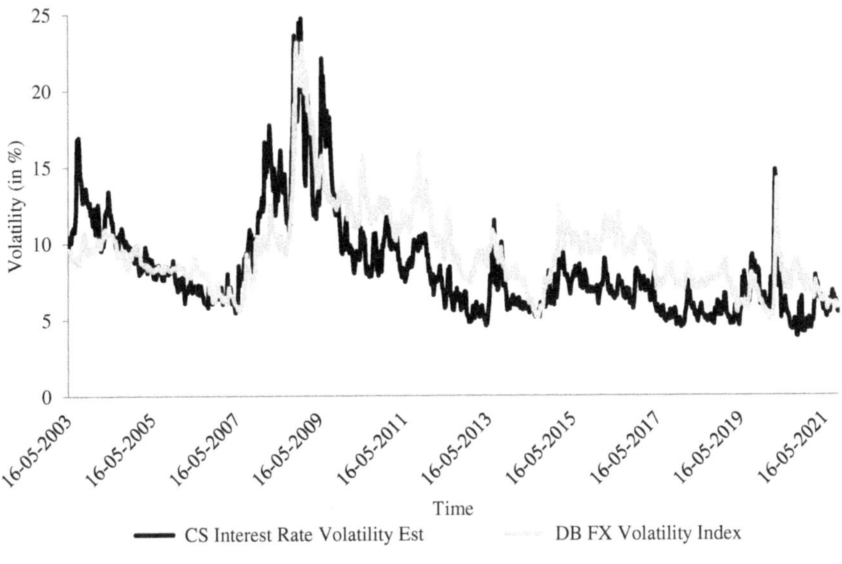

Figure 6.1: Interest Rate and Currency Implied Volatility

Notes: The DB FX Volatility Index is the Deutsche Bank FX Implied Volatility Index as provided by Bloomberg (CVIX Index). The CS Interest Rate Volatility Est is the Credit Swiss Interest Rate Volatility Estimation Index (CIRVE Index). Data obtained by the authors from Bloomberg, LLC.

---

[14]See for example, Chen (1999), Duarte and Rajagopal (1999), Baz *et al.* (2001), Huttman and Harris (2006), Bisat (2010), Alonso and Barnes (2017), Iborra and Chabane (2020), and Arruda *et al.* (2021).

Because the variance of currency movements in a portfolio accounts for a large proportion of portfolio risk, one practical optimization technique for managing FX risk in a portfolio is minimum variance optimization (MinVO) advocated by Arnott and Pham (1993), Jorion (1994), and Baz *et al.* (2001). Deriving a currency allocation with MinVO is a straightforward process given that it does not require the estimation of expected returns which are the input parameters most susceptible to misspecification.

Currency exposure can have a varying impact on portfolio volatility depending on the portfolio's asset mix. For example, in equity and multi-asset portfolios, currency often has a lower impact on portfolio volatility relative to bond portfolios. This is because equities and other assets such as commodities are contributors to portfolio volatility similar to the significant volatility contributions of currencies.[15] In multi-asset portfolios, hedging currency risk can be challenging. Levich and Thomas (1993) identified two ways to approach currency risk in a portfolio: (1) regard it as a return strategy in line with an MVO approach to optimization or (2) regard it as a source of risk only in line with a MinVO approach to optimization.

A crucial aspect of currency risk management in bond portfolios is to consider it from the standpoint of a base currency. In Chapter 3, we showed that for any currency pair, EUR/USD, for example, the first currency in the pair is assumed to be the long currency position, while the second currency refers to the short currency position. Because some currency pairs are expressed in unit notations and not in price notations, to determine proper currency allocation from a specific portfolio base currency, it is necessary to convert all unit notations into prices to derive the currency's returns. The base currency of a fund is the currency in which the fund's NAV is denominated and estimated. Most global emerging market bond portfolios are denominated in US dollars. Note that this approach also assures proper variance–covariance estimation.

In Figure 6.2, we show the magnitude of FX volatility from the perspective of a portfolio manager trading in different currencies. We see that the currency volatility for assets denominated in US dollars is different in magnitude compared to that of assets denominated in euros.

---

[15] See, for example, Guo and Ryan (2018), Bush and Woodham (2018), Iborra and Chabane (2020), and Arruda *et al.* (2021).

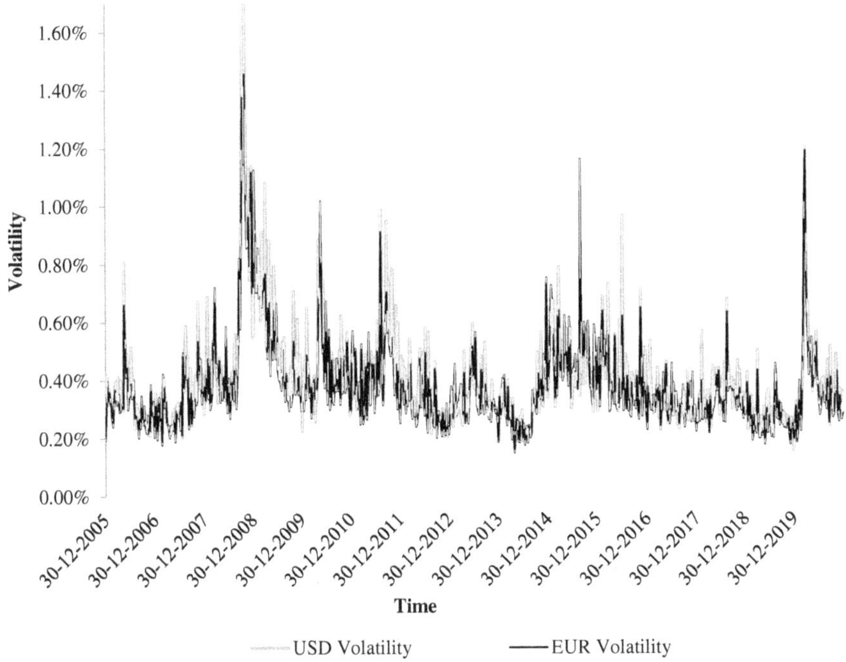

Figure 6.2: Weekly Global Foreign Exchange Volatility for Portfolios Based on U.S. Dollar (USD) and Euro (EUR): December 2005–December 2020

Source: Constructed by the authors from data obtained from Bloomberg, LLC.

It is possible to use MinVO to optimize a portfolio of currencies. However, it must be kept in mind that like other assets, currency returns are not normally distributed. For this reason, it may be desirable to utilize an optimization framework that accounts for the skewness and kurtosis of currency returns. While closed-form analytical approaches to implementing mean–variance–skewness–kurtosis optimization may be practically intractable for large portfolios, numerical optimization may be invoked to build portfolios based on the four moments of an asset's return distribution. Harvey *et al.* (2010) showed that asset returns are not normally distributed and provide solutions to implement higher moments of a distribution in portfolio optimization. Again such a procedure is reasonable for global bond portfolios because currency and bond returns have distributions that strongly deviate from the normal distribution. Exhibiting fat tails and skewness might bias the return estimations, which in turn might bias the portfolio allocation estimation.

6.4.2 *Country portfolio allocation*

Country portfolio allocation is also an important dimension of building emerging market bond portfolios. Each country offers unique risks and opportunities. Country exposure also presents a relatively straightforward way for portfolio managers to express views on the prudence of the monetary and fiscal policies of governments, as well as country political risk. Separating country allocation decisions from hard and local currency allocation decisions broadens the opportunity space for possible effective portfolio solutions. That said, when allocating among countries, it is of utmost importance that investors account for the level of diversification each country brings to the portfolio, in light of its expected risk and return contributions. Robust portfolio optimization techniques, which we discuss next, are intended to enhance diversification and optimal portfolio construction when confronted with estimation error regarding model input parameters.

6.5 Robust Portfolio Optimization

In this section, we provide robustness extensions to our two models for portfolio allocation — the traditional MVO model and the BL approach.

6.5.1 *Robust mean–variance optimization*

In the mean–variance model of portfolio optimization, one of the critical assumptions is that the asset returns, variances, and covariances are known with certainty. Analysts have rarely questioned this assumption, believing that covariances, for example, are fairly stable over time and further that MVO is relatively insensitive to the covariance assumption altogether.[16] Parameter uncertainty is real, however, and introduces the potential for model misspecification.

For some time now, there has been a drive to extend the static maxmin expected utility theory of Gilboa and Schmeidler (1989) to a dynamic environment that can be fruitfully exploited in various areas of finance, including portfolio theory. Gilboa and Schmeidler's theory provides an elegant framework for modeling decision-making that incorporates investors' aversion to uncertainty and ambiguity in the sense described by Ellsberg (1961).

[16]See, for example, Best and Grauer (1991, 1992) and Chopra and Ziemba (1993).

For example, Fabozzi *et al.* (2007) showed how to apply robust portfolio optimization to the mean–variance portfolio allocation problem. Equation (6.1) then becomes a modified optimization problem. To achieve a greater accuracy for the optimization, the model is modified such that the portfolio weights remain robust and thus agnostic to all values of expected returns that have large estimation errors that are close to the estimates of expected returns. To gain an intuition, suppose, for example, that we estimate the expected currency returns of, say, G10 currencies in which a portfolio should allocate. In the original MVO model given by equation (6.1), the portfolio manager would include a vector of expected returns $E(r)$. In the modified version, the optimization includes a set of vectors that comprise possible expected returns $\widehat{E(r)}$. In this example, the vectors might comprise expected returns for currency depreciation and appreciation.

The modification is therefore robust because it minimizes the worst-case expected return in a portfolio allocated to assets, countries, rating segments, currencies, and factors. In other words, the variables of portfolio allocation (assets, countries, rating segments, currencies, and factors) whose return estimations have a large amount of error will receive a lower portfolio weight. The interaction of several bond-related risks like interest rates, currencies, and spreads (among others) elevates the risk of misevaluations and estimation errors that might have a substantial impact on the portfolio allocation. Therefore, it is critical for global bond portfolios that use the Markowitz framework to revise the portfolio optimization techniques using a formal expression that adjusts for estimation errors. The following formula shows how to account for estimation errors in the MVO framework:

$$\operatorname*{Arg\,max}_{w} \widehat{E(r)}' w - \delta'\psi - \lambda w'\Sigma w, \quad \text{with } w'l = 1 \tag{6.17}$$

where δ is the estimation error of expected returns, ψ is a $(1 \times n)$ vector that captures the weights that react to estimation errors, w is the $(n \times 1)$ vector of portfolio allocation weights, Σ is the variance–covariance matrix of factor returns, and l is a vector of ones.

Note that the term $-\delta'\psi$ decreases the optimization function. This is not surprising as the model searches for weights that are adjusted by the estimation error of expected returns. Put differently, the robust optimization model decreases (or "shrinks") the weights of assets, countries, rating segments, currencies, and factors with large estimation error and thus decreases the maximized expected return of the overall portfolio.

6.5.2 *Robust Black–Litterman optimization*

Another example of robust portfolio optimization is that provided by Simonian and Davis (2011), who extend the work on robust portfolio theory developed by Garlappi *et al.* (2007) and apply it to the BL model. One way of accommodating uncertainty within economic models is through the use of multiple priors (Hansen and Sargent, 2001).[17] The robust Black–Litterman (rBL) approach described below is motivated by a desire to design an asset allocation framework based on the BL methodology that directly incorporates uncertainty about the covariance matrix Σ in a simple yet coherent manner.

To begin, let's assume that we can describe the uncertainty about Σ using a distribution derived via bootstrap or asymptotic approximation to the sampling distribution of the covariance matrix estimator. Based on the BL methodology, there exists a systematic correspondence between each covariance matrix and the resulting BL-derived posterior distribution. In the rBL model, we begin by characterizing a neighborhood of alternative prior distributions that are also likely based on the sampling distribution of the covariance matrix Σ.

One measure that captures the relative log-likelihood of one distribution Q conditional on another distribution P is Kullback–Leibler (KL) divergence:

$$D(P|Q) = \int_{-\infty}^{\infty} \log\left(\frac{p(x)}{q(x)}\right) p(x)\, dx \tag{6.18}$$

KL is a measure of the distance between two probability distributions. It is an information theoretic concept that compares the entropy of two distributions over the same random variable. The normal distribution p is compared to an approximating model, denoted by q. $D(P|Q)$ represents

[17]Examples of the wide variety of applications of robust methods in finance include Hansen and Sargent (2001, 2007), Garlappi *et al.* (2007), Fabozzi *et al.* (2007), Hansen and Sargent (2007), Simonian and Davis (2010, 2011), and Simonian (2011).

the information lost when one uses model q to approximate p. Conditional on the reference prior distribution, here given by a multivariate normal with parameters μ_0 and Σ, we can calculate the expected relative log-likelihood of an alternative multivariate normal with parameters μ_a and Σ_a and in closed form as

$$D(N_a|N) = \frac{1}{2}\left(\ln\left(\frac{|\Sigma_a|}{|\Sigma|}\right) + \mathrm{tr}\left(\overset{-1}{\underset{a}{\Sigma}}\Sigma\right) + (\mu_a - \mu_0) - n\right) \tag{6.19}$$

where we constrain the alternative prior distribution to be consistent with the benchmark by requiring the following additional constraint to hold:

$$\mu_a = \gamma \Sigma_a w_0 \tag{6.20}$$

The distribution of this statistic can be found empirically by repeatedly drawing from the sampling distribution of Σ.

In the rBL model, we introduce another parameter to describe the confidence the portfolio manager has in their estimate of the covariance matrix, similar to the concept behind the BL parameter τ that scales the portfolio manager's confidence in their views. Define the hyperparameter p to be the portfolio manager's confidence in the estimate of the covariance matrix, which in turn implicitly defines a value η that will be used in the rBL model. This is given by the following function:

$$P\left(D(N_a|N) \le \eta\right) = 1 - p \tag{6.21}$$

Thus, the portfolio manager's confidence level determines a neighborhood of alternative prior distributions that is a direct function of the sampling error of the covariance estimator. As the portfolio manager loses confidence in the quality of the covariance matrix estimate, the space of priors determined to be "*ex ante* plausible" expands.

Acknowledging the potential imprecision of parameter estimates alters the portfolio allocation process by imposing two constraints on the mean–variance objective function. The first constraint stipulates that mean excess return and covariance parameters for each asset must lie within a specified confidence interval of their estimated value. This constraint implies that the investor explicitly recognizes the possibility of model misspecification. The second constraint is that a minimization over the choice of mean excess returns and covariances must be performed.

The two constraints effectively transform the mean–variance objective function into a maxmin utility function, where the portfolio manager selects a probability distribution that maximizes utility while "nature" simultaneously selects a probability distribution that minimizes utility.[18] The modified utility function can be formalized as

$$\max_{w}\left\{\min_{\tilde{\Sigma}_a} w'\mu_a - \frac{\gamma}{2} w'\tilde{\Sigma}_a w\right\} \tag{6.22}$$

subject to the following constraint on the KL divergence of the alternative prior from the reference prior:

$$D(N_a|N) = \frac{1}{2}\left(\ln\left(\frac{|\Sigma_a|}{|\Sigma|}\right) + \mathrm{tr}\left(\overset{-1}{\Sigma}\underset{a}{\Sigma}\right) + (\mu_a - \mu_0) - n\right) \leq \eta \tag{6.23}$$

where the following BL relationships hold:

$$\tilde{\mu} = \mu_a + \tau\Sigma_a C\left[\tau\left[C'\Sigma_a C\right] + \Omega_a\right]^{-1}\left[M - C'\mu_a\right] \tag{6.24}$$

$$\tilde{\Sigma}_a = \Sigma_a + \left(\frac{\Sigma_a^{-1}}{\tau} + C'\Sigma_a C\right)^{-1} \tag{6.25}$$

$$\Omega = \tau \times \mathrm{diag}(C'\Sigma_a C) \tag{6.26}$$

$$\mu_a = \gamma\Sigma_a w_0 \tag{6.27}$$

The end result is that the perturbed prior alters the entire BL process. Through robust optimization, the pivotal role of the covariance matrix in BL is brought to the fore within the framework of a Bayesian formalism that explicitly incorporates the uncertainty that investors often have in their capital market assumptions.

6.6 Key Takeaways

- Successful optimization of portfolio allocations for global bond portfolios depends on several factors. Portfolio optimization requires time series data. Proper quantification of the input parameters is essential

[18] See Gilboa and Schmeidler (1989).

and the input variables in optimization should reflect the portfolio's economic and statistical exposures. The input variables refer to expected returns, risk measures, and portfolio constraints.

- Traditional portfolio allocation frameworks take a single objective function and attempt to solve for it given any constraints imposed by a portfolio manager's investment process. However, it is also possible to implement multi-objective optimization during portfolio selection. In this type of framework, more than one objective function is solved simultaneously. The final solution represents a compromise between the various investment goals being solved for.
- Robust portfolio optimization is an important extension of the minimum-variance optimization approach, as many types of fixed income assets and currencies are susceptible to significant model misspecification. However, because bonds have other important dimensions of risk aside form variances and covariances, optimization techniques that solely rely on a covariance matrix must be supplemented with additional risk management tools during the investment process.

References

Alonso, N. and M. Barnes. 2017. "What is Missing in Common Minimum Volatility Strategies? The Ignored Impact of Currency Risk". *Journal of Index Investing* 8(2): 77–88.

Arnott, R. D. and T. K. Pham. 1993. "Tactical Currency Allocation". *Financial Analysts Journal* 49(5): 47–52.

Arnott, R. D., C. R. Harvey, V. Kalesnik, and J. Linnainmaa. 2019. "Alice's Adventures in Factorland: Three Blunders That Plague Factor Investing". *Journal of Portfolio Management* 45(4): 18–36.

Arruda, N., A. Bergeron, and M. Kritzman. 2021. "Optimal Currency Hedging". *Journal of Alternative Investments* 23(4): 122–130.

Baz, J., F. Breedon, V. Naik, and J. Peress. 2001. "Optimal Portfolios of Foreign Currencies". *Journal of Portfolio Management* 28(1): 102–111.

Bisat, A. 2010. "Sources of Return within an Emerging Markets Fixed-Income and Foreign Exchange Portfolio". *Journal of Alternative Investments* 13(1): 79–86.

Bush, R. and A. Woodham. 2018. "The New Neutral: The Long-Term Case for Currency Hedging". *Journal of Investing* 27(2): 105–114.

Chen, C. 1999. "Currency Hedging, Currency Overlay Strategy, and the Performance of Closed-End Country and International Equity Funds". *Journal of Alternative Investments* 2(2): 42–55.

Chopra, V. K. and W. T. Ziemba. 1993. "The Effect of Errors in Means, Variances, and Covariances on Optimal Portfolio Choice". *Journal of Portfolio Management* 19(2): 6–11.

Dym, S. I. 1991. "Measuring the Risk of Foreign Bonds". *Journal of Portfolio Management* 17(2): 56–61.

Duarte, A. M. and R. Rajagopal. 1999. "A Scenario-Based Approach to Optimal Currency Overlay". *Journal of Portfolio Management* 25(4): 51–59.

Ellsberg, D. 1961. "Risk, Ambiguity, and the Savage Axioms". *Quarterly Journal of Economics* 75: 643–669.

Fabozzi, F. J., P. N. Kolm., D. A. Pachamanova, and S. M. Focardi. 2007. "Robust Portfolio Optimization". *Journal of Portfolio Management* 33(3): 40–48.

Garlappi, L., R. Uppal, and T. Wang. 2007. "Portfolio Selection with Parameter and Model: A Multi-prior Approach". *Review of Financial Studies* 20: 41–81.

Gilboa, I. and D. Schmeidler. 1989. "Maxmin Expected Utility with a Non-unique Prior". *Journal of Mathematical Economics* 18: 141–153.

Guo, H. and L. Ryan. 2018. "Currency-Hedging Optimization for Multi-Asset Portfolios". *Journal of Portfolio Management* 44(2): 100–113.

Harvey, C. R., J. C. Liechty, M. W. Liechty, and P. Müller. 2010. "Portfolio Selection with Higher Moments". *Quantitative Finance* 10(5): 469–485.

Hansen, L. P. and T. J. Sargent. 2001. "Robust Control and Model Uncertainty". *American Economic Review* 91: 60–66.

He, G. and R. Litterman. 1999. "The Intuition Behind Black-Litterman Model Portfolios". *Investment Management Research*, Goldman, Sachs & Company, December.

Huttman, M. and L. Harris. 2006. "Generating Alpha from Currency Programs". *Journal of Alternative Investments* 8(4): 48–54.

Iborra, R. and I. Chabane. 2020. "Strategic Currency Hedging in Multi-Asset Portfolios". *Journal of Investing* 29(5): 31–57.

Jones, D. F. and M. Tamiz. 2010. *Practical Goal Programming*. New York: Springer.

Jorion, P. 1994. "Mean/Variance Analysis of Currency Overlays". *Financial Analysts Journal* 50(3): 48–56.

Kazemi, H., K. H. Black, and R. D. Chambers. 2016. *Alternative Investments: CAIA Level II*. 3rd Edition. Hoboken, New Jersey: John Wiley & Sons.

Koijen, R. S. J. , T. J. Moskowitz, L. H. Pedersen, and E. B. Vrugt. 2018. "Carry". *Journal of Financial Economics* 127: 197–225.

Kolm, P. N., G. Ritter, and J. Simonian. 2021. "Black -Litterman and Beyond: The Bayesian Paradigm in Investment Management". *Journal of Portfolio Management* 47(5): 91–113.

Konstantinov, G. 2014. "Active Currency Management of International Bond Portfolios". *Financial Markets and Portfolio Management* 28(1): 63–94.

Konstantinov, G. S. 2022. "Emerging Market Bonds: Expected Returns and Currency Impact". *Journal of Portfolio Management* 48 (8): 139–158.

Lee, W. 2000. *Advanced Theory and Methodology of Tactical Asset Allocation.* Hoboken, NJ: John Wiley & Sons.

Lee, W. and P. Liu. 2021. "Work Harder: Diligent Rebalancing and Investment Horizon". *Journal of Portfolio Management* 47(3): 17–34.

Levich, R. M. and L. R. Thomas. 1993. "The Merits of Active Currency Risk Management: Evidence from International Bond Portfolios". *Financial Analysts Journal* 49(5): 63–70.

Masters, S. J. 2002. "Emerging Markets". *Journal of Portfolio Management* 28(3): 96–101.

Markowitz, H. 1952. "Portfolio Selection". *Journal of Finance* 7(1): 77–91.

Martens, M., P. Beekhuizen, J. Duyvesteyn, and C. Zomerdijk. 2019. "Carry Investing on the Yield Curve". *Financial Analysts Journal* 75(4): 51–63.

Nucera, F. and G. Valente. 2013. "Carry Trades and the Performance of Currency Hedge Funds". *Journal of International Money and Finance* 33: 407–425.

Rattray, S., N. Granger, C. R. Harvey, and O. Van Hemert. 2020. "Strategic Rebalancing". *Journal of Portfolio Management* 46(6): 10–31.

Satchell, S. and A. Scowcroft. 2000. "A Demystification of Black-Litterman Model: Managing Quantitative and Traditional Portfolio Constructions". *Journal of Asset Management* 1(2): 138–150.

Simon, H. A. 1956. Rational Choice and the Structure of the Environment. *Psychological Review* 63, 129–138.

Simonian, J. 2011. "A Bayesian Approach to Building Robust Structural Credit Default Models". *Applied Economics Letters* 18(14): 1397–1400.

Simonian, J. 2021. "Factor Allocation as Reverse Attribution". *Journal of Portfolio Management* 47(5): 65–71.

Simonian, J. and J. Davis. 2010. "Robust Value-at-Risk: An Information-Theoretic Approach". *Applied Economics Letters* 17(16): 1551–1553.

Simonian, J. and J. Davis. 2011. "Incorporating Uncertainty into the Black–Litterman Portfolio Selection Model". *Applied Economics Letters* 18(17): 1719–1722.

Simonian, J. and G. Barschdorff. 2013. "Liabilities — A Multi-Objective Approach" *Applied Economics Letters* 20(8): 763–766.

Tamiz, M., D. F. Jones, and C. Romero. 1998. "Goal Programming For Decision Making: An Overview of The Current State-of-the-Art". *European Journal of Operational Research* 111: 569–581.

Thornton, D. L. and G. Valente. 2012. "Out-of-Sample Predictions of Bond Excess Returns with Forward Rates: An Asset-Allocation Perspective". *Review of Financial Studies* 25: 3141–3168.

Chapter 7

Bond Selection

In contrast to portfolio level allocation described in the previous chapter, bond selection is concerned with determining which individual bonds to include in a portfolio from a universe of candidate bonds based on criteria relating to factor exposures, duration, ratings, and spread risk. In this chapter, we discuss different aspects of bond selection and consider the challenges in applying a number of traditional optimization techniques like the mean–variance optimization (MVO) and Black–Litterman frameworks described in the previous chapter to the allocation of individual bonds.

The focus of this chapter is the bottom-up process in which the portfolio is constructed using the characteristics of individual bonds. Following a bottom-up approach, a portfolio's ultimate weights are the result of an evaluation of individual bond risk and expected returns. Rigorous analysis is a necessary step to extend the bottom-up process to other sub-asset classes and to asset classes like currencies, countries, or sectors.

7.1 Optimization at the Single Bond Level

While it is possible to apply standard optimization techniques such as MVO to the allocation of individual bonds, doing so is not always ideal for two reasons. First, the use of a covariance matrix at the individual bond level can be problematic. Second, the complexities in global bond portfolios that arise from investing in a broad array of asset classes and sectors often make covariance matrix-dependent frameworks such as MVO impractical.

For these two reasons, there is a need for dimension reduction when building portfolios at the individual bond level. It is natural therefore to defer to a factor model, in which a parsimonious set of drivers is assumed to explain the return behavior of the multitude of bonds that are candidates for inclusion in the portfolio. The construction of factor-tracking portfolios can be presented as a simple exercise solved in a straightforward manner by well-worn optimization methods. In the following, we demonstrate how to use bottom-up optimization to optimize baskets of individual securities in the manner described. In particular, we show how linear programming can accommodate consideration of the entire spectrum of portfolio risk-and-return drivers including duration, spread, notional size, currency, country risk, and rating, among others.

Formally, linear programming is an optimization problem in which a linear function is maximized or minimized given various constraints. The following input parameters are often used when applying linar programming to a bond portfolio:

- vector of individual bond expected returns;
- portfolio overall duration as the weighted sum of the sector durations. Portfolio duration can function as an objective or a constraint;
- maturity buckets (e.g., 1–3 years, 3–5 years, 5–7 years, 7–10 years, and more than 10 years) in every single currency/country in the portfolio;
- individual bond minimum/maximum weights and additional constraints on individual bonds, sector, and/or country weights in the portfolio;
- sectors and countries (e.g., specific weights on sectors and countries);
- individual bond option-adjusted spread (OAS) or duration-times-spread (DTS);
- credit ratings on the individual bonds;
- specific individual bond factor sensitivity to the yield curve factors (level, steepness, and curvature);
- interactive exposure to complex categories that determine the individual bond weights (e.g., the portfolio could comprise U.S. dollar- and EUR-denominated corporate bonds, but no British pound-denominated (GBP-denominated) corporate bonds.

A bottom-up optimization approach has been previously applied to global bond portfolio selection by Walter and Zimmerer (2000) who applied the framework to European bond portfolios in the absence of currency risk and Konstantinov (2014) and Konstantinov and Fabozzi (2021) who provide an approach to address the specific needs of global bond portfolios. The bottom-up optimization approach follows the intuition of a bottom-up investment process and uses the individual bonds' expected returns and portfolio constraints to derive a portfolio's allocation.

Formally, the optimization of the bond selection portfolio is defined as an objective function of the product of the desired portfolio weights as decision variables and the expected individual bond returns:

$$\underset{w}{\operatorname{Arg\,max}} = w'E(r) \tag{7.1}$$

where w' is the transposed vector of portfolio weights and $E(r)$ represents the expected individual bond returns.

The maximization of expected individual bond portfolio returns is only possible under specific constraints. They can be client-specific, portfolio-manager-specific, or regulatory restrictions, all of which are expressed as follows:

$$\begin{gathered} Aw = c \\ \text{with } 0 < w_k \leq 1 \end{gathered} \tag{7.2}$$

where A is an $(m \times n)$ matrix of portfolio constraints including slack variables and identity and zero matrices, w' is the $(n \times 1)$ transposed vector of portfolio weights, $E(r)$ is the $(n \times 1)$ vector of expected single bond returns, c is the $(m \times 1)$ vector of portfolio constraints, n is the number of individual bonds under consideration, and m is the number of portfolio constraints. Non-negativity constraints $0 < w_k \leq 1$ (no short-selling) assure that the portfolio invests 100% of funds available without borrowing.

Equations (7.1) and (7.2) require further explanation. To provide an in-depth analysis of how to implement portfolio optimization for bond portfolios, we describe its separate components in the following sections of the chapter.

7.1.1 *Expected single bond returns and weights*

The optimization procedure maximizes expected portfolio return by adjusting the portfolio's weights. Formally, the optimization problem regarding portfolio expected return and the weights defined in equation (7.1) can be expressed using vectors:

$$\operatorname*{Arg\,max}_{w} = (w_1,\ldots,w_k,tc_1,\ldots,tc_k)\begin{pmatrix} E(r)_1 \\ \vdots \\ E(r)_k \\ tc_1 \\ \vdots \\ tc_k \end{pmatrix} \tag{7.3}$$

where w' is the transposed vector of portfolio weights that includes the bonds to purchase or sell, $E(r)$ is the transposed vector of expected returns for all single bonds, and tc is a single value for transaction costs which serves as a penalty parameter.

Note that the size k of the return and weight vectors must be equal, including the variables that govern transaction costs. We can further split the transaction costs that reflect buying and selling orders. Using one value for tc is problematic for heterogeneous bond portfolios, since the transaction costs in different currencies, sectors, sub-asset-classes, etc., cannot be the same. For example, the transaction costs for U.S. Treasuries cannot be the same as those for trading Indonesian government bonds in Indonesian rupiah (IDR). The purpose of tc is to act as a penalty function in an optimization process.

Transaction costs can be split into two categories: explicit costs and implicit costs. Explicit costs include bid-ask spreads, brokerage fees, and trade and custodian commissions. Implicit costs include costs related to the market mechanism of matching buyers with sellers along with the decision process associated with trading. Market mechanisms and decision processes are intertwined with each contributing to market impact costs.[1] Market mechanism costs result when traders are competing to

[1]Market impact costs can be decomposed into temporary and permanent components. Security prices change when market participants adjust their views and perceptions as they observe news. The permanent component of market impact costs reflects this information through trading by market participants. The market reacts to this information because the trade could be signaling superior information asymmetric to what the markets already know about a security's price. This permanent component reflects how private information becomes impounded in prices. The temporary component is considered unrelated to the underlying value of the security. It represents price concessions

execute trades. That is, it is the price concession that traders make to complete their trades and tends to be the dominant cost in trading. Market impact costs are important in deciding on the investment vehicle to use to obtain a targeted portfolio exposure. For example, the use of derivative instruments like futures and forwards is in some markets a better choice than using cash bonds. Derivative instruments like futures or forwards allow fast execution and portfolio managers are able to quickly gain exposure in the market. Cash bonds have higher market impact costs associated with trading (bid-ask spreads, notional amounts, and market volatility among others).

In general, large global bond funds have an advantage with respect to explicit costs; however, very large global bond funds have a strong market impact and might move markets if engaged in specific currencies or bonds. For example, the relatively low spot liquidity and daily average turnover volume of US $5,017 million of the Polish zloty (PLN) against the US dollar might be challenging for a multi-billion global bond fund taking a spot 10% bet of its volume in USD/PLN.[2]

However, the maximization of expected bond returns is only one part of the bond selection process as global bond portfolios have a lot of variables to consider. These variables are modeled in an extended matrix that allows more flexibility than a simple variance–covariance matrix.

7.1.2 *Estimating expected individual bond returns and risk*

Selection optimization uses single bond expected returns, which are usually derived from the underlying single yield curves used in the entire investment process (highlighted in Chapters 4 and 6). Similarly, to derive

---

needed to attract traders within the recent time interval. It can represent the liquidity concession necessary for the liquidity provider (e.g., the market maker) to the order, inventory effects (price effects due to broker–dealer inventory imbalances), or imperfect substitution (for example, price incentives to induce market participants to absorb the additional shares). For a further discussion of implicit costs associated with trading, see Cerniglia and Fabozzi (2022).

[2]Bank of International Settlements, "Triennial Central Bank Survey: Global Foreign Exchange Market Turnover in 2019." Monetary and Economic Department, 2019.

expected returns for the portfolio allocation in a portfolio that includes currencies, there are two possible solutions: (1) derive local currency bond returns from the underlying local or sector yield curves or (2) estimate domestic or expected bond returns adjusted for the base (domestic) portfolio currency.

The estimation of individual expected bond returns is associated with several estimation risks, as the expected returns in both local currency and in domestic currency impact the portfolio. There are two approaches to estimate expected individual bond returns: (1) in local currency and (2) in expected returns adjusted for foreign exchange (FX) risk.

To estimate expected single bond returns, we can use the formulation suggested by Zimmerer (2003) and apply it to local currency bonds. This is shown in Konstantinov (2014, 2022) and Konstantinov and Fabozzi (2021). The following formulation allows us to derive expected individual bond returns in a manner similar to the equation used to determine expected returns for bond indexes. The basic formula is as follows:

$$E(R)_t^{\text{LC Bond}} = D_t^{\text{LC Bond}} \Delta y_t^{\text{LC Bond}} + y_t^{\text{LC Bond}} \Delta t \tag{7.4}$$

where $D_t^{\text{LC Bond}}$ is the bond's duration, $y_t^{\text{LC Bond}}$ is the bond's yield to maturity, Δt denotes the change in time, and $E(R)_t^{\text{LC Bond}}$ is the local currency expected bond return.

Note that in equation (7.4) all terms are in local currency and referred to as bond carry. In other words, the individual bond returns are unhedged positions. As a consequence, both the single bond expected returns and the portfolio expected returns are in local currency and should match the portfolio allocation to local currencies in an unhedged portfolio.

An alternative approach for deriving expected bond returns is to use forward rates or expected spot rates for individual bonds.[3] Formally, expected bond local currency returns are converted into domestic or base currency returns using expected spot rates and the current FX rates as follows:

$$E(R)_t^{\text{BC Bond}} \equiv y_t^{\text{BC Bond}} = (1 + y_t^{\text{LC Bond}}) \frac{E(S_{t+1})}{S_t} - 1 \tag{7.5}$$

[3] See Thornton and Valente (2012), Nucera and Valente (2013), and Konstantinov (2022).

where $y_t^{\text{LC Bond}}$ is the bond yield of the foreign currency bond, $E(S_{t+1})$ is the expected spot rate at time $t+1$, S_t is the current FX rate, and $E(R)_t^{\text{BC Bond}}$ is the expected bond return in domestic currency.

A few observations regarding equations (7.4) and (7.5) are in order. First, the expected returns in equation (7.4) always denote local currency returns; the bond yield expression in equation (7.5) converts local currency bond yields into domestic yields using the current and expected spot FX rate. In other words, the expression in equation (7.4) is purely yield curve driven and the expression of expected returns in equation (7.5) is currency and individual bond return driven. Note that the change in currency effect on every individual bond in a global bond portfolio depends on the duration, yield, coupon, and maturity of the bond.

The uncertainty in the return estimation defined in equation (7.4) arises due to the assumption of a constant yield curve and is dependent on the holding period. The uncertainty in equation (7.5) might arise due to miscalculation of the expected currency spot returns, $E(S_{t+1})$. As pointed out in Chapter 3, expected spot rates are only to some extent a reliable predictor of future realized spot rates.

In general, for unhedged bond selection portfolios, it is convenient to use equation (7.4). If the bond portfolio selection optimization should result in a hedged portfolio, then adjusting the bond yields by expected FX rates might be the preferred solution. However, building a hedged portfolio on a single bond level might be more expensive than on an allocation level. That is, often it is more cost effective to hedge portfolio exposure to sectors or assets than to hedge individual bonds. For example, knowing the weighted yield, coupon, or maturity exposure, portfolio managers might implement direct hedging policies using the relevant futures contracts (e.g., Bund futures for long-term bonds (10-year maturity) or the Bobl futures for 5-year bonds).[4]

In terms of bond risks, when using linear programming, we abandon a variance–covariance matrix. Given this, we need to approach bond risk from the standpoint of common bond risk factors such as spread, duration, convexity, and currency risks. Decomposing the factor impact of curve level, steepness, and curvature using sector- and country-specific yield curves is a powerful tool that offers valuable insights on bond risks. As

[4] We discuss hedging policies in Chapter 9.

explained in Chapter 4, DTS is one of the major risk indicators for individual bonds.

Additionally, the portfolio duration is the weighted sum of individual bond durations. However, the total bond portfolio duration as a weighted sum of individual bond durations is often not representative of the sensitivity of bond prices to changes in interest rates. To understand why, suppose, for example, that a global bond portfolio comprises multiple currencies and bonds from different countries. What is the portfolio duration and what sensitivity to interest rates does a portfolio duration represent? The weighted sum of the individual bond durations captures the total portfolio duration; however, the individual currencies and countries are exposed to different interest-rate dynamics and risks. As a result, the portfolio duration of the portfolio's European bond exposure might better represent an individual bond's interest-rate risk than the overall bond portfolio duration. In this respect, it is often more convenient to measure the sensitivity of interest-rate changes according to the currency and country buckets than to consider a total bond portfolio duration. We note that, in addition to "direct" bond factors such as those mentioned above, we may also utilize "indirect" bond factors such as those discussed in Chapter 5.

7.1.3 *Modeling risk, restrictions, and constraints*

The management of risk — client-specific, portfolio-manager-specific, and regulatory restrictions — as well as constraints in a bond portfolio, requires their representation in matrix form. This is the most significant and important property of bond selection optimization. We will demonstrate how linear programming is a powerful tool for optimization of bond portfolios comprising a large number of individual bonds and for modeling a large number of individual bond constraints.

In general, a matrix comprising raw single bond data and dummy variables helps to model portfolio constraints. The dummy variables are necessary to deal with possible portfolio restrictions. In global bond portfolios, for example, every bond is often assigned a value of 1 if it is denominated in U.S. dollars and zero otherwise. Modeling these types of restrictions is important in global bond portfolio management due to the lack of liquidity in specific markets. For example, U.K. gilts or U.S. Treasuries have very different liquidity than emerging market sovereign bonds. This fact becomes highly significant in times of financial stress, as liquidity dries up. Market liquidity issues are common when emerging market currencies depreciate heavily, bond yields rise, and low-yielding currencies appreciate as investors seek to shelter their capital in liquid markets. Examples of such markets are the U.S. dollar and U.S. Treasuries, Japanese yen and Japanese government bonds, and Swiss franc and Swiss government bonds.

A matrix representation provides managers of global bond portfolios with unique opportunities to manage their funds. Separating specific country and currency interest-rate sensitivity and risk is necessary to properly capture the drivers of bond portfolio risk and return. It also allows managers to adjust for multiple duration constraints and manage both the overall portfolio allocation and bond selection toward desired sectors and maturity buckets. Bond selection also allows us to model individual country-specific durations. For example, a manager may wish to have a barbell allocation in U.S. Treasuries and a bullet allocation in South African bonds. However, portfolio managers must be vigilant because the dimension of the matrix can cause serious estimation problems if the constraints and input information are large.

The dummy variables for the portfolio holdings govern single bond restrictions. Turnover constraints can be adjusted to consider specific market-related transaction costs. For example, the transaction costs for trading Hungarian government bonds are different from the costs of trading U.S. Treasuries or Malaysian government bonds. Similarly, transaction costs on emerging market corporate bonds are different from G10 government bonds. Buy and sell orders can be modeled using the corresponding transaction costs associated with buying or selling individual bonds. These costs can differ according to the economic cycle or financial market conditions.

Additional constraints that are applied during the optimization process include those pertaining to country and industry exposure, ratings, and spreads among others. Sometimes, it is also convenient to expand the matrix by more detailed duration, spread, and convexity decomposition.

We can employ matrix decomposition to account for the universe of portfolio risk drivers. We show a basic schematic of our matrix decomposition below where we have the product of an $n \times m$ matrix A and the vector of weights w as an $m \times 1$ vector containing the portfolio constraints:

$$
A = \left(\begin{array}{cccc|cccc|cccc}
\multicolumn{4}{c|}{\text{matrix}} & 0 & & \cdots & 0 & 0 & & \cdots & 0\\
\multicolumn{4}{c|}{E} & & 0 & & \vdots & & 0 & & \vdots \\
 & & & & \vdots & & \ddots & & \vdots & & \ddots & \\
 & & & & 0 & \cdots & & 0 & 0 & \cdots & & 0\\
\hline
1 & & \cdots & 0 & -1 & & \cdots & 0 & 1 & & \cdots & 0\\
 & 1 & & \vdots & & -1 & & \vdots & & 1 & & \vdots\\
\vdots & & \ddots & & \vdots & & \ddots & & \vdots & & \ddots & \\
0 & \cdots & & 1 & 0 & \cdots & & -1 & 0 & \cdots & & 1\\
\hline
0 & 0 & \cdots & 0 & 1 & 1 & \cdots & 1 & 0 & 0 & \cdots & 0
\end{array}\right)
\begin{pmatrix} w_1\\ \vdots \\ w_k \\ b_1 \\ \vdots \\ b_k \\ s_1 \\ \vdots \\ s_k\end{pmatrix}
$$

$$
\begin{array}{c}
>\le \\ >\le \\ >\le \\ >\le \\ = \\ = \\ = \\ = \\ \le
\end{array}
\left(\begin{array}{c}
\text{currencies} \\ \text{sectors} \\ \text{maturities} \\ \text{curve factors} \\ \hline \text{bond}_1 \\ \text{bond}_2 \\ \vdots \\ \text{bond}_n \\ \hline \text{pt}
\end{array}\right)
$$

$$\text{with } 0 < w_1,\ldots,w_n \le w_{Max}, \qquad b_1,\ldots,b_n \ge 0, \qquad s_1,\ldots,s_n \ge 0 \tag{7.6}$$

where the upper left matrix E is an $m \times n$ country-maturity-allocation matrix which captures information pertaining to sectors (S), factors (F), maturities (M), countries (C), ratings (R), and currency exposure (FX), among others.

The other variables are defined as follows: w is the vector of portfolio weights that represents security buys and sells, b is the vector that represents buy orders, s is the vector that represents sell orders, w_{Max} is the maximum weight of an individual bond, m is the number of variables and constraints, n is 3 times (see the lower row of matrix A) the number of individual bonds, and pt is the turnover constraint.

Matrix A, which we defined in equation (7.2), comprises portfolio constraints including slack variables and identity and zero matrices. The upper left part of the matrix A captures all possible exposures in the portfolio (modified duration, currency, sector, and asset class). In addition, the matrix E represents exposures to the yield curve factors, country of issuance, country risk, and maturity buckets, among others. This is matrix E. The three zero matrices and identity matrices in the middle section of equation (7.6) capture the changes in the single bond weights in the portfolio. This assures us that the new and old bond weights are properly modeled. In other words, adding the sells and subtracting the buys to the new bond weights produces the old bond weights. In the last row of the matrix given by equation (7.6), the turnover constraints are modeled.

Of particular interest are the matrices that govern portfolio constraints and restrictions. They control for the portfolio holdings and the buying and selling of bonds. This extension to standard optimization is important for frequently rebalancing bond portfolios because transaction costs play an important role that might cause the target selection to deviate from the current or estimated selection.

However, the inclusion of selling and buying orders increases the complexity and computational power required to solve the optimization. Note that a much simpler and practical way to estimate portfolio selection is to run the optimization without buying/selling constraints. For this purpose, let us focus on the most important matrix in equation (7.6), matrix E.

Matrix E deserves special discussion because it is central for quantitative bond portfolio management and portfolio rebalancing. We have already shown in Chapter 2 that the matrix decomposition of benchmarks and portfolios is the most convenient way to not only represent exposures but also to compute various portfolio allocation and risk metrics. We note that for the sake of implementation efficiency, the components included in matrix E should be the most relevant drivers of portfolio risk and return.

The most useful way to model constraints for global bond portfolios is to use a currency-maturity matrix with additional spread, duration, yield curve components, factor, sector, and rating vectors among others as follows:

$$\begin{pmatrix} E & FX_l & M_i & R_h & \cdots & E_h \\ bond_1 & bond_1 FX_l & bond_1 M_i & bond_1 R_h & \cdots & bond_1 E_h \\ bond_2 & bond_2 FX_l & bond_2 M_i & bond_2 R_h & \cdots & bond_1 E_h \\ bond_3 & bond_3 FX_l & bond_2 M_i & bond_3 R_h & \cdots & bond_1 E_h \\ \vdots & \vdots & \vdots & \vdots & & \vdots \\ bond_n & bond_n FX_l & bond_n M_i & bond_n R_h & \cdots & bond_n E_h \end{pmatrix} \tag{7.7}$$

Note that this matrix comprises a large number of sub-matrices. The number of sub-matrices is proportional to the most important drivers of portfolio risk and return. Specifically, it can be formed by considering yield curve components, countries, and maturities or currencies and maturities. Portfolio managers can expand and model the size of the different components as they see fit.

For example, FX_l allows a portfolio manager to include l number of currencies that the portfolio might invest in, which can exceed 60 if the bond portfolio uses a global aggregate government bond index in local currencies (e.g., the J.P. Morgan GBI Government Broad Index). Similarly, for the maturity sub-matrix M_i, there are i number of maturity buckets to consider. A detailed bucket decomposition allows for a more granular overview of the maturity allocation in portfolio positioning. Note that this granular maturity bucket decomposition is more relevant for multi-currency bond portfolios that underlie multiple yield curves. For the rating buckets R_h, there are many possible solutions. For example, a portfolio manager can use credit ratings from ratings agencies such as Moody's, Standard & Poor's, or Fitch, use composite ratings like the Bloomberg composite rating, or devise proprietary credit ratings.

Another widely used option is to add a sub-matrix E with dummy variables that represent country exposures. Country risk is an important consideration for hard currency bond portfolios with minimal currency risk.

In short, the elements of matrix E can be expanded to conform to the specific requirements of a portfolio manager's investment process. However, it is important to bear in mind that the more granular the matrix E is, the more detailed the portfolio optimization will be, which will in turn entail greater computational complexity.

Mathematically, the algorithm assigns a value of 1 if a bond matches a certain category, say, currency, rating, country, or sector. A bond can be assigned a value of 1 to only one category. However, cross relations are easily modeled as two categories can be integrated. For example, certain currency and country restrictions can be modeled so that a bond might be assigned to that category. The first row of the matrix includes all relevant constraints. The inclusion of zero matrices and identity matrices allows the portfolio manager to also model buy and sell orders in the optimization.

7.2 Practical Examples of Bond Selection Optimization

To illustrate the importance of single security selection, we provide two practical examples with real bond portfolios: (1) a hard currency emerging market bond portfolio and (2) an unconstrained government bond portfolio. To highlight the different roles of the portfolio allocation and portfolio selection optimizations, we assume that for the global unconstrained bond portfolio, the currency allocation is the result of the portfolio allocation. That is, the currency allocation is fixed and not changed in the portfolio selection optimization. For the emerging market bond portfolio, we do not assume a fixed portfolio allocation.

In the next section, we analyze each portfolio and discuss their primary points of difference with one another. The most important difference between the models in Chapter 6 and the models in this chapter is that the allocation models in Chapter 6 are only intended to be used for asset allocation. In contrast, bond selection models can be used to drive both asset allocation and security selection. Our two examples highlight this. In the first, the allocation is already given — assumed to be derived using an allocation model. In the second example, allocation and selection are derived simultaneously.

7.2.1 *Global unconstrained government bond portfolio*

Our first example portfolio is an unconstrained global government bond portfolio. For illustrative purposes, we assume that the portfolio has the J.P. Morgan GBI Broad Bond Index as its benchmark. Assumptions, objectives, and constraints for the global unconstrained bond portfolio optimization are as follows:

- maximize expected returns,
- fixed currency allocation determined in a previous stage (portfolio allocation),
- duration neutrality,
- no leverage.

Table 7.1 captures the optimization vector c of equation (7.2) comprising the portfolio exposure compared to the benchmark exposure. The portfolio currency allocation is the result of the portfolio allocation process explained in the previous chapter. The task of the bond selection optimization is to select the bonds that fit within the currency allocation. An additional purpose of the bond selection optimization is to fulfill specific constraints, and allow for flexibility in maturity, duration, currency, sector, and credit rating exposure that were not part of the portfolio allocation process.

Note that the column in Table 7.1 labeled "Portfolio" is already a portfolio with exposures to specific currencies, sectors, maturity buckets, and ratings. The column "Benchmark" shows the benchmark exposure, and the column "Difference" shows the deviations between the portfolio and benchmark. The maximized bond portfolio return for a monthly holding period according to equation (7.1) is 35 bps. While the coupon, spread, and yield to maturity are not constrained and are not subject to the optimization, the portfolio has a higher yield to maturity and higher coupon than the benchmark. One condition that must be satisfied in the optimization process is duration neutrality, which is satisfied in our

Table 7.1: Portfolio Selection Optimization for an Unconstrained Government Bond Portfolio

	Portfolio	Benchmark	Difference
Expected return	0.35%	–0.03%	0.38%
Spread	–12.21%	5.10%	–17.30%
Coupon	2.57%	2.24%	0.33%
Yield to maturity	1.48%	0.95%	0.53%
Duration	5.698	5.698	0.00%
USD	0.0%	32.8%	–32.8%
JPY	6.2%	20.0%	–13.8%
CAD	5.5%	1.5%	3.9%
GBP	8.9%	5.8%	3.1%
AUD	5.5%	1.3%	4.1%
CZK	6.4%	0.2%	6.2%
EUR	8.1%	21.7%	–13.6%
HUF	18.8%	0.1%	18.6%
MXN	0.0%	0.4%	–0.4%
NZD	17.0%	0.2%	16.8%

Table 7.1: (*Continued*)

	Portfolio	Benchmark	Difference
PLN	5.6%	0.3%	5.3%
ZAR	5.2%	0.4%	4.8%
SEK	6.4%	0.2%	6.3%
NOK	6.4%	0.1%	6.3%
Industrials	0.0%	0.0%	0.0%
Covered	0.0%	0.0%	0.0%
Financial	0.0%	0.0%	0.0%
Quasi & Foreign Government	0.0%	0.0%	0.0%
Utility	0.0%	0.0%	0.0%
Sovereign	100.0%	100.0%	100.0%
Securitized	0.0%	0.0%	0.0%
<1.5	14.5%	7.2%	7.2%
1.5<2.5	2.8%	11.7%	–8.9%
2.5<3.5	2.2%	8.9%	–6.7%
3.5<4.5	3.4%	9.0%	–5.6%
4.5<5.5	14.0%	7.3%	6.6%
5.5<6.5	7.0%	6.1%	1.0%
6.5<7.5	6.6%	5.6%	1.1%
7.5<8.5	16.9%	4.3%	12.6%
8.5<9.5	23.3%	5.4%	17.8%
9.5<	9.4%	34.3%	–24.9%
AAA	43.4%	41.6%	1.8%
A1	6.2%	26.6%	–20.4%
A2	5.6%	0.6%	5.0%
A3	0.0%	3.6%	–3.6%
AA1	0.0%	1.1%	–1.1%
AA2	0.0%	6.8%	–6.8%
AA3	15.7%	7.7%	8.0%
BBB1	0.0%	0.4%	–0.4%
BBB2	18.8%	0.1%	18.6%
BBB3	5.1%	7.4%	–2.3%
Total	100.0%	100.0%	0.0%
Number of bonds	65	2409	–2317

example. The portfolio duration is equal to 5.7, which is the same as the benchmark. Obviously, the bond portfolio selection is not only driven by the portfolio allocation to currencies, and bonds with specific maturity buckets and ratings (among other characteristics) but also selects the optimal bonds that satisfy portfolio constraints and maximize expected returns. The bottom-up optimization uses expected returns as inputs. And the example represents an integrated approach that follows the bottom-up intuition of an investment process. Furthermore, the currency allocation is quite aggressive compared to the benchmark. Similarly, both the maturity and rating allocation deviate from the benchmark. The final portfolio comprises 65 bonds, whereas the benchmark comprises more than 2,400 bonds.

It is worth discussing the potential portfolio management implications for this portfolio. The bond portfolio bears substantial risks, and they come from multiple sources. The first is the large deviation in the currency allocation compared to the benchmark. Such large deviation increases the portfolio's tracking error risk. The economic intuition behind such aggressive positioning might be the expected currency depreciation of the G3 currencies, which would generate outperformance of the portfolio compared to the benchmark.

Additionally, the expectations of the portfolio manager in this example might be that lower-rated bonds will outperform better rated bonds. The underweight in the A1 credit rating bucket and the overweight in BBB2 are indications that the portfolio manager expects the lower credit ratings (BBB2) to outperform the higher rating bonds (A1). Figure 7.1 shows the currency, maturity, and credit rating exposures of the portfolio. To provide a more granular understanding of the portfolio, we provide both allocation information for the portfolio and its active positioning.

The current portfolio shows strong currency deviation relative to the currency weights of the benchmark. In addition, the bond portfolio maturity allocation is heavily concentrated in the long-term maturity buckets. The active maturity allocation reveals the tactical positioning of the overall portfolio compared to the benchmark. Decomposing the currency allocation for a specific maturity would indicate a more insightful picture of the interest-rate risk in the different currency exposures of the portfolio.

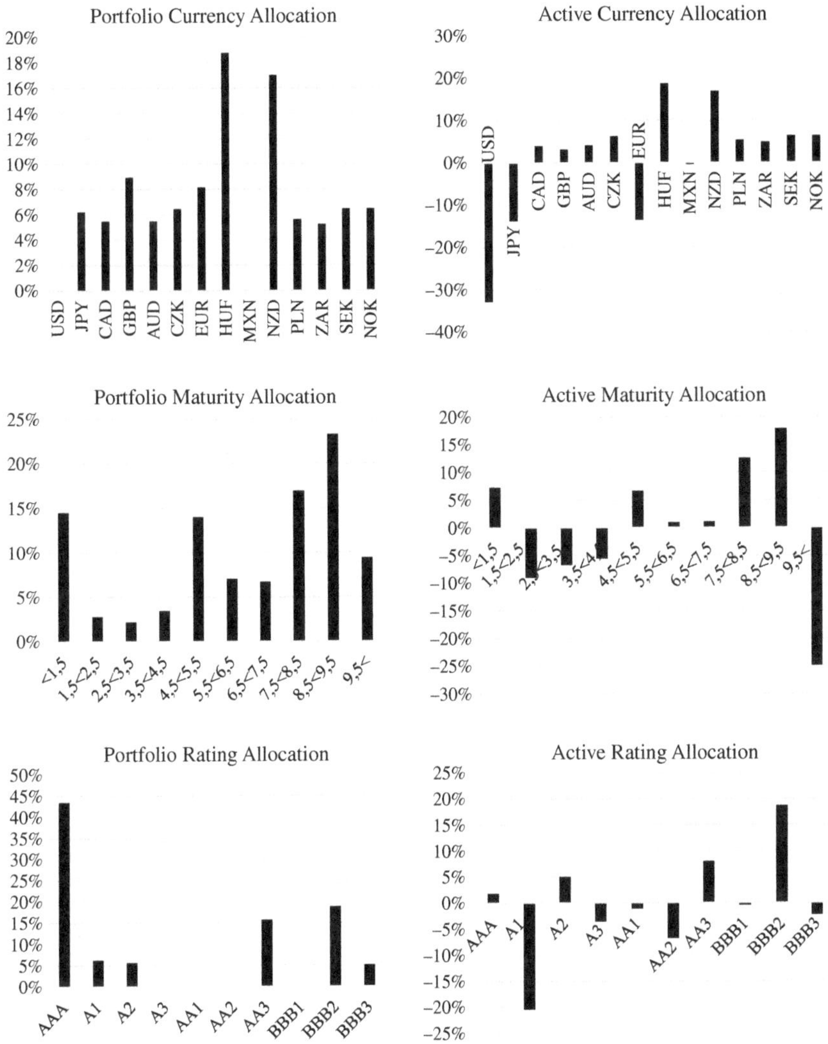

Figure 7.1: Optimization: Global Unconstrained Government Bond Portfolio

7.2.2 *Emerging market bond portfolio*

Our second example is an emerging market bond portfolio. The hard currency portfolio is managed against the J.P. Morgan EMBI Global Composite Index, which is a U.S.-dollar-denominated bond benchmark.

Because the portfolio's base currency is the U.S. dollar, there is no currency risk. If the bond portfolio had a different base currency than the benchmark, the currency effect might result in substantial risk and return contributions. However, compared to an unconstrained bond portfolio with local currency exposure, the FX risk is not coming from multiple currencies, but only from the U.S. dollar. This is the case when the emerging market bond portfolio has a base currency different from the U.S. dollar. Thus, the main risks of a hard currency emerging market portfolio are countries, credit ratings, and maturities. Table 7.2 shows the bond portfolio selection optimization.

Table 7.2: Portfolio Selection Optimization for an Emerging Market Bond Portfolio

	Portfolio	**Benchmark**	**Difference**
Expected return	0.56%	0.33%	0.23%
Convexity	1.12	1.21	–0.10
Spread	405.73	372.86	32.86
Coupon	6.19	5.38	0.82
Yield to maturity	4.6%	4.4%	0.3%
Duration	8.09	8.09	0.00
ARMENIA	0.00%	0.18%	–0.18%
ARGENTINA	0.00%	1.56%	–1.56%
AZERBAIJAN	0.00%	1.17%	–1.17%
BOLIVIA	0.00%	0.33%	–0.33%
BRAZIL	3.53%	3.82%	–0.29%
BELARUS	4.91%	0.65%	4.26%
BELIZE	0.00%	0.04%	–0.04%
COTE D'IVOIRE	0.00%	0.58%	–0.58%
CHILE	1.51%	3.69%	–2.17%
CHINA	9.87%	5.30%	4.57%
COLOMBIA	1.88%	3.76%	–1.88%
COSTA RICA	4.02%	1.02%	3.00%
DOMINICAN REPUBLIC	2.17%	3.11%	–0.94%
ECUADOR	0.00%	1.73%	–1.73%
EGYPT	0.00%	3.16%	–3.16%
GABON	0.00%	0.41%	–0.41%

Table 7.2: (*Continued*)

	Portfolio	Benchmark	Difference
GEORGIA	0.00%	0.09%	–0.09%
GHANA	0.00%	1.48%	–1.48%
GUATEMALA	0.00%	1.02%	–1.02%
HONDURAS	0.00%	0.35%	–0.35%
CROATIA	0.00%	0.75%	–0.75%
HUNGARY	0.01%	1.47%	–1.46%
INDONESIA	2.54%	5.93%	–3.39%
JAMAICA	1.76%	1.01%	0.75%
JORDAN	0.00%	0.87%	–0.87%
KENYA	0.00%	1.11%	–1.11%
KAZAKHSTAN	3.03%	3.31%	–0.29%
SRI LANKA	0.00%	1.62%	–1.62%
LITHUANIA	0.00%	0.28%	–0.28%
MOROCCO	0.17%	0.45%	–0.28%
MONGOLIA	0.00%	0.55%	–0.55%
MEXICO	6.24%	5.78%	0.46%
MALAYSIA	0.26%	3.43%	–3.17%
MOZAMBIQUE	0.00%	0.13%	–0.13%
NAMIBIA	0.00%	0.23%	–0.23%
OMAN	6.64%	2.90%	3.74%
PANAMA	0.00%	3.75%	–3.75%
PERU	4.36%	3.50%	0.87%
PHILIPPINES	6.31%	4.01%	2.29%
POLAND	4.44%	1.66%	2.78%
PARAGUAY	2.80%	1.13%	1.67%
ROMANIA	4.79%	1.99%	2.81%
RUSSIA	3.77%	4.35%	–0.58%
SLOVAK REPUBLIC	0.00%	0.28%	–0.28%
SENEGAL	0.00%	0.46%	–0.46%
EL SALVADOR	6.05%	1.15%	4.90%
TAJIKISTAN	0.00%	0.07%	–0.07%
TUNISIA	0.00%	0.16%	–0.16%

(*Continued*)

Table 7.2: (*Continued*)

	Portfolio	**Benchmark**	**Difference**
TURKEY	5.91%	4.00%	1.91%
TRINIDAD AND TOBAGO	0.00%	0.59%	–0.59%
UKRAINE	8.07%	2.94%	5.13%
URUGUAY	2.97%	3.20%	–0.23%
VIETNAM	0.00%	0.20%	–0.20%
SOUTH AFRICA	1.97%	3.03%	–1.06%
ZAMBIA	0.00%	0.25%	–0.25%
<1	0.00%	0.16%	–0.16%
1<3	8.99%	12.28%	–3.29%
3<5	15.60%	15.60%	0.00%
5<7	12.00%	12.00%	0.00%
7<10	16.21%	16.21%	0.00%
<10	47.19%	43.74%	3.45%
Sovereign Bonds	78.22%	78.22%	0.00%
Quasi-Sovereign Bonds	21.78%	21.78%	0.00%
A	1.88%	1.88%	0.00%
A–	4.70%	4.70%	0.00%
A+	5.55%	5.55%	0.00%
B	16.99%	7.86%	9.14%
B–	6.05%	6.05%	0.00%
B+	7.68%	7.68%	0.00%
BB	2.80%	2.11%	0.69%
BB–	14.35%	14.35%	0.00%
BB+	0.00%	0.84%	–0.84%
BBB	15.69%	15.69%	0.00%
BBB–	13.76%	13.76%	0.00%
BBB+	10.54%	10.54%	0.00%
CCC–	0.00%	0.25%	–0.25%
CCC+	0.00%	2.07%	–2.07%
NR	0.00%	6.68%	–6.68%
$\sum$	100.00%	100.00%	0.00%
Bonds	49	699	–650

Assumptions for the emerging market bond portfolio optimization are as follows:

- maximize expected returns,
- no fixed country allocation from portfolio allocation process,
- duration neutrality,
- maturity neutrality,
- no leverage.

Observe that the optimization is implemented using equations (7.1) and (7.2). The maximized bond expected return is 56 bps compared to the benchmark expected return of 33 bps. The maximization of portfolio expected returns is derived using the individual bond expected returns. In this case, the currency exposure in the portfolio is the result of the optimization and subject to the individual bond returns. This is an integrated approach that allows for both portfolio selection and allocation, or stated more succinctly a *bottom-up approach* to portfolio allocation. Note that this approach is not a mainstream approach to portfolio allocation because more traditional techniques follow a *top-down approach* in which the portfolio allocation optimization precedes the portfolio selection optimization.

The portfolio convexity of 1.12 is less than the convexity of the benchmark. This means that the portfolio's value would be less sensitive to overall interest rate changes than the benchmark. The portfolio spread is 405 bps higher than the spread of the benchmark. This means that despite duration and maturity neutrality, the portfolio has both higher interest-rate and spread risks compared to the benchmark. The interest-rate and spread risks depend on the active country weights or the extent to which a portfolio's credit ratings deviate from the credit ratings of the benchmark.

The outperformance in such quantitative bond portfolios are driven by the country bets. Recall that the most severe hard currency emerging market risks are associated with country risks. From a practitioner's perspective, the portfolio has higher expected return than the benchmark, but also exhibits higher risks as measured by the larger spread and lower convexity.

The emerging market bond portfolio comprises 49 bonds, whereas the benchmark has roughly 700 bonds. Figure 7.2 shows the optimization results for the emerging market bond portfolio.

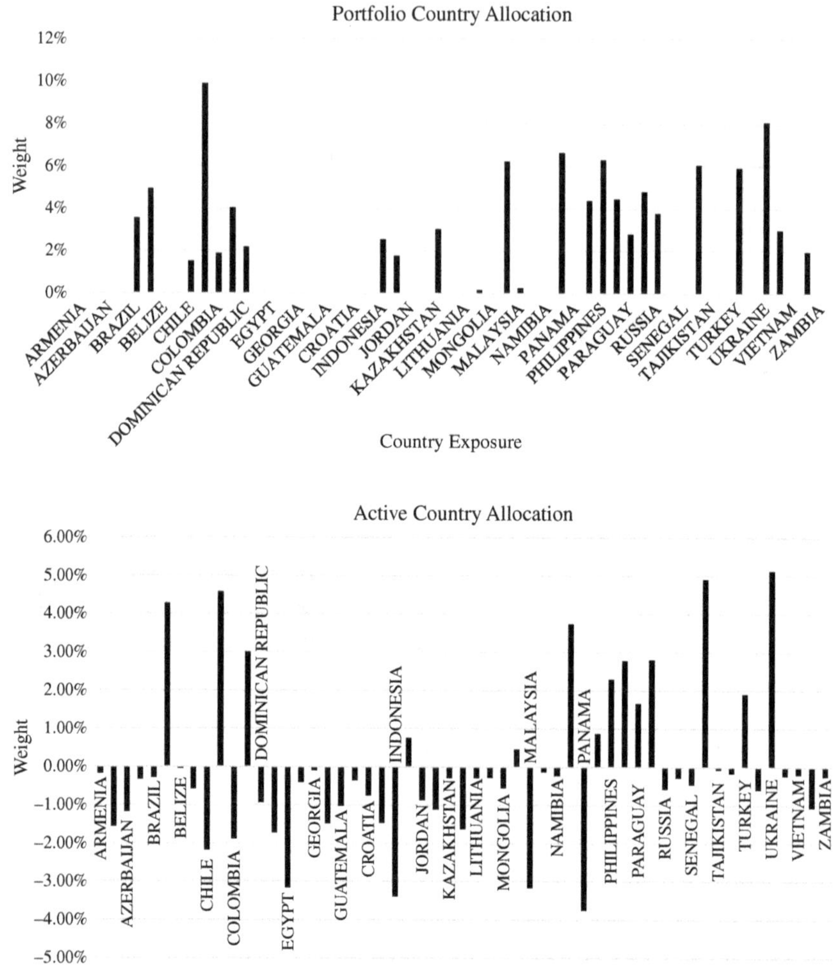

Figure 7.2: Optimization: Emerging Market Hard Currency Bond Portfolio

The difference between the portfolio weights and the benchmark weights shows the active risk of a portfolio. The risk might be from the deviation of country, currency, maturity, credit rating, or sector weights among others. Each risk must be analyzed in its own right. For example, the active credit risk and country risk are different and their respective active deviations might require specific risk models to understand and monitor these risks. Credit spread models for default risks and macroeconomic models for interest rates are examples of such models.

Bond selection optimization has the advantage that the final weights are used to determine the notional size of the individual bonds given the portfolio's total assets. Note that these amounts are adjusted for liquidity constraints such as the outstanding notional amount of a specific bond, the bid-ask spreads, bond volatility, and the maximum deviation from the benchmark weights, among others. We explain the calculation of notional amounts and bond exposure in the next chapter.

We close this chapter by noting that just as in the case of portfolio allocation, selection at the security level also entails model misspecification risks. As such, robust optimization techniques such as those described in the previous chapter may be helpful in minimizing the effects of parameter misestimation during the portfolio construction process.

7.3 Key Takeaways

- The MVO technique is not ideal for allocating single bonds. The reason is that the variance–covariance matrix is difficult to obtain from bond price data, and bond price dynamics do not reflect bond market risk. More precisely, bond prices are not directly observed like equity prices but are quoted prices.
- Alternative optimization techniques are necessary for capturing the risk and return of bond portfolios that contain a large number of bonds. Such portfolios are computed using benchmark indexes that comprise several hundred bonds. An appropriate technique should also be capable of incorporating a large number of constraints and reflect the investment universe represented by the benchmark.
- It is important to add relevant variables that capture and represent the most critical drivers of global bond portfolio risk and return. These risks can be captured in a constraint matrix which can include durations, spreads, convexities, currencies, sector, countries, and asset classes (covered bond, government bond, financial, corporates, high-yield bonds, etc.), in addition to the yield curve factor exposures,

country of issuance, country of risk, maturity buckets and other relevant risk exposures.

- Modeling buying and selling orders increases the computational challenge of optimization. It is often much easier to model portfolios without buy and sell transactions in order to reduce the complexity of bond selection.

References

Cerniglia, J. A. and F. J. Fabozzi. 2022. "A Practitioner Perspective on Trading and the Implementation of Investment Strategies". *Journal of Portfolio Management* 48(6): 30–44.

Konstantinov, G. S. 2014. "Active Currency Management of International Bond Portfolios". *Financial Markets and Portfolio Management* 28(1): 63–94.

Konstantinov, G. S. 2022. "Emerging Market Bonds: Expected Returns and Currencies Impact". *Journal of Portfolio Management* 48(8): 139–158.

Konstantinov, G. S. and F. J. Fabozzi. 2021. "International Bond Portfolio Management". Chapter 57 in F. J. Fabozzi (ed.), *The Handbook of Fixed Income Securities.* 9th Edition. New York: McGraw Hill.

Nucera, F. and G. Valente. 2013. "Carry Trades and the Performance of Currency Hedge Funds". *Journal of International Money and Finance* 33: 407–425.

Thornton, D. L. and G. Valente. 2012. "Out-of-Sample Predictions of Bond Excess Returns with Forward Rates: An Asset-Allocation Perspective". *Review of Financial Studies* 25: 3141–3168.

Walter, U. and T. Zimmerer. 2000. "Ansätze zum Management europäischer Renten-Spezialfonds". Chapter in Kleeberg, J. M. and C. Schlenger (ed.), *Handbuch Spezialfonds: Ein praktischer Leitfaden für institutionelle Anleger und Kapitalgesellschaften*. Uhlenbruch Verlag, pp. 541–568.

Zimmerer, T. 2003. "Der Roll Down im Bondmanagement: Theoretisches Phänomen und praktische Implementierung". *Finanz Betrieb* 4: 234–252.

Chapter 8

Bond Trading, Portfolio Rebalancing, and Electronic Exchanges

The decision pertaining to when and how to trade in the bond market is essential for bond portfolios. After executing the initial trades in a portfolio allocation, a portfolio manager may need to periodically modify their portfolio holdings and adjust their exposure to accommodate changes in the market environment. This activity is referred to as *portfolio rebalancing*. Trading and rebalancing are natural processes associated with portfolio management as risk and returns change over time and new allocations are desired. Over time, developments in bond markets and technological progress have improved the velocity and efficiency of trading. However, the basic mechanics of how managers trade remain essentially the same. This chapter explains how rebalancing and trading work depending on portfolio management style — discretionary or systematic.

8.1 Economic Principles for Trading in Global Bond Portfolios

Market risk premiums are time varying, and different economic regimes and market situations require different portfolio allocations. In other words, time-varying risk premiums require portfolio rebalancing because the portfolio allocation might not properly capture market premiums at a given time. Moreover, with the passage of time, a given portfolio allocation changes with market fluctuations and the portfolio's exposures naturally drift from their target allocations.

Portfolio rebalancing might be required to reinvest maturing or called bonds, because of new inflows, allocation adjustments, regulatory issues, or a client's needs for liquidity. That said, the question "when do bond managers trade?" is to some extent misleading as it might refer to market timing, capital requirements, idiosyncratic risks, and many other drivers of trading activity.

Portfolio rebalancing is often determined by the investment process. For example, a buy-and-hold portfolio that invests in specific bonds might hold them until they mature. Such a portfolio does not call for rebalancing because it does not actively trade. In the same vein, a quantitative strategy using short-term market signals might require frequent rebalancing. In this respect, a portfolio manager's style and investment process determines the frequency and complexity of their bond trading. The two major style alternatives that impact trading are *discretionary* and *systematic* trading.

8.1.1 *Discretionary trading*

Discretionary trades are trades executed on an individual basis. Discretionary trades can be motivated by active portfolio decisions, portfolio redemptions, capital withdrawal, or risk management considerations. These trades are often associated with the fundamental approach to investing, relying on the individual judgment of the portfolio manager or a portfolio management team, without an overreliance on quantitative models. While discretionary managers may utilize quantitative models, their portfolio decisions are primarily based on their "real-time" qualitative judgments, which are in turn informed by their experience and interpretation of the evidence at the time an investment decision is made.

In the case of discretionary investing, trading is often focused on relative value analysis, rich/cheap valuation, new issues placed on the primary market, portfolio adjustments involving high conviction trades based on news flows, changes in single bond picking fundamentals, corporate events, and downgrading or upgrading of ratings, among others. The trading frequency of discretionary bond portfolios is not uniform. A portfolio managed in a discretionary manner might implement bets sporadically as an immediate consequence of information flow arriving from the markets. For example, in the case of an ad hoc increase in interest rates in a country, a portfolio manager might sell long-term bonds and buy short-term bonds. This exposure seeks to gain from movement in the local currency, which based on the carry is expected to appreciate. The reduction of the bond exposure is based on the negative impact that an interest rate increase has on long-term bonds. Alternatively, the portfolio manager might sell their entire bond exposure in a given country and sell forward contracts in the expectation that the country's currency appreciates against the U.S. dollar. Again, the ultimate trading decision may be based on a combination of qualitative and quantitative analysis.

8.1.2 *Systematic trading*

Systematic trades are generally automated and may be triggered by various market signals. Examples for such events might be index rebalancing associated with index exclusion or inclusion of countries, currencies, and individual securities due to downgrades, defaults, or illiquidity.

Systematic trading strategies are often executed via basket trades. This is due to the large number of individual instruments usually involved in rebalancing or otherwise adjusting (e.g., factor tilting) a portfolio. Within a quantitative investment process, the duration, maturity allocation, sector and asset class exposure, and other risk–return metrics are all considered in the process of rebalancing; thus, basket trades add to the efficiency of the latter process.

We next discuss the determinants of bond pricing and liquidity, which are of course important to both discretionary and quantitative asset managers.

8.2 Determinants of Bond Prices and Liquidity

The primary determinants of bond prices are interest rates, coupons, spreads, liquidity, and foreign exchange. Understanding the role of each of these variables is crucial to successfully trading global bond portfolios.

The price of a bond $P(t, q)$ at time t depends on the notional amount q. The underlying spot curve and additional factors can be expressed as

$$P(t, q) = T(t, \mathrm{CF}, s_t + \mathrm{OAS}_t + l_t + e_t) \tag{8.1}$$

where s is the underlying spot rate curve, OAS_t is the option-adjusted spread at time t, CF is the bond's cash flow, l_t is a measure of price liquidity, and e_t is the residual term.

The observed bond price $P(t, q)$ at time t from equation (8.1) is a function of the (local currency) spot rate curve s used to discount the coupons. We add to the underlying spot curve risk premiums for the option-adjusted spread (OAS) as compensation for credit risk, the liquidity premium (l) (the degree of difficulty to buy or sell a bond), and other residual factors e. Note that the foreign exchange (FX) rate here is excluded as the spot curve is quoted in local currency terms. The FX rate affects the price, but the effect is purposely excluded here.

A large OAS or widening spread is an indication of higher risk and vice versa. It is important to note that a fair value model based on a sector-specific spot curve is commonly used to estimate the OAS. This is done by minimizing the squared errors of the difference between the estimated and observed bond prices; however, the true or real price might diverge from the estimated fair value due to liquidity risk and/or other factors. The liquidity premium also affects the bond price via spreads (see, for example, Ericsson and Renault, 2006). Empirical research conducted by Jankowitsch *et al.* (2006) on EMU government bonds suggested that bond yields also react to liquidity and yields change according to changing bond liquidity. Given the importance of liquidity risk in all aspects of bond trading, we provide a detailed treatment of it in the following section.

8.2.1 *Bond liquidity*

There are several factors that have a major impact on bond liquidity. The most important is the strong relationship between notional amounts and bond prices. Bond liquidity is generally measured by the bid-ask spreads of fixed income instruments. The most important determinants of liquidity for individual securities are the notional amount of the bond traded and the bond's country of issue and sector. The high-yield market has significantly different liquidity than that of developed market sovereign bonds. Similarly, emerging market bonds have much less liquidity than U.S. Treasury bonds.

A bond market's sector liquidity is the sum of the specific single liquidity metrics of the bonds within the sector. For example, a specific sector bond index's liquidity would be the weighted sum of its individual bond liquidities. However, index liquidity is only representative for the bonds with the same notional amounts included in the index. A bond portfolio with different notional amounts than the index would have different liquidity compared to the index because the notional amounts of the bonds determine both bond prices and liquidity metrics. Consequently, bond market liquidity is a highly specific metric that applies to a market portfolio whose capitalization is a function of the notional amounts of its individual bonds.

Tradable securities and new issues generally have different liquidity profiles. In general, newly issued bonds by the same issuer enjoy higher tradability and liquidity than older bonds. To mitigate the impact of liquidity and tradability for market indexes that represent market segments like sectors, countries, or industries, some index providers apply certain criteria for index inclusion, such as requiring a minimum of the outstanding amount of the bond and minimum issue size. When considering bond sector liquidity — say, emerging markets, corporate bonds, or high-yield markets — it is convenient to analyze the whole market with all traded notional amounts. A tradable index with the index constituents' notional amounts is only an approximate data source as the bonds are not really traded. There are several factors that impact portfolio trading and specifically the choice of trading method, functionality, and success:

- bid-ask spreads
- portfolio size
- portfolio allocation
- persistent illiquidity in certain bond markets (e.g., emerging market high-yield bonds, or private placements in high-yield bonds and loans)
- market volatility (equity, interest rate, and bond market specific volatility)
- transaction costs

These challenges affect the bond manager's activities to a larger extent when markets change significantly (e.g., during regime shifts) and bond portfolio complexity increases. These factors are closely related and interact with each other.

8.2.2 *Liquidity and portfolio management*

The determinants of liquidity and its impact on bond portfolios depend on all the factors mentioned in the previous section.[1] Here, we focus on the most relevant issues to global bond portfolio management.

Financial analysis that focuses on liquidity and pricing is called financial market microstructure analysis. The transactions made between buyers and sellers are the main focus of inquiry. Market microstructure refers to features of the market such as market depth, pricing, trading, and the interactions among market players.

Several studies attempted to explain bond market liquidity and its determinants. The research on bond market liquidity has its foundation in equity market research, most notably motivated by the research on equity market liquidity conducted by Pastor and Stambaugh (2003) and Sadka (2006), who used regression models to estimate liquidity on a monthly basis. However, bond markets have some unique features relative to other markets. In general, we observe that low interest-rate environments are supportive for new issuance, which is supportive of more liquid bond markets. Further we note that on-the-run bonds are more liquid relative to their off-the-run counterparts.

8.2.2.1 *Bid-ask spreads*

Bid-ask spreads represent the difference between the highest price that a buyer is willing to pay for a security and the lowest price that a seller is willing to accept. Bid-ask spreads are often considered a liquidity proxy. However, the bid-ask spread is only a reliable liquidity indicator for a bond trade only after the trade is made. This is due to the fact that bond trading depends on information regarding size and not merely on pricing data. The intuition behind using bid-ask spreads as a liquidity indicator is that lower liquidity drives bond yields higher and higher liquidity means lower bond yields (see Jankowitsch *et al.*, 2006). Often, bid yields and ask yields differ substantially, indicating that the bond is relatively illiquid. This is one of the reasons that trading such bonds is challenging, as market depth and bid/ask prices are more sensitive to different notional amounts.

[1] Fabozzi and Fabozzi (2021) provide a comprehensive overview on bond liquidity and a detailed discussion of liquidity analytics.

The bid-ask spread of a single bond at time t is

$$\text{Bid} - \text{Ask Spread}_t = \ln(P_t^{\text{ask}}) - \ln(P_t^{\text{bid}}) \tag{8.2}$$

where P_t^{ask} is the bond ask price at time t and P_t^{bid} is the bond bid price at time t.

The bid-ask spread of a bond in (8.2) is computed as a logarithmic return of the ask and bid price of the bond at time t. Historical prices are usually available from data providers (e.g., Bloomberg) and used for simple calculations of bond market spreads and liquidity. Several studies have extensively investigated bid-ask spreads and liquidity risk inherent in bond prices and pointed out the relationship between bond liquidity and bond bid-ask spreads. However, it seems that with only one exception, these studies do not investigate the impact of the notional size of the bonds traded.[2] A notable exception is the study conducted on corporate high-yield bonds by Alexander *et al.* (2000), who investigated trading volumes in the bond pricing mechanism. As we shall see, order placement in bond markets is very different from placing orders in equity markets as notional sizes determine bond prices, which are not observable *ex ante* compared to equity market prices. Not only does fixed income behave differently from equities, where prices are directly observable, but the metrics applied to analyzing trading activities, as well as the process and protocols for executing trades, are also different for bonds. The observed pricing data and price returns for bonds are not a clear indication of liquidity and market depth. The continued development of the capabilities of electronic exchanges and the application of algorithms from financial data science and big data today provide us with the ability to gain much broader and deeper information on bond market microstructure.

Financial market microstructure analysis requires new and sophisticated tools to allow for the gathering of appropriate information that can serve as a reliable basis for the comprehensive investigation of liquidity, spreads, and other trading variables (e.g., bond notional sizes traded and their corresponding prices) (See Roth, 2018). The analysis of bond spreads should arguably be focused on high-frequency data, as thousands

---

[2]See Roll (1984), Amihud (2002), Lou and Sadka (2011), Ben Slimane and de Jong (2017), Helwege *et al.* (2014), and Schestag *et al.* (2016).

of bond market transactions occur within the span of minutes. Thanks to the development of financial data science, there exist analytical tools that allow data analysis using notional sizes, pricing, and time.

Bid-ask spreads in the secondary markets are affected by supply and demand. Demand for bonds from institutional investors often drives the bid-ask spreads in one direction. Central banks also have an outsized impact on bond market liquidity given their standard and non-standard (e.g., quantitative easing) operations. Because the direction of bid-ask spreads in large part depends on the volume of the transactions, it is not surprising that institutions and central banks have an outsized influence on them.

8.2.2.2 *Portfolio size*

Portfolio size directly impacts bid-ask spreads and bond market liquidity. There are two important issues to consider with regard to portfolio size. The first is the difference between concentrated and diversified portfolios. Concentrated portfolios have fewer portfolio holdings; thus, the bonds they buy and sell might directly impact portfolio size. Larger portfolios trade larger notional sizes on bonds. In this case, tradability and liquidity might become significant issues. Diversified portfolios comprise a larger number of securities. Larger portfolios usually trade larger amounts of bonds with small notional amounts. Trading a small number of bonds with large notional amounts might be a challenging task. This applies especially to emerging markets as developed markets experience less tradability and liquidity problems relative to emerging markets.

8.2.2.3 *Portfolio allocation*

In bond trading, portfolio allocation directly affects liquidity considerations. In general, including "exotic" asset classes such as emerging market bonds or CCC rated debt, for example, detracts from portfolio liquidity. If such assets comprise a significant portion of a portfolio, then the ability of a portfolio manager to effectively rebalance or otherwise adjust portfolio positioning without entailing significant transaction costs may be adversely impacted. This will especially be the case in challenging market environments when rates are rising or spreads are widening.

8.2.2.4 *Illiquidity in bond markets*

Often, global bond markets of small and emerging economies are considered attractive from a total return standpoint. One of the reasons these assets provide an attractive potential return is the relatively large risk premiums associated with such markets and their persistent illiquidity. That said, we note illiquidity might not be a major concern for small tradable sizes of, say, 200,000 notional amount for a local currency bond, but might be persistent for larger transactions in portfolios that require significant exposure in the market.

A practical way to mitigate these challenges is for broad global portfolios to trade large baskets of individual bonds and thus to obtain, for example, a 0.01% exposure in a smaller market. Such bond portfolios might be very well diversified with a large number of individual securities. In practice, global bond portfolios comprising more than 1,000 bonds are quite common.

The level of liquidity of any market is dynamic because there is a natural tendency for markets to adapt, to develop, and to change. Some markets deemed illiquid today may become more liquid over time as investor sentiment, regulations, and technology evolve in a way that contributes to the increased tradability of these markets. The development of emerging markets globally is a good example of such an evolution. Brazil, Russia, India, and China, collectively referred to as the BRIC countries, were relatively inaccessible to investors in the early 1990s but are now considered relatively "mainstream" investments that are accessible to a wide range of investors. These countries now comprise the core of most emerging market indices. Their increased attractiveness to investors was in large part driven by increased liquidity, lower settlement and transaction costs, and higher integration in the global bond market (primarily driven by index inclusion).

8.2.2.5 *The market cycle and volatility*

Market volatility directly affects bid-ask spreads. In a calm market environment, transactions are generally easily executed as buyers and sellers adjust their expectations quickly without much "friction". During financial market turmoil, however, liquidity dries up and investors begin to feel anxiety and fear as bid-ask spreads widen because sellers find it difficult to sell their bonds due to increasingly reluctant buyers. Selling pressure gets amplified in such periods, often resulting in a cascading and spiraling effect that further deteriorates market liquidity.

Usually, volatile market periods are favorable for "safe haven" bonds such as U.S. Treasuries. Counter-examples are emerging markets and high-yield bonds that usually decrease in value while their tradability deteriorates substantially. In such environments, widening bid-ask spreads become misleading for bond market pricing as the bid-ask spreads indicate only a tradable market in which bid and offer prices are "derived" from quoted prices. However, quoted prices are only indicative prices. In fact, valuation based on bid-ask spreads in the case of financial market stress becomes a less reliable indicator and source of information. As a result, portfolio turnover and rebalancing in times of strong market volatility are highly problematic, as desired allocations derived from portfolio optimization might depart significantly from realized allocations using actual bond prices.

8.2.2.6 *Transaction costs*

Bond markets also differ with respect to the transaction costs associated with different fixed-income sectors. For example, the transaction cost for buying and selling sovereign bonds in the G3 bond markets (U.S., Eurozone, and Japan) is completely different compared to less liquid emerging markets. For emerging markets, the transaction costs might exceed 10 bps even for the most liquid bonds. Even within emerging markets countries, some bond markets are associated with higher transaction costs compared to others. Note that "transaction cost" refers not only to the cost of trading securities but also to the settlement and other operational expenses that might arise. These costs can be substantial depending on the market, and their negative impact on a bond portfolio's performance may be significant, especially in times of heightened financial market volatility.

In comparison to the more uniform costs for hard currency bonds, the transaction costs for local currency bonds can diverge substantially. Trading hard currency bonds is in general more cost effective than trading local currency bonds. Trading hard currency debt is associated with lower costs and higher market liquidity. The primary reason for this is that fewer investors prefer local currency risk compared to hard currency risk.

8.3 Trading Approaches

There are three basic types of bond trades: request for quote, order placement, and new issues.

Request for quote (RFQ) is a convenient way for a bond manager to request bond prices from multiple dealers. Upon receipt of a request, the dealers can respond with price quotes on specific notional sizes. Execution occurs if an offer is hit or ask is lifted. If bonds are in local currencies, FX transactions can be executed prior to the bond trade or afterward. Because of the variability of bond prices due to differences in notional size, bonds are often traded first, and FX transactions placed afterward. However, if an FX transaction is prioritized, bid-ask spreads can help estimate the notional sizes and amounts in the local currency that needs to be traded.

Order placement comprising specific notional amounts is submitted to the market and is matched with the notional amounts traded by the market-makers. This is the most important trading mechanism for bond markets as prices are usually quoted but depend on the notional size of the orders. Bonds with less than investment-grade ratings are quoted, but order execution depends on the size.

As an example, consider the case where a US-based investor buys an Italian government bond and a German corporate bond with notional of 20 million and 10 million, at the price of 105 and 111, respectively. There are three options. The first option, which is the most inconvenient order execution for portfolio managers, is to require automatic conversion of the local currency amount in the basis currency. Automatic conversion of the exchange rate is the most unfavorable choice because the seller (bank or market-maker) usually converts the amount using a price close to the middle price (between the bid and ask price) for the FX spot transaction. The second option is for a bond manager to place FX orders separately and thus use electronic trading for FX spot transactions, which allow for narrow bid-ask spreads and low costs. The third option is for the bond manager to apply an overlay strategy for the foreign exchange exposure of their portfolio.

In general, the investment process determines the order sequence — which exposure is prioritized, the FX transaction or the bond order. In general, a discretionary manager responsible for both fixed-income and FX trading can apply different strategies on a tactical basis.

New issues (*auctions*) are primarily used in new issues or book-building. In the general case, the lead manager of the underwriting group of an issue supplies information (e.g., issue size, maturity, yield, spread, issuer rating, and specific covenants). Relative value analysis is essential for new issues. Often, the relevant industry, or peer yield curve, is used to evaluate the bond. Similar bonds issued by the same corporation are also referenced for pricing guidance. Properly pricing a bond requires a careful choice of the underlying sector, country, currency, and rating yield curves. The primary risks in bond pricing are the use of inappropriate yield curves and miscalculation of important metrics (e.g., spreads).

For example, suppose a U.S.-dollar-based global bond portfolio with assets under management of USD 400 million is investing in a euro-denominated corporate bond. The bond is a newly issued BBB+ rated, 9-year corporate bond, with an issue size of EUR 500 million. An order of 10 million is placed with the prime lead manager of the issue with a spread limit of +70 basis points above the relevant spot curve. Once this order and others are placed, they will be aggregated by the lead manager of the issue and an allocation is made after closing the deal. If the issue is in high demand (e.g., oversubscribed), the manager placing the order may be allocated less of the issue than initially placed. In our example, we also note that in addition to the notional bond amount received for the portfolio, an FX transaction is necessary — in this case, the portfolio has to sell U.S. dollars and buy euros to cover the proceeds from the new issue.

8.4 Electronic Trading

Electronic exchanges are modern platforms that allow immediate trading action and portfolio rebalancing and significantly lower trading costs and high execution velocity. In this section, we explain the development and the principles of electronic exchanges and how they enhance the functioning of the global bond market.

8.4.1 *Development of electronic exchanges*

Trading in fixed-income securities differs from trading in equities or other asset classes. One of the reasons is that notional amounts and prices are not disclosed and transparent to other market participants. Therefore, the quoted bid-ask spreads for fixed-income securities observed from data providers like Bloomberg and Thomson Reuters are only approximate indications of the actual liquidity of a specific bond or bond market. Depending on the sector and asset class, real bid-ask spreads may diverge significantly from quoted values. Given the difference between quoted and traded prices, one of the primary applications of the algorithms used in electronic trading is to facilitate the more efficient gathering of data so as to generate a much more reliable picture of bond market liquidity. The impact of greater efficiency due to electronic trading has perhaps been felt the most in the trading of corporate bonds. Corporate bonds are mostly executed in the over-the-counter market (OTC), but ever since the Global Financial Crisis (GFC) in 2008, a major liquidity event, corporate bonds have been more frequently traded through electronic exchanges.

One drawback in the recent development of electronic exchanges is that their data remain proprietary for large dealers and market-makers. This is because the brokerage firms and trading institutions invest a substantial amount in the development of trading algorithms, which gives these providers a competitive edge in the marketplace. Consequently, they are reluctant to share what they view as part of the return on their investment.

The rise of electronic trading has been driven by three factors, whose development accelerated after the GFC of 2008. According to the Committee on Global Financial System Fixed Income Market Liquidity (2016), there are three reasons for the growing need for liquidity in bond markets: supply and demand, market complexity, and structural change. We discuss these three drivers of liquidity, which have shaped markets and are responsible for the development of electronic exchanges.

8.4.1.1 *Supply and demand for bonds*

The change in the supply of and demand for liquidity is an important property of bond markets in the new millennium compared to the market environment several decades ago.[3] One of the important determinants has been the ever-growing demand for liquidity since the GFC. Today, we can observe an asymmetric market, with a high demand for liquidity driven by asset managers, investors, central banks, and corporations. Individual investors have also been more sensitive to liquidity since the GFC. This is one reason that U.S. Treasuries continue to enjoy strong demand as they are considered a safe haven during times of heightened financial market stress and uncertainty. Similarly, the U.S. dollar is (still) the world's reserve currency, whose demand peaks at times of financial market stress when market participants seek shelter in the form of liquidity, reliability, and reduced risk of default.

As a consequence of this liquidity supply-and-demand asymmetry in bond markets, investors need immediate, transparent, cost-efficient, and reliable order matching provided by electronic exchanges.

8.4.1.2 *Market complexity*

Market complexity is perhaps the most important driver for the rise of electronic exchanges. There are several components of market complexity: regulation, technology, and monetary policy.

Changing regulations have been strong drivers for the development of electronic exchanges. Driven by a growing need to prevent fraud and enable a much higher level of transparency, financial institutions and investors have faced the challenge of reshaping their market-making activities. This change has forced market participants to restructure their risk-taking behavior and has led to decreasing inventories of bonds. This was especially the case for investment banks and their proprietary trading desks, which traded bonds and took risk for the accounts of investment banks. As a consequence, market-makers and trading firms are now most comfortable engaging in transactions only if they can easily and quickly match and execute orders. However, in the case of large market volatility, reduced market-making activities can increase the risk in the markets. This has had an enormous effect on the availability of market liquidity when it is most needed.

Global monetary policy has been a further catalyst for the change in demand for liquidity that has resulted in the rise of electronic exchanges.

[3] See Konstantinov and Pojarliev (2021).

Specifically, low growth and slowing economies worldwide have caused more interventionist behavior on the part of central banks in the form of increased bond purchases. Note that central banks have much larger capacity and capital reserves to conduct bond purchases than traditional market participants. As a result, central banks are now considered *de facto* "liquidity providers of last resort" for the global economy and markets.

8.4.1.3 *Structural market change*

The asset management industry has witnessed remarkable growth in the use of exchange-traded funds (ETFs) for exposure to both investment-grade (IG) and high-yield (HY) bonds, which is a consequence of the development of electronic exchanges. While it is difficult to determine cause and effect — whether the development of the ETF market led to the development of electronic exchanges, or if the advent of electronic exchanges spurred the development of ETF products. Nevertheless, market and technological progress has had a positive impact on bond markets and improving liquidity.[4] Major brokerage houses like Citi, Société Générale, J.P. Morgan, and BNP Paribas run electronic exchanges.

According to reports from SIFMA Insights — the Electronic Trading Market Structure Primer (2019), the Markets Committee "Electronic Trading in Fixed Income Markets" and a report conducted by the Bank of International Settlements (2016), there was more than a twofold increase in the assets under management in ETFs between 2014 and 2019. As a consequence of all these factors, the asset management industry has moved to the rapid development of and movement to electronic platforms. This is a sign of structural market change that has significantly impacted global bond markets.

At first glance, these three determinants seem directly related to the drivers of bond market liquidity, but technology has had a very specific influence. In fact, technology has been used to lower the costs of portfolio management and trading. Asset managers face rising pressure with financing as global yields have declined and it is increasingly difficult to pass costs on to investors. In other words, asset management

[4]See Hanif and Smith (2012) for a comprehensive analysis of the rise of algorithmic, electronic, and automated trading platforms. See Cohen *et al.* (2022) for more details on the growth of ETFs and their relationship to fixed-income markets.

expenses are difficult to cover as bond yields decline. This development also parallels the rise of new products and market segments.

Additional financial market evolution has had an enormous effect on electronic exchanges. The rise in electronic trading has significantly contributed to the growth of *robo-advisors*. Robo-advisors provide direct business-to-business (B2B) and business-to-clients (B2C) services. As a consequence, the lack of middle counterparties provides a very cost-effective way to execute trades, which increases bond liquidity. Large asset management firms also provide B2B and B2C solutions, resulting in low bid-ask spreads and better liquidity.

8.4.2 *Trading platforms*

Nicholson (2012) explains the development and rise of trading platforms. Trading platforms differ by the number of participants and specific structure. *Exchanges* are anonymous trading platforms in which buyers and sellers directly match trades. Exchanges are thus liquidity providers. Liquidity is directly provided by the trading parties — for example, two portfolio managers trading baskets for their portfolios: one portfolio manager that is selling bonds and another who is buying these bonds.

The factors that drive liquidity that we highlighted in the previous section and the drivers of the evolution of electronic exchanges have given birth to several cutting-edge platforms. According to Nicholson (2012), electronic exchanges originated with application program interfaces (APIs), which replaced the old graphical user interfaces (GUIs). The common properties of electronic exchange platforms are algorithm-based, cloud-supported, and data-driven.

In all of the above platform types, accurate and efficient bond pricing is the result of the application of ultra-fast algorithms, large data storage facilities, and strict best execution policies. In the following, we list some well-known platforms that specialize in fixed income and FX trading[5]:

- Tradeweb — a broad platform for multiple bond asset classes
- TruMid — a fixed-income specialist platform that is driven by machine learning

---

[5] See Konstantinov and Pojarliev (2021).

- MarketAxess — the largest platform for corporate bonds
- Liquidnet — an open-source artificial intelligence platform
- Flextrade — an all-in order management and execution system
- Algomi — a fixed-income market aggregation and market surveillance tool
- Bloomberg — a well-known comprehensive trading and database platform

The algorithms employed in trading platforms and by investment banks with large trading desks are vast. Two algorithms are worth highlighting as several platforms and investment banks were the originators of them.[6]

A *matrix algorithm* uses methods from financial data science to detect commonalities between recently traded bonds with similar characteristics (e.g., maturity, rating, size, and liquidity), and thus derives a comparable price. The mathematical method applied behind this system is called "eigenvector centrality". The higher the centrality score, the greater the liquidity of the bond. The advantage in using this algorithm is that it provides pricing for less liquid bonds as well as liquid issues. In technical terms, the centrality of less liquid bonds is lower than more liquid bonds. A disadvantage of the matrix algorithm is that it tends to "data snoop".

An *evaluated pricing algorithm* is based on quantitative analysis and human judgment and is used to evaluate new issues, current pricing, and broker/dealer quotes. The main objective of this algorithm is to apply utility functions that model trader behavior, order books, and transactions. Such utility functions are the domain of quantitative behavioral finance and aim at explaining how market prices result from notional amounts exchanged in real financial markets. A model that applies to such analysis is the discrete choice model developed by McFadden (2001).[7]

[6] *Trumid* is an example of a high-tech platform whose pricing is based on two different algorithms https://www.trumid.com/files/FVMP-Whitepaper-10-20-17.pdf; https://www.liquidnet.com; https://www.algomi.com; https://www.flextrade.com; https://www.content.marketaxess.com; https://www.tradeweb.com.

[7] Also see Train (2003), Loistl *et al.* (2004), Prix *et al.* (2007), and Loistl and Konstantinov (2020).

8.4.3 *Bond trading and basket trades*

One way to govern the informational opacity of the bond trading process is by applying what is called *Bid Wanted in Competition* (BWIC). This procedure works by using a vector comprising the bonds to be traded with their corresponding notional sizes (e.g., selling 2 million of a bond in USD and buying 5 million of a bond denominated in EUR). Upon agreement, the basket is executed within a specific, reasonable time. Achieving the ideal of selling at the highest possible prices and buying at the lowest prices is generally not possible. The individual bond prices in a basket will deviate from a median price of the portfolio trade. In other words, the median price of a portfolio basket is usually better than the individual bond prices. This is especially the case for emerging market bonds, where pricing and liquidity have improved substantially since the GFC thanks to the rising appetite for emerging market debt and the relative ease in trading it due to the development of electronic platforms.

Traditional bond order execution is limited to discretionary managers and a small number of trades, is cost intensive, and time consuming. There are clear advantages to electronic trading in terms of gains in pricing accuracy and speed. We close this section by summarizing the most prominent ones.

- Basket trades comprising multiple bonds eliminate inefficiencies and increase transparency by reducing costs, the time to implement new allocations, and the rebalancing of portfolios due to their reliance on ETFs and passive product index matching.
- Electronic exchanges reduce operational issues related to back and middle offices in asset management firms.
- Electronic exchanges allow optimized beta hedging and factor models for risk management and liquidity.
- Electronic platforms contribute to volatility reduction in a portfolio, compared to single bond trades as bond price fluctuations are lower. This is because trading individual bonds generally causes more portfolio volatility than electronically driven portfolio basket trades comprising ETFs.

8.4.4 *Foreign exchange trading and basket trades*

The trade execution in foreign exchange markets has become increasingly automated as well, moving away from traditional "voice" execution to electronic trading. The main drivers are the same as for the bond market — cost saving and lower transaction costs. The Bank for International Settlement 2019 Triennial Survey shows that the share of FX trading executed electronically is currently close to 60%. The spot foreign exchange market is perhaps the most relevant for global bond portfolios, whose share of all transactions remains roughly 75%. Note that more than 90% of the total amount of directional trading in the spot FX market is in the US dollar, euro, and the Japanese yen.

Somewhat unsurprisingly, inter-dealer markets have experienced a decline, which is in line with the growth of electronic exchanges. Transaction costs are among the most important costs in portfolio management. Thus, minimizing such costs can be challenging in portfolios that must be rebalanced frequently. Although transaction costs in foreign exchange markets are far lower than in bond markets, the globalization of markets and the desire to lower costs have been among the main drivers for direct settlement of transactions and the reduction of the role of intermediaries. This decline in electronic inter-dealer trading is driven principally by "internalization", whereby dealers try to match demand for risky currency investments to the supply of risky foreign exchange capital flows as discussed in Chapter 3.

Important evidence reported by the Bank of International Settlement in its 2019 Triennial Survey is that electronic trading is not progressing uniformly across all instruments and market segments. For example, inter-dealer trading of FX swaps — the other major instrument used in global bond portfolios to manage exposure in currency markets — has remained heavily voice reliant. The reasons for voice retaining a higher share in FX swaps are straightforward. First, swap trades involve particularly large notional amounts and, second, FX swaps are more difficult to price because balance sheet considerations play a larger role.

8.5 Portfolio Rebalancing

In a portfolio context, bond trading is intimately connected to portfolio rebalancing. Quantitatively managed portfolios should generally be rebalanced in a conventional way. Masters (2003) discussed several ways of evaluating the cost-effectiveness of rebalancing portfolios without harming portfolio allocation and strategic targets. Further research by Lee and Liu (2021) showed that the constant information flow in the markets impacts portfolio allocation and rebalancing needs. They find that often the predefined holding period for an estimated allocation (e.g., monthly) is not adequate to reflect the changing market landscape and conditions. Brown (2018) further argued that fixed holding periods are most harmful for portfolios. Expected and realized returns might deviate substantially when rebalancing is forced in this manner.

To provide a more detailed picture of the process of rebalancing global bond portfolios, it is useful to consider the activity of bond selection and compare the desired versus the realized allocations. The treatment of cash deserves special attention. Adequate cash in a portfolio is essential if the portfolio manager wants to increase invested capital, or to decrease the funds allocated. To illustrate this point, consider a simple example. Suppose a 500 million portfolio is 90% invested in global bonds and 10% in cash. This means that 450 million is invested in individual securities. If the portfolio manager decides to increase investments simultaneously while rebalancing the portfolio by 5%, then the portfolio's rebalancing needs should be covered with cash. However, given a quantitative investment process, the portfolio baskets comprising old and new allocations and the selection portfolio should be matched to the new investment exposure of 475 million.

However, modern front-office management tools like the ones provided by Aladdin, FactSet, and Bloomberg, among others, offer complete monitoring, trading, management, and attribution services, where portfolio managers can track the trading and attribution effects of their portfolios in real time.

We show the steps involved in portfolio rebalancing in Figure 8.1. We highlight several important aspects of the portfolio rebalancing process. We discuss the important aspects of each step in turn.

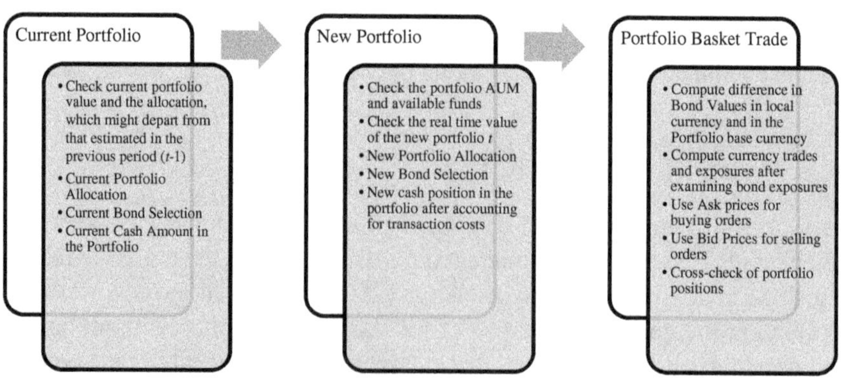

Figure 8.1: Steps in Portfolio Rebalancing

Note: Created by the authors.

8.5.1.1 *Current portfolio*

The current portfolio must be evaluated using the current prices and notional amounts because the current allocation might have departed from that estimated in the previous rebalancing. Suppose, for example, that a bond portfolio is rebalanced monthly. Portfolio allocation at the beginning of the month (in the case of monthly rebalancing) will experience market fluctuations and the portfolio allocation and bond price changes (market risk) might result in a different portfolio prior to the next rebalancing.

Similarly, the portfolio's cash position changes during the course of time due to portfolio redemptions, currency movements, portfolio transactions, and regular fees that might occur. In addition, some bonds might mature during the holding period (say 30 days for monthly rebalancing). The maturing of a bond increases the cash holdings in the respective currency. For example, a South African bond that matures during the holding period increases the South African rand cash ledger. The price and market risk of bonds with embedded options might impact the cash ledgers as well. Exercising a call option embedded in a bond would mean that the bond is paid off by the issuer before it matures. In this case, the redemptions increase the cash in a portfolio. In the case of a concentrated bond portfolio, such portfolio exposure might be large — say 5% in a single bond. As a consequence, the cash increase might be higher compared to a diversified bond portfolio where the largest individual bond weights do not exceed 1%. In the same manner, severe market fluctuations might cause the portfolio weight of, say, the South African rand-denominated bonds to decrease in value causing their allocation to be different from the allocation at the beginning of the month.

8.5.1.2 *Portfolio trading and rebalancing*

Estimating the current portfolio is entirely associated with estimating the current exposure of bonds required according to the portfolio weights computed in the portfolio allocation and selection process, often implemented using some type of optimization. Determining the value of the current portfolio and the desired portfolio guarantees that the changes in cash and foreign exchange will be reflected properly. This is even more important if the rebalancing not only changes a substantial part of the portfolio but also if the portfolio invested capital changes from, say, USD

400 million to USD 450 million. A critical part of the entire procedure is to compute the exposure that goes into the basket trade using appropriate prices — bid for selling securities and ask for buying them. This also guarantees the correct estimation of foreign exchange volume that needs to be reallocated.

Satchell and Scherer (2010) showed that the portfolio weights estimated in a mean–variance framework are only dependent on prices. That is, notional amounts are irrelevant. Unfortunately, this is not true for bond portfolios. We provide an example that shows how bond pricing and sizing influence the determination of portfolio weights. To begin, we assume that the following expression captures the relationship between portfolio volume, bond (ask) price, and portfolio weight:

$$q_i = \frac{\text{Portfolio Exposure}_{\text{Base Currency}}}{P_i^{\text{ASK}}} = \frac{V_{\text{PF}} * w_i}{P_i^{\text{ASK}}} \tag{8.3}$$

where q_i is the notional amount of a bond in a portfolio, V_{PF} is the portfolio volume (or portfolio exposure), w_i is the portfolio weight of the specific bond, and P_i^{ASK} is the bond ask price in percent that is required to estimate the bond notional amount that corresponds to the portfolio weight w_i.

Now, let us assume we have a USD 300 million emerging market bond portfolio. We have the portfolio weights derived from an optimization and have the current bid and ask price indications. To size a particular bond, a BRAZIL 5 5/8 02/21/47 bond, for example, we apply equation (8.3), multiply the portfolio size of 300 million with the bond weight of 1.3%, and divide the product by the bond ask price of 96.09%.The correct notional amount would be 4,058,906; however, this notional amount is usually not tradable as the tradable notional size for bonds is expressed as 100, 1,000, or 10,000. Therefore, we round the size to 4,100,000 (or to 4,000,000). We estimate the tradable notional sizes for the other bonds in a similar way.

Using equation (8.2), we can calculate the bid-ask spread and by multiplying it by the notional size, we can estimate the dollar amount of market depth. Let's consider an illustrative example. Assume, that the total dollar amount of a bond we want to trade is roughly USD 99,000. If we take the ratio of the market dollar debt to the total portfolio size, we derive the cost of our trade which is 3 basis points (i.e., (99,000/300,000,000) ×10,000 = 3 bps). Note that the transaction cost of 3 bps is price indicated based on the quoted prices. The reason for the differences between estimations and tradable sizes and costs lies in the notional amount that determines the bond prices.

8.5.1.3 *Portfolio trading and rebalancing with foreign exchange*

In the previous example, we showed notional estimation with no currency risk. To derive the impact of currency on portfolio size, notional amounts, and trading, we extend our original example. Suppose now that we have an emerging market bond portfolio with EUR 300 million. To show the difference that currency exposure makes to a global bond portfolio, we use an extension of equation (8.3) provided by Konstantinov and Pojarliev (2021) given by the following:

$$q_i = \frac{\text{Portfolio Exposure}_{\text{Base Currency}}}{P_i^{\text{ASK}}} = \frac{V_{\text{PF}} \times w_i \times fx_{qx/\text{BC}}}{P_i^{\text{ASK}}} \qquad (8.4)$$

where $fx_{qx/\text{BC}}$ is the currency exchange rate expressed as a currency pair of the counter currency (local) versus the base or numeraire currency of the portfolio, and the other variables are as defined earlier.

To correctly estimate portfolio exposure in a currency pair, the choice of the currency pair (numeraire/counter currency) must reflect the base currency of the portfolio. In other words, the first currency of a currency pair is the counter currency and the second is the numeraire or base currency. The following example shows the importance of the choice of the numeraire. Suppose EUR/USD = 1.1192, which means that the US dollar price of 1 euro is 1.1192.[8] Using equation (8.4), we see that the notional amounts are different.

Again, for our BRAZIL 5 5/8 02/21/47 bond, we assume a 300 million portfolio, multiplied by the bond weight of 1.3%. Then, we again divide the product by the ask price of the bond (96.09%). However, to compute the notional amount that corresponds to 1.3% in the portfolio, we divide the amount by the EUR-USD exchange rate of 1.1193, which is the

[8] Similarly, we can say that the EUR/USD is the U.S. dollar per euro, which is the American convention and USD-EUR is the European convention which refers to the EUR units expressed in euro per U.S. dollar. The Japanese yen price of 1 U.S. dollar is usually quoted in the foreign exchange market as USD/JPY = 115.

foreign exchange ask price we need to buy US dollars in the portfolio. The notional amount of that bond is now 4,500,000. Note that the bid-ask notional weighted spread of USD 25,386 is higher for the 4.5 million of the bond compared to the previous example using a bond with 4,100,000 notional amount. The total bid-ask spread in EUR is not 22,680. Because the EUR/USD is the most liquid currency pair characterized by a very narrow bid-ask spread, the FX market depth impact on the trade is very low.

It is worth discussing the impact of currency appreciation or depreciation in our example. In general, portfolio exposure in the numeraire of a currency pair (in this case the euro) is considered neutral. However, the bonds in the preceding example are in US dollars. Portfolio exposure in US-dollar-denominated bonds is long and an appreciation of the US dollar against the euro would be a gain for the portfolio. Conversely, a depreciation of the US dollar against the euro would be a loss for the portfolio. The reason is that because of the US dollar depreciation against the euro, the US-dollar-denominated bonds would decrease in value. Following the above intuition, for a EUR-based portfolio, the increase of the EUR-USD from 1.1192 to, say, 1.20 (in this case, a depreciation of the US dollar, or EUR appreciation) would be a loss for the US-dollar-denominated bonds in the portfolio.

Pojarliev and Levich (2012) and Taleb (1997) demonstrated that although the prices are inverse (USD/EUR = 1/(EUR/USD)), the profit or loss would diverge.[9] Again, some of the inverse pricings are not traded, but portfolios cannot translate their profit or loss in foreign exchange exposure without also having exposure to one of the currency pairs in their portfolios. Summarizing, based on the EUR-USD exchange rate of 1.1193, the portfolio denominated in the euro must invest more in the US-dollar-denominated bonds in order to achieve the estimated weights.

8.5.1.4 *Portfolio trade basket*

The portfolio trade basket comprises all bonds that must be traded — both sold and bought — in order to achieve the new portfolio allocation.

---

[9]The pricing is not affected by inversion. However, we show in Chapter 9 using binomial trees that the different pricing notations diverge as expectations are made using volatility and the passage of time. This issue is discussed in Taleb (1997).

Mathematically, this is a vector of notional amounts with a negative (selling) and positive (buying) sign that the bond manager trades. In Chapter 7, the vector of portfolio trades might be computed within an optimization problem. The important dimension of basket trading is to determine how currency and notional amounts impact the portfolio holdings and allocation when some bonds must be sold while others are purchased. To show this, we extend our example from the previous section. In the example, we make use of the information that is based on Table 8.1.

Suppose that for our EUR 300 million emerging market bond portfolio from the previous section we are selling three bonds and buying two bonds. We show the buys and sells in Table 8.1 on the far right of the table. Selling the notional amounts of the three bonds is known in advance as they represent portfolio holdings. When selling them, bid prices are used. Since the bonds are in US dollars, the portfolio manager sells the respective sizes using the bid prices for both bonds and currency. As a result, the portfolio receives a total of USD 10,332,524, which corresponds to EUR 9,232, 062. Note that converting the decimal amounts into suitable trading sizes is essential.

Conversely, the buying of the bonds is slightly different and equation (8.4) applies as the portfolio manager has to estimate the amounts that the portfolio has to buy in order to maintain the portfolio allocation. For buying BRAZIL 5 5/8 02/21/47 and HAOHUA 4 1/8 07/19/27, both bond and currency ask prices apply and the total amount sums up to the total amount of USD 7,309,997 and corresponds to EUR 6,530,865.

This example also reveals a complication that is often experienced in practice when managing portfolios. Specifically, the total amount of purchases is less than the amount of bonds sold. The difference in our example is roughly USD 3,022,527 and corresponds to EUR 2,701,197. Here the portfolio manager has two options depending on the their strategy for the portfolio. The portfolio manager might leave the US dollar amount in cash. In this case, the portfolio has a larger amount in cash than the exposure in underlying bonds. This represents additional foreign exchange risk and would imply that the portfolio still exhibits a larger US dollar risk, but less interest-rate risk. Conversely, if the amount is exchanged to euros, the total portfolio exposure to the US dollar, comprising interest-rate and foreign-exchange risk, decreases. As the euro is the assumed numeraire or base currency of the portfolio in this example, the cash in euros represents a neutral position. As may be expected, the foregoing risks will be even more pronounced in the case of multiple currencies.

Table 8.1: Portfolio Trading with Foreign Exchange

Bond	**Weight**	**Notional**	**FX**	**Bid**	**Ask**	**Bid-Ask Spread**	**Depth (LC)**	**FX Bid**	**FX Ask**	**FX Bid-Ask Spread**	**Depth (in EUR)**	**Buy (LC)**	**Sell (LC)**	**Buy (EUR)**	**Sell (EUR)**
BRAZIL 5 5/8 02/21/47	1.3%	4,500,000	USD	95.55	96.09	0.0056	25.386	1.1192	1.1193	0.0001	22.680	4.323.825		3.862.972	—
BRAZIL 8 1/4 01/20/34	1.0%	–2,600,000	USD	127.06	127.81	0.0059	15.245	1.1192	1.1193	0.0001	13.621		–3.303.612	—	–2.951.762
HAOHUA 4 1/8 07/19/27	0.9%	2,800,000	USD	106.16	106.65	0.0046	12.951	1.1192	1.1193	0.0001	11.570	2.986.172		2.667.892	—
COLOM 7 3/8 09/18/37	1.2%	–3,600,000	USD	112.39	113.22	0.0074	26.586	1.1192	1.1193	0.0001	23.755		–4.045.968	—	–3.615.054
COSTAR 7 04/04/44	0.9%	–3,200,000	USD	93.22	94.11	0.0095	30.484	1.1192	1.1193	0.0001	27.237		–2.982.944	—	–2.665.247
Total							**110.651**				**98.863**	**7.309.997**	**–10.332.524**	**6.530.865**	**–9.232.062**

Note: Data obtained by the authors from Bloomberg, LLC.

8.6 Key Takeaways

- Changing regulations have been strong drivers for the development of electronic exchanges. Driven by a growing need to prevent fraud and enable a much higher level of transparency, financial institutions and investors have faced the challenge of reshaping their market making activities. This change forced investors to restructure risk taking, which in turn led to decreasing inventories of bonds.
- Bid-ask spreads are strongly impacted by supply and demand, preferred allocations, interest-rate dynamics, fundamentals, business cycle and market volatility, and the quantities exchanged.
- Bid-ask spreads and portfolio weights depend on the portfolio size, notional exchanged, and market segment liquidity. The liquidity for lower-rated bonds is less than the liquidity and tradability for higher-rated bonds.
- Usually, volatile market periods are favorable for safe haven bonds or bonds that enjoy investor preference in times of increased uncertainty. Widening bid-ask spreads become even more misleading for bond market pricing as the bid-ask spreads indicate only a tradable market in which bid and offer prices are "derived" from quoted prices. However, quoted prices are not traded.
- Portfolio weights and portfolio size are directly related to bid-and ask prices and currencies. Diversified and concentrated portfolios might experience a different cost impact when trading bonds. More diversified portfolios have a large number of bonds with lower notional sizes. Concentrated bond portfolios trade a small number of bonds with large notional sizes. Diversified portfolios invested in broad markets can be easily traded on electronic exchanges as portfolio managers are able to rebalance their portfolios in a more cost-effective manner and decrease transaction costs.

References

Alexander, G. J., A. K. Edwards, and M. G, Ferri. 2000. "The Determinants of Trading Volume of High-Yield Corporate Bonds". *Journal of Financial Markets* 3(2): 177–204.

Amihud, Y. 2002. "Illiquidity and Stock Returns: Cross-Section and Time-Series Effects". *Journal of Financial Markets* 5(1): 31–56.

Ben Slimane, M. and M. de Jong. 2017. "Bond Liquidity Scores". *Journal of Fixed Income* 27(1): 77–82.

Brown, R. A. 2018. "Intelligent Rebalancing". *Journal of Investing* 27(1): 31–42.

Cohen, S., S. Laipply, A. Madhavan, and J. Mauro. 2022. "The Primary Market Process for Fixed Income Exchange-Traded Funds Under Market Stress". *Journal of Fixed Income* 31(3): 66–78.

Ericsson, J. and O. Renault. 2006. "Liquidity and Credit Risk". *Journal of Finance* 61(5): 2219–2250.

Fabozzi, F. J. and F. A. Fabozzi. 2021. *Bond Markets, Analysis, and Strategies*. 10th Edition. Cambridge, MA: MIT Press.

Hanif, A. and R. E. Smith. 2012. "Algorithmic, Electronic, and Automated Trading". *Journal of Trading* 7(4): 78–86.

Helwege, J., H. Z. Huang, and Y. Wang. 2014. "Liquidity Effects in Corporate Bond Spreads". *Journal of Banking and Finance* 45(1): 105–116.

Jankowitsch, R., H. Mosenbacher, and S. Pichler. 2006. "Measuring the Liquidity Impact on EMU Government Bond Prices". *European Journal of Finance* 12(2): 153–169.

Konstantinov, G. S. and F. J. Fabozzi. 2021. "International Bond Portfolio Management". Chapter 57 in F. J. Fabozzi (ed.), *The Handbook of Fixed Income Securities*. 9th Edition. New York: McGraw Hill.

Konstantinov, G. S. and M. Pojarliev. 2021. "International Bond Portfolio Management". Chapter 44 in F. J. Fabozzi (ed.), *The Handbook of Fixed Income Securities*. 9th Edition. New York: McGraw Hill.

Lee, W. and P. Liu. 2021. "Work Harder: Diligent Rebalancing and Investment Horizon". *Journal of Portfolio Management* 47(3): 17–34.

Loistl, O. and G. S. Konstantinov. 2020. "Interactions and Interconnectedness Shape Financial Market Research". *Journal of Financial Data Science* 2(2): 51–63.

Loistl, O., B. Schossmann, and A. Veverka. 2004. "Tick Size and Spreads: The Case of Nasdaq's Decimalization". *European Journal of Operational Research* 155: 317–334.

Lou, X. and R. Sadka. 2011. "Liquidity Level or Liquidity Risk? Evidence from the Financial Crisis". *Financial Analysts Journal* 67(3): 51–62.

Masters, S. J. 2003. "Rebalancing". *Journal of Portfolio Management* 29(3): 52–57.

Nicholson, M. 2012. "Electronic Trading For Fixed Income Markets". Chapter 4 in Frank J. Fabozzi (ed.), *The Handbook of Fixed Income Securities*. 8th Edition. New York: McGraw-Hill.

Pastor, L. and R. F. Stambaugh. 2003. "Liquidity Risk and Expected Stock Returns". *Journal of Political Economy* 111(3): 642–685.

Pojarliev, M. and R. Levich. 2012. *A New Look at Currency Investing*. CFA Institute.

Prix, J., O. Loistl, and M. Huetl. 2007. "Algorithmic Trading Patterns in Xetra Orders". *The European Journal of Finance* 13: 717–739.

Roll, R. R. 1984. "A Simple Implicit Measure of the Effective Bid-Ask Spread in an Efficient Market". *Journal of Finance* 39(4): 1127–1139.

Roth, A. E. 2018. "Marketplaces, Markets, and Market Design". *American Economic Review* 108(7): 1609–1658.

Sadka, R. 2006. "Momentum and Post-Earnings-Announcement Drift Anomalies: The Role of Liquidity Risk". *Journal of Financial Economics* 80(2): 309–349.

Satchell, S. and B. Scherer. 2010. "Fairness in Trading: A Microeconomic Interpretation". *Journal of Trading* 10(1): 40–47.

Schestag, R., P. Schuster, and M. Uhrig-Homburg. 2016. "Measuring Liquidity in Bond Markets". *Review of Financial Studies* 29(5): 1170–1219.

Taleb, N. N. 1997. *Dynamic Hedging: Managing Vanilla and Exotic Options.* Hoboken, NJ: John Wiley & Sons.

Train, K. E. 2003. *Discrete Choice Methods with Simulation.* Cambridge, UK: Cambridge University Press.

Chapter 9

Portfolio Risk Management

Portfolio risk management is a critical aspect of managing a global bond portfolio. It begins with identifying the major risks to which the portfolio is exposed, how those risks are interrelated, and how they are measured. In Chapters 3 and 4, we described those risks and how they are interrelated in global bond portfolios. Once those risks are measured, the next step in portfolio risk management is to control those risks to increase the likelihood that the portfolio will achieve its strategic objectives.

When a portfolio's risk profile has fallen out of line with its risk targets, it will typically be rebalanced. This can be accomplished by transacting in the cash market or the derivatives market. Typically, the derivatives market is the preferred forum for altering risk exposure because it is less costly (both explicit and implicit costs) and not disruptive to the manager's investment process. Effectively, the portfolio can be viewed as having two parts: a cash portfolio and a derivatives portfolio. It is the derivatives portfolio that is used to alter the risk exposure of the portfolio. When derivatives are employed to adjust a portfolio's risk exposures, the strategy is referred to as overlay management or simply an overlay strategy.

In this chapter, we discuss how portfolio managers control risk for two interrelated risks in global bond portfolios: interest-rate and currency risk. However, from the standpoint of portfolio risk management, these risks are best considered as independent exposures. We include several practical examples that demonstrate how interest-rate and currency risk exposures can be controlled using derivatives. In the use of one type of derivative, options, we show how the estimation of volatility can help to manage the risk in global bond portfolios. Finally, we focus on the importance of overlay management and discuss both currency and interest-rate overlay management for global bond portfolios that aim to neutralize — rather than hedge — currency and interest-rate risks. Here, we also provide examples that illustrate how the various techniques we describe can be used to implement an effective overlay management program.

Before doing so, it is important to note that market practitioners commonly refer to risk management as "hedging". Hedging is actually a special case of risk management. Risk management involves controlling the level of portfolio risk. The focus of risk management is not to forecast asset returns or changes in foreign exchange rates, but to analyze possible market scenarios and quantify how such scenarios could impact the portfolio's performance. Based on the different scenarios, the risk management team selects the appropriate instruments (typically derivatives) to hedge particular risks (e.g., interest-rate risk, currency risk, and credit risk among others). For example, a global bond portfolio manager may want to reduce a portfolio's interest-rate risk, as measured by duration, in some country. The portfolio manager is still willing to accept interest-rate risk, but the targeted level of that risk may differ from the current exposure. In "pure" hedging, the objective is to eliminate interest-rate risk (i.e., change the portfolio's duration from its current value to zero). Despite this more restrictive meaning of hedging, we will continue to use the term hedging in the latter sense. What we will show is that if a global bond portfolio manager wants to change a given risk exposure in a portfolio, it is equivalent to taking a portion of the portfolio and hedging it completely (e.g., creating a duration of zero to hedge interest-rate risk for a particular country). We also note at the outset that the focus of this chapter is risk management at the portfolio level and not the individual bond level.

9.1 Hedging Interest-Rate Risk of Global Bond Portfolios

The most fundamental risk for all bonds is interest-rate risk. It is a primary risk because interest-rate dynamics impact the market value of all the portfolio's holdings and thus the value of the entire portfolio. Therefore, the term structure of interest rates, and interest-rate volatility risk, is where hedging efforts should be concentrated. If a global bond portfolio is managed against a benchmark, the proper way to minimize interest-rate risk is to adjust the bond portfolio duration to be neutral to that of the benchmark. This can be done by buying or selling specific instruments.

Before we hedge interest-rate risk, we need a metric that faithfully captures systematic properties. The most widely used metric is portfolio beta. Beta refers to the overall market risk of a portfolio and is a weighted sum of the individual bond betas in the portfolio:

$$\beta_P = \sum_i \beta_i w_i \tag{9.1}$$

where β_i is the beta of bond i and w_i is the weight of bond i in the portfolio.

However, because bond instruments are nonlinear we need an extension to beta that more effectively gauges systematic risk and an extension to duration that more efficiently captures the changes in bond prices due to changes in interest rates and spreads. For this purpose, convexity can be used. However, before discussing convexity, we need a detailed understanding of duration. The duration of the portfolio is a weighted sum of the individual bond durations:

$$D_P = \sum_i D_i w_i \tag{9.2}$$

where D_i is the duration for bond i.

Relationships between portfolio risk and benchmark risk are best represented as ratios. For this purpose, a ratio of the portfolio duration relative to the benchmark duration provides insights about the interest-rate risk relationship between a portfolio and its benchmark. Similar to foreign exchange, the ratio shows the amount of risk that a portfolio is exposed to over and above the benchmark risk. The beta on the other hand shows how the portfolio responds to benchmark movements and measures the market or systematic risk of the portfolio.

Beta can be estimated in two ways. The first is to use linear regression models, where the derived estimate is referred to as empirical duration (see Ben Dor *et al.*, 2022). It is common to use regression to estimate the sensitivity of a bond portfolio value change against changes in the US Treasury or benchmark yields. A beta coefficient greater (less) than 1 indicates higher (lower) systematic risk relative to a reference variable such as a yield change or asset return. However, this measure — which is commonly used in equity portfolio management — is limited when applied to measuring the beta of bond portfolios due to the nonlinearity of bond returns. As Ben Dor *et al.* (2022) point out, empirical duration might deviate significantly from the bond portfolio's analytical duration. Therefore, here we focus on analytical duration.

The second approach to measuring a portfolio's beta is to use a relational model. Baltussen *et al.* (2021) noted that an active manager might view a portfolio's beta as a relation between the portfolio duration and the benchmark duration. This relationship is given by the following:

$$\beta_{\text{simple}} = \frac{D_P}{D_B} \tag{9.3}$$

where D_P is the portfolio duration and D_B is the benchmark duration.

A major drawback of simple beta estimation is the incomplete nature of the price changes that it captures. In other words, nonlinear movements are not captured. In contrast, convexity does capture nonlinear bond price changes. Similar to duration, portfolio convexity is also a weighted sum of the individual bond convexities as given by

$$C_P = \sum_i C_i w_i \tag{9.4}$$

where C_i is the convexity of bond *i*. This also applies to the benchmark.

In general, global bond portfolios and the benchmarks used by portfolio managers have different yields. The different allocations and exposures in the portfolio and in the benchmark might underlie different yield dynamics and changes of the yield to maturity due to different asset exposures. Different maturity allocations and currency exposures might also drive such differences in the yield to maturity of the portfolio. By considering the portfolio and benchmark durations and convexities as weighted sums, and the change in yields of the portfolio and the benchmark, we can approximate the *active beta* of the portfolio. The latter measure accounts for nonlinear changes in bond prices and uses the bond portfolio and benchmark yields, which are weighted sums of the individual bonds included in a portfolio and a benchmark[1]:

$$\beta_{\text{active}} = \frac{-D_P(\Delta y_P) + 0.5C_{PF}(\Delta y_P)^2}{-D_B(\Delta y_B) + 0.5C_B(\Delta y_B)^2} \tag{9.5}$$

[1]This is derived by using the Taylor expansion.

where C_P and C_B are the portfolio convexity and benchmark convexity, respectively, and Δy_P and Δy_B are the changes in the portfolio and benchmark yield, respectively. All other variables are as defined previously.

In order to accurately assess the level of portfolio systematic risk relative to the benchmark, including the change in credit risk measured by the spread, it is necessary to add the changes in spread. The main advantage of the active beta computation using yields and spreads compared to the simple beta estimation lies in the nonlinear adjustments that the active beta measure allows:

$$\beta'_{\text{active}} = \frac{-D_P(\Delta y_P + \Delta s_P) + 0.5C_P(\Delta y_P + \Delta s_P)^2}{-D_B(\Delta y_B + \Delta s_B) + 0.5C_B(\Delta y_B + \Delta s_B)^2} \tag{9.6}$$

where Δs_P is the change in spread of the portfolio and Δs_B is the change in spread of the benchmark. All other variables were defined previously.

To illustrate the importance of computing a more accurate beta coefficient for bond portfolios, we provide an example using an emerging market global bond portfolio whose benchmark is the J.P. Morgan EMBI Global Diversified Bond Index.

Table 9.1 provides the relevant data and the different beta parameters computed using equations (9.1)–(9.5). The simple beta computation results in a beta equal to 1. In other words, the portfolio moves in unison with the benchmark. *Active risk beta* is the ratio of the portfolio beta to the benchmark beta in equations (9.3) and (9.6). In Table 9.1, we see that the active risk beta is 0.77. If we take spread effects into account, the beta

Table 9.1: Emerging Market Bond Portfolio vs Benchmark

	Portfolio	**Benchmark**
Yield-To-Maturity (y)	3.49%	3.78%
Spread (bps) (s)	202	241
Duration (D)	8.99	8.93
Convexity (C)	1.21	1.40
Beta	1.0	
Beta (Δy)	0.77	
Beta ($\Delta y + \Delta s$)	1.03	

Note: The benchmark index used in this illustration is the J.P. Morgan EMBI Global Diversified Index.

rises to 1.03. So in this example we see that spreads add more systematic risk (1.03) than the active beta which only considers interest-rate risk (0.84). The primary lesson here is that bond portfolios with large exposure to credit risk like emerging market bond portfolios often exhibit large deviations between simple beta and active beta.

Notably, computing active beta provides insightful information about the relative position of the portfolio versus the benchmark. However, because some bond portfolios are not managed against a benchmark, active beta is arguably of less interest. Risk measurement is of course only one component of the risk management process. Hedging the risks in a portfolio is critical to establishing the desired level of risk control in a portfolio. Typically, various types of derivative instruments are used to hedge portfolio risks. In the remainder of this chapter we provide detail on several ways to establish portfolio hedges using derivatives.

9.1.1 *Bond portfolio hedging with futures*

The two most widely used instruments for bond portfolio hedging are the US Treasury and the Euro bund futures. One of the most desired properties for risk management instruments is their liquidity. Both the US Treasury and the German bund futures are among the most liquid futures contracts, along with the UK gilt and Japanese government 10-year bond futures. While there are many other liquid futures contracts for different countries (e.g., Italy, Spain, Switzerland and Sweden), their liquidity is still less than that required to implement a maximally effective hedging policy. Emerging market bond futures contracts also exist, but they are less suitable for dynamic risk management due to their relative lack of market depth and sufficient trading volumes.

One of the economic reasons for using futures contracts is that they are often considered a proxy for expected central bank policy. Specifically, bond portfolio managers use bond futures as reliable predictors and indicators of central bank interest-rate policy because futures prices react immediately to any market news regarding changes in interest-rate policy.

When discussing hedging, the first concept that needs to be introduced is the hedge ratio. Hedge ratios show the relationship between the risk of the portfolio that is to be hedged and the instruments that are used to hedge the risk. Specifically, if a bond portfolio is hedged against interest-rate risk with futures, the hedge ratio captures the relationship between the portfolio and the futures contract that is required to hedge the portfolio. Using the approach shown in Bierwag (1987) and Pitts and Fabozzi (1990, Chapter 9), the hedge ratio for a bond duration hedge is expressed as the relationship between the portfolio duration and the futures contract duration adjusted by the portfolio volume and the size of the futures contract:

$$h = -\frac{-D_P V_P}{-D_F V_F} \tag{9.7}$$

where h is the optimal hedge ratio required to hedge the portfolio against parallel yield curve changes, D_P is the portfolio duration, D_F is the futures contract duration, V_P is the market value of the portfolio, and V_F is the market value of the position in the futures contract. To hedge against parallel shifts in the yield curve, investors typically use long-term bond futures.

Like beta, the hedge ratio between the portfolio and futures contract might be expanded using portfolio duration and convexity. We define this expanded measure as the *extended hedge ratio* and calculate it as follows:

$$h_{\text{extended}} = -\frac{-D_P(\Delta y_P) + 0.5C_P(\Delta y_P)^2}{-D_F(\Delta y_F) + 0.5C_F(\Delta y_F)^2}\frac{V_P}{V_F}\beta_{\text{CTD}} kf_{\text{CTD}} \tag{9.8}$$

where h_{extended} is the optimal hedge ratio required to hedge the portfolio against parallel yield curve changes, β_{CTD} is the beta of the cheapest-to-delivery bond that underlies the futures contract,[2] kf_{CTD} is the conversion factor of the cheapest-to-delivery bond, and all other variables are as defined previously.

Table 9.1 illustrates the importance of accurately measuring portfolio risk to hedging. If the wrong risk metric is used, the portfolio may

---

[2]This is because in the case of bond futures, the seller of the contract has to deliver a bond at the contract's maturity. It is up to the seller to find the cheapest bond to deliver among those acceptable to the exchange. Since the deliverable bonds have different maturities and coupons, the conversion factors adjust for the differences. In the case of US Treasury bond futures, the conversion factors indicate by how much the bond price should be adjusted in order to have the appropriate yield.

over- or under-hedge. An overhedge has a similar adverse impact on a portfolio as an underhedge. An overhedge means that the hedged exposure changes less than expected. Underhedging means that the hedge does not properly reflect the market changes in portfolio exposure when interest rates decrease and the portfolio experiences a loss despite being hedged.

Futures contracts have maturities. Rolling positions in the futures contracts from maturing contracts into the future assures hedge continuance but requires specific adjustments. However, the rolling of futures contracts that are close to maturity creates risk for the portfolio due to transaction costs and pricing mismatches and also presents the risk of underhedging or overhedging. For example, suppose a portfolio manager sold 100 bund futures contracts (the long-term German 10-year bond futures contract with Bloomberg ticker RX1 Comdty for the generic time series) for the purpose of hedging the interest-rate risk of the euro-exposure in a global bond portfolio. The current contract has a 6-month maturity and expires in September. For the purpose of rolling the futures contracts, the portfolio manager needs to buy the March contract at 149.10 (due in September) and sell short the new100 futures contract at 149.34. In other words, the portfolio manager needs to buy back the futures contract that was sold (in June) to hedge the interest-rate risk of the portfolio because the old contract is expiring. The manager buys the contract at the price of 149.10. At the same time, the bond portfolio must be hedged and the manger needs to sell the new futures contract. For this purpose, the manager sells 100 futures contracts at the price of 149.34. Table 9.2 captures the procedure of rolling futures contracts. We note that the difference in pricing is a common risk in rolling futures contracts.

Table 9.2: Rolling Euro Bund Futures Contracts

Open/Close in	Close	Open
March	100 Euro Bund Future March at 170.58	−100 Euro Bund Future June 167.55
June	100 Euro Bund Future June at 149.10	−100 Euro Bund Future September at 149.34

Note: Data obtained by the authors from Bloomberg, LLC.

9.1.1.1 *Alternative hedging approaches*

Alternative solutions for interest-rate hedging involve using bond options and/or interest-rate swaps. For heterogeneous bond portfolios with exposure to multiple countries and significant currency risk, interest-rate swaps offer one of the most convenient ways to hedge interest-rate risk. For example, if a portfolio manager expects interest rates to rise, it may be favorable for the portfolio manager to pay a fixed interest rate and to receive a floating interest rate. This strategy applies to global bond portfolios with large exposure to markets with distinctive currency and interest-rate risk. Local currency emerging market bond portfolios with exposure to hard currency denominated bonds (e.g., in euro or in US dollar) are an example.

In the previous sections we discussed the hedging of systematic risk. However, aside from recurring systematic risks there are risks that might be triggered by single events like a political crisis or unique economic disruptions. History offers numerous examples of events like these such as the Asian currency crisis and the European Monetary Union crisis in the case of Greece and Cyprus.

9.1.2 *Credit risk*

For hedging credit risk, a credit default swap (CDS) on a single issuer is the most commonly used instrument in global bond portfolios. Issuers might be sovereigns or corporates. However, the focus of risk management for global bond portfolios is often dedicated to sovereign single credit risks. Therefore, CDSs on specific countries are much more common than CDS on corporate issuers. Note that portfolio credit risk might be expressed as a weighted sum of the individual bond ratings (using credit ratings). The credit risk for global bond portfolios increases in a manner that is inversely proportional to the credit rating of the bonds in the portfolio. That is, the higher the exposure to high-yield bonds, the higher the credit risk and the necessity to buy CDS protection against country credit risk.

Ben Dor and Guan (2017) showed that high-yield bond portfolios might be hedged using CDS. However, as mentioned above, global bond portfolios might be more interested in CDSs to hedge the credit risk at the individual country level (e.g., Argentina, Russia, or Venezuela). Country CDSs are often useful instruments to consider when political or economic risk in a country heightens. The credit event is the default or deterioration of the creditworthiness of the country. CDS contracts reflect the economic fundamentals of a country and the price of the protection which a CDS contract represents rises when the economic fundamentals deteriorate. Single countries with elevated default or restructuring risk are vulnerable to financial market fragility and/or deterioration in macroeconomic conditions. When a bond portfolio has exposure to such countries, the portfolio manager might want to buy portfolio credit protection.

Emerging markets are vulnerable to various risks. However, we note that large and even diversified bond portfolios might experience losses due to unexpected credit defaults. In the case of financial stress, it is often impossible to shift portfolio exposures even when the portfolio manager is willing to realize heavy losses. CDS contracts on Russia, Argentina, Kenya, Venezuela, and Pakistan, to name a few, are good examples of countries that have experienced defaults in the past. Such defaults might harm even well-diversified bond portfolios. Suppose, for example, that a country in a well-diversified bond portfolio of, say, USD 500 million invested in broad emerging markets, experiences a default. If that country has a 2% weighting in the portfolio, this might result in a loss of USD 10 million. Default events in emerging markets have occurred several times in the past and have caused large losses in emerging market bond portfolios. As a result, CDS contracts have become mainstay instruments to hedge country credit risk.

9.1.3 *Hedging currency risk*

Currency hedging has a long academic history tracing back to the works of Black (1989) and Perold and Schulman (1998). The primary risks with currency exposure are foreign exchange price risk and the volatility of foreign exchange. However, foreign exchange is also sensitive to the local-term structure of interest rates and the volatility of the yield curve. As a result, currency exposure is vulnerable to the same risks associated with bond portfolios. The foreign exchange risk-adjusted duration model suggested by Bierwag and Fooladi (2006) and Fouladi *et al.* (2021) for foreign government bonds implies that when interest-rate parity holds, there is no diversification benefit in using foreign bonds that are hedged against foreign exchange risk. However, currency movements can wipe out the entire profit generated by the price changes in fixed-income instruments. Thus, while currency exposure can potentially enhance a portfolio's returns, currency depreciation can significantly detract from a portfolio's performance.

In the previous section, we discussed managing interest-rate risk and spread risk. However as we have emphasized in much of this book, the risk of currency depreciation might be the most severe risk for bond portfolios. This risk might be amplified in the case of a so-called black swan event, where a country defaults on its debt, which in turn will result in currency depreciation and bond spread widening. In this case, the corporate bonds of issuers in that country may also be adversely impacted. For example, the default of Russian debt in 1997 caused spread widening of the country's government bonds and the depreciation of the Russian ruble. This also impacted corporate bonds issued in Russia's financial and industrial sectors. Emerging markets are more vulnerable to black swan events relative to developed markets. For this reason, research has focused on the risks of unexpected events that might cause significant portfolio losses, especially in emerging markets, and the instruments that can be used to mitigate those risks (see Estrada, 2009).

But again, currency risk in global bond portfolios might be more central than spread risk, given the large impact that an adverse currency movement can have on portfolio holdings. Afik *et al.* (2018) proposed an integrated approach that applies *ex ante* a two-factor duration model that accounts for both foreign interest-rate and exchange rate exposures. Whereas these authors provide an integrated approach to considering currency and interest-rate risk, we show how currency hedging can be implemented as a separate process. The economic rationale for this is that often, currency hedging and currency overlay management might be outsourced and detached from direct bond portfolio management. This type of bifurcated approach has been proposed by Jorion (1994) and Levich and Thomas (1993), in which bond and currency exposure are managed separately using the Markowitz mean–variance framework.

In this section, we focus explicitly on currency hedging. The most commonly used instruments for this purpose are forwards, futures, options, and other derivative strategies like currency straddles and strangles. Foreign exchange swaps are also part of the hedging instrument toolkit. It is imperative to understand how currency hedging works. So let us first discuss why currency hedging plays an important role in global bond portfolios.

There are two important points regarding implementation when hedging currency risk and currency hedging. The first concerns the depreciation of local currencies in a portfolio. For example, if a portfolio holds European government bonds denominated in EUR and the latter currency depreciates, then the value of euro-denominated government bonds in the portfolio will also decrease. The second point concerns the appreciation of the portfolio base currency or the total currency risk of a portfolio. For example, if a portfolio's base currency is USD, and the latter appreciates against the other currencies held in a portfolio, then losses may be incurred.

9.1.3.1 *Modeling foreign exchange as a lattice tree*

The modeling of prices is critical in risk management. However, modeling and predicting foreign exchange prices has historically proven to be challenging. One promising approach to modeling the dynamics of foreign exchange prices is to use lattice trees. Representing currencies and interest rates as a lattice tree allows for the computation of possible price realizations of foreign exchange using observable parameters like volatility and interest rates. The approach we use in our discussion is widely utilized in the literature and shows the future price of an asset within a binomial tree. Fabozzi *et al.* (2021) provide examples of interest-rate lattices. Here, we demonstrate how the approach can be applied to foreign exchange using a practical example.

Let us assume that the foreign exchange price follows a binomial random walk. That is, the price of the currency pair in the next period can either go up by a factor u or go down by a factor d. Note that the factors u and d are proportional to the volatility of the foreign exchange price. The factor u is defined by $u = \exp(\sigma\sqrt{\Delta t})$, where σ is the foreign exchange price volatility and the Δt denotes the length of one period in the tree. The time period might be a day, week, or any other unit of time. The factor d is given by $d = 1/u$. The current price of the currency S can either go up to S $\times$ u, or decrease to S $\times$ d in period 1. Similarly, the price in period 2 can go to S $\times$ u^2 or S $\times$ d^2. In Figure 9.1, we provide an example for a two-period tree with possible foreign exchange prices.

Following the binomial tree approach suggested by Cox, Ross, and Rubinstein (1979), we can construct risk-neutral pricing at any time in

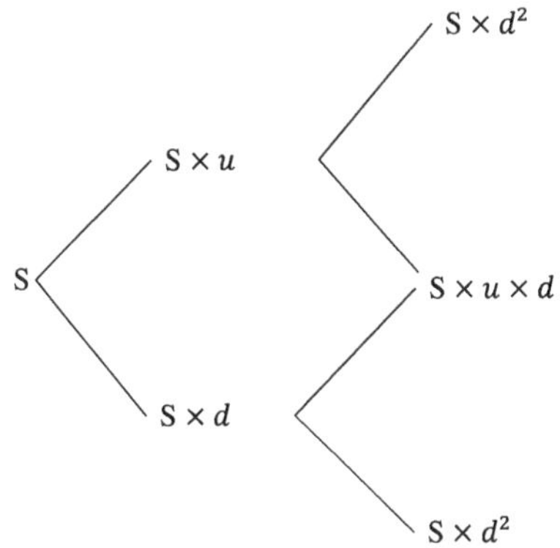

Figure 9.1: Possible Currency Movements (Two Periods)

the future. Suppose, for example, that the EUR/USD exchange rate is currently at 1.06. Let us assume that the exchange rate follows a log-normal distribution and that its expected volatility is 10.74% per annum. The price of the currency exchange rate, in our case the EUR/USD, is estimated using the expected volatility and the probabilities that the price rises or falls in subsequent periods. We assume the risk-free rate for the EUR/USD exchange rate to be zero. The time step is 30/360 using the 30/360 daycount convention. Note that in the binomial model the prices in the future period depend on the current node and have two possible outcomes — higher or lower. The price in the current node is given by the sum of the prices in the future period nodes given a specific probability:

$$S(t) = S_u(t + 1)\,p + S_d(t + 1)(1 - p) \qquad (9.9)$$

where $S(t)$ is the spot price, $S_u(t + 1)$ is the up price at time $t + 1$, $S_d(t + 1)$ is the down price at time $t + 1$, p is the probability of the price going up, and $1 - p$ is the probability of the price going down.

The currency exchange price at every node in the binomial tree is the product of the preceding node price multiplied by the product of the expected volatility and the square root of the time between the nodes:

$$S_u(t+1) = S(t)\exp(\sigma\sqrt{\Delta t}) \quad \text{and} \quad S_d(t+1) = S(t)\exp(-\sigma\sqrt{\Delta t}) \qquad (9.10)$$

where σ is the volatility of the exchange rate, and Δt is the time step or time step in the tree, with all other variables defined previously.

The risk-neutral probability of the price going up is given by the parameters u and d, which are proportional and inverse-proportional to the time-weighted volatility, respectively:

$$p = \frac{\exp(r\Delta t) - d}{u - d}, \text{ with } u = \exp(\sigma\sqrt{\Delta t}) \text{ and } d = \exp(-\sigma\sqrt{\Delta t}) \tag{9.11}$$

where $\sqrt{\Delta t}$ is the risk-free rate, or the local currency money market rate weighted by the change in time Δt,[3] u is the probability of the foreign exchange price going up, d is the probability of the foreign exchange price going down, and all other variables are as defined previously.[4]

Let us assume that we have a tree with three 1-month nodes. Then, $u = \exp(10.74\%\sqrt{0.08}) = 1.03$ and $d = 1/u$, which is 0.97. The risk-neutral probability (equation (9.12)) that the foreign exchange price moves up is 49.22%. Conversely, the probability of the exchange rate going down is $(1 - p)$, or 50.77%. Thus, for the EUR/USD, there is slightly higher probability of the euro depreciating against the US dollar, or the US dollar appreciating against the euro. Note that the pricing notation of the currency exchange rate differs from unit notations. As a result, the risk-neutral probability for the EUR/USD and USD/EUR remains the same, but the price movement is different, and this difference plays an important role depending on the currency denomination of the portfolio and thus the hedging policy.

The next example will show that for a US-dollar-based bond portfolio, the EUR/USD portfolio exposure is different in price than for a European global bond portfolio. Suppose the EUR/USD with a current price of 1.06 is going to 0.87. Consider two portfolios — a US-dollar-based portfolio and a euro-based global bond portfolio. A EUR/USD move from 1.06 to 0.87 is a US dollar appreciation for the euro-based bond portfolio, but it is a euro depreciation for the US-dollar-based portfolio. Table 9.3 shows the

---

[3] Practitioners often assume the risk-free rate to be zero when analyzing both emerging and developed markets.

[4] Note that the life of the tree is set to equal the life or analyzing period of the exchange rate for hedging purposes. That is, for hedging with options with a maturity of one month, the tree life is one month with daily observations.

Table 9.3: Binomial Trees for Currencies (Three Periods)

Panel A: EUR/USD				**Panel B: USD/EUR**			
$t = 0$	$t = 1M$	$t = 2M$	$t = 3M$	$t = 0$	$t = 1M$	$t = 2M$	$t = 3M$
			1.16				1.04
		1.13				1.00	
	1.09		1.09		0.97		0.97
1.06		1.06		0.94		0.94	
	1.03		1.03		0.91		0.91
		1.00				0.89	
			0.97				0.86

Panel C: EUR/USD expectation for EUR				**Panel D: Reversed**			
$t = 0$	$t = 1M$	$t = 2M$	$t = 3M$	$t = 0$	$t = 1M$	$t = 2M$	$t = 3M$
			0.86 (1/1.16)				0.97 (1/1.04)
		0.89 (1/1.13)				1.00 (1/1.00)	
	0.91 (1/1.09)		0.91 (1/1.09)		1.03 (1/0.97)		1.03 (1/0.97)
0.94 (1/1.06)		0.94 (1/1.06)		1.06 (1/0.94)		1.06 (1/0.94)	
	0.97 (1/1.03)		0.97 (1/1.03)		1.09 (1/0.91)		1.09 (1/0.91)
		1.00 (1/1.0)				1.13 (1/0.89)	
			1.04 (1/0.97)				1.16 (1/0.86)

Note: Three-step nodes for EUR/USD currency pair with constant volatility of 10.74% per annum.

complexity of currency pricing that is brought about by this example.[5] Note that the goal of the model is not predicting currency prices, but computing the possible market scenarios in order to understand how currency price movements could impact the portfolio.

[5] Similar examples are provided by Taleb (1997).

In panel A of Table 9.3, we compute a simple price tree with a time step of one month for the EUR/USD with a current price of 1.06. This is the most common view of the exchange rate. However, it depends on one's point of view. Given a volatility of 10.74%, the EUR/USD can rise to 1.16 (USD depreciation against the EUR for a EUR investor, or EUR appreciation against the USD for a USD investor). It can conversely go down to 1.04, which is an appreciation of the USD against the EUR for a EUR-based portfolio.

Panel B of Table 9.3 shows the reciprocal notation. That is, the USD/ EUR of 0.94 = 1/1.06. The price can rise in three months to 1.04 or decrease to 0.86. In this case, the rise to 1.04 represents an appreciation and the decrease to 0.86 a depreciation of the USD against the EUR. This is the common view for a EUR-based investor using price notation. This is the EUR per USD expectations for a USD-based investor.

The reciprocal price notation of the EUR/USD for an US-centric investor or the EUR/USD expectations for a Euro-centric investor is shown in panel C of Table 9.3. The first node is 0.94 = 1/1.06. Given the same expected volatility of 10.74%, the price can be 0.86 in three months or 1.04. This is the common EUR-USD expectation for a EUR-based investor. Panel D of Table 9.3 provides a reversed pricing of the expected price development of the USD/EUR.

In general, hedging currency risk requires thinking about the underlying economics. Note that an intuitive way to think about hedging is to consider the currency movement into infinity or to zero. A simple example illustrates this logic. Consider a US dollar-based portfolio with exposure in EUR/USD. Economically, the movements are limited to zero. A change from say 0.90 to 0 is finite, and the price cannot become negative. Suppose now that the EUR/USD moves up, which represents a euro appreciation and US dollar depreciation. In this case, the loss that a euro-based portfolio might experience in EUR/USD exposure due to the US dollar depreciation might be unlimited. Specifically, an upward movement of the EUR/USD from 1.06 has the potential to move to infinity. In such a case, the portfolio loss is more-or-less unlimited. The moves (depreciation) of the Russian ruble in 1997 and the Argentinian peso in 1993 and 2005, as well as the experience of other emerging market countries after they experienced a default, are examples of currency meltdowns that have caused massive portfolio losses.[6]

[6]Papaioannou and Tsetsekos (2018) provide a list of emerging market countries that experienced restructuring after severe macroeconomic crises and defaults.

Hedging currency portfolio risk is a complex undertaking which requires an understanding of what should be hedged and how the required hedging should be implemented. Next, we provide an overview of the two most commonly used currency futures and forwards and options.

9.1.3.2 *Currency forwards and futures*

In this section, we discuss cross-currency contracts that comprise two currencies. Cross-currency contracts are popular because they are liquid and easy to implement. Moreover, their transaction costs are negligible compared to other derivatives.

Cross-currency contracts are either futures or forwards. A currency forward or futures contract is an obligation to exchange one currency into another at a specified date in the future at a pre-specified price. Forwards and futures contracts on EUR/USD, the USD/JPY, and the GBP/USD are the most widely utilized. The main difference between the forward and futures contracts is that forward contracts are not standardized contracts and are traded in the over-the-counter market. In contrast, futures contracts are standardized instruments.

The interest-rate differential between two countries determines the forward/futures price. Suppose that one currency is expressed as units in terms of the other currency. The forward/futures price is the product of the current spot price and the cost of carry (i.e., the difference between the two interest rates of the currencies in the pair):

$$F = e^{(r_{fx1} - r_{fx2})t} S \tag{9.12}$$

where F is forward/futures price, S is the spot price of the currency pair, t is the time to delivery (360/360 daycount), r_{fx_1} is the interest rate of currency 1, and r_{fx_2} is the interest rate of currency 2.

It is important to understand not only the specific exposure at risk but also the relative currency to which the foreign exchange risk is to be hedged. The base currency, or the currency in which the profit and loss will be expressed, is the currency that determines the direction of the trade. In the EUR/USD, the unrealized profit and loss can be either in US dollars or in euros. In other words, without exposure to one of the currencies — EUR or USD — the conversion of profit and loss is not possible. Figure 9.2 shows the profit and loss of a forward contract on the EUR/USD exchange rate with a spot price of 1.06.

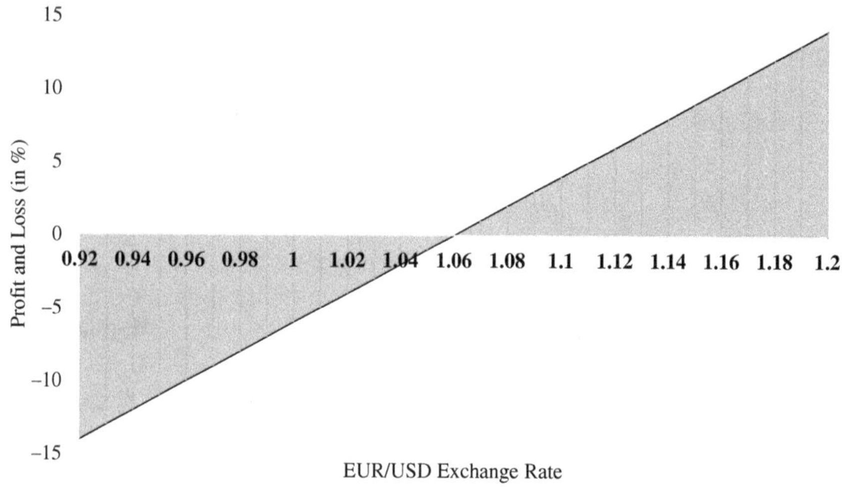

Figure 9.2: EUR/USD Exchange Rate Forward (Futures) Contract

Note that the EUR/USD ranges from 0.92 to 1.20 and a long forward (futures) contract in the EUR/USD results in a gain if the price rises above 1.06. However, this price increase is a depreciation of the US dollar against the euro and an appreciation of the euro against the US dollar. A long futures (forward) in this case would be favorable for a euro-based portfolio with US dollar exposure because it would hedge the portfolio exposure against US dollar depreciation. Alternatively, a US-dollar-based portfolio with euro exposure would need a short forward on the EUR/USD to hedge its euro exposure against depreciation of the euro. Note that the choice of the numeraire, or currency, in which the exposure is calculated is essential for the success of the hedge. Accordingly, there is a wide range of possibilities that involve numeraire flipping (i.e., estimation of the base currency and currency exposure that needs to be hedged).

9.1.3.3 *Currency options*

While managing foreign exchange risk with options is common among global bond portfolio managers, using this type of derivative is far more complex and challenging than when using forwards and futures for risk management. This is in part due to the fact that options can also be used as part of an active management strategy as well as for risk management.[7] Compounding the challenge in using currency options is the fact that changes in the underlying affect both the portfolio value as well as the prices of the options in the portfolio. Further, options are often not the most cost-effective hedging instruments. Thus, utilizing currency options demands careful consideration.[8]

Buyers of long options profit from rising volatility; sellers of options profit from declining volatility and from the time decay that options experience with the passage of time (referred to in option terminology as *theta*). In general, long call and put options are used for hedging purposes. Currency options are widely used but their pricing is sometimes challenging. The challenge stems from the duality of option direction and the numeraire. The currency used to report profit and loss has an additional impact on the portfolio. Suppose, for example, that a US dollar-based bond portfolio has exposure in EUR/NOK. The price and premium amount might be in euro, Norwegian krone, or US dollar. Therefore, we need to determine what should be hedged and what option position — "long/short", "put", or "call" — should be used.

Figure 9.3 shows the P&L range for the EUR/USD depending on option position. Here, we plot the price of the EUR/USD in the range from 1.029 to 1.095 and plot the profit and loss for the four major plain vanilla option contracts — long call, short call, long put, and short put with a spot price of 1.06.

In general, hedging currency risk is done using a long contract in a put or call option. The reason for this is that the portfolio manager typically wants to express a view on the direction of a given currency. Obviously, the direction in which a currency depreciates is the one which determines the option contract to be used. In other words, the numeraire (i.e., the base currency) determines the direction (see Taleb, 1997). For example, for a euro-based investor, it is more intuitive to use the USD/EUR notation to

---

[7] Fabozzi and Vohra (2022) provide an overview of the foreign exchange option payoff and strategy in active portfolio and risk management.

[8] Garman and Kohlhagen (1983) extended the option pricing model of Black and Scholes (1989) to currency options. The difference between the original Black–Scholes model and the extension provided by Garman and Kohlhagen is the inclusion of both domestic and foreign interest rates to calculate the option value. Note that the same extension applies when we discuss the valuation of foreign exchange futures contracts later in this chapter.

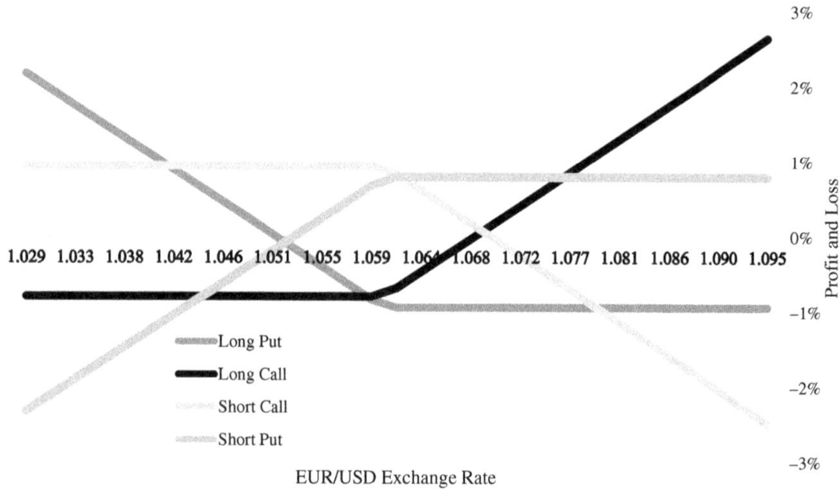

Figure 9.3: EUR/USD Options with a Spot of 1.06

Table 9.4: Currency Options

FX	EUR/USD	USD/JPY	GBP/USD
Spot Price	1.06	134.16	1.2409
Time (30 days, basis 360 days)	0.0833	0.0833	0.0833
Expected Volatility (in % per annum)	10.74	12.75	9.54
Call Price	0.94%	1.87%	1.35%
Put Price	0.79%	1.73%	1.35%
Delta FX Call	52.433%	49.232%	50.508%

Note: The data used in this table are for illustration purposes. The option prices are calculated using a binomial tree for option pricing.

determine the correct P/L. Similarly, using EUR/USD is more intuitive for U.S. dollar investors. However, because not all currency pairs (conventions) exist, it is important to determine the proper currency pair and the appropriate option. Table 9.4 summarizes the option prices and the data for three currency options with 1-month maturity. These data were used to construct both Figure 9.3 and Table 9.4.

There is an important property of currency options to bear in mind. And this is that a call on a EUR/USD is a put on the USD/EUR. However, the prices of the call and put options will be different depending on the currency numeraire. In our example, the long put and the long call serve as hedging instruments, depending on the portfolio's exposure. The intuition is that a call option is used as a hedge against an appreciating euro, or equivalently a depreciating US dollar. A put option is used to protect against a depreciating euro, or equivalently an appreciating US dollar.

Let's now discuss the hedging mechanism. A put on the EUR/USD (the right to sell euros and buy US dollars) is a call on the USD/EUR. The long call in EUR/USD with a strike price of 1.06 is equivalent to a USD/EUR with a strike price of 0.9433 (0.9433 = 1/1.06). The long call would be in the money if the EUR/USD moves higher than 1.068. The EUR/USD move from 1.06 to levels above 1.068 means that the euro appreciates against the US dollar. From the perspective of a US-dollar-based investor in euro-denominated bonds, this is a positive outcome. However, from the perspective of a euro-based portfolio manager, the move would be a currency depreciation of the US dollar, resulting in a loss to the portfolio. Therefore, a long call in EUR-USD with a strike of 1.06 would be beneficial for euro-based portfolios which might suffer from a weaker US dollar. The opposite is true for a US-dollar-based portfolio. In this case, a long put in the EUR/USD would allow the portfolio to benefit in case the EUR depreciates.

A simplified example using three currency options is provided in Table 9.5 which illustrates the foregoing points for a USD 500 million global bond portfolio.

Table 9.5: Currency Options for a Currency Hedge

Currency Pair	FX Price	Strike	Option Price (in %)	Portfolio Exposure (in USD)	Option Premium (in USD)	Volatility (%)	Weights (%)
EUR/USD	1.061	1.06	0.94%	261,318,709.84	2,456,395.87	10.7	52.3
USD/JPY	134.2	134	1.87%	178,013,017.93	3,328,843.44	11.5	35.6
GBP/USD	1.241	1.24	1.35%	60,668,275.50	819,021.72	14.3	12.1
Total Cost					6,604,261.03		
% of AUM					1.32%		

Note: The numbers are simplified for illustrative purposes for a hypothetical global bond portfolio of USD 500 million.

Let's assume the portfolio allocates to euros, Japanese yen, and the British pound. Remember that the base currency of the portfolio is the US dollar. The notional amount of the portfolio (i.e., hedging exposure) is estimated using the portfolio size and the exposure at risk, which is 52.3% based on euros (as shown in Table 9.5.) By multiplying the portfolio size of USD 500 million by the portfolio weight, the EUR exposure of the portfolio can be estimated. Dividing the exposure by the EUR/USD exchange rate gives the estimated local currency exposure. Using the trade size and price of the option contracts (0.94% for the EUR/USD option), we can estimate the cost to hedge the euro exposure, which is USD 2,456 million (or €2.317,354). Visual inspection of Table 9.5 shows that the cost to hedge with currency options with one-month maturity is approximately 1.3% of the total portfolio.

In the above example, we have multiple currency options in the global bond portfolio, which represent a currency option portfolio. When a global bond portfolio comprises several currency options, we can determine the portfolio basket using the correlations or variance–covariance matrix.[9] Using minimum-variance optimization, we can determine the optimal currency option weights based on our objective, e.g., having the lowest volatility currency portfolio. In the case of having multiple currency options in a global bond portfolio, it makes sense to estimate the volatility of the basket and to monitor the changes in the correlations between currency pairs and the changes in their volatilities. Once again, numeraire equality is essential. That is, the base currency of the portfolio should reflect the base (numeraire) currency of the portfolio basket of currency options.

The portfolio optimization process would have as an objective function minimizing the matrix product of the transposed vector of portfolio weights, multiplied by the product of the $(k \times k)$ variance–covariance matrix of currency returns and the vector of currency option portfolio weights. The sum of the currency options in the global bond portfolio can be at most 1. This is equivalent to minimizing portfolio risk of the currency option basket as shown in the following:

---

[9]Note that the currency exposure for a global bond portfolio is often used in currency overlay programs with external managers who are hired to replicate the portfolio exposures.

$$
\underset{w}{Arg\min} = (w_1^k,\dots,w_{fx}^k)\begin{pmatrix} \sigma_1^2 & \cdots & \rho_{1fx1}\sigma_1\sigma_{fx} \\ \vdots & \ddots & \vdots \\ \rho_{fx1}\sigma_{fx}\sigma_1 & \cdots & \sigma_{fx}^2 \end{pmatrix}\begin{pmatrix} w_1^k \\ \vdots \\ w_{fx}^k \end{pmatrix},
$$

$$
\text{with } (w_1,\dots,w_{fx})\begin{pmatrix} 1 \\ \vdots \\ 1 \end{pmatrix} = 1 \tag{9.13}
$$

where w_{fx} are the asset weights, ρ is the pairwise correlation coefficient between currency options, and the $\sigma's$ are the covariances between the currency pair return parameters.

For a US-dollar-based portfolio, we can use the EUR/USD, JPY/USD, and GBP/USD pricing to compute the expected portfolio basket volatility. We continue using the data provided in Table 9.5. Assume that (1) the correlation between the EUR/USD and USD/JPY is 0.7, (2) the correlation between the EUR/USD and GBP/USD is 0.6, and (3) the correlation between the USD/JPY and GBP/USD is 0.5. Using minimum-variance optimization, the optimal currency weights and the expected currency option basket portfolio volatility can be estimated. Solving for the weights of the two currency pairs gives us 52.3% for the EUR/USD, 35.6% for the JPY/USD, and 12.1% for the GBP/USD.[10]

The portfolio basket volatility σ_b is the square root of the variance var_b:

$$
\text{var}_b = \sqrt{\begin{aligned} &0.523^2 \times 0.1074^2 + 0.356^2 \times 0.115^2 + 0.121^2 \times 0.143^2 \\ &+ 2\times 0.523\times 0.356\times 0.7\times 0.1074\times 0.115 \\ &+ 2\times 0.523\times 0.121\times 0.6\times 0.1074\times 0.143 \\ &+ 2\times 0.121\times 0.356\times 0.5\times 0.115\times 0.115 \end{aligned}}
$$

$$
\sigma_b = \sqrt{\text{var}_b{}^2} = \sqrt{0.0102} = 10.1\% \tag{9.14}
$$

In our three-instrument example, the currency basket volatility is 10.1%. We see in equation 9.14 how the derivation of portfolio volatility,

[10] We note that a portfolio of currency options generally makes sense only if the options being used possess sufficient liquidity.

and by extension the derivation of the minimum-variance portfolio weights, depends on the correlation coefficients between the currencies.

However, as Lagnado and Taleb (2022) pointed out, correlations are nonstationary and change across time, including in periods of financial turmoil when hedges are needed most (see Cornell (2018) for a discussion).

As an alternative to mean–variance optimization, we can use a factor framework of some type to gauge the changes in both correlations and volatilities. One such portfolio factor is the one developed by Konstantinov and Fabozzi (2022a). Using empirical data, the latter authors developed a factor that captures changes of both currency-implied correlation and volatilities. The construction of such a factor is based on the application of the Guldin-Pappus theorem in Euclidean space for rotating triangles. This factor is defined as the gravity radius.[11] Figure 9.4 shows the currency triangle composition.

Visual inspection of Figure 9.4 shows the expected currency triangle that captures both expected volatilities and correlations comprising the currency pairs USD/JPY, EUR/USD, and EUR/JPY. Specifically, the factor that captures changes in expected correlations and volatilities has the length of GR or G'R' in the case of a change in the volatilities of EUR/USD and USD/JPY. The larger the volatilities, the longer the length of the gravity radius (GR). Again, we note that the correlation (the β angle between EUR/USD and USD/JPY) in this visualization is held constant.[12]

The foregoing approach allows the construction of a portfolio index aggregating all currency pairwise trades. Indeed, portfolio managers and

---

[11] The Guldin-Pappus theorem states that the surface area of the solid figure generated by rotating a plane curve is equal to the product of the perimeter (arc length) P of the figure and the distance travelled by the center of gravity of the figure. There are four axioms: (1) volatilities are non-negative, (2) currency volatilities are reciprocal, (3) the volatility of the target pair is less than or equal to the sum of the reciprocal directed pairs, and (4) volatilities are symmetrical or invariant with respect to the numeraire or base currency. As an example of the first three axioms, the currency volatility between the euro and US dollar (EUR/JPY) for a US dollar (USD) based investor is equal to or less than the sum of the USD/EUR and USD/JPY currency pairs. As an example of the application of the first and second axioms, a volatility of 10.74% for the EUR/USD is the same as for the USD/EUR. According to the fourth axiom, the volatility of the USD/EUR and EUR/USD is 10.74%.

[12] See Konstantinov and Fabozzi (2022a) for a detailed explanation of the gravity radius.

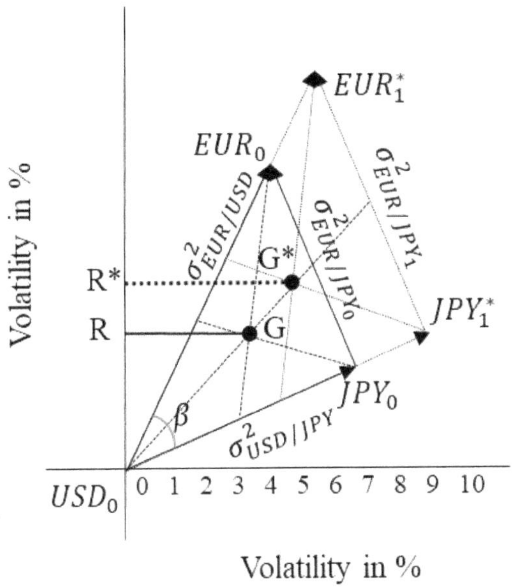

Figure 9.4: Currency Gravity Factor with Changing Expected Volatilities and Constant Correlation with USD as a Base Currency

Note: The assignment of a currency pair is done on the horizontal axis. The US dollar is used as the base currency in the illustration. Every currency can be used at the zero point (base), and it is useful to choose the base currency as the reporting currency, or the currency in which the trade payoff is calculated in. The change from USD/EUR to USD/EUR* and from USD/JPY to USD/JPY* reflects an increase in volatility by a constant correlation value coefficient β between the currency pairs USD/EUR and USD/JPY. The change of EUR/JPY to EUR*/JPY* also reflects an analogous increase in the volatility of the currency pair. As a result, the gravity factor increases from RG to R*G*.

risk managers can use the new metric to identify correlation and volatility changes that dynamically react to new information. The factor can thus serve as a practical risk indicator.

9.1.3.4 *Hedging impact and portfolio management*

The role of successful portfolio hedging with currency options depends on the relationship between realized and implied volatility, and the overall frequency of portfolio rebalancing and re-hedging. A critical aspect of hedging is the ongoing assessment of option price behavior in changing market conditions. To the latter end, the so-called "Greek" measures in option pricing models aim to gauge the changes in option pricing due to changes in various market parameters. Specifically, option values in the portfolio change with changes in the underlying (*delta*), changes in delta (*gamma*), time (*theta*), volatility (*vega*), and interest rates (*rho*).

9.1.3.4.1 Realized vs implied volatility

The purpose of hedging activities with currency options is not to generate profits, but to protect the portfolio from unintended currency losses. The success of hedging strategies that use options depends on the proper estimation of implied and expected volatility. In other words, a successful hedging strategy depends on identifying options with implied volatility that deviate from expected realized volatility.

Taleb (1997) suggested two approaches to hedging: strategic and dynamic hedging. In the case of unexpected events that might arise due to political risk and exogenous shocks, the most successful strategy is to use judgment and not apply continuous hedging, focusing on the strike price of specific option positions. This is called *strategic hedging*. In the case of a high variance, the more effective portfolio hedging strategy might be to continuously hedge using a variety of strike prices. This is an example of dynamic hedging (with risk-neutral valuation).

9.1.3.4.2 Portfolio rebalancing and re-hedging

Transaction costs are an important part of any hedging strategy because their drag often causes a drift of the portfolio return from desired or expected returns. Frequent rebalancing and re-hedging increase transaction costs and the drift of portfolio returns. The success of both frequent and infrequent balancing depends on developments in the markets and their impacts on the portfolio's delta neutrality.

Often, systematic strategies employed by global bond portfolio managers rely on frequent rebalancing. That is, the portfolio exposure is changed periodically, say, monthly, quarterly, or even weekly. In the case of frequent rebalancing, the underlying principles of random walk or mean-reverting markets may apply, and the portfolio will gain from delta neutrality.

In the case of infrequent rebalancing, the market has to exhibit trending behavior for the portfolio to gain from market movements. The reason is that the options in the portfolio might lose from market movements. In this case, a delta-neutral, long gamma portfolio would be beneficial.

9.2 Overlay Management

The purpose of overlay management is to offset a portfolio's specific risk by using a strategy that is unrelated to the underlying primary strategy of the portfolio. Overlay management might be treated as a risk management technique or as a portfolio strategy. Because overlay programs aim at managing and neutralizing a specific risk in a portfolio (e.g., interest-rate risk), we argue that overlay management is an integral part of risk management.

In this section, we discuss the two most widely used overlay strategies — currency overlays and interest-rate overlays. Whereas currency overlays are used to offset the risk associated with adverse currency movements, the purpose of an interest-rate overlay is to neutralize adverse interest-rate movements that might affect the value of the bonds comprising a portfolio. The most widely used approach to overlay strategies is to utilize derivative instruments like futures, swaps, and forwards. The reason for this is that by using derivative instruments, market impact costs can be reduced and because they allow direct exposure at low cost to the underlying bond and currency markets.

The overlay approach to risk management is to some extent a replication approach that aims at replicating the return and risk profile of a benchmark index, or underlying security like EUR/USD. Dynkin *et al.* (2006) identified three types of replication strategies: (1) cash instruments like bonds or currency pairs, (2) derivatives, and (3) total-return swaps. The most commonly used approaches for both currency and interest-rate overlay management involve the use of derivatives that aim to replicate the movement of the underlying asset — currency exchange rate or bond instrument.

Fundamental portfolio analysis of the underlying investment universe is necessary to provide sound economic rationale for the use of derivative instruments in the overlay strategy. For example, using a derivative-based equity momentum strategy in a global government bond portfolio might be statistically valid, but economically less meaningful than using a currency overlay strategy or US Treasury and European bond futures. The reason is that the overlay strategy should offset specific risks in a portfolio not prioritize the generation of alpha. Following this line of thought, using an equity momentum strategy or a credit derivatives strategy might be more appropriate for corporate bond portfolios (see Ben Dor *et al.* (2022)). There are four possible approaches to index overlay and replication:

- stratified sampling
- duration-matched
- minimum-variance optimization
- momentum replication

Whereas the stratified sampling approach divides the index or underlying benchmark into several risk dimensions, the duration-matched approach uses duration buckets to replicate yield curve movements. The minimum-variance approach tries to find the minimum risk exposure required to replicate the portfolio against the index. The momentum approach tries to replicate the momentum exposure of an index. In practice, momentum overlay strategies using futures and forwards are the most widely used.

9.2.1 *Currency overlay management*

Currency overlay management has two purposes. First, it isolates the currency movements that need to be offset in the portfolio. In other words, the primary task of currency overlay management is risk reduction. The challenge stems from the fact that the short-term movement of exchange rates is unpredictable, and the most consistent movement is associated with a random walk assuming no drift. In this framework, it is impossible to predict currency market movements and therefore currency returns are assumed to be zero. This conclusion can be traced back to the early work of Meese and Rogoff (1983) and Rogoff (2002). Empirical analysis supports the claim that currency prices are unpredictable in the short run.

The main objective of currency overlay management is to hedge some portion or the entire pre-existing currency risk in a global bond portfolio. Given the risk management role of currency overlay strategies, the generation of additional return via selective hedging is not its primary task. Currency overlay management might be focused on the benchmark exposure of the portfolio or might be the result of an absolute return strategy that a global bond portfolio might implement. In the case of an absolute return strategy, the currency overlay has the role of reducing the risk of the exposures.

The development of institutional investing and the proliferation of professional currency managers has increased the role of institutionalization of currency investing and specifically currency overlay management. Pojarliev and Levich (2012) showed that currency overlay programs should be differentiated based on funded and unfunded mandates. The difference is common for large global bond portfolios, or multi-asset bond portfolios with significant exposure to foreign exchange. In the case of funded mandates, an investor might assign specific funds that are placed in accounts which the currency manager is permitted to manage. This might be the case when the currency management of a large global bond portfolio is detached from its fixed-income management. For example, investors might allocate USD 100 million to a currency overlay funded program.

The second application of currency overlay management is the unfunded currency overlay program, which is also common for global bond portfolios. In an unfunded program, the investor monitors the currency exposure of the portfolio. Using portfolio assets as collateral, the investor assigns a specific amount of capital to a currency manager. As previously mentioned, measuring and monitoring the real-time exposure of the portfolio and determining the portfolio weights and notional amounts in the various portfolio currencies are essential for the success of the overlay program.

As an example of how unfunded programs work, let us suppose that USD 50 million in cash of a USD 500 million bond portfolio is dedicated for overlay management. In an unfunded program, the currency overlay is implemented without assets, and the currency overlay focuses on trading activities using established currency management strategies like momentum, carry, or value. Institutional investors often prefer currency overlay programs as add-ons to global bond portfolios. For example, a global bond portfolio might be part of a large multi-asset strategy of, say, USD 10 billion. The global bond portfolio manager of a USD 500 million sleeve in a larger multi-asset portfolio might have exposure to currency risk and full discretion of the currency exposure. However, investors might add a currency overlay program to the entire portfolio and consider all currency exposure at risk using the portfolio weights.

We also note that the base currency of the portfolio plays a central role in currency overlay management. This is because the base currency of a portfolio is the reporting currency of the portfolio holdings. For example, a USD 500 million global bond portfolio might invest in Japanese government bonds. In this case, the USD/JPY is used to calculate the exposure.

While currency overlay management may utilize the four currency styles identified by Pojarliev and Levich (2008), in the next section, we focus on two popular currency overlay approaches — momentum and volatility strategies.

9.2.1.1 *Currency overlay management using a momentum approach*

Perhaps the most widely used currency overlay management technique is the currency momentum or trend-following strategy that tries to replicate currency price movements.[13] Compared to fundamentally based strategies like carry and value, trend-following strategies are based on the simple assumption that there is a persistent pattern in currency movements. Momentum strategies are widely used for all traditional asset classes like equities and bonds, but empirical evidence supporting them has also been found in alternative asset classes like currencies and commodities. Technical indicators like moving average, the 200-day line, and short- and medium-term trend signals are often used to detect trends. The underlying principle of momentum strategies is to buy currencies that have been appreciating and sell currencies that have been depreciating. The strategy is maintained until the trend pattern breaks and the opposite strategy appears. Suppose, for example, that the EUR/USD exchange rate is 1.03 at time $t-1$ and 1.056 at time t. Because the euro has appreciated against the US dollar, a simple momentum strategy would be to buy the EUR/USD. This position is maintained, for example, until the EUR/USD changes to 1.07.

Because global bond portfolios have exposure to multiple currencies, a currency momentum overlay strategy will take long positions in the currencies that have appreciated against the portfolio base currency and short positions in the currencies that have depreciated against the portfolio base

[13]An extensive overview of currency momentum strategies is provided by Menkhoff *et al.* (2012).

currency. Fixing the portfolio base currency assures that the overlay strategy fully covers the portfolio's currency risk. Pukthuanthong-Le, Levich, and Thomas (2007) found that the effectiveness of trend-following strategies in currency markets declined with time. Because trend-following strategies are short-lived, and trading signals appear and vanish in the short-term, positioning adjustments and close monitoring of the markets are essential for successful momentum overlay management.

9.2.1.2 *Currency volatility overlay management*

Another commonly employed currency overlay strategy is the volatility strategy. The latter uses options to gain exposure to and benefit from currency movements. While, popular, one of the challenges in implementing volatility overlay strategies is the transaction costs associated with replication of currency movements. Option transaction costs are much higher than spot transaction costs. Therefore, directional trades or trades that replicate the price movements of foreign exchange often require significant transaction costs for option risk management (managing the so-called "Greek measures"). Pojarliev and Levich (2012) provide an example for the AUD/USD exchange rate and show that the option costs deviate substantially from the spot transaction costs. Specifically, the spot changes by 0.03%, but the options on AUD/USD are quoted by 0.05 steps. As a result, the volatility of the AUD/USD has to increase by 5% to cover transaction costs, while the spot changes by 0.03%. Note that the AUD/USD is a highly liquid currency pair. The transaction costs of emerging market currencies might be significantly higher.

9.2.2 *Interest-rate portfolio overlay example for futures*

The main goal of interest-rate overlay management is to replicate the interest-rate behavior of an index as interest-rate risk represents the primary source of risk in bonds. Interest-rate overlays are an important tool for all types of bond portfolios (see Dynkin *et al.*, 2002). In interest-rate overlays the decomposition of key-rate durations is essential.[14] The portfolio duration contributions in each duration bucket are matched with

[14] The concept of key-rate durations was introduced by Ho (1992). The main intuition behind the concept is to decompose duration contributions into maturity buckets. In other

appropriate futures contracts. Liquid instruments like US Treasury futures can be used successfully in overlay strategies in cases in which the corporate bond exposure of a global bond portfolio does not dominate the entire portfolio exposure. This is not surprising because spread risk and interest-rate risk show different dynamics and portfolio managers might choose to avoid one but build exposure to the other.

The main function of an interest-rate overlay is to neutralize the impact of changing interest rates that might harm the bonds in a portfolio without requiring explicit duration management. For this purpose, interest-rate overlays with futures are the most widely applied structure. The reason for this is that bond futures are highly liquid and are transparent, standardized instruments. Bond futures are available for the most liquid bond markets worldwide (e.g., US Treasury futures in the United States, bund futures in Germany/Eurozone, and yen futures in Japan). The most liquid futures reference the bonds with a 10-year maturity, which are often used as a proxy for the prevailing level of interest rates. The main risk when implementing interest-rate overlays with futures is the existence of basis risk. Basis risk arises due to differences between the prices of futures contracts and the spot prices of their underlying assets.

Futures contracts are available at various maturities in all major markets. This allows portfolio managers the ability to build customized hedging strategies. However, hedging and overlay with futures still require constant risk monitoring. Dynkin *et al.* (2002) showed that a US Treasury futures overlay on a US Treasury index generates significant tracking error. Basis risk further increases during times of volatile financial markets. Similar tracking error concerns might arise when using a set of futures for the other currencies in a portfolio. In general, for passively investing bond portfolios, the replication and overlay with cash bonds is less problematic. The exposure to major currencies such as the USD, EUR, GBP, and JPY is more than 90% in passive portfolios. However, actively managed portfolios with aggressive positioning and exposure in emerging markets might try to apply derivatives strategies using liquid instruments. This is due to the fact that emerging markets show significant exposure to U.S. Treasuries and the U.S. dollar.

---

words, the key-rate duration of a portfolio is the bond portfolio sensitivity to a change in the benchmark yield curve at specific maturities.

The development of emerging markets has resulted in the rise of futures contracts on many EM exchanges. However, futures instruments in the G10 markets remain the most liquid and widely adopted instruments in interest-rate overlay programs. The more heterogeneous the global bond exposure in a portfolio, the greater the complexity to implement an interest-rate futures overlay. An example of such a portfolio might be a global bond portfolio with a large number of single bonds, say 500, and multiple currency and country exposures. In these types of portfolios, factor models are often used to explain bond dynamics. Principal component analysis or other statistical techniques can be successfully applied to find the relevant factors. Once the appropriate factors have been identified, the next step is to find futures instruments that match the behavior of the factors.

Here, economic and econometric analyses can be invoked and co-integration tests specifically help in this endeavor.[15] Following Wu (1999), co-integration tests might be applied to find the non-stationary movement of the portfolio returns and the futures returns. A test that is widely used is the Augmented Dickey–Fuller test (Dickey and Fuller (1979)). The portfolio and futures instrument are said to be co-integrated if a linear combination of the time series results in a stationary process.[16] A stationary process means that there is no change in mean or standard deviation through time. However, because non-stationary time series exist in markets, the convergence between futures and the portfolio is time varying. The reason might be a shift in the portfolio exposure to specific assets, for example, or a decrease or increase in a country or currency exposure. Co-integrated portfolio and futures time series should converge over time. Therefore, overlay management and the instruments used to implement it require frequent adjustments and monitoring of the spread between the co-integrated portfolio and futures time series.

Setting a threshold level for the spread volatility between the bond and futures contracts might help to prevent the divergence of the series and possible malfunctioning of the overlay strategy. With the foregoing in

[15] Phillips and Ouliaris (1989) were among the first who combined principal component analysis and co-integration analysis.

[16] See Crowder (1996), Engle and Yoo (1997), Wu (1999), and Jondeau and Ricart (1999) for co-integration tests and application of co-integration to different financial markets.

mind, we can outline the following steps for the analysis of strategies for overlay management:

- Find an economically meaningful variable that might explain the portfolio.
- Analyze the time series and test for co-integration.
- Apply econometric analysis (e.g., regression analysis, seasonality tests, vector autoregression).
- Set threshold levels for the spread between the two time series and monitor the dynamics.

Formally, bond portfolio and futures time series will be co-integrated if the following is stationary:

$$e_t = \ln(R_t^{PF}) - a\ln(R_t^{F}) \tag{9.15}$$

where a is a constant, e_t is a stationary random variable, R_t^{PF} is the natural logarithm of the portfolio price, and R_t^{F} is the natural logarithm of the futures prices.

Co-integration assumes that the portfolio and futures instrument should follow an econometric process with common trends. That is, the bond portfolio and futures instrument are modeled as a trend series with noise terms:

$$\ln(R_t^{PF}) = \phi_{PFt} + \epsilon_t \quad \text{and} \quad \ln(R_t^{F}) = \phi_{Ft} + \upsilon_t \tag{9.16}$$

where ϕ_{PFt} and ϕ_{Ft} are common trends that should be related, and ϵ_t and υ_t are stationary random noise terms.

It can be shown that if the two trend variables ϕ_{PFt} and ϕ_{Ft} are related, then the linear combination in equation (9.15) is stationary and the portfolio and futures time series in our example are co-integrated.

A simple example is shown in Table 9.6 that illustrates the results of co-integration tests for an anonymized bond portfolio and bund futures time series with 180 monthly observations in the period from 2001 to 2016. Note that the portfolio and the futures instruments might have the same currency, something which will reduce the basis and currency risks in the overlay.

Here, we see that the test results for the two time series are broadly similar, with the tau-statistic uniformly rejecting the null hypothesis of no co-integration. Both the tau-statistic (t-statistic) and the normalized autocorrelation coefficient (z-statistic) for residuals are obtained using each

Table 9.6: Co-integration Tests for a Global Bond Portfolio and Euro Bund Futures

Dependent	**Tau-statistic**	**Prob.***	***z*-statistic**	**Prob.***
Global Bond Portfolio	−11.84	0.000	−157.81	0.000
Euro Bund Future	−13.03	0.000	−176.11	0.000

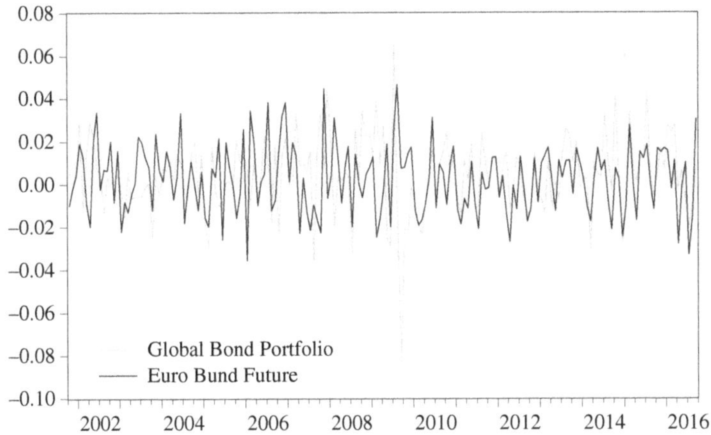

Figure 9.5: Global Bond Portfolio and Euro Bund Futures Returns

Notes: This figure includes anonymized monthly returns of a global bond portfolio and the Euro Bund Futures (RXA Commodity). The returns of the time series are plotted on the left-hand side. Data obtained by the authors from Bloomberg, LLC.

series in the group as the dependent variable in a co-integrating regression. The results for the *z*-statistics (used to test for residuals) are uniform, for both the Global Bond Portfolio and the Euro Bund Futures, rejecting the unit root null at the 5% level.

Figure 9.5 shows an example of the monthly returns of a global bond portfolio and the German Euro Bund Futures contract. We run the co-integration tests described above and plot the monthly returns in Figure 9.5.

The test results clearly suggest that the portfolio returns and bund futures returns are co-integrated and converge to a linear stationary term. Notably, the common average (stationary) value may well indicate a common factor exposure. Note that the time series diverge in some cases.

Applying econometric analysis, we can show that the correlation between the portfolio returns and the Euro bund futures returns is 0.23.

Regressing the portfolio returns against the Euro bund future returns shows that the beta of the portfolio returns to the Euro bund futures is 0.25 (t-statistics of 2.88) with an intercept of 34bps (t-statistic 2.24). That is, the Euro bund futures explain a small part of the portfolio returns. The R^2 of the regression is 0.06 (i.e., the variance of Euro bund futures returns explains only 6% of the variance of global bond portfolio returns).

However, visual inspection of Figure 9.6 and statistical analysis show that the spread is close to normally distributed. This can be visually observed in the histogram plotted on the left-hand side of the figure. Note that the normally distributed spread between the global bond portfolio returns and the Euro bund futures returns is an indication that applying a threshold level might be reasonable.

To further investigate the spread between the two time series, we can plot the autocorrelograms as shown in Figure 9.7. Specifically, small plots within the dashed lines are the first indication of low autocorrelations. The spread exhibits autocorrelation (significant first and second lag of the autocorrelograms). The pattern indicates that the autocorrelations follow a random walk. In our case, we use 12 monthly lagged periods, which are identified in the third column. In other words, we show the correlations with a time lag of up to 12 months. The autocorrelations' values are shown in the fourth column. For example, the correlation of the original series

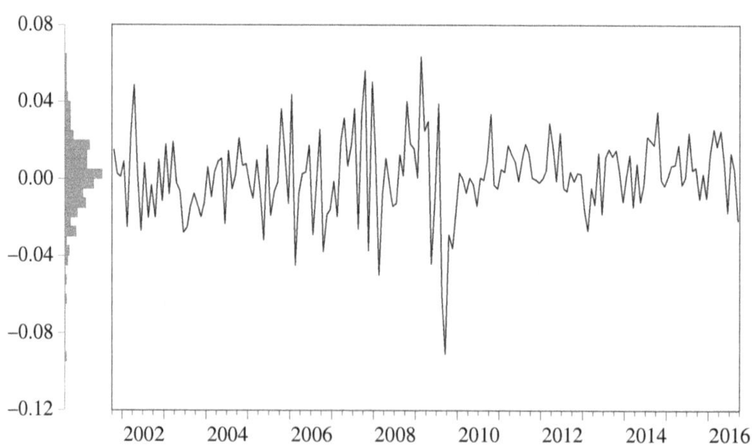

Figure 9.6: Spread between the Global Bond Portfolio Returns and the Euro Bund Futures Returns

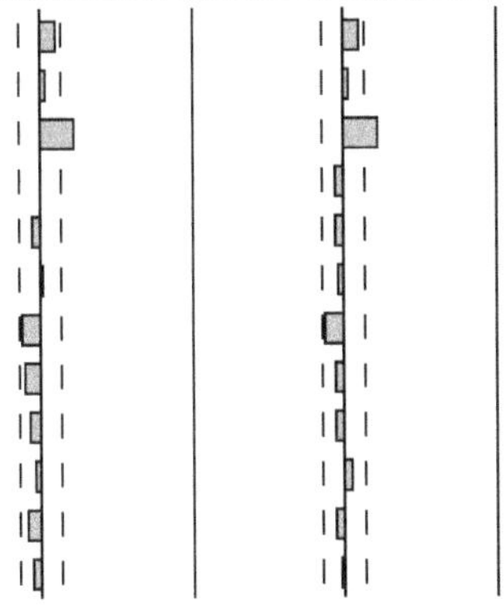

Autocorrelation	Partial Correlation		AC	PAC	Q-Stat	Prob
		1	0.11	0.11	2.20	0.14
		2	0.04	0.03	2.47	0.29
		3	0.24	0.24	13.12	0.00
		4	0.00	-0.05	13.12	0.01
		5	-0.05	-0.06	13.67	0.02
		6	0.01	-0.03	13.70	0.03
		7	-0.13	-0.12	16.86	0.02
		8	-0.11	-0.06	18.99	0.01
		9	-0.08	-0.06	20.21	0.02
		10	-0.03	0.05	20.39	0.03
		11	-0.09	-0.06	22.03	0.02
		12	-0.05	-0.02	22.59	0.03

Figure 9.7: Spread Autocorrelation

Note: Authors' own estimates; correlations with a time lag of up to 12 months.

with the time series of lag 1 (one monthly observation) is 0.11. The *Q*-stat is reported in the fifth column; the large *p*-values of the *Q*-stat indicate that the error terms are white noise.

9.3 Takeaways

- The focus of this chapter is on two major topics — hedging interest-rate risk and currency risk. There are two important issues to consider when implementing a hedging policy in global bond portfolios. The first relates to the interest-rate risk that arises due to changing bond yields. Options and futures are widely used to hedge interest-rate and currency exposure. Volatility is the most important variable in analyzing and pricing options, and transaction costs are an important consideration in the implementation of option strategies.
- Both currency and interest-rate overlay management use derivatives to replicate the movement of the underlying asset and their implementation is based on a specific style or strategy. Momentum strategies are the most widely used in practice.
- Alpha generation is not a central objective of overlay programs. Rather, the main objective of overlay management is to hedge some

portion of or the entire pre-existing currency and/or interest-rate risk in a global bond portfolio. Various econometric tools can be employed to help craft effective overlay strategies.

References

Afik, Z., G. Jacoby, and Z. Wiener. 2018. "Duration and Globalization". *Journal of Fixed Income* 28(2): 31–43.

Baltussen, G., P. Houweling, M. Martens, and O. Penninga. 2021. "Factor Investing in Fixed Income Securities". Chapter 47 in F. J. Fabozzi (ed.), *The Handbook of Fixed Income Securities.* 9th Edition. New York: McGraw Hill.

Ben Dor, A., L. Dynkin, and J. Hyman. 2021. "Managing the Spread Risk of Credit Portfolios Using the Duration Times Spread Measure". Chapter 53 in F. J. Fabozzi (ed.), *The Handbook of Fixed Income Securities.* 9th Edition. New York: McGraw Hill.

Ben Dor, A., A. Desclee, L. Dynkin, J. Hyman, J. Meli, and S. Polbennikov. 2022. "Quantitative Management of Credit Portfolios". *Journal of Fixed Income* 32(2): 93–141.

Ben Dor, A. and J. Guan. 2017. "Hedging Systematic Risk in High Yield Portfolios with a Synthetic Overlay: A Comparative Analysis of Equity Instruments vs. Credit Default Swaps". *Journal of Fixed Income* 26(4): 5–24.

Bierwag, G. O. and I. Fooladi. 2006. "Duration Analysis: A Historical Perspective". *Journal of Applied Finance* 16(2): 144–160.

Black, F. 1989. "Universal Hedging: Optimizing Currency Risk and Reward in International Equity Portfolios". *Financial Analysts Journal* 45(4): 16–22.

Black, F. and M. Scholes. 1973. "The Pricing of Options and Corporate Liabilities". *Journal of Political Economy* 81(3): 637–654.

Cornell, B. 2018. "Taking Stationarity Seriously". *Journal of Portfolio Management* 44(3): 1–3.

Cox, J., S. Ross, and M. Rubinstein. 1979. "Option Pricing: A Simplified Approach". *Journal of Financial Economics* 7: 229–263.

Crowder, W. J. 1996. "A Note on Cointegration and International Capital Market Efficiency: A Reply." *Journal of International Money and Finance* 15(4): 661–664.

Dickey, D. A. and W. A. Fuller. 1979. "Distribution of the Estimators for Autoregressive Time Series with a Unit Root". *Journal of the American Statistical Association* 74: 427–431.

Dynkin, L., J. Hyman, and P. Lindner. 2002. "Hedging and Replication of Fixed-Income Portfolios". *Journal of Fixed Income* 11(4): 43–64.

Dynkin, L., A. Gould, and V. Konstantinovsky. 2006. "Replicating Bond Indices with Liquid Derivatives". *Journal of Fixed Income* 15(4): 7–19.

Engel, C. 1996. "A Note on Cointegration and International Capital Market Efficiency". *Journal of International Money and Finance* 15(4): 657–660.

Engle, R. F. and B. S. Yoo. 1997. "Forecasting and Testing in Co-integrates Systems". *Journal of Econometrics* 35: 143–159.

Estrada, J. 2009. "Black Swans in Emerging Markets". *Journal of Investing* 17(3): 20–34.

Fabozzi, F. J. and S. Vohra. 2022. "Applications of FX Derivatives in Active Currency Risk Management". *Journal of Derivatives* 29(4): 168–191.

Fabozzi, F. J., A. Kalotay, and M. Dorigan. 2021. "Valuation of Bonds with Embedded Options". Chapter 36 in F. J. Fabozzi (ed.) *The Handbook of Fixed Income Securities*. 9th Edition. New York: McGraw Hill.

Fooladi, I. J., G. Jacoby, and L. Jin. 2021. "Real Duration and Inflation Duration: A Cross Country Perspective on a Multidimensional Hedging Strategy". *Journal of International Financial Markets, Institutions and Money* 70: 101265.

Garman, M. B. and S. W. Kohlhagen. 1983. "Foreign Currency Option Values". *Journal of International Money and Finance* 2: 231–237.

Ho, T. S. Y. 1992. "Key Rate Durations". *Journal of Fixed Income* 2(2): 29–44.

Jondeau, E. and R. Ricart. 1999. "The Expectation Hypothesis of the Term Structure: Tests on US, German, French, and UK Euro-rates". *Journal of International Money and Finance* 18: 725–750.

Jorion, P. 1994. "Mean/Variance Analysis of Currency Overlays". *Financial Analysts Journal* 50(3): 48–56.

Konstantinov, G. S. and F. J. Fabozzi. 2022a. "The Geometry of the World of Currency Volatilities". *Computational Economics* 60(1): 125–145.

Lagnado, R. and N. N. Taleb. 2022. "Pension Funds Should Never Rely on Correlation". *Journal of Alternative Investments* 24(4): 8–17.

Meese, R. A. and K. Rogoff. 1983. "Empirical Exchange Rate Models of the Seventies: Do they Fit Out of Sample?" *Journal of International Economics* 14(1–2): 3–24.

Menkhoff, L., L. Sarno, M. Schmeling, and A. Schrimpf. 2012. "Currency Momentum Strategies". *Journal of Financial Economics* 106(3): 660–684.

Levich, R. M. and L. R. Thomas. 1993. "The Merits of Active Currency Risk Management: Evidence from International Bond Portfolios". *Financial Analysts Journal* 49(5): 63–70.

Papaioannou, M. G. and G. Tsesekos. 2018. "Regaining Access to Capital Markets: An Overview of Issues and Strategies". *Journal of Investing* 27(3): 45–52.

Perold, A. and E. Shulman. 1998. "The Free Lunch in Currency Hedging: Implications for investment Policy and Performance Standards". *Financial Analysts Journal* 44(3): 45–50.

Phillips, P. C. B. and S. Ouliaris. 1989. "Testing for Cointegration Using Principal Components Methods". *Journal of Economic Dynamics and Control* 12: 205–230.

Pitts, M. and F. J. Fabozzi. 1990. *Interest Rate Futures and Options*. Chicago, IL: Probus Publishing.

Pojarliev, M. and R. M. Levich. 2008. "Do Professional Currency Managers Beat the Benchmark? *Financial Analyst Journal* 64(5): 18–32.

Pojarliev, M. and R. M. Levich. 2012. *A New Look at Currency Investing*. CFA Institute.

Pukthuanthong-Le, K., R. M. Levich, and L. R. Thomas. 2007. "Do Foreign Exchange Markets Still Trend? *Journal of Portfolio Management* 34(1): 114–118.

Taleb, N. N. 1997. *Dynamic Hedging: Managing Vanilla and Exotic Options*. Hoboken, NJ: John Wiley & Sons.

Wu, J. L. 1999. "A Re-examination of the Exchange Rate-Interest Differential Relationship: Evidence from Germany and Japan". *Journal of International Money and Finance* 18: 319–336.

Part 3

Performance Analysis and Attribution

Chapter 10

Factor Models in Performance Analysis

Global bond portfolio managers use factor models for different purposes. Some factor models are utilized *ex ante* within the optimization process, while others are used in in order to understand portfolio behavior *ex post*. In this chapter, we focus on the latter application — explaining bond portfolio risk and return. We place special emphasis on model specification given that different types of bond portfolios may require different models to explain their behavior.

Global bond portfolio managers might use qualitative and quantitative criteria to select factors. Qualitative criteria are typically rooted in economic intuition. In this case, portfolio managers might base their selection of factors based on specific economic evidence or theories. Quantitative criteria typically connect factor desirability to the statistical properties of a candidate factor, such as it being additive to the explanatory power of a model or it being uncorrelated with the other factors in the model. Beyond differentiating between qualitative and quantitative criteria for factor selection, we can group factors according to investment themes, using the factor classifications which we defined in Chapter 5 — market yield and currency factors, asset-based factors, equity market factors, and strategy (style) factors.

In this chapter, we discuss two important applications of factor models. In the first application, factor models are used *ex ante* to create portfolios based on appropriate risk factors with the objective of minimizing tracking error to a specific benchmark, as well as to achieve diversification, monitor risks, and capture the time-varying nature of each factor. The second application of factor models is to explain portfolio returns *ex post* and (eventually) identify alpha, which is used for performance measurement and performance attribution. Since these topics are of critical importance to global bond portfolio management, we discuss both applications in this chapter.

Of course, the considerations that are used to select factors in relation to managed portfolios are also important for the analysis of benchmarks. To the latter end, we describe the methods that can be used to select factors to explain the returns of the most widely used benchmark index for global bonds, the Bloomberg Barclays Global Aggregate Bond Index. Despite the large number of factors we identified in the four factor groups, in practice, a more restricted set of factors are typically utilized by portfolio managers. This results in an increased exposure to common factors across funds. Global bond portfolios are no exception. This is known as *factor crowdedness* in global bond portfolio management. Accounting for and measuring factor crowdedness is an important aspect of manger performance evaluation.

10.1 Methodology for Building Factor Models for Bond Portfolios

Modeling factors and their relationship to asset returns can be done in a number of ways. The most common way is to use a linear model such as an ordinary least squares (OLS) regression. Linear models are useful in explaining basic relationships between variables and are often a good starting point for researchers before moving on to more sophisticated frameworks.

We can illustrate the utility of linear models with an example. Ben Dor *et al.* (2007) derived a duration-times-spread (DTS) factor to explain bond market returns and return volatility. Let us suppose that we are trying to explain portfolio returns using the DTS factor. Note that the DTS factor uses spreads stated in basis points and durations stated in years. For example, a portfolio with duration of, say, 7, and a spread of, say, 250 bps (2.5%) would have a DTS of 7 × 2.5 = 17.5. The model has the following form:

$$R_{\text{Portfolio}} \approx \alpha_i + \beta \text{DTS} + \varepsilon_t \tag{10.1}$$

where β is the sensitivity (beta) of bond portfolio returns to a given factor, DTS is the duration-times-spread factor, and ε_t is a randomly distributed error term.

For example, suppose that the estimated beta coefficient (β) is −0.2. This implies that for a 1% increase in the DTS portfolio, returns decrease by approximately 20%. In other words, a duration weighted spread widening has a negative impact on the bond portfolio. Linear models are easy to interpret in this way.

While linear models have their advantages, they often fail to provide the level of analytical insight required to confidently manage portfolios. This is often the case with bond portfolios, which generally contain debt instruments with significantly complex return behaviors. Some of the challenges posed by the complexities of the bond market can be overcome by avoiding the use of linear models. A linear factor model that restricts itself to a small number of factors faces the risk of providing an inadequate picture of portfolio return behavior over a given measurement period. As a result, such models are not maximally informative because of their inability to account for the nonlinear return behavior of and/or interaction effects among factors.

Indeed, James *et al.* (2013) listed the following challenges (and potential solutions to them) when applying linear models to global bond portfolios:

- nonlinearity in the data, mitigated by inclusion of squared terms and interactions;
- correlation of error terms, detected using autocorrelograms[1];
- heteroskedastic variance of error terms, detected using the White test;
- outliers as predicted values, detected using residual plots;
- high leverage points associated with outliers of the exogenous data, and;
- collinearity which arises due to highly correlated explanatory factors.

A natural response to the shortcomings of linear factor models is to employ nonlinear factor models; however, parametric nonlinear models also have a number of shortcomings. First, the structure of nonlinear models is often heavily dependent on the sample data. As the sample expands or contracts, we at times find that the function specified by the model

[1]An autocorrelogram, also called an autocorrelation function, indicates how observations in a time series are related to past observations and how significant the relationship is.

changes, sometimes dramatically. Second, unlike linear models, parameter estimates cannot always be derived analytically. Rather, solutions are often found using iterative methods, in which initial values are posited for each unknown. Although iterative methods can be useful, the optimizations that drive them may ultimately fail to converge if the initial values are too distant from possible solution values. Initial values that are remote from optimal values can also cause convergence to a local solution rather than a global solution.

As a remedy to the drawbacks of both linear models and parametric nonlinear models, many machine learning algorithms can be used to model financial data in a more efficient manner. Machine learning models are non-parametric and capture nonlinear return behavior and interaction effects without convoluted formalism. In the equity space, a well-known application of a machine learning algorithm to modeling equity factors was provided by Simonian *et al.* (2019) where the random forest algorithm is applied to the Fama–French–Carhart model. In the realm of fixed income, Konstantinov and Rusev (2020) model interaction effects between bonds and equity funds by applying a graph theoretical approach. They conclude that equity factors drive the relationship between the two categories of global equity and bond funds.

10.2 How to Select Factors

Which factors are relevant is the key question that a portfolio manager must answer when using a factor model. Before providing answers to this question let us take a look at the correlational relationships among some of the factors we discussed in Chapter 5.

Computing pairwise return correlations is a convenient place to start factor analysis. In Table 10.1, we report the monthly pairwise return correlations of several factors for the period November 2000 to December 2019. The low correlations between the factors suggest that they are not direct substitutes. Low correlations between factors are desired from a diversification perspective. This means that factors with low correlations might reduce the risk of a portfolio when a factor model is used for factor allocation in portfolio management. In the table, we see that currency volatility has a negative correlation to yield volatility (–0.360). This suggests that the currency and yield volatility risk factors are inversely related. Similarly, currency momentum and bond carry have a correlation of 0.105. This means that both factors are not associated. Low historical

Table 10.1: Correlations of Monthly Factor Returns November 2000–December 2019

	UMD	MKT	SMB	HML	RMW	CMA	BAB	Currency Volatility	Currency Carry	Currency Momentum	Currency Value	Bond Trend	Bond Carry	Rate Volatility
UMD	1.000													
MKT	–0.475	1.000												
SMB	–0.196	0.252	1.000											
HML	0.061	–0.076	–0.014	1.000										
RMW	0.423	–0.472	–0.364	0.136	1.000									
CMA	0.330	–0.435	–0.229	0.689	0.231	1.000								
BAB	0.550	–0.246	0.051	0.392	0.488	0.314	1.000							
Currency Volatility	–0.047	0.084	–0.016	0.125	–0.100	0.112	–0.059	1.000						
Currency Carry	–0.046	0.083	0.006	–0.059	–0.050	–0.136	0.025	–0.529	1.000					
Currency Momentum	0.115	–0.055	–0.049	0.085	–0.150	0.217	–0.058	0.198	–0.132	1.000				
Currency Value	–0.067	–0.013	–0.067	–0.009	0.041	0.008	–0.080	0.167	–0.058	–0.070	1.000			
Bond Trend	–0.022	–0.070	0.015	0.019	–0.076	0.023	0.025	–0.009	0.015	–0.010	–0.067	1.000		
Bond Carry	0.126	–0.224	–0.187	0.118	0.144	0.251	0.050	0.183	–0.243	0.105	0.027	0.300	1.000	
Rate Volatility	–0.027	0.111	0.165	–0.031	–0.023	–0.078	0.128	–0.360	0.260	–0.161	–0.182	0.050	–0.198	1.000

Notes: The factors in the table are discussed in Chapter 5. Monthly data obtained by the authors from Bloomberg LLC.

correlations between factors are a positive indicator, which analysts and portfolio managers consider when applying factor models. Another interesting case is the correlation between the Betting-against-Beta (BAB) and the momentum (UMD) factor, which is 0.550. The correlation coefficient is much higher compared to the correlation coefficients between the other factors. Nevertheless, both factors might be included in a factor model for several reasons. First, factor inclusion might be based on economic theory and not purely based on statistical analysis. Second, significant positive correlation can still be meaningful from a statistical point of view, as long the factors do not exhibit multicollinearity.[2]

Both academic research and practitioner research emphasize the use of linear models to construct portfolios. Linear models have the advantage of being easy to interpret. Nevertheless, a key question that is often asked is which factors are relevant? Which factors should be considered in global bond portfolios if there are so many factors, and novel developments constantly present new solutions? Factor identification is essential because of the sheer number of potential factors (Harvey and Liu (2014) have identified more than 300 factors). Traditional linear models like OLS regression do not provide the means for factor selection.

There are two models that can be efficiently utilized to select factors: least absolute shrinkage and selection operator (LASSO) and orthogonal regression models. Another tool used by researchers to identify important factors involves the process of building orthogonal regressions, we describe each model in turn below.

10.2.1 *LASSO and ridge regression models*

The LASSO model posits absolute terms for the β_j coefficients, which means that they are given a value of zero if their impact is significantly small. The aim of a LASSO analysis is to find the best regression model by minimizing the squared errors between the portfolio returns R_i and a model $\widehat{R}_i$ fitted to explain portfolio returns.[3]

---

[2]The Variance Inflation Ratio (VIR) is computed for the risk factors in order to identify possible multicollinearity in a factor model.

[3]James *et al.* (2013) provide an extensive review and explanations of LASSO and ridge regression models along with code for implementing them in the programming language R.

The LASSO model has the following form:

$$\underset{\beta \in R^p}{\text{Arg min}} \left[\sum_{i=1}^{K} (R_i - \widehat{R}_i)^2 \right] = \sum_{i=1}^{K} \left(R_i - \alpha - \sum_{j=1}^{P} \beta_j F_{ij} \right)^2 + \lambda \sum_{j=0}^{P} |\beta_j| \quad (10.2)$$

where R_i is the portfolio's return, α_i is an intercept, $F_{j,t}$ are style factors, and β_i is a coefficient that measures the sensitivity of the portfolio's return to the factor.

The novel part of equation 10.2 is the last term on the right-hand side. This term defines the values that calibrate the β_i coefficients, which are in absolute terms $|\beta_j|$. This step is called *factor shrinkage*. Note that the shrinkage effect depends on the penalty parameter λ. A λ value of zero will produce the same model as the ordinary least squares model. However, a sufficiently large value of λ would force some of the coefficients β_j to become zero. Thus, different λ estimations determine the outcome of a model. λ is also known as a "tuning" parameter.

An alternative to LASSO is ridge regression. In this model, there are squared terms for the β_j parameter, which is the only difference compared to LASSO. Because the β_j parameters are squared, they can take on values close to but not equal to zero.[4]

$$\underset{\beta \in R^p}{\text{Arg min}} \left[\sum_{i=1}^{K} (R_i - \widehat{R}_i)^2 \right] = \sum_{i=1}^{K} \left(R_i - \alpha - \sum_{j=1}^{P} \beta_j F_{ij} \right)^2 + \lambda \sum_{j=0}^{P} \beta_j^2 \quad (10.3)$$

As mentioned above λ is an important parameter that determines the model outcome, and the major difference in the models is how the β_j parameters are expressed. A squared β_j parameter in equation (10.2) cannot be negative, thus the coefficient would preserve even a small value. In contrast, the absolute values of the coefficients $|\beta_j|$ might become zero and disappear from the model.

The most important formal difference between the two models, and in fact the property that defines LASSO as a factor selection model, is that

[4]Note that the shrinkage effect depends on the penalty parameter λ. Obviously, a λ value of zero will produce the same model as the ordinary least square model. However, a sufficiently large value of lambda would force some of the coefficients β_j to become zero. Thus, different λ estimations determine the outcome of a model and the variability of coefficients.

LASSO and ridge regression perform different shrinkage procedures. Specifically, LASSO shrinks the least squares coefficients toward zero by the same amount. In contrast, ridge regression shrinks the least squares coefficients by a constant amount. From a portfolio management perspective, LASSO is most commonly used for dimension reduction because it allows investors to start with an expansive set of factors and narrow it down to a more parsimonious set. It presents an advantage over other commonly used dimension reduction methods like PCA because it allows us to retain economically interpretable factors versus the synthetic constructs generated in PCA. Ridge regression on the other hand, is typically used to combat overfitting in an existing model so that it generalizes on new data. In statistical terms, ridge regression increases bias in order to reduce variance. Ridge regression also reduces multicollinearity through the penalty parameter λ. When the penalty parameter is applied to the diagonal of the regression matrix, it forces the columns of the matrix to be linearly independent (for an investment application of ridge regression see Simonian and Wu, 2019).

10.2.2 *Illustration of LASSO and ridge regression models*

Let's illustrate the application of LASSO and ridge regression for factor selection. Table 10.2 shows the weights of the asset classes of a global bond portfolio estimated using predictive regressions and a broad set of factors described in Chapter 5. We assume that a portfolio manager starts with a blended set of 17 factors. By a "blended set", we mean that the portfolio manager might want to pick up factors from each of the four groups we identified — market yield and currency factors, asset-based, equity market, and strategy (style) factors. Again, whereas ridge regression would preserve all factors in the model, only LASSO would help to select the most important factors.

In the next two sections we examine how LASSO and ridge regression would respectively handle the case study presented here.

10.2.2.1 *Ridge regression*

Let's first look at the results for ridge regression. Ridge regression assigns weights to all the factors in the model. If a factor model is used to determine portfolio weights and factor exposures, ridge regression generates factor exposures that are broad and thus diversified. In this case, all the

Table 10.2: Coefficients for the Bloomberg Barclays Global Aggregate Bond Index November 2000–December 2019

Ridge		LASSO	
Factor	**Coefficient**	**Factor**	**Coefficient**
Intercept	0.00291	Intercept	0.00276
UMD	–0.03058	UMD	–0.02665
MKT	–0.00942	MKT	—
SMB	–0.01166	SMB	—
HML	–0.00756	HML	—
RMW	0.03675	RMW	0.05632
CMA	0.00375	CMA	—
BAB	–0.04534	BAB	–0.02901
Currency Carry	0.00832	Currency Carry	—
Currency Momentum	0.05374	Currency Momentum	0.03098
Currency Value	–0.12298	Currency Value	–0.14183
Bond Trend	0.08445	Bond Trend	0.05173
Bond Carry	0.16859	Bond Carry	0.24884
Level	0.33101	Level	0.40170
Steepness	–0.23904	Steepness	–0.04284
Curvature	–0.00619	Curvature	—
Currency Volatility	0.19647	Currency Volatility	—
Yield Volatility	–0.20009	Yield Volatility	–0.16736

Notes: The predictive regressions are based on separating the time series in training and a test samples. We compute the LASSO and ridge regression models in the statistical software R using the "glmnet" package. Monthly data obtained by the authors from Bloomberg LLC.

factors are assumed to explain the Bloomberg Barclays Global Aggregate Bond Index.

However, as we see from Table 10.2, many of the factors have low magnitude. This is due to its retention of the entire factor set. As mentioned previously, ridge regression is not a dimension reduction tool in the way that LASSO is.

10.2.2.2 *LASSO*

In contrast to ridge regression, LASSO will assign zero weights to some factors, essentially excluding them from the model. In this case, the equity market factors are no longer retained except for the equity momentum (UMD) factor which has a very low magnitude. The yield volatility beta is –0.21, and 0.16 for the ridge regression and LASSO models, respectively, when blended factors are used. In both models the bond carry and bond trend factors are explanatory variables with large magnitude. As for the currency styles of value and momentum, the bond index has a negative beta to currency value and a positive exposure to currency momentum.

It is notable that no equity market factor has any explanatory power here, except for the equity momentum factor. However, this factor has a much lower magnitude for the global aggregate bond market than suggested in academic research. For example, Frazzini and Pedersen (2013) found evidence of the BAB factor in several markets, but the factor loadings for the global aggregate bond index exhibits a negative low-volatility exposure. Put differently, the Bloomberg Barclays Global Aggregate Bond Index is not a low-volatility market portfolio, but it is a high currency volatility market portfolio. In the LASSO model for example, a percentage change in yield volatility decreases the index returns by more than 16%.

This illustration provides an overview as to how bond and currency volatility affect the global bond markets represented in the Bloomberg Barclays Global Aggregate Bond Index. But the most important feature of the regression models shown in Table 10.2 is that the possibilities for factor selection for global bond portfolios are highly versatile. We also note the implications of the results in Table 10.2 for bond portfolio optimization. For a bond manager, the curve shift and steepness are variables that might find special focus in an optimization process. Zaremba (2019) found that there is a significant role played by cross-sectional seasonalities in global government bond returns, which are supported by the bond trend style. Bektic (2019) documented equity momentum in bond markets, but the momentum coefficient has a negative sign. Comparing the coefficients for the equity momentum (UMD) and the currency momentum factors, currency momentum deserves more attention than equity momentum from a global bond portfolio manager's point of view.

10.2.3 *Orthogonal regressions for selecting factors*

Another approach to factor analysis developed in academic research provides an alternative solution to test the available factors and to decide if they are suitable for explaining global bond portfolio returns. The intuition behind this approach is straightforward and involves estimating an orthogonal regression. To investigate the importance of factors, each factor is regressed against the others using a linear model. Finding significant beta coefficients and insignificant intercepts would mean that a specific factor can be constructed as a linear combination of the other factors. We provide an example by estimating orthogonal regressions for the factors BAB, bond trend, and currency value in Table 10.3. For this purpose, we regress each of the three factors against the other factors.

An important issue to highlight is that a factor might not have a significant intercept, but might still be a valuable source of information in the model. One such example is the factor intercept of the currency value factor, which although significant at the 5% level (t-statistic = 1.975), has a beta to the curvature factor of 0.08 (t-statistic = 4.238). Does this mean that the factor is related to the bond market curvature? Investigating the economic relationship between the currency value factor and other significant factors is crucial to determining factor relevance in an overall portfolio context. Statistically and mathematically, results might be meaningful, but it is always essential to provide evidence of a factor's economic relevance.

10.2.4 *Application of factor models in investment management*

Investment style analysis is a widely used framework for implementing factor models in portfolio construction. This is not surprising because factors help reduce dimensionality and complexity. Consider a broadly diversified portfolio with exposure to multiple asset classes. It is desirable for both portfolio and risk managers using a factor model to reduce the complexity of the portfolio to a simple set of factors that explain the volatility of returns.[5]

Style analysis often lends itself to the analysis of bond funds because bond managers often do not have specific views on style components. According to Leibowitz (2005), bond managers simply exploit different styles. In contrast, fund managers with a large exposure to some factors or

[5] Bolla (2017) suggested a factor model that explained more than 90% of the variance of global bond benchmark returns.

Table 10.3: Example of Orthogonal Regressions for BAB, Bond Trend, and Currency Value

BAB	**Coefficient**	***t*-statistic**	**Bond Trend**			**Currency Value**		
Intercept	0.0042	2.831	Intercept	0.0039	3.142	Intercept	0.0035	1.975
Bond carry	–0.0409	–0.531	Steepness	–0.5269	–1.207	Steepness	–0.5181	–1.130
Bond trend	0.0855	1.387	Curvature	0.0347	1.712	Curvature	0.0871	4.238
CMA	–0.1006	–0.607	Bond carry	0.3186	5.350	Bond carry	–0.0076	–0.107
Curvature	0.0231	0.813	CMA	–0.0618	–0.445	Bond trend	–0.0778	–0.891
Level	–0.2923	–1.845	Level	0.3849	1.914	CMA	0.1204	0.692
Steepness	–0.5996	–1.790	Currency carry	0.0258	0.675	Level	0.1320	0.690
Currency carry	0.0403	0.696	Currency momentum	–0.0382	–0.607	Currency carry	0.0436	0.589
Currency momentum	–0.0654	–0.998	Currency value	–0.0641	–0.921	Currency momentum	–0.0810	–1.012
Currency value	–0.0994	–1.171	Currency volatility	–0.0474	–0.110	Currency volatility	0.8794	1.713
Currency volatility	0.4608	0.939	HML	0.0338	0.348	HML	–0.0166	–0.157
HML	0.5167	3.949	MKT	–0.0710	–1.448	MKT	–0.0071	–0.129
MKT	0.0457	0.907	RMW	–0.2802	–2.387	RMW	0.1137	0.885
RMW	0.7695	6.417	SMB	0.0281	0.312	SMB	–0.0452	–0.454
SMB	0.4026	3.139	UMD	–0.0448	–1.207	UMD	–0.0311	–0.457
UMD	0.3361	6.120	BAB	0.0746	1.392	BAB	–0.1053	–1.154
Yield volatility	0.0100	0.050	Yield volatility	–0.1509	–1.022	Yield volatility	0.3074	1.487
R-squared	0.58		*R*-squared	0.19		*R*-squared	0.14	

Note: Monthly data from November 2000 to December 2019, obtained by the authors from Bloomberg LLC.

style are defined as "beta grazers", relying only on these style factors, and they do not generate significant positive excess returns. One way to perform a style-based regression analysis that mitigates the challenging issue of identifying factor risk and market risk for bonds is to construct factors from observable market data — bond yields, exchange rates, asset returns, index returns, and the like. The advantage of this method is that the factors have both statistical properties and are directly observable in the market.

A well-known approach to applying factors in investment management is the returns-based style analysis introduced by Sharpe (1992). It is a way of analyzing and replicating investment strategies by means of investable proxies. The analysis is regression based and expressed formally as

$$R_t^m = \alpha + \sum_{i=1}^{I} \beta_i R_t^i + \epsilon_t \tag{10.4}$$

where R_t^m is the return stream for the investment strategy to be replicated, R_t^i is the set of return streams for the proxy returns, I is the number of investable proxies, and ϵ_t is the error term.

There are two important constraints that are imposed in order to produce a combination of investable proxies suitable for a long-only strategy implementation. First, each beta coefficient is constrained to be greater than zero. Second, the sum of the betas is constrained to equal 1 (i.e., $\sum_{i=1}^{I} \beta_i = 1$). As such, each beta is interpreted as a weight assigned to a particular investable proxy in a replication portfolio.

In addition to style analysis, applying cross-sectional regressions in the manner of Fama and MacBeth (1973) is also a popular way to analyze factor exposures in bond funds. Academic research provides evidence that both time series regressions and cross-sectional regressions are appropriate for fund return analysis. The aim for global bond portfolio analysis is to estimate the premiums for both bond and currency strategies unit exposure. Estimating bond and currency market premiums allows for the identification of not only the time-variation of factor loadings but also the static factor risk premium in the market for both the bond and currency components. According to Goyal (2012), applying both cross-sectional and regression-based time series analysis allows for robustness for both tradable and non-tradable risk factors. However, given the dynamic and ever-evolving nature of fund factor exposures, a time-varying framework for measuring market risk is usually a necessity.

10.3 Capturing Time-Varying Factor and Style Exposure: Crowded Trades

In the previous sections, we showed how to construct and select factors, and showed their application in factor models. Factor models are highly versatile. They can be used to define expected returns for the investments in a portfolio or to build a portfolio that mimics or replicates the views of other portfolios, clients, or benchmarks. They can also be used to detect similar factor exposures among managers.

As mentioned above, an important application of factor models is their use in replication strategies. We mentioned in the introduction that global bond portfolios are often highly complex and their exposure comprises multiple bonds in different asset classes. Broad global bond portfolios that have the Bloomberg Barclays Global Aggregate Bond Index as a benchmark, which comprises more than 20,000 bonds, are examples of such diversified portfolios. In the vast majority of cases, complete benchmark replication is impossible. Therefore, factor replication models are needed to reduce complexity, and to identify and explain a significant amount of bond portfolio returns. A factor model would be used to minimize the tracking error to a benchmark by indicating a set of securities (often index funds) with the exposures needed to replicate it.[6] Such portfolios are called *trackers* or *clones* because they are designed to track benchmark performance and to generate alpha. Because bond benchmarks are almost impossible to replicate using individual bonds, the factor models using liquid assets are efficient solutions to the replication problem.[7]

10.3.1 *Definition and intuition of crowded trades*

In this section, we turn our attention to performance-based factor models, which have important risk management implications. We investigate crowded trades, which might be the result of two types of management

[6] See Kazemi *et al.* (2016). Factor replication models can be traced back to the hedge fund industry and the works of Hasanhodzic and Lo (2007) and Lee and Lo (2014) who applied factor models to replicate hedge fund returns.

[7] Ben Dor *et al.* (2021) provided an approach to replicate corporate bond indexes using the DTS. DTS successfully gauges the risk of corporate bonds. However, in Chapter 9, we explain the major problems that global bond portfolios face when they try to passively replicate broad benchmark indexes and discuss the overlay techniques that help to mitigate these problems.

style — deriving expected returns (closely related to the risk and return evaluation), and the behavioral and momentum tendencies (without explicit estimation requirement).

Let's first define what is meant by a crowded trade and the drivers of a crowded trade.[8] Two expressions are used in both the academic and practitioner literature to describe the same phenomenon: *crowdedness herding* and *view commonality*. Whereas crowdedness and herding apply to the same phenomenon, the origin of crowdedness can be traced back to behavioral economics. A brief overview of the literature provides an informative picture of this important phenomenon.[9] Holland (2012) defined crowding effects as the decreasing payoff for individuals in the case of an increasing number of players in a strategy. An increase in the number of players in a strategy leads to the decreasing profitability of that strategy — it becomes overcrowded. Crowding can be driven by any segment of the market. The defining properties of crowded trades are competition and mutualism.

Surowiecki (2005) argued that broad consensus views are more accurate than specialist opinions. That said, crowding behavior is often caused by biased estimations and observations dependent on fund managers' behavior. Following this line of thought, crowdedness should decrease as soon as fund managers' market views start to diverge again. Mackay (2003) extensively analyzed the three most important examples of crowded trades that occurred in the past and resulted in disastrous consequences for investors. Historically, although crowded trades often produced negative results, this is not always the case. However, the negative outcomes of crowded trades in portfolio management generally have greater magnitude than the upside effects of crowdedness.

Nofsinger and Sias (1999) found evidence of crowded trades and positive feedback trading resulting from trading in the same direction over a period of time and the correlation of lagged returns. According to Pojarliev and Levich (2012), if portfolio managers generate returns by following a simple strategy that is easily replicable, then such a return could be regarded as beta factor return that is susceptible to crowding.

---

[8] We use the term "crowdedness" and "crowded trades" interchangeably in this chapter.

[9] Several studies measured the effect of common exposure to the same investment vehicle — fund, style, factor, or asset classes — for equities (Cahan and Luo, 2012), for volatility (Marmer, 2010), for currencies (Pojarliev and Levich, 2011), and for hedge funds, Bussiere *et al.* (2014), Bayraktar *et al.* (2015), and Konstantinov and Rebmann (2020), among others.

The intuition behind crowded trades in global bond portfolios is similar to that found in other asset classes in that positive returns on a particular factor will attract other investors to invest in the same factors. A simple example illustrates this idea. Suppose that the level factor is implemented in several portfolios and generates positive returns. This may cause other portfolio managers to implement the level factor in their portfolios. At a certain time, the level factor attracts portfolio managers that start to run a similar factor exposure. This results in level factor crowdedness.

Similarly, the same strategy might be crowded due to negative factor returns. For example, negative returns associated with the currency trend factor might be a positive signal for other portfolio managers to follow the crowd and implement short positions. As a consequence, the number of portfolios that have a short position in the currency momentum factor increases. In both cases, the factor exposure might be a profitable undertaking, but represents a serious risk when many investors close their exposure. Following the crowd when it invests in a factor is known as *protrarian* behavior. Conversely, some investors may take positions in opposition to the crowd. In this case, portfolio managers build *contrarian* positions by shorting the crowded factor.

As we see, the factor exposure of a portfolio must be evaluated relative to other portfolios. As factor and style investing has become an important topic in portfolio management, it is important to identify not only the factors relevant for a portfolio but to also investigate the crowdedness of these factors. There are two approaches to this — cross-sectional and time series estimation of crowdedness. In this chapter, we focus on time series regression-based estimation of factor crowdedness.

The time variation of fund exposures to factors or style indices is captured by the model originally proposed by Pojarliev and Levich (2011b) as shown in the following equation[10]:

$$C_{\beta,t} = \sum_i f_{\beta,t}^{+} - \sum_i f_{\beta,t}^{-} \tag{10.5}$$

[10]Furthermore, this metric is also applied to Euro-denominated global bond funds by Konstantinov (2016), to European bond funds by Konstantinov and Fabozzi (2020a), and to hedge fund exposure by Konstantinov and Rebmann (2020). It has been applied to crowdedness estimations of US-dollar-denominated global bond funds by Konstantinov (2017b).

The time variation for factor $C_{\beta,t}$ at time t is expressed as the percentage of funds with significant positive exposure to style $f^{+}_{\beta,t}$, less the percentage of funds with significant negative exposure to the same style $f^{-}_{\beta,t}$ (see also Bayraktar *et al.* (2015)). In equation (10.5), $f^{+}_{\beta,t}$ represents the percentage of funds with significant positive exposure to factor β over the period t–k through t, and $f^{-}_{\beta,t}$ represents the percentage of funds with significant negative exposure to risk factor β over the period t–k through t. To identify significant exposure, the standard 95% confidence level and t-statistic value with an absolute value greater than or equal to a threshold have been used by researchers.[11] In this respect, this method is a reliable tool for explaining the time-varying behavior of funds relating to both risk factor exposure and excess return. By considering only the funds with significant exposure to a specific factor, the funds with non-zero, but insignificant exposure, are excluded. Drachman and Little (2010) and Kazemi *et al.* (2016) define the common style or factor exposure of managers or funds by aggregating their views in an index. Computing the crowdedness on every point at time t with a rolling time period of t–k generates a time series of crowdedness values.

The crowdedness approach is not restricted to measuring the beta exposure of funds. It can also be successfully applied to measure performance or alpha. The same approach is used by Konstantinov (2016) and Konstantinov and Fabozzi (2021b) to measure fund performance, but the cumulative metric is extended to calculate the alpha of funds. If the sum of the negative alpha exceeds the sum with positive intercepts, the result would be negative, and the data series would show up as a negative sign. Mathematically, it is clear that the time-varying exposure $C_{\beta,t}$ in equation (10.5) can be a positive or a negative number.

Next we apply the foregoing framework to take a look into the crowded behavior of global bond portfolio managers.

10.3.2 *Currency crowdedness of global bond funds*

Konstantinov (2017) documented currency crowdedness in global bond funds in the currency factors FX Momentum, FX Carry G10, FX Carry Global, FX Value, and FX Volatility in the period from May 2007 to

[11] Usually, the t-statistic level of ±1.96 is used; however, financial research suggests use of other threshold levels depending on the total number of tests done to develop a model.

January 2015.[12] In the analysis, 310 funds were selected from Lipper's Investment Management Database using Lipper Global Classifications. The selected mutual funds with Lipper Classification extension Global Bonds invest in the global bond markets in both local and hard currency government, corporate, and collateralized bonds. The selected funds correspond to the following classifications: Bond Global, Emerging Markets Global in LC and HC, Global High Yield, Global Short Term, Global Corporates, Emerging Markets Corporates, Bonds Asia Pacific in LC and HC, Emerging Markets LatAm, and Emerging Markets Europe.

The interaction of currency risk factors has been extensively studied in previous research. Menkhoff *et al.* (2012b) observe that carry trades underperform when there is a rise in FX Volatility and the change in currency volatility does not compensate for the carry return. Thus, FX Carry is negatively related to FX Volatility. In this respect, FX Volatility risk exceeds liquidity risk. As such, rising volatility, or at least its change in the case of underperforming carry trades, could — via its connectivity between strategies and cross-relationships — generate crowdedness in the market during which liquidity spirals are formed.[13] In such scenarios, crowdedness and liquidity spiral effects may make it difficult for a portfolio manager to decrease exposure to a particular strategy. This is particularly the case if more and more investors try to exit the strategy. We note however that the causation in the latter scenario remains uncertain. That means that it is not completely clear whether liquidity causes spiral effects or crowdedness causes liquidity to dry out.

An important attribute of crowded trades in specific currency factors is that global bond portfolio managers typically do not have any specific views on currency factors. According to Leibowitz (2005), these portfolio managers simply exploit them. This is an important topic we described at the beginning of this sub-section; that is, global bond portfolio managers often follow the currency bets and exposure of other fund managers. One reason could be that participating in crowded trades does not require estimation of expected returns. If estimating currency expected returns can

[12] For readability purposes, we use the term "FX" instead of "currency" when dealing with currency-related factors. The study uses strategy (style) factors provided by investment banks and not the market yield and currency factors defined in Chapter 5.

[13] Liquidity spirals result in times of financial market turbulence as market players try to sell bonds in the market, but no buyers exist. This causes prices to decrease further, magnifying the losses, which in turn results in even worse liquidity in the market.

be considered a skill in portfolio management, following the crowd implies that skill in currency investing is not important.

The following style equation is a five-factor model that was applied by Konstantinov (2017a) to investigate the currency crowdedness of global bond funds[14]:

$$R_{n,t} = \alpha_n + \beta_{1,n}\, r_t^{\text{FX Carry } G10} + \beta_{2,n}\, r_t^{\text{FX Carry Global}} + \beta_{3,n}\, r_t^{\text{FX Momentum}} + \beta_{4,n}\, r_t^{\text{FX Value}} + \beta_{5,n}\, r_t^{\text{FX Volatility}} + \varepsilon_t \quad (10.6)$$

where $R_{n,t}$ is the return of fund n at time t and $\sum_{i=1}^{5} \beta_{i,n}$ is the exposure of the fund's return n associated with the currency investing related risk factors at time t.

10.3.2.1 *Overview of bond portfolio crowdedness*

According to the study by Konstantinov (2017a), global portfolio managers have mainly focused on carry and specifically on FX Carry Global.[15] This is quite surprising given the fact that the average return of FX Carry Global has been on average negative.

Global bond funds have relied heavily on both FX Carry Global and FX Value. Pojarliev and Levich (2010) found that currency managers are often engaged in carry and momentum strategies. Contrarian positions, to both the FX Momentum and FX Value strategies, on average, have reduced the total return of the funds, because both strategies had positive returns. In general, the evidence supports the claim that crowdedness increased after the Global Financial Crisis (GFC) in 2008.[16]

We next discuss specific factor crowdedness in order to gain more insights into the behavior of global bond portfolios. We also explain the economic rationale and motivations for following FX strategies in bond portfolios. We start with FX Carry crowdedness.

---

[14]The Carry G10 comprises G10 currencies, the Carry Global comprises global currencies including emerging markets. The author used separate strategy (style) factors for currency carry to show the importance of emerging markets and developed markets in currency investing.

[15]FX strategies are discussed in the Chapter 3.

[16]Konstantinov and Rebmann (2020) observed an increase in crowded trades in common style factors since the GFC for hedge funds as well.

10.3.2.2 *FX carry crowdedness*

Academic research has shown that one of the most widely used strategies in currency investing is carry. Depending on the state-of-affairs in the markets, the performance of global carry could be the opposite to that of the G10, due to the significant weight of emerging market currencies in FX Carry Global. This was the case after the collapse of Lehman Brothers. The results of decreasing G10 and increasing FX Carry Global crowdedness were coincident with the underperformance of the FX Carry G10 strategies beginning in the summer of 2009 and the outperformance of global carry strategies starting at that time (see Pojarliev and Levich, 2011). Konstantinov (2017a) found that global bond managers over-crowded currency carry during that period.

Interestingly, global bond portfolio managers preferred global markets as opposed to the narrower G10 group. This has especially been the case in carry trades, where higher yielding currencies have been favored over lower yielding developed market currencies. Recall that portfolios are often managed in a developed market base currency such as the U.S. dollar, euro, Japanese yen, British pound, and Swiss franc, among others. As a portfolio follows crowded trades in high-yielding global currencies (including emerging markets), portfolios with a G10 base currency are directly exposed to high-risk carry trades. The primary risk is that emerging market currencies depreciate and G10 currencies appreciate. If emerging market currencies depreciate suddenly then the currency depreciation may offset the gain in yield from emerging market currencies.[17]

Peaks in FX Carry G10 crowdedness are often observed in cases of market turmoil such as in the Euro crisis in 2011, 2012, and 2013, during the Fed tapering in 2013, and the emerging markets sell-off in early 2014. The economic motivation for this behavior is that during times of financial stress, the demand for liquidity and less risky G10 currencies increases. That said, the FX Carry G10 had a negative return on average. The picture of portfolio manager behavior that emerges is one where crowding oscillates between emerging market currencies and G10 currencies. Portfolio managers are willing to accept "crash risk" for positive carry. However, once a market crash occurs, there is a

[17]See Pojarliev and Levich (2008, 2011a, 2012).

reactionary crowing into G10 currencies. Then, when markets stabilize, the cycle repeats.

10.3.2.3 *FX momentum crowdedness*

FX Momentum has historically been less preferred by bond portfolio managers. The reason for this is explained in the academic literature. Menkhoff *et al.* (2012a) found empirical evidence that FX momentum returns are risky in that their returns are volatile over short time horizons. Thus, their risk cannot be captured by traditional fund covariance risk measures and are thus different from carry trades. FX momentum returns stem primarily from currencies that are difficult to hedge, have high country risk, and are not driven by currency regimes and policy interventions. These are generally emerging markets currencies, which are significantly less efficient than developed markets. Punkthuanthong-Le and Thomas (2008) argued that the weak-form efficiency in the currency markets in relation to trend-following strategies, explains the short-term character of FX Momentum. Abbey and Doukas (2012) analyzed the use of technical analysis in currency markets and found that though it is widely used, most technical analysis indicators are simply too crowded and do not deliver noteworthy performance.

It is interesting to see whether bond portfolios' behavior contradicts the academic research. In theory FX Momentum crowdedness should be contrarian to carry crowdedness. Historically, global bond managers who implemented long positions in FX Momentum earned positive returns on several occasions; however the factor does not produce positive average returns as a buy-and-hold strategy. As mentioned previously in our discussion of carry strategies, factors will often change from being crowded to uncrowded depending on the state of the market. The trigger for the shift in factor crowdedness is often elevated market stress and heightened risk aversion. The GFC was such a period. Contrarian FX Momentum views rise in times of financial turmoil such as in October 2008 with the collapse of Lehman Brothers and again in the autumn of 2011 and in the autumn of 2013 as the European debt crisis adversely impacted the euro. In the period prior to and after the financial crisis in 2008, the performance of the FX Momentum strategy and its crowdedness was highly correlated. FX Momentum is much more easily implemented relative to carry or value strategies in currency investing, which makes it a convenient "go-to" strategy during times of financial market uncertainty.

10.3.2.4 *FX value crowdedness*

Konstantinov (2017a) found that bond portfolio managers are to some extent contrarian value investors, which is surprising since the value factor represents a "fundamental" exposure to currencies. In the latter study bond fund managers were found to be positioned against Purchasing Power Parity (PPP) and FX Value crowdedness was observed to generate a small payoff for those adopting the same trading positions. In other words, following the crowd with FX Value is not a profitable strategy, which is the case for both currency and global bond portfolio managers.

It is important to be clear why FX Value is so often a contrarian strategy. As we showed in Chapter 3, contrarian bond manager exposure to the value factor is not surprising as relative PPP models require an estimate of inflation. However, inflation data arrive with a time lag, and important determinants of inflation are expected and unexpected inflation rates. Thus, as new macroeconomic and market information arrives, a gap forms between the two metrics. As a result, spot foreign exchange prices might react much faster to new information than inflation data. Therefore, the PPP equilibrium price cannot be in equilibrium as steady information flow exists that adjusts foreign exchange data.[18] Although macroeconomic data and PPP require longer periods to be realized, global bond portfolio managers have much shorter holding periods and implement strategies that require much more frequent turnover.

10.3.2.5 *FX volatility crowdedness*

When a FX volatility factor has a positive return, betting against exchange rate volatility generates a negative return. This means that managers who were buying volatility by being long currency options and thus hedging currency risk are able to increase returns. There are important takeaways from this relationship that need explanation.

First, bond portfolio managers often regard currency volatility as a major source of risk. The evidence shows that bond portfolio managers have, in fact, strong views on the volatility factor. Similar to the FX Momentum factor, FX Volatility is driven by short-term market dynamics.

---

[18]Grossmann and Stiglitz (1980) explain why equilibrium is not possible in financial markets.

In the case of contrarian exposure to FX Volatility, investors expect that the combination of risk and return provides better exposure than being long the risk reversal differential between implied and historical currency volatility. Given this, FX Volatility is not a crowded place, but contrarian positions might still be costly. Selling options to gain the option premium can be a profitable strategy. Buy-and-hold contrarian FX Volatility strategies have generally underperformed because FX Volatility spikes generate negative option price payoffs during market dislocations which wipes away the accumulated premiums in more tranquil times (Pojarliev and Levich (2012)). A breakdown of carry trades is anticipated to be a source risk for depreciating currencies, causing FX Volatility exposure to increase. This is always the case as currency risk protection is needed. Therefore, global bond portfolio managers overcrowd currency volatility only in times of heightened risk and uncertainty, and do not regard it as a primary source of return.

10.4 Model Selection

We have discussed several models in this chapter. The choice of which one to use should be based upon clear statistical criteria. While no model can provide a completely accurate representation of the phenomena it is attempting to describe, for a given application, some models will be more informative than others. To that end, in this section we describe two model selection frameworks that are designed to evaluate the informativeness of models. They are the Akaike Information Criterion (AIC) and Schwarz Criterion (SC)[19] and are formally described thus:

$$\text{AIC} = 2k - \ln\left(\frac{\text{RSS}}{n}\right) \tag{10.7}$$

$$\text{SC} = n\ \ln\left(\frac{\text{RSS}}{n}\right) + k\ \ln(n) \tag{10.8}$$

where n is the number of data points in the time series, RSS is the residual sum of squares, and k is the number of factors in a model.

---

[19] James *et al.* (2013) show how machine learning algorithms can also be used in model selection.

The intuition behind model selection in the AIC and SC is that when researchers identify a model, there is always a certain amount of information loss. That is, a factor model applied to portfolio returns cannot be better than the "true" model that describes the portfolio returns. However, because we can never know the true model, portfolio managers should select the model with the smallest information loss, which is what the AIC and SC seek to do. Application of the AIC and SC produces a negative number that ranges from $-\infty$ to zero. The smaller the number, the smaller the information loss, and the closer the model is to the true model. Therefore, for both criteria, the model with the lowest value is preferred.

Both the AIC and SC consider the number of explanatory variables. However, there is an advantage to using the SC for models where there are a large number of explanatory variables. This is due to the fact that if the number of factors in a model exceeds seven, then the SC adds a higher penalty to the model. Thus the SC also considers model parsimony within its framework, which is an important element in model selection.

Table 10.4 provides an illustration of an application of the AIC and SC. The models comprise five and six factors, respectively.[20] Note that the model selection here is unrelated to the selection of factors, but is an evaluation of a model once the factors in the model have already been selected. As we see in the table, a higher adjusted R^2 does not necessarily identify a better model. The six-factor model has a lower adjusted R^2, but the six-factor model has lower AIC and SC indicating that it has lower information loss compared to the five-factor model.

Table 10.4: Akaike Information Criterion (AIC) and Schwarz Criterion (SC) for Model Selection

Model (k)	**Adjusted R^2**	**RSS**	**AIC**	**SC**
Five Factor Model	0.62	325.24	–459,124.34	–459,077.71
Six Factor Model	0.55	283.74	–470,727.33	–470,671.38

[20]The estimates in the table are based on weekly returns for 310 global bond portfolios from November 2006 to January 2015 obtained from the Lipper for Investment Management Database. The adjusted R^2 refers to the fit of the regression — AIC and SC are computed using equations (10.7) and (10.8), respectively.

10.5 Key Takeaways

- Factor models find broad applications in portfolio management. They are used to create portfolios based on appropriate risk factors with the objective of minimizing tracking error to a specific benchmark, achieving diversification, and monitoring portfolio risks. Factor models are also used to explain portfolio returns and identify alpha, which is important in performance measurement.
- Deciding which factors to include in a factor model is an important but challenging task. The criteria used to select factors should be based on economic principles, market intuition, and quantitative metrics. LASSO, ridge regression, and orthogonal regression are three frameworks that can aid portfolio managers in factor selection.
- Crowding refers to the tendency of market participants to focus on similar sets of strategies or factors. When excess capital follows a restricted set of investment strategies, there is a heightened risk of a liquidity event or large drawdown when the tide turns and investors begin to liquidate their positions.
- If estimating currency expected returns can be considered a skill in portfolio management, following the crowd implies that skill in currency investing is not important, and neither is the estimation of expected currency returns.
- It is important to model and monitor crowdedness. From a risk management standpoint, it is best to also monitor the crowded trades of peer groups.

References

Abbey, B. S. and J. A. Doukas. 2012. "Is Technical Analysis Profitable for Individual Currency Traders?" *Journal of Portfolio Management* 39(1): 142–150.

Bayraktar, M., S. Doole, A. Kassam, and S. Radchenko. 2015. "Lost In the Crowd? Identifying and Measuring Crowded Strategies and Trades". MSCI Research Insight.

Bektić, D. 2019. "Residual Equity Momentum Spillover in Global Corporate Bond Markets". *Journal of Fixed Income* 28(3): 46–54.

Bektić, D., J. S. Wenzler, M. Wegener, D. Schiereck, and T. Spielmann. 2019. "Extending Fama–French-Factors to Corporate Bond Markets". *Journal of Portfolio Management* 45(3): 141–158.

Ben Dor, A., L. Dynkin, and J. Hyman. 2021. "Managing the spread Risk of Credit Portfolios Using the Duration Times Spread Measure". Chapter 53 in F. J. Fabozzi (ed.) *The Handbook of Fixed Income Securities.* 9th Edition. New York: McGraw Hill.

Ben Dor, A., L. Dynkin, J. Hyman, P. Houweling, E. van Leeuwen, and O. Penninga. 2007. "DTS (Duration Times Spread)". *Journal of Portfolio Management* 33(2): 77–100.

Bolla, L. 2017. "Fundamental Indexing in Global Bond Markets: The Risk Exposure Explains It All". *Financial Analysts Journal* 73(1): 101–120.

Brooks, J., D. Palhares, and S. Richardson. 2018. "Style Investing in Fixed Income". *Journal of Portfolio Management* 44(4): 127–139.

Bussiere, M., M. Hoerova, and B. Klaus. 2014. "Commonality in Hedge Funds Returns: Driving Factors and Implications". ECB Working Article Series No. 1658 (March).

Cahan, R. and Y. Luo. 2013. "Standing Out From the Crowd: Measuring Crowding in Quantitative Strategies". *Journal of Portfolio Management* 39(4): 14–23.

Carhart, M. 1997. "On Persistence in Mutual Fund Performance". *Journal of Finance* 52(1): 57–82.

De Jong, M. and F. J. Fabozzi. 2020. "The Market Risk of Corporate Bonds". *Journal of Portfolio Management* 46(2): 92–105.

Drachman, J. and P. Little. 2010. "Enhancing Liquidity in Alternative Portfolios". Credit Swiss Asset Management, White Paper.

Fama, E. F. and K. R. French. 1992. "The Cross-Section of Expected Stock Returns". *Journal of Finance* 47(2): 427–465.

Fama, E. F. and K. R. French. 1993. "Common Risk Factors in the Returns on Stocks and Bonds". *Journal of Financial Economics* 33(1): 3–56.

Fama, E. F. and K. R. French. 2015. "A Five-Factor Asset Pricing Model". *Journal of Financial Economics* 116: 1–22.

Fama, E. F. and J. D. MacBeth. 1973. "Risk, Return, and Equilibrium: Empirical Tests". *Journal of Political Economy* 81(3): 607–636.

Frazzini, A. and L. Pedersen. 2014. "Betting Against Beta". *Journal of Financial Economics* 111(1): 1–25.

Goyal, A. 2012. Empirical Cross-sectional Asset Pricing: A Survey. *Financial Markets and Portfolio Management* 26(1): 3–38.

Grossmann, S. and J. Stiglitz. 1980. "On the Impossibility of Informationally Efficient Markets". *American Economic Review* 70(3): 393–408.

Harvey, C. R. and Y. Liu. 2014. "Evaluating Trading Strategies". *Journal of Portfolio Management* 40(5): 110–118.

Hasanhodzic, J. and A. W. Lo. 2007. "Can Hedge-Fund Returns Be Replicated?" *Journal of Investment Management* 5(2): 5–45.

Holland, J. 2012. *Signals and Boundaries: Building Blocks for Complex Adaptive Systems*. Cambridge, Massachusetts: The MIT Press.

James, G., D. Witten, T. Hastie, and R. Tibshirani. 2013. "*An Introduction to Statistical Learning: With Applications in R*". Springer Science+Business Media New York.

Kazemi, H., K. H. Black, and R. D. Chambers. 2016. *Alternative Investments: CAIA Level II*. 3rd Edition. Wiley.

Konstantinov, G. S. 2016. "Capturing Short-term and Long-term Alpha of Global Bond Portfolios: Evidence from EUR-Investors' Perspective". *Financial Markets and Portfolio Management* 30(3): 337–365.

Konstantinov, G. S. 2017a. "Currency Crowdedness Generated by Global Bond Funds". *Journal of Portfolio Management* 43(2): 123–135.

Konstantinov, G. S. 2017b. "On the Dynamics of EMU Bond Portfolios". *Journal of Investing* 27(2): 99–110.

Konstantinov, G. S. 2021b. "Towards a Dead End? EMU Bond Market Exposure and Manager Performance". *Journal of Global Money and Finance* 116: 102433.

Konstantinov, G. S. 2022. "The Geometry of the World of Currency Volatility". *Computational Economics* 60(1): 125–145.

Konstantinov, G. S. and F. J. Fabozzi. 2021a. "Carry Strategies and the U.S. Dollar Risk of U.S. and Global Bonds". *Journal of Fixed Income* 30(3): 26–46.

Konstantinov, G. S. and M. Pojarliev. 2021. "Trading in the Bond Market", Chapter 44 in Frank J. Fabozzi (ed.) *The Handbook of Fixed Income Securities*. 9th Edition. New York: McGraw-Hill.

Konstantinov, G. S. and J. Rebmann. 2020. "Different in Nature, Common in Style: View Commonality of Single Hedge Funds and Funds of Hedge Funds". *Journal of Alternative Investments* 23(2): 49–66.

Konstantinov, G. S. and M. Rusev. 2020. "The Bond-Equity Fund Relation Using the Fama–French–Carhart Factors: A Practical Network Approach". *Journal of Financial Data Science* 2(1): 24–44.

Lee, P. A. and A. W. Lo. 2014. "Hedge Fund Beta Replication". *Journal of Investment Management* 12(3): 5–18.

Leibowitz, M. (2005). "Alpha Hunters and Beta Grazers". *Financial Analysts Journal* 61(5): 32–39.

Mackay, C. 2003. *Extraordinary Popular Delusions and the Madness of Crowds*. Petersfield, United Kingdom: Harriman House Ltd.

Marmer, H. S. 2015. "Fire! Fire! Is U.S. Low Volatility a Crowded Trade?" *Journal of Investing* 24(3): 17–37.

Menkhoff, L., L. Sarno, M. Schmeling, and A. Schrimpf. 2012a. "Carry Trades and Global Foreign Exchange Volatility". *Journal of Finance* 67(2): 681–718.

Menkhoff, L., L. Sarno, M. Schmeling, and A. Schrimpf. 2012b. "Currency Momentum Strategies". *Journal of Financial Economics* 106(3): 660–684.

Nofsinger, J. and R. Sias. 1999. "Herding and Feedback Trading by Institutional and Individual Investors". *Journal of Finance* 54(6): 2263–2295.

Pojarliev, M. 2019. "Some Like It Hedged" *CFA Institute Research Foundation.* Available at https://www.cfainstitute.org/-/media/documents/article/rf-brief/some-like-it-hedged.pdf.

Pojarliev, M. and R. M. Levich. 2008. "Do Professional Currency Managers Beat the Benchmark?" *Financial Analysts Journal* 64(5): 18–32.

Pojarliev, M. and R. M. Levich. 2010. "Trades of the Living Dead: Style Differences, Style Persistence and Performance of Currency Fund Managers". *Journal of Global Money and Finance* 29: 1752–1775.

Pojarliev, M. and R. M. Levich. 2011a. "Detecting Crowded Trades in Currency Funds". *Financial Analysts Journal* 67(1): 26–39.

Pojarliev, M. and R. M. Levich. 2011b. "Are All Currency Managers Equal?" *Journal of Portfolio Management* 37(4): 42–53.

Pojarliev, M. and R. M. Levich. 2012. *A New Look at Currency Investing*, Research Foundation of CFA Institute. Available at https://www.cfainstitute.org/-/media/documents/book/rf-publication/2012/rf-v2012-n4-1-pdf.ashx.

Punkthuanthong-Le, K. and R. Thomas III. 2008. "Weak-Form Efficiency in Currency Markets". *Financial Analysts Journal* 64(3): 31–52.

Sharpe, W. 1992. "Asset allocation: Management Style and Performance Measurement". *Journal of Portfolio Management* 18(2): 7–19.

Simonian, J. and C. Wu. 2019. "Factors in Time: Fine-Tuning Hedge Fund Replication". *Journal of Portfolio Management* 45(3) 159–164.

Simonian, J., C. Wu, D. Itano, and V. Narayanam. 2019. "A Machine Learning Approach to Risk Factors: A Case Study Using the Fama–French–Carhart Model". *Journal of Financial Data Science* 1(1): 32–44.

Surowiecki, J. 2005. *The Wisdom of Crowds*. New York: Anchor Books.

Zaremba, A. 2019. "Cross-sectional Seasonalities in Global Government Bond Returns". *Journal of Banking and Finance* 98: 80–94.

Chapter 11

Performance Analysis

The focus of this chapter is on the performance analysis of global bond portfolios. Performance analysis has three basic dimensions: performance measurement, performance attribution, and performance evaluation.

Performance measurement involves the calculation of the return realized by a portfolio manager over some interval of time (referred to as the *evaluation period*) and is the starting point for performance attribution and evaluation. There are several important issues that must be addressed in developing a methodology for calculating a portfolio's return. There are different methodologies that can be used but these can lead to quite disparate results regarding portfolio performance. To deal with this problem, the CFA Institute has promulgated a set of industry-wide principles, referred to as the Global Investment Performance Standards (GIPS), for calculating and presenting performance results. Return calculations are the primary inputs into performance attribution and evaluation. In addition, performance measurement also involves presenting basic descriptive statistics pertaining to a fund such as the standard deviation, range, skewness, and drawdown.

Performance attribution involves the determination of the sources of a manager's performance, especially its performance relative to a benchmark. The starting point for attribution analysis is the calculation of the difference between a manager's return and the benchmark return. This difference is known as the *active return*. If the computed active return is positive, the portfolio manager has outperformed the benchmark; if it is negative, the portfolio manager has underperformed the benchmark.

Performance attribution goes beyond performance measurement by addressing the question of how the portfolio manager generated their active return. Was it due to overweighting the countries or currencies that performed well or underweighting the sectors within a country that performed poorly. Performance attribution analysis decomposes the portfolio manager's decisions showing why there was over- or underperformance. The most commonly used performance attribution model is that described by Brinson and Fachler (1985). However, in this chapter we focus on factor-based approaches to performance attribution and evaluation. Our approach is motivated by the complexity of global bond portfolios, whose performance analysis often require more fine-grained methods.

Basic performance measurement does not consider the risks that a portfolio manager undertook to produce the return that they did. To address the latter issue, performance evaluation is used to measure a manager's risk-adjusted performance in various ways. Various metrics such as the Sharpe ratio and Sortino ratio, among others, can be invoked to this end. Beyond the use of risk metrics, regression analysis can be used to produce a finer grained picture of a portfolio's risk–return profile.

11.1 Manager Skill and Performance: What Does Alpha Measure?

The return that a manger generate in excess of a benchmark is commonly referred to as *alpha* and is widely used by practitioners as a measure of manager skill. However, the time period over which alpha is measured is critical to determining a manager's true skill level. Simple estimation of alpha is often not enough to answer important questions. Some of the most important questions in assessing performance relate to its persistence, its source in manager skill or luck, and its statistical significance. When measuring alpha, it is important to control for relevant factors when estimating returns and evaluating performance, as well as interpreting manager performance. With respect to these issues, Campisi (2000) emphasized that bond portfolios are significantly different from equity portfolios. Therefore, it is imperative to identify the factors that are specific to global bond portfolios. Factor models can assist in this regard as they can often help explain manager performance in a more granular fashion.

Portfolio managers of global bond funds are focused on implementing strategies whose goal is to increase returns and minimize risks with respect to both the interest-rate and currency exposure in their portfolios. In fact, global bond portfolios can be considered multi-strategy portfolios. As such, in this chapter, we pay special attention to factor-based performance measurement, which is often useful in decomposing the returns of complex portfolios. Moreover, in today's global market, approximately 75% of the total number of global bond funds are not run against a benchmark (Konstantinov, 2016), so a benchmark-agnostic approach to performance measurement, such as that provided by factor analysis, is appropriate from a practical standpoint. Although attribution is an *ex-post* endeavor, it can nevertheless be used as input in the *ex-ante* factor allocation process. Factor allocation is typically implemented against a type of benchmark called a tracking portfolio — a portfolio of assets that matches a specific set of factor sensitivities.

We begin by reviewing some well-known approaches to the performance measurement of global bond portfolios.[1] Various studies have identified specific metrics that are useful in evaluating manager skill, performance, and persistence. Determining whether performance is driven by skill is considered a fundamental aspect of performance evaluation by most practitioners. On this point, Berk and Green (2004) and Berk *et al.* (2020) argue that there is an important difference between performance persistence and manager skill.

Jensen (1968) proposed regression analysis for evaluating the factor exposure and alpha of funds. However, heterogeneous benchmarks pose serious challenges to applying performance evaluation to bond funds. This is especially the case for global bond portfolios as only a small proportion of the funds report an official benchmark. Angelidis *et al.* (2013), for example, pointed out that ignoring self-reported benchmarks might misstate manager skill. To deal with this concern, they propose both static and dynamic models utilizing selection and market timing to explain excess returns. Ben Dor *et al.* (2008) recommend an alternative approach for measuring bond fund performance and style. They demonstrate that a

[1]This section is based on the bond fund alpha analysis conducted by Konstantiov and Fabozzi (2020b).

single index or passive benchmark might be an inefficient way to evaluate the performance of multi-sector bond funds that invest in different asset classes. Consequently, factor models that include active indexes or strategies, such as long/short carry, value, and momentum factors that reflect the active management approach of global bond portfolios can be useful tools for performance measurement in more complex portfolios.

Several studies have analyzed the role of risk factors in performance evaluation. In fact, it is a challenging task for investors to identify relevant factors that explain fund returns. Indeed, Harvey *et al.* (2016) identified more than 300 potential factors that may be relevant to analyzing equity returns alone.

The most widely accepted approach to investigating equity factor exposures and fund returns is to use the factors proposed by Fama and French (1992, 1993) and Carhart (1997). The Fama–French–Carhart (FFC) factors are systematic risk factors that are intuitive and have a strong theoretical and empirical foundation. The applicability of the FFC factors is not limited to equities, and research has identified their influence on other asset classes. The use of the FFC factors in other asset classes — size, value, and market, and the term and default factors — can be traced to the work of Leibowitz (2011), who suggested that every asset class has equity exposure. Indeed, the FFC factors can be used to analyze global bond portfolios. Baltussen *et al.* (2022) applied value and momentum factors to sovereign bond markets. Similarly, Duyvesteyn and Martens (2014) applied equity market momentum and equity market risk factors to emerging market government bonds. Bektić (2019) and Bektić *et al.* (2019) applied the classical FFC factors to corporate bonds and reported evidence of equity market factors driving bond returns.

However, the FFC factors might be less suitable for the performance measurement of global bond portfolios because they do not account for currency, interest-rate, sovereign and corporate bond spreads, and market sector risks, at least not explicitly. This is important because, in global bond portfolios, the exposures to currencies, countries, spreads, and interest-rate regimes are the most important drivers of performance. Adjusting equity market factors for currency risk cannot properly reflect the currency risk exposure of a global bond portfolio. Similarly, the value factor for bonds might be different from the value factor for equities because bond risk premiums differ from equity risk premiums in important ways.

11.1.1 *How to evaluate global bond portfolios*

Several studies have shown that the underlying dynamics in bond markets that differ from those explained by the FFC factors.[2] Berk *et al.* (2015, 2017) argued that measuring manager skill requires a realistic portfolio with tradable instruments instead of synthetic factor loadings. This is an important point because sometimes commonly used factors cannot explain the underlying dynamics of bond portfolio returns. This is the reason why bond market-specific factors have been introduced and tested.

Research on the dynamics of bond markets has shown that directly observable factors are more suitable than the synthetic or latent factors created from principal component analysis. It is therefore important to clarify the difference between synthetic factors and bond factors derived from market data. In Chapter 10, we grouped factors into four clusters. As we noted, the complex and heterogeneous investment universe of global bond portfolios requires a more nuanced treatment relative to less complex investment vehicles. Global bond portfolio managers typically not only invest in government bonds, corporate bonds, covered bonds, high-yield bonds, and quasi-sovereigns but also in derivative instruments like futures, forwards, swaps, and options on foreign exchange and fixed-income securities. It is imperative to have factors that track these markets.

Estrada, Kritzman, and Page (2006) argued that it is more convenient to focus on countries than on industries when evaluating investments in emerging markets. Although their research applied to equities, the same intuition extends to bond portfolios, where performance measurement should also focus on country and currency exposure rather than industry exposure. As with any type of investment analysis, bond portfolio analysis should focus on the investment universe of a given global bond portfolio to determine the relevant factors. If the portfolio manager is focusing on currency risk, countries and more broadly defined asset classes like corporate and government bonds, then factors reflecting the dynamics of corporate and government bond risk should be considered. If a global bond portfolio includes corporate bonds with a strong differentiation of

[2] See, for example, Parikh and Fabozzi (2018), Mladina and Germani (2019), de Jong and Fabozzi (2020), and Maeso *et al.* (2020).

credit risk (e.g., industrials, financials, and utilities), appropriate factors that explain such risks must be incorporated into the factor model that explains portfolio returns.

In a similar vein, changes in sovereign bond spreads are important drivers of performance in global bond portfolios. Research has identified indexes that serve as risk and fear indicators for sovereign bond spreads. One such indicator is the Cboe Volatility Index (VIX). Rocha *et al.* (2007) and Remolona *et al.* (2008) demonstrate that the changes in equity market volatility as measured by the Cboe VIX can have a large impact on emerging market spreads. Specifically, factors that explain sovereign risk spreads in global bond portfolios should gauge global risk aversion, economic fundamentals, liquidity, and the effects of government policies. These are important determinants of sovereign bond spreads that affect not only emerging markets but also developed markets.

Ladekarl and Peters (2013) performed statistical tests and principal component analysis and found that the currency factor remains one of the most important factors in measuring portfolio returns. Therefore, currencies have to be accounted for in performance evaluation. Whereas the latter authors focused on emerging markets, Konstantinov and Fabozzi (2021a) documented that the currency risk of the U.S. dollar is the most important for global bond portfolios. The foregoing research underscores the importance of currency risk in performance measurement, and highlights one of the primary ways in which the decomposition of global bond portfolios requires a unique set of analytical tools.

A practical way to select a set of factors to analyze a portfolio is to begin with a large set of economically relevant factors, and gradually narrow the relevant factors down to a smaller subset that has the most explanatory power. The following categories of risk may serve as a guide in factor selection for performance evaluation:

- Credit risks of sovereign, high-yield, corporate bonds,
- Developed and emerging market exposures,
- Duration and maturity allocation,
- Liquidity risks and derivative instruments,
- Local currency and country risk.

It is important to note that there is strong interaction between the risk categories listed above. That is, credit, country, duration, and liquidity risks might affect a single security (e.g., an emerging market bond) simultaneously. A benchmark's universe is generally a strong indicator of a portfolio's potential risks. For example, an unconstrained bond portfolio that is not run against a benchmark might potentially invest in every bond market. As a result, when conducting performance measurement and attribution, either a broad benchmark index like the Bloomberg Barclays Global Aggregate Index can be used to represent the investment universe or alternatively, a set of global factors that track the portfolio's assets may be used.

11.1.2 *A more nuanced treatment of factors*

To properly evaluate the performance of global bond portfolio managers, it is imperative to apply factors that make economic sense and reasonably explain the performance of a portfolio. The broad investment universe of global bond portfolios makes it difficult to extract information about performance, risk, and portfolio strategy using a single index. Therefore, regression-based analysis might be used to employ a wider set of factors. However, because factors measure the systematic risk in a portfolio and provide information about the systematic bets of the portfolio manager they do not provide insight into the idiosyncratic risks which also need to be analyzed when evaluating manager performance. (see Fischer and Wermers, 2013).

According to Chen and Knez (1996), return-based approaches should satisfy the following criteria. First, the models should capture the factors that reasonably explain portfolio performance. For example, a factor that gauges currency risk should be considered in the performance measurement of a global bond portfolio with currency exposure. Second, the performance measure should be scalable and allow the linear combination of factors. Third, the performance model should be continuous and performance measures should be the same unless a style drift is evident and detectable using a regression model. For example, suppose a global bond portfolio experiences a strategy change — it no longer invests in corporate bonds, but only in FX and money market instruments. In this case, a DTS factor should be omitted from the model as the portfolio does not have any exposure to credit risk. A credit risk factor for government bond portfolios with heavy exposure to country and currency risk might very well explain the performance of the fund, but we must nevertheless be mindful that the credit risk for government bonds is different from the credit risk for corporate bonds. If, for example, the credit risk for government bonds is measured as the spread above the U.S. Treasury spot rate curve (AAA rating) and the credit risk for corporate bonds is measured as the spread above a credit yield curve then the credit risk for government bonds and corporate bonds cannot be the same.

Because factors play a key role in explaining security behavior, model specification is critical in measuring and analyzing portfolio performance. The most widespread factor frameworks apply regression-based models of time series to assist in performance attribution. We turn to a discussion of such models in the next section.

11.1.3 *Factor models and performance measurement*

When measuring alpha using factor models, the focus is on fund returns rather than portfolio holdings. As discussed above, the objective when using factors for performance measurement is to apply the proper factor model. However, there is another important issue when analyzing alpha. Specifically, what can be called "alpha returns" when measured against an incomplete set of factors might be considered "beta returns" when measured against an appropriate and complete set of factors. For example, a statistical evaluation of global bond portfolio returns using the market equity factor might provide evidence of "alpha", but statistical tests using currency and global bond factors might properly identify the portfolio returns as being entirely driven by systematic exposures. Therefore, factor exposure is highly specific depending on the style and composition of a portfolio, and factor choice should reflect the investment universe and markets in which the bond portfolio manager invests.

Leibowitz (2011) argues that every portfolio has equity exposure to some degree. In the case of bond portfolios, while they may not have any direct equity exposure, the performance of some of the instruments contained in them, like corporate bonds, is directly related to the fortunes of the company that issued the bonds. Alternatively, in other cases, the equity beta stems not from any direct connections to a company's performance, but to the more equity-like behavior of the instrument, namely, relatively higher return and volatility. For example, lower-rated emerging market bonds have been observed to behave much more like equities and less like fixed-income-related instruments due to their "riskier" equity-like characteristics.

The factors that explain global bond portfolio returns can be expressed in a linear regression model. One of the main reasons for choosing a linear multi-factor model is that it is usually fairly easy to interpret results and because it is possible to derive portfolio returns as a linear combination of several explanatory variables. In the previous chapter, we identified the following model for the returns of a portfolio $R_{i,t}$:

$$R_{i,t} = \alpha + \sum_i \beta_i F_{i,t} + \varepsilon_t \tag{11.1}$$

where R_t is return of a fund (regressed against the factor returns), α is a parameter that measures manager skill, β is the coefficient or factor loading that measures the sensitivity of the manager's return to factor F, and ε is the random error term. Usually, a $t-k$ period might be $t-52$ weeks or $t-60$ months.

As noted by Peterson *et al.* (2011), the alpha (α_i) from equation (11.1) can be interpreted as the contribution to returns resulting from managerial skill. The coefficients β_i in equation (11.1) represent factors that are a proxy for factors $F_{i,t}$ which global bond portfolio managers are likely to be exposed to, and ε_t is a normally distributed error term.[3]

Timing ability is an important consideration when evaluating fund performance. The most widely used framework for measuring skill and timing abilities is the Treynor–Mazuy model (Treynor and Mazuy, 1966). This model indicates that increasing (decreasing) the exposure to the factor F_i when the returns of this factor are rising (decreasing) shows positive timing abilities. In general, the intuition behind the model is that the portfolio manager forecasts the market and if this is the case, a significant alpha might be the result of timing. To control for timing skill separately from selection skill, we can use the following formalism:

$$R_t = \alpha + \sum_i \beta_i F_{i,t} + \sum_i \gamma_i F_{i,t}^2 + \varepsilon_t \tag{11.2}$$

[3] See Chapter 5.

where R_t is the return of the fund regressed against the factor returns, $F_{i,t}^2$ is the squared factor returns, and α, β, and ε are as defined earlier.

The γ coefficient seeks to capture the timing abilities of the squared factor returns $F_{i,t}^2$. Manager market timing abilities are positive when the estimated coefficients in the regression model in equation (11.2) are positive and statistically significant. Negative and statistically significant coefficients in equation (11.2) mean that the manager does not have market timing abilities. With bond funds, there is evidence that significant values in the timing coefficient decreases the intercept α in equation (11.2).[4]

The Treynor–Mazuy model is often desired for measuring the market timing activities of global bond portfolios because the relationship between the portfolio returns and explanatory factors is nonlinear. A simple linear equation might not identify this. Because bonds and currencies often exhibit non-normal returns, it night be preferable to use a nonlinear model to evaluate bond portfolio performance.

Because global bond portfolios can exhibit especially complex behavior, choosing an appropriate model to explain their returns is often not a simple affair. To assist in model selection, we can apply the Akaike Information Criterion and Schwarz Information Criterion and select the model with the lowest criterion value (which we explained in the previous chapter).

11.1.4 *The information ratio as a performance measure*

The increasing complexity of global bond portfolios and investment research has led to the rising role of asset allocation in portfolio management. Allocating to different asset classes and using benchmark portfolios requires appropriate performance measurement tools. One of the most widely used performance evaluation measures is the *information ratio* (IR) proposed by Grinold (1989), and Grinold and Kahn (2000). The IR is an integral part of the Fundamental Law of Active Management, which describes the relationship between skill — defined as the ability to predict

[4]Konstantinov and Fabozzi (2021b) investigated EMU bond manager performance and found significant timing coefficients and intercepts indicating low alpha. However, intercepts of the funds decreased with timing abilities.

asset returns — and the number of independent views that the portfolio manager might have. The Fundamental Law states that the optimal expected active return is the product of the assumed information coefficient (IC), the square root of breadth (B), and the active portfolio risk. We describe these terms below.

11.1.4.1 *Evaluating global bond portfolios with the information ratio*

Following Kahn (1998), the IR can also be applied to bond managers, whose management styles can be described as active duration, sector rotation, opportunistic sector rotation, mortgage specialist, and global bond. Modern complex global bond portfolios typically incorporate all the above styles. The IR is given as follows:

$$\mathrm{IR} = \mathrm{IC}\sqrt{\mathrm{B}} \tag{11.3}$$

where IR is the information ratio, or the ability of the portfolio manager to generate alpha, IC is the information coefficient which measures the ability of the portfolio manager to accurately predict asset returns, and B is the breadth which represents the number of independent manager views or portfolio positions.

The IR increases as both the number of independent positions and predictive skill of the manager increase. A simple example illustrates this.

Consider a portfolio manager who selects bonds from 10 currencies and has an IC of 0.05 and a portfolio manager who selects from 100 currencies and has the same IC of 0.05. The IR of the first portfolio manager is $0.15 = 0.05 \times \sqrt{10}$, and the IR of the second portfolio manager is $0.5 = 0.1 \times \sqrt{100}$.

Often, the number of assets depends on a manager's benchmark exposure and investment universe. For example, an emerging market hard currency benchmark comprising, for example 60 countries with bonds denominated in the U.S. dollar is different from the local currency Bloomberg Barclays Global Aggregate Government Bond Index that comprises more than 40 currencies and countries.

When applied to global bond portfolios, the estimation of the IR becomes more challenging compared to equity portfolios. The reason lies in the assumption that portfolio positions or views on assets are interdependent of one another. But this is clearly not the case in most instances. For example, forming a view on the Mexico peso is likely not independent from a manager's view on Mexican bonds. The higher the complexity of a global bond portfolio and the more heterogeneous the asset classes in which the portfolio manager invests, the more problematic the formulation of independent views becomes.

According to Kazemi *et al.* (2016), however, determining the IC is the most challenging task when estimating the IR. Regression-based models can be used to gain reasonable assessment of manager skill.[5] Specifically, portfolio returns are regressed against lagged portfolio returns. The time lag used is often based on statistical tests related to the autocorrelation of current portfolio returns to past returns.[6] The IC is the correlation coefficient of the predicted and realized portfolio returns. If the IC is zero, then the portfolio manager has no skill in predicting returns. The R^2 of the regression model can be used to determine the correlation coefficient, which is the square root of R^2 of the regression. A higher correlation coefficient ($IC = \sqrt{R^2}$) is an indication of better predictive skill.

Xia and Simonian (2021) provided an alternative approach to deriving the IC. Specifically, they show how the weighted rank correlation measure provides an intuitive and transparent version of the IC, which can be applied to global bond portfolios. Their approach uses a simulation-based framework that helps analyze the impact of asset allocation skill and its implications for estimating reasonable expectations of asset allocation alpha.

Often, bond portfolios have various constraints that must be complied with during portfolio construction. These might be associated with the prevention of the violation of regulatory issues, short selling, currency or country exposure, transaction costs and trading restrictions, or even the explicit prohibition to invest in certain assets. These issues represent limitations which have to be taken into account when estimating the IR. The

---

[5] See Kahn and Rudd (1995).

[6] Autocorrelation analysis is important in financial time series research. Autocorrelations help to investigate time series dependencies. Specifically, the time series of portfolio returns can be investigated to discover the dependencies of current portfolio returns with past portfolio returns up to a specific time period. Autocorrelations are simply computed using the original time series of the portfolio returns with the series lagged a certain number of periods.

IR estimation is then adjusted by the transfer coefficient (TC), which reflects the level of constraints in a portfolio. We can formally incorporate the TC into the derivation of the IR as follows:

$$\mathrm{IR} = \mathrm{IC}\sqrt{\mathrm{B}}\ \mathrm{TC} \tag{11.4}$$

where IR IC, and B, are described earlier, and TC is the measure of the extent that a bond portfolio manager is able to apply an unconstrained version of a strategy.

A TC level of one means the portfolio manager faces no constraints. Values less than one mean that the portfolio manager is bound by some strategy constraints. In general, a lower TC will imply transaction cost and liquidity challenges in a manager's investment process. Relatively illiquid markets such as emerging and high yield markets often serve to degrade the TC for managers.

11.1.4.2 *Evaluating absolute return global bond portfolios*

The IR is a powerful instrument for performance measurement and can be applied to both portfolios run against a benchmark and measuring the performance of absolute return bond portfolios. Absolute return bond portfolios are often unconstrained bond portfolios, that invest in a variety of asset classes, utilizing both long and short positions, with relaxed constraints on position size and holding period. These types of funds also often make use of derivative instruments like swaps, futures, forwards, and customized derivative products.

Because these portfolios may change their exposures frequently, they will often contain more liquid investments rather than relatively illiquid securities like high-yield bonds and corporate bonds with small issue sizes. One of the major challenges when evaluating the performance of such portfolios is that no proper bond benchmark index might represent their investment style. Nevertheless, they still need a reference return by which to measure their performance. Often, money market rates plus an added premium, are used to represent the absolute return level that a bond portfolio must achieve. For example, three-month U.S. T-bill rate plus 100 bps might be an appropriate benchmark.

For some, selecting a benchmark return of zero for absolute return portfolios may be seem intuitive. However, given that an absolute return portfolio will be taking on some level of risk, a non-zero return that is commensurate with that risk needs to be stipulated. To mitigate the benchmark problem, portfolio managers have applied regression-based performance measurement and investigated portfolio performance against factor exposures that reflect a portfolio's investment universe. Of course, alpha estimation will vary depending on the selection of factors and model specification.

Waring and Siegel (2006) and Pojarliev and Levich (2014) show that regression-based style analysis can be applied to estimate *ex-post* alpha and to define an alternative IR as the manager's active return (alpha) divided by its standard deviation of excess returns. Pojarliev and Levich label this ratio the *alpha ratio.* To calculate the IR, the Pojarliev and Levich estimate alpha after stripping out factor beta exposures by modifying equation (11.1) to

$$\hat{\alpha} = R_t - \sum_i \hat{\beta}_i F_{i,t} + \varepsilon_t \tag{11.5}$$

where $\hat{\alpha}$ is the estimated measure of active manager skill, $\hat{\beta}_i$ is the estimated coefficient of factor loadings that measures the sensitivity of the portfolio returns to a factor, $F_{i,t}$'s are the factors representing different investing styles, and ε_t is a randomly distributed error term.

Now, the alternative IR is the excess return divided by the standard deviation of the excess return after controlling for the risk factors. That is,

$$\text{IR} = \frac{\hat{\alpha}}{\sigma(\hat{\alpha})} \tag{11.6}$$

where $\sigma(\hat{\alpha})$ is the standard deviation of $\hat{\alpha}$.

Style-based models using relevant style factors like momentum, carry, value, or quality are often a reasonable choice in performance measurement. *Style drift* refers to changing investment behavior. For example, a global bond portfolio manager might choose to switch from a carry strategy to a momentum strategy. The style drift might be driven by algorithms trying to catch the change in market cycles and market regimes. For unconstrained global bond portfolios that often experience style drift, performance measurement using a return-based style model is an especially appropriate choice.

11.1.5 *Performance measurement and contribution to risk: An illustration*

In this section, we illustrate performance measurement using factor models with an approach suggested by Konstantinov (2016) and further developed by Zaremba (2019). The framework consists of the following seven-factor model that includes both currency and bond factors:

$$\begin{aligned} R_{i,t} = \alpha_i &+ \beta_1 r_{i,t}^{Bond\ Momentum} + \beta_2 r_{i,t}^{Bond\ Carry} + \beta_3 r_{i,t}^{Rate\ Volatility} \\ &+ \beta_4 r_{i,t}^{FX\ Carry} + \beta_5 r_{i,t}^{FX\ Trend} + \beta_6 r_{i,t}^{FX\ Value} + \beta_7 r_{i,t}^{FX\ Volatility} \\ &+ \beta_8 r_{i,t}^{Term} + \beta_9 r_{i,t}^{Default} + \varepsilon_{i,t} \end{aligned} \tag{11.7}$$

We can use the model given by the above equation to take a closer look at the drivers of global bond portfolio performance. To do this, we use two example portfolios that reported their returns on the MercerInsight database between January 2001 and December 2020 (see Table 11.1).

We see in Table 11.1 that our model is quite informative. First, we see that the respective R^2 of each portfolio is quite high, 46% and 48% for Fund F1 and Fund F2, respectively. A high R^2 means that the variance of portfolio returns is well explained by the regression model. In other words, 46% and 48% of the variance of portfolio returns for Fund F1 and Fund F2, respectively, is explained by the factors.

There are important conclusions that can be drawn after estimating performance measurement using factor models. Because factor models show the systematic exposures of a portfolio, controlling for global bond exposures is important for gaining insight into the skill level and longer-term alpha generating capacity of portfolio managers.

Risk decomposition aims at investigating the risk exposure that a portfolio has to a specific factor. For this purpose, the total risk of a portfolio is separated into the contributions of its individual factors. The estimated effects of the individual risk factors are the sum of the factor contributions to the total portfolio risk:

$$\sigma_P = \sum_i \rho_{i,P} \sigma_{F_i} F_i \tag{11.8}$$

where σ_P is the portfolio's total risk as measured by standard deviation, $\rho_{i,P}$ is the correlation coefficient of factor i with the returns of the

Table 11.1: Factor Model Regressions for Two Global Bond Portfolios: January 2001–December 2020

R^2	Fund		FX Value	FX Momentum	FX Carry	FX Volatility	Rate Volatility	Bond Carry	Bond Momentum	Term	Default	Intercept
0.46	F1	Coef.	–0.27***	0.16***	0.21***	–0.14	0.08	–0.03	0.02	0.87***	0.15**	0.0050***
		t-stat.	–4.331	2.793	3.452	–1.492	1.298	–0.447	0.247	5.680	2.460	3.490
0.48	F2	Coef.	–0.29***	0.02	0.06	0.20**	–0.06	0.01	–0.14**	1.35***	0.29***	0.0036***
		t-stat.	–4.957	0.514	1.111	2.171	–1.155	0.108	–2.100	9.325	4.888	2.695

Note: Bond fund data obtained from MercerInsight. *** denotes significance at the 1% level, ** denotes significance at the 5% level, * denotes significance at the 10% level.

portfolio, $\sigma_{F_{i,t}}$ is the standard deviation of the factor $F_{i,t}$, and $F_{i,t}$ is the estimated factor effect (coefficient) on the portfolio from the *i*th factor.

A simple example illustrates this point. Suppose that the total risk as measured by the standard deviation of the F1 global bond portfolio in Table 11.1 is 6.2%. If the correlation between changes in the term factor and the return of the portfolio is 0.7, the standard deviation of the FX term factor changes is 4.5%, and the estimated factor effect is 0.87, then applying equation (11.8), we see that the risk contribution of the term factor to the total risk of the portfolio is $0.045 \times 0.87 \times 0.7 = 2.74\%$. In other words, the changes in the term factor account for approximately 44% (2.74/6.2%) of the total portfolio risk.

Finally, factor models and attribution models can be successfully combined in portfolio management. For example in a framework called *reverse attribution*, Simonian (2021) shows how to use attribution models to generate forward looking factor allocations. A notable feature of the methodology is how it generates expected factor alphas. Given the difficulty in generating accurate point estimates for *ex ante* factor returns, the reverse attribution framework describes a technique that gives managers the ability to generate expected factor alphas from factor volatilities. It also allows managers to adjust factor volatility values in a manner that is consistent with their subjective beliefs regarding a factor's likely marginal alpha contribution.

11.2 Key Takeaways

- Performance measurement is critical for assessing, *ex post*, the drivers of portfolio performance and the skill level of portfolio managers over discrete investment horizons.
- The factors applied in return-based factor models should have sound economic reasoning and a robust statistical foundation. Applying factor models to performance measurement requires the choice of appropriate factors. The factors should reflect a portfolio manager's style and investment approach.
- Estimating factor models and identifying risk factor contributions should be conducted on an ongoing basis because of the time-varying nature of factor behavior and changing market conditions.
- In any given performance measurement model, it is important to control for the market timing skills of managers. The Treynor–Mazuy model is the standard framework for measuring market timing skill.

- The information ratio is one of the most common metrics for performance evaluation and has been successfully applied to global bond portfolios. Factor models can also be effectively employed to evaluate manager performance.
- Return-based factor models are not only useful for performance evaluation but also can be applied to future portfolio allocations using predictive models and inverse attribution approaches.

References

Angelidis, T., D. Giamouridis, and N. Tessaromatis. 2013. "Revisiting Mutual Fund Performance Evaluation". *Journal of Banking and Finance* 37(5): 1759–1776.

Baltussen, G., M. Martens, and O. Panninga. 2022. "Factor Investing in Sovereign Bond Markets: Deep Sample Evidence". *Journal of Portfolio Management* 48(2): 209–225.

Bektić, D. 2019. "Residual Equity Momentum Spillover in Global Corporate Bond Markets". *Journal of Fixed Income* 28(3): 46–54.

Bektić, D., J. S. Wenzler, M. Wegener, D. Schiereck, and T. Spielmann. 2019. "Extending Fama–French-Factors to Corporate Bond Markets". *Journal of Portfolio Management* 45(3): 141–158.

Ben Dor, A., V. Budinger, L. Dynkin, and K. Leech. 2008. "Constructing Peer Benchmarks for Mutual Funds: A Style Analysis-Based Approach". *Journal of Portfolio Management* 34(2): 65–77.

Berk, J. B. and R. C. Green. 2004. "Mutual Fund Flows and Performance in Rational Markets". *Journal of Political Economy* 112(6): 1269–1295.

Berk, J. B. and J. H. van Binsbergen. 2015. "Measuring Skill in the Mutual Fund Industry". *Journal of Financial Economics* 118(1): 1–20.

Berk, J. B. and J. H. van Binsbergen. 2017. "Mutual Funds in Equilibrium". *Annual Review of Financial Economics* 9: 147–167.

Berk, J. B., J. H. van Binsbergen, and M. Miller. 2020. "Mutual Funds: Skill and Performance". *Journal of Portfolio Management* 46(5): 17–31.

Brinson, G. and N. Fachler. 1985. "Measuring Non-U.S. Equity Portfolio Performance". *Journal of Portfolio Management* 11(3): 73–76.

Campisi, S. 2000. "Primer on Fixed Income Performance Attribution". *Journal of Performance Measurement* 4(4): 14–25.

Carhart, M.M. 1997. "On Persistence in Mutual Fund Performance". *Journal of Finance* 52(1): 57–82.

Chen, Z. and P. Knez. 1996. "Portfolio Performance Measurement: Theory and Application". *Review of Financial Studies* 9(2): 511–556.

De Jong, M. and F. J. Fabozzi. 2020. "The Market Risk of Corporate Bonds". *Journal of Portfolio Management* 46(2): 92–105.

Duyvesteyn, J. and M. Martens. 2014. "Emerging Government Bond Market Timing". *Journal of Fixed Income* 23(3): 36–49.

Estrada, J., M. Kritzman, and S. Page. 2006. "Countries Versus Industries in Emerging Markets: A Normative Portfolio Approach". *Journal of Investing* 15(4): 19–28.

Fama, E. F. and K. R. French. 1992. "The Cross-Section of Expected Stock Returns". *Journal of Finance* 47(2): 427–465.

Fama, E. F. and K. R. French.1993. "Common Risk Factors in the Returns on Stocks and Bonds". *Journal of Financial Economics* 33(1): 3–56.

Fama, E. F. and K. R. French. 2015. "A Five-Factor Asset Pricing Model". *Journal of Financial Economics* 116: 1–22.

Fischer, B. and R. Wermers. 2013. *Performance Evaluation and Attribution of Security Portfolios*. Oxford: AP Elsevier.

Grinold, R. C. 1989. "The Fundamental Law of Active Management". *Journal of Portfolio Management* 15(3): 30–37.

Grinold, R. C. and R. Kahn. 2000. *Active Portfolio Management: A Quantitative Approach for Providing Superior Returns and Controlling Risk*. New York, NY: McGraw-Hill.

Harvey, C. R., Y. Liu, and H. Zhu. 2016". … and the Cross-Section of Expected Returns". *The Review of Financial Studies* 29(1): 5–68.

Jensen, M. C. 1968. "The Performance of Mutual Funds in the Period 1945–1964". *Journal of Finance* 23(2): 389–416.

Kazemi, H. B., K. H. Black, and D. R. Chambers. 2016. *Alternative Investments*. 3rd Edition, Hoboken, NJ: John Wiley & Sons.

Kahn, R. N. 1998. "Bond Managers Need to Take More Risk". *Journal of Portfolio Management* 24(3): 70–76.

Kahn, R. N. and A. Rudd. 1995. "Does Historical Performance Predict Future Performance?" *Financial Analysts Journal* 51(6): 43–52.

Konstantinov, G. 2016. "Capturing Short-term and Long-term Alpha of Global Bond Portfolios: Evidence from EUR-Investors' Perspective". *Financial Markets and Portfolio Management* 30(3): 337–365.

Konstantinov, G. and F. J. Fabozzi. 2021a. "Carry Strategies and the U.S. Dollar Risk of U.S. and Global Bonds". *Journal of Fixed Income* 30(3): 26–46.

Konstantinov, G. and F. J. Fabozzi. 2021b. "Towards a Dead End: EMU Bond Market Exposure and Manager Performance". *Journal of International Money and Finance* 116: 102433.

Ladekarl, J. and E. E. Peters. 2013. "Emerging Market Currency: The Common Risk Factor in Emerging Markets". *Journal of Investing* 22(3): 135–143.

Leibowitz, M. L. 2011. "Alpha Orbits". *Financial Analysts Journal* 67(4): 6–7.

Maeso, J. M., L. Martellini, and R. Rebonato. 2020. "Factor Investing in US Sovereign Bond Markets: A New Generation of Conditional Carry Strategies with Applications in Asset-Only and Asset-Liability Management". *Journal of Portfolio Management* 46(2): 121–140.

Mladina, P. and S. Germani. 2019. "Bond-Market Risk Factors and Manager Performance". *Journal of Portfolio Management* 45(6): 75–85.

Parikh, H. and F. J. Fabozzi. 2018. "The Impact of Market Conditions on Bond Fund Managers". *Journal of Fixed Income* 27(3): 6–22.

Peterson, J. D, M. J. Iachini, and W. Lam. 2011. "Identifying Characteristics to Predict Separately Managed Account Performance". *Financial Analysts Journal* 67(4): 30–41.

Pojarliev, M. and R. M. Levich. 2014. "Evaluating Absolute Return Managers". *Financial Markets and Portfolio Management* 28(1): 95–104.

Remolona, E., M. Scatigna, and E. Wu. 2008. "The Dynamic Pricing of Sovereign Risk in Emerging Markets: Fundamentals and Risk Aversion". *Journal of Fixed Income* 17(4): 57–71.

Rocha, K., R. Siqueira, and F. Pinheiro. 2007. "Vulnerability of Emerging Markets to Global Shocks: The Role of Debt and Governance on Sovereign Spreads". *Journal of Fixed Income* 17(2): 77–91.

Simonian, J. 2021. "Factor Allocation as Reverse Attribution". *Journal of Portfolio Management* 47(5): 65–71.

Treynor, J. and K. Mazuy. 1966. "Can Mutual Funds Outguess the Market?" *Harvard Business Review* 44: 131–136.

Waring, B. M. and L. B. Siegel. 2006. "The Myth of the Absolute Return Investor". *Financial Analysts Journal* 62(2): 14–21.

Xia, S. Q. and J. Simonian. 2021. "Measuring Investment Skill in Multi-Asset Strategies: An Empirical Study of the Information Coefficient as Weighted Rank Correlation". *Journal of Portfolio Management* 47(4): 135–144.

Zaremba, A. 2019. "Cross-sectional Seasonalities in International Government Bond Returns". *Journal of Banking and Finance* 98: 80–94.

Chapter 12

Yield Curve Attribution for Global Bond Portfolios

Performance attribution is critical for every type of investment management style — both discretionary and systematic — and is important for both portfolio managers and investors. The concerns that managers and investors have are fourfold: (1) assessing portfolio manager skill, (2) measuring returns, (3) identifying the sources of risk, and (4) identifying the sources of drawdowns or losses. These four concerns are related to managers' and investors' concern with their portfolios outperforming their respective benchmarks. The focus of this chapter is to describe a yield curve-based approach to performance attribution for global bond portfolios.

We begin by discussing an approach to performance attribution that decomposes all sources of bond portfolio return and then adds the impact of foreign exchange exposure to the total sum of bond returns in local currencies. An important advantage of this approach over return-based regression-based models is that no assumption of model composition, parameters, and explanatory factors is made. Furthermore, the model is nonlinear and thus faithfully captures the dynamics of bond prices. Second, we show how a bond portfolio's return components (summarized as bond and currency effects) behave depending on the base currency of the fund. Third, we discuss the interaction between pricing and data quality, which is related to model estimation and the estimation of errors in performance attribution analysis. Whereas pricing and data quality might be considered exogenous factors, model specification, model estimation, and model errors are fundamental determinants of the outcome of performance attribution analysis.

12.1 Theoretical Framework

Decomposing the drivers of portfolio returns *ex post* can be challenging for multi-currency bond portfolios. However, several approaches are now widely accepted for this purpose. While asset allocation-oriented approaches to attribution such as that of Brinson, Hood, and Beebower (1986) and Brinson, Singer, and Beebower (1991) can be applied to bond portfolios, to really account for the specificities of bonds, we need additional tools in order to produce meaningful and correct attribution analysis. Campisi (2000) was among the first to highlight the incompatibility of equity models when applied to fixed-income attribution. McLaren (2001, 2002) presented models suitable for multi-currency bond portfolios, as these models incorporate appropriate yield curves and separate currency effects. The most significant aspect of the studies by McLaren is the inclusion of a yield curve-based reference portfolio. Adding a reference portfolio allows for the estimation of specific yield curve contributions. This is very useful for multi-yield curve bond portfolios with broad country and sector exposures.

Menchero and Davis (2009) propose a model that expresses the currency effects in the corresponding base currency of the portfolio. This approach is particularly useful for multi-currency bond portfolios because it shows the direct currency attribution in absolute terms.

For global bond portfolios, other models also provide useful information. The approach suggested by van Breukelen (2000) emphasizes duration and investigates attribution effects across markets in a top-down structure which is suitable for quantitative bond portfolios that are driven by duration style. Local market effects are a central focus of this analysis. A primary characteristic of this model is that it separates the currency attribution from fixed-income effects.

Perhaps the most important bottom-up framework is the model suggested by Lord (1997). The most distinguishing characteristic of this model is that, for every single bond in a portfolio, it computes bond attribution effects. The results are then aggregated to sectors and other categories.

12.1.1 *Yield curve-based effects*

Because yield curve management has been a central concern of global bond portfolio managers, in this section, we provide an analysis that is consistent with the approaches presented by Lord (1997), Menchero and

Davis (2009), McLaren (2002) and van Breukelen (2000). However, our approach is most similar to that described by Dai and Elliot (2014/2015), in which bond carry is explained by yield curve effects.

A yield curve-based attribution model allows information to be gained regarding the different curve dynamics in the underlying currency exposures and different interest-rate regimes. For example, the curve dynamics of US Treasuries differ from the yield curve changes for Hungarian government bonds. The specific stage of the business cycle also influences these changes.

Litterman and Scheinkman (1991) showed that three yield curve factors — level, slope, and curvature — explain roughly 95% of the volatility of interest rates. Baek *et al.* (2019) show that at the portfolio level, quantifying the factors in the different currency exposures in a portfolio reveals the underlying complex dynamics of both currency and fixed-income effects. The return attribution of a portfolio can be decomposed using the five factors in Figure 12.1, as well as local currency returns. We can further decompose currency returns into three factors: carry, value, and trend.

The roll down and the coupon factors are return effects resulting from the passage of time, while the remaining four factors — parallel, twist, butterfly, and spread — are yield curve based. Measuring the effects in local currency in every sector, country, and asset class allows identification of the source of return by taking different bets on different yield curves. The currency effects reveal the magnitude of currency depreciation or appreciation as a result of curve management. The price change from t_0 to t_1 is decomposed into separate steps using the underlying spot curve to evaluate the impact of the five factors. The procedure is formally expressed as follows:

$$R_t = \frac{T(t_1, s_1 + \text{OAS}_1) - T(t_0, s_0 + \text{OAS}_0)}{T(t_0, s_0 + \text{OAS}_0)} \approx \frac{P(t_1, s_1) - P(t_0, s_0)}{P(t_0, s_0)} \quad (12.1)$$

where R_t is the total bond price return, $T(t_0, s_0)$ is the theoretical bond price at time $t = 0$ estimated with the spot curve at time $t = 0$, $T(t_1, s_1)$ is the

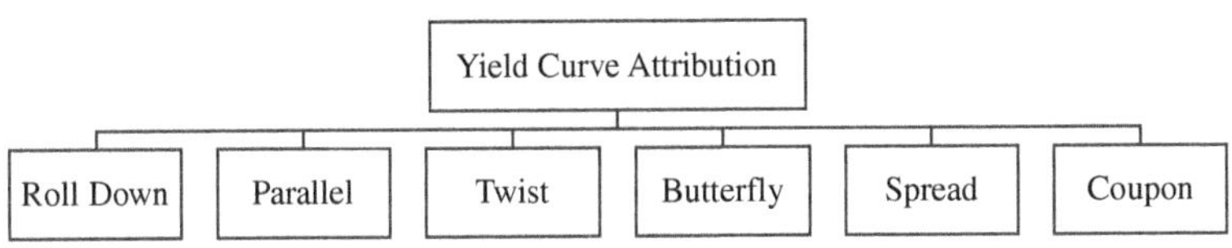

Figure 12.1: Yield Curve Attribution Factors Excluding Currency Effects

theoretical bond price at time $t = 1$ estimated with the spot curve at time $t = 1$, OAS_1 is the option-adjusted spread at time $t = 1$, OAS_0 is the option-adjusted spread at time $t = 0$, $P(t_1, s_1)$ is the market bond price observable at time $t = 1$, and $P(t_0, s_0)$ is the market bond price observable at $t = 0$. The model then needs to estimate the specific drivers of bond prices while accounting for dirty prices which include the accrued interest on the clean price at a given point in time, i.e., $t_0(P_0 + AI_0)$.

Let us now turn to bond price return decomposition, which is shown in Figure 12.2. Here, the price movement from the beginning of the period to the end of the holding period is additive. That is, first the roll down effect is computed followed by the parallel effect. Then, the structure effect is estimated or separated into a twist and butterfly effect. Finally, after all yield curve-related effects are considered, the spread effect is calculated. The spread effect captures all price changes due to a change in the OAS. Figure 12.2 shows the theoretical, idealized computation of yield curve-based attribution. It is of course necessary to estimate the spot curves at the beginning and end of the desired period.[1]

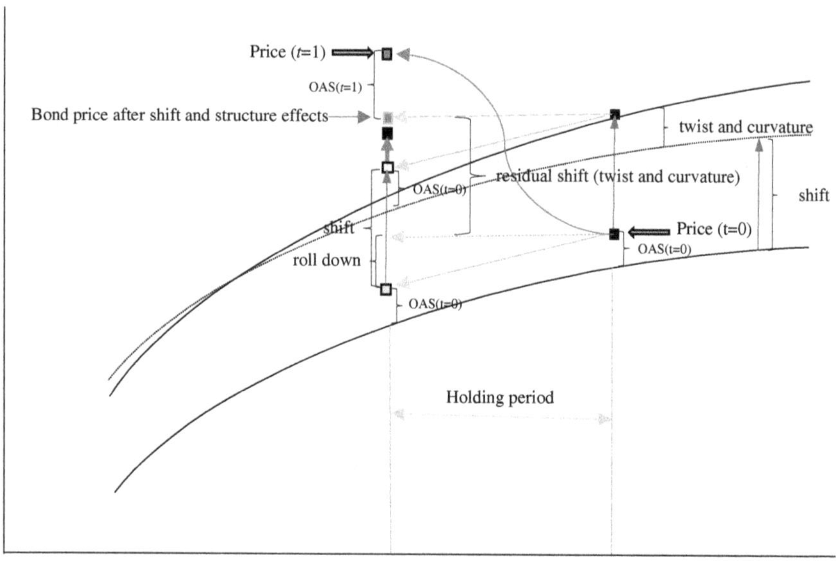

Figure 12.2: Idealized Illustration of the Yield Curve Attribution Effects

[1] Yield curve-based attribution is based on the bond index rules and definitions used by the Merrill Lynch and ICE Bond Index methodologies, whose foundation can be traced back to the work of Lord (1997), van Breukelen (2000), and McLaren (2002).

In Chapter 4, we showed that the parameters level, slope, and curvature are the building blocks of a spot curve. For this reason, the change in the β_0 parameter is regarded as a yield curve shift:

$$\text{shift} = \beta_0(t_1) - \beta_0(t_0) \tag{12.2}$$

where $\beta_0(t_1)$ is the β_0 parameter of the Nelson-Siegel polynomial at time $t = 1$ and $\beta_0(t_0)$ is the β_0 parameter of the Nelson-Siegel polynomial at time $t = 0$.

It is important to note that, while formally simple, the estimation of the *shift effect* in practice is not trivial. According to Colin (2005, 2006), its difficulty is due to the fact that for most portfolios, the shift is estimated using 10-year local currency bond yields or the arithmetic average of the changes in local currency yields.

An alternative approach is to estimate the shift at the portfolio and/or portfolio currency/country segment level. For every bond in the portfolio, the shift factor is computed using the bond's own maturity and corresponding Nelson-Siegel parameters, and summed up at the segment level (e.g., Australian government bonds in local currency (AUD) or European exposure in EUR). The mathematical formulation of the country or sector yield curve average shift is as follows:

$$\text{shift}^{C_k} = \frac{1}{n}\sum_{i=1}^{n} \partial s_n^c \tag{12.3}$$

where s_n^c is the average change of the yield curve k across all n maturities.

This approach has the advantage that it separates the spot curve shifts and precisely measures the portfolio pure shift in every segment but does *not* measure shifts across yield curves. Estimating an overall shift should be made for only the relevant sectoral spot curves. A portfolio shift is then the weighted sum of all sector specific yield curve shifts. Measuring bond shifts for the benchmark and then computing active metrics would show the allocation and selection contributions in the manner suggested by Brinson, Hood, and Beebower (1986) and Brinson, Singer, and Beebower (1991). The disadvantage of this approach is that in large and diversified global bond portfolios (e.g., a portfolio comprising several hundred bonds), the approach grows in complexity.

12.1.1.1 *Roll down effect*

The *roll down* is the return due to the passage of time and results from the difference of a bond price discounted with the same spot curve and the option-adjusted spread OAS_0 at time t_1 and t_0. The calculation considers only the change in time t. Based on the definition of the roll down return, the yield curve at the beginning of the holding period is held constant, and so changes that occur in the yield curve shape during the holding period are ignored. The realism of this assumption, already considered in the previous chapter, can be ignored over short holding periods. In practice, such periods are usually one month. A further assumption of most roll down calculations is a constant OAS, whose changes will be captured in the spread effect evaluation. The roll down effect incorporates the pull to par effect in bonds. That is, it is the effect of price convergence toward nominal value (e.g., 100). The roll down calculation is stated formally in the following equation:

$$\text{Roll Down} = \frac{T(t_1, s_0 + \text{OAS}_0) - T(t_0, s_0 + \text{OAS}_0)}{P_0 + AI_0} \tag{12.4}$$

where $T(t_1, s_0)$ is the theoretical bond price at time $t = 1$ estimated with the spot curve at time $t = 0$, $T(t_0, s_0)$ is the theoretical bond price at time $t = 0$ estimated with the spot curve at time $t = 0$, AI_0 is the bond's accrued interest at time $t = 0$, OAS_0 is the OAS at time $t = 0$, and P_0 is the market bond price observable at time $t = 0$.

12.1.1.2 *Parallel effect*

The *parallel effect* results as a consequence of a shift in the initial spot curve at time t_1. More precisely, the bond price at t_1 is discounted using the spot curve at s_0 with the option-adjusted spread OAS_0. The shift is added to the bond price at t_1 using the spot curve s_0 and the OAS_0. Starting with the initial curve, we simply add the shift to the starting spot curve. We thus create a "new" curve using an initial spot curve plus a shift. Again, it is necessary to calculate the roll down effect, as shown below:

$$\text{Parallel} = \frac{T(t_1, s_0 + \text{OAS}_0 + \text{shift}) - T(t_1, s_0 + \text{OAS}_0)}{P_0 + AI_0} \tag{12.5}$$

where $T(t_1, s_0)$ is the theoretical bond price at time $t = 1$ estimated with the spot curve at time $t = 0$, AI_0 is the accrued interest of the bond at time $t = 0$, OAS_0 is the OAS at time $t = 0$, and P_0 is the market bond price observable at time $t = 0$. Shift is the shift parameter estimated using equation (12.2).

12.1.1.3 *Structure effect*

The twist and butterfly effects add up to what is known as the *structure effect*, which reflects the change in the yield curve shape, complementary to the parallel effect. Note that we now add the yield curve shift defined in equation (12.2) to the yield curve at the beginning of the holding period. In contrast to the parallel effect, the measurement of the structure effect starts once the initial curve is shifted. This is its major difference with the parallel effect. The structure effect is formally described as follows:

$$\text{Structure} = \frac{T(t_1, s_1 + \text{OAS}_0) - T(t_1, s_0 + \text{OAS}_0 + \text{shift})}{P_0 + AI_0} \tag{12.6}$$

where $T(t_1, s_1)$ is the theoretical bond price at time $t = 1$ estimated with the spot curve at time $t = 1$, and the other variables are as defined earlier.

A decomposition of the structure effect is necessary to evaluate the returns from changes in steepness (twist) and curvature (butterfly). Note that the decomposition of the structure effect into twist and butterfly effects is done by considering yield curve shifts. Within this framework, we start where we stopped with the parallel effect. Mathematically, by adding the twist and butterfly effects, the term $T(t_1, s_1 + \text{OAS}_0 + \text{shift})$ cancels out, resulting in the structure effect. The simplicity in decomposing the structure effect using the yield curve shift from equation (12.2) stems from the fact that the yield curve shift is straightforward to compute. The computation of a steepness, or slope parameter of the local yield curves, is more sensitive and difficult to estimate. Several approaches use the additional Nelson-Siegel or Svensson components. However, shift is usually preferred for practitioner purposes and easier to implement.

An alternative way to show the twist and butterfly effects is to derive them using the spot curve parameters suggested by Colin (2005) and Fischer and Wermers (2013). However, such estimations bear several idiosyncratic and model specification risks, rendering them less meaningful in practice because the shift component typically explains roughly 90% of the variance of bond returns (according to Litterman and Scheinkman (1991)).

12.1.1.4 *Twist effect*

After adding a shift to the initial spot curve at t_0, we now measure the effect on bond prices between that price and the completely new price resulting from the spot curve at t_1. This is known as the *twist effect* which is measured as follows:

$$\text{Twist} = \frac{T(t_1, s_1 + \text{OAS}_0 + \text{shift}) - T(t_1, s_0 + \text{OAS}_0 + \text{shift})}{P_0 + AI_0} \tag{12.7}$$

where the variables are as defined earlier.

12.1.1.5 *Butterfly effect*

The *butterfly effect* can be derived as a residual effect of the entire movement of the curve. Specifically, the butterfly effect captures the residual effect in excess curve shift between s_0 and s_1 spot curves and is measured as follows:

$$\text{Butterfly} = \frac{T(t_1, s_1 + \text{OAS}_0) - T(t_1, s_1 + \text{OAS}_0 + \text{shift})}{P_0 + AI_0} \tag{12.8}$$

where the variables are as defined earlier.

12.1.1.6 *Spread effect*

The *spread effect* is simply the bond price change at t_1 using the spot curve s_1 due to a change in the OAS between OAS_0 and OAS_1:

$$\text{Spread} = \frac{T(t_1, s_1 + \text{OAS}_1) - T(t_1, s_1 + \text{OAS}_0)}{P_0 + AI_0} \tag{12.9}$$

where $T(t_1, s_1)$ is the theoretical bond price at time $t = 1$ estimated with the spot curve at time $t = 1$, OAS_1 is the OAS at time $t = 1$, and the other variables are as defined earlier.

12.1.1.7 *Coupon effect*

The *coupon effect* measures the amount of interest accrued during the holding period as follows:

$$\text{Coupon} = \frac{\text{AI}(t_1) - \text{AI}(t_0) + \text{CF}(t_0, t_1)}{P_0 + \text{AI}_0} \tag{12.10}$$

where $\text{CF}(t_0, t_1)$ is the coupon due between $t = 0$ and $t = 1$, AI_1 is the accrued interest of the bond at time $t = 1$, and the other variables are as defined earlier.

12.1.2 *Currency effects*

Decomposing the *currency effect* is an important aspect of fixed-income attribution and as we have emphasized, it is usually estimated and shown to be separate from yield curve and spread effects. An advantage of separating currency effects from bond effects is that it is possible to show the net effects of currency management regardless of the base currency — whether it be euro, US dollar, Swiss franc, or Japanese yen. The attribution analysis starts with estimating the spot curves and determining the yield curve shift.

Next, we show all currency effects as price effects. It is essential to convert all unit notations into prices in order to derive returns. Specifically, the EUR/USD notation and time series reflect a US-dollar-based portfolio. However, a global bond fund with a euro base currency has to convert the unit notation into a price notation. The rule of thumb is that the first currency in a pair denotes the reference, or base currency (BC), and the second term refers to the "foreign" currency (qx). A similar convention applies to all currencies. In the case of a US-dollar-based investor, the euro investment in a portfolio at time t uses the following price notation:

$$\frac{qx}{\text{BC}} = \text{Price} \rightarrow \text{EUR/USD} = 1.083 \rightarrow \text{EUR/USD} = \frac{1}{1.083} = 0.9233$$

Thus, the return of a currency in a given period can be computed using only price notation:

$$fx_t^{\text{Base Currency}} = \ln(qx/\text{BC})_t - \ln\left(\frac{qx}{\text{BC}}\right)_{t-1} \tag{12.11}$$

where qx is the foreign exchange denomination of a currency pair and BC is the portfolio's base currency.

This approach helps to reveal one of the most important dimensions of managing global multi-currency or hard currency bond portfolios. Specifically, the return decomposition shows that the local currency bond effects are equal for all investors holding the same portfolio, but the base currency of the fund causes the differentiation in their returns (see Konstantinov, 2022).

To show the separate currency effects as a total sum, it is necessary to determine the single bond currency impact using the price notation and multiply it by the portfolio weight. The sum is simply the total bond portfolio currency impact. Further, it is possible to use discrete or continuous notation when estimating the currency impact on an asset. For a continuous return estimation with long holding periods, it is convenient to use the following notation:

$$r_t^{\text{Base Currency}} = (1 + r_t^{\text{LC}})(1 + fx_t^{\text{Base Currency}}) - 1 \tag{12.12}$$

where r_t^{LC} is the local currency return, $fx_t^{\text{Base Currency}}$ is the foreign exchange with the adjusted base currency of the portfolio, and $r_t^{\text{Base Currency}}$ is the return in the base currency of the portfolio. Then, the bond return in the base currency r_t^{LC} is the product of the local currency return r_{lc} and the currency return $fx_t^{\text{Base Currency}}$ at time t.

As we showed in Chapter 3, currency returns can be decomposed into four major factors: carry, value, momentum, and volatility. We describe the mathematical derivation of the returns for each factor below.

12.1.2.1 *FX carry effect*

FX carry is the difference in the expected spot rate and the realized spot rate. If the expected spot rate is higher than the realized spot rate, then the carry return is positive and vice versa. The returns are calculated in the following manner:

$$\begin{aligned} R_t^{\text{FX Carry}} &= \ln(E(S_{t+1})/S_{t+1}) \quad \text{if } E(S_{t+1}) > S_t \quad \text{and} \\ &\quad \ln(S_{t+1}/E(S_{t+1})) \quad \text{if } E(S_{t+1}) < S_t \end{aligned} \tag{12.13}$$

where $E(S_{t+1})$ is the expected spot rate of the currency pair at time $t + 1$, S_{t+1} is the spot rate at time $t + 1$, and S_t is the spot rate of a currency at time t.

12.1.2.2 *FX value effect*

Relative to FX momentum and FX carry, FX value is fundamentally driven by the long-term value of an exchange rate. To calculate FX value returns, it is necessary to compute the relative Purchasing Power Parity (PPP), which assumes that exchange rates and inflation rates in two countries should converge over time. The FX value returns are positive if the long-term fair value price is higher than the current spot price and vice versa. Formally, the returns for FX value are as follows:

$$R_t^{\text{FX Value}} = \begin{array}{ll} \ln(S_{t+1}/S_{\text{PPP}}) & \text{if } S_{\text{PPP}} > S_t \quad \text{and} \\ \ln(S_{\text{PPP}}/S_{t+1}) & \text{if } S_{\text{PPP}} > S_t \end{array} \tag{12.14}$$

where S_{t+1} is the spot rate at time $t + 1$, S_t is the spot rate of a currency at time t, and S_{PPP} is the fair value of the currency spot rate according to PPP.

The relationship between the currencies and inflation rates of the base and foreign countries can be expressed as follows:

$$\frac{S_{\text{PPP}}}{S_t} = \frac{1+\inf_{\text{base}}}{1+\inf_{qx}} \tag{12.15}$$

where $\inf_{\text{base}}$ is the inflation rate of the portfolio base currency, $\inf_{qx}$ is the inflation rate of the foreign currency, and the other variables are as defined earlier.

12.1.2.3 *FX momentum effect*

The *FX momentum effect* is the result of the foreign exchange price at the end of period $t + 1$ and the foreign exchange price at a specified period $t - h$. Note that FX momentum can have a dual meaning. Alternatively, the FX momentum might also be positive if the currency appreciates. In other words, FX positioning is crucial to determining negative or positive momentum. Therefore, portfolio managers should be careful to adjust the currency pair and properly identify the short or long position in FX momentum trades. To compute the profit and loss from FX momentum, we use the following formula:

$$R_t^{\text{FX Momentum}} = \ln(S_{t+1}/S_{t-h}) \quad \text{if } S_{t-h} - S_t > 0 \quad \text{and}$$
$$\ln(S_{t-h}/S_{t+1}) \quad \text{if } S_{t-h} - S_t < 0 \tag{12.16}$$

where S_{t-h} is the spot rate of a currency at time t minus a specific period length of h periods, and the other variables are as defined earlier.

12.1.3 *Portfolio weights and returns*

After estimating the yield curve-based effects and the FX return effects, it is necessary to compute the portfolio and benchmark weighted return vectors. The return vectors are the product of the weights and the attribution effects for roll down, spread, parallel, twist, butterfly, coupon, and spread, as well as the currency effects for carry, momentum, and value. To compute the contribution to portfolio return in that month, it is necessary to multiply the portfolio weights w_i by the corresponding return components — roll down, parallel, and currency in every segment — as shown below:

$$R_t^{C_k} = \sum_{i=1}^{n} r_n^c w_n \tag{12.17}$$

where r_n^c is the return effect for roll down, spread, parallel, twist, butterfly, coupon, and spread, as well as the currency effects for carry, momentum, and value, and w_n represents the portfolio weights.

The same procedure applies when managing to a benchmark. In that case, the active decisions are the differences between the portfolio and benchmark components, both currency and bond exposures. However, active portfolio management focuses on both active weights and returns. The active returns (r_{Active}) are simply the difference between portfolio returns ($r_{\text{Portfolio}}$) and benchmark returns ($r_{\text{Benchmark}}$); that is,

$$r_{\text{Active}} = r_{\text{Portfolio}} - r_{\text{Benchmark}} \tag{12.18}$$

The active weights of a portfolio (w_{Active}) are the difference between the portfolio weights ($w_{\text{Portfolio}}$) and benchmark weights ($w_{\text{Benchmark}}$). That is,

$$w_{\text{Active}} = w_{\text{Portfolio}} - w_{\text{Benchmark}} \tag{12.19}$$

To properly summarize the attribution effects, it is important to express every segment (e.g., currency exposure) as a separate portfolio. For example, if a portfolio comprises 20 European bonds and the euro has a weight of 15%, it is necessary to express this exposure as a separate portfolio. Thus, the 15% euro is rescaled to 100% and all constituents have a rescaled weight that sums up to 100%. Matrix notations can help simplify the relevant calculations.

Finally, a note on practical implementation is necessary. In general, performance attribution is not computed by portfolio managers, but by the risk management and performance measurement team within an organization. However, portfolio managers should have at least a basic knowledge of performance attribution in order to understand the sources of their portfolios' performance.

12.2 Case Studies: Holdings-Based Attribution of a Global and Emerging Market Bond Portfolios

To provide a practical overview of the attribution models applied in global bond portfolios, in this section we provide two case studies of yield curve-based attribution models where in each we separate the currency effects. Both case studies assume that the holding period for each portfolio is one month. That is, the returns of the portfolio and the benchmark are measured from the beginning of the month to the end of the month. Attribution models use the portfolio and benchmark weights at the beginning of the period to measure the specific return effects. An important assumption of the case studies is that the portfolio holdings do not change during the holding period. This is consistent with a quantitative allocation model that is applied on a monthly basis where portfolio rebalancing is carried out monthly. The first case study is focused on the yield curve and currency return attribution of a global bond portfolio. The second case study analyzes an emerging markets hard currency bond portfolio allocated to US-dollar-denominated bonds.

There are two major issues that these case studies highlight. The first is to show how different local currency bonds and spot curves result in different attribution effects. The second issue is related to the different impacts of currency risk. Specifically, for the global bond portfolio case study, we show the portfolio effects of local currency exposure according to different portfolio base currencies (USD, EUR, CAD, AUD, GBP, CHF, and JPY). In the case of an emerging market bond portfolio, the bond exposure is in US dollars, but we vary the base currency of the portfolio.

The two case studies address two different issues when managing currency exposure. For the global bond portfolio case study, we demonstrate the effects of active currency management (different bond exposures and different base currencies). For the hard currency emerging markets bond portfolio, the case study provides an overview of the return attribution impact of the base currency. In doing so it sheds light on the need to consider currency risk overlays.

12.2.1 *Global bond portfolio case study*

The first case study involves a global bond portfolio with local currency exposure. The global bond portfolio comprises 50 individual government bonds in local currency in both developed and emerging markets. The maximum weight of an individual bond is limited to 5%, and the minimum weight of an individual security is 0.5%. The currency exposure is in USD, JPY, CAD, AUD, HUF, CZK, ZAR, MXN, NZD, ILS, NOK, CHF, and EUR. The base currency of the portfolio is EUR. The portfolio is duration neutral; that is, the overall portfolio duration equals the benchmark index duration. To provide more insight regarding the different impacts of currency management, we use different base currencies in the portfolio — AUD, GBP, EUR, USD, CHF, JPY and CAD.

Our analysis starts with a sample plot of local currency spot curves estimated using the Nelson-Siegel model (see Figure 12.3). Note that the country risk equals the currency risk. Thus, the local currency spot curve for Australia is the same as the country spot curve (e.g., Australia = AUD).

In Figure 12.4, we show the currency allocation of the portfolio. Notably, the largest allocations are to the currencies AUD, USD, CAD, HUF, and MXN. The portfolio exposure is tilted to developed markets with an emerging market exposure of roughly 30%.

An overview of the portfolio allocation is only the first step in analyzing the return attribution of global bond portfolios. We also need to compare the portfolio allocation to the benchmark allocation. Because the currency exposure constitutes a large portion of risk and return, we focus

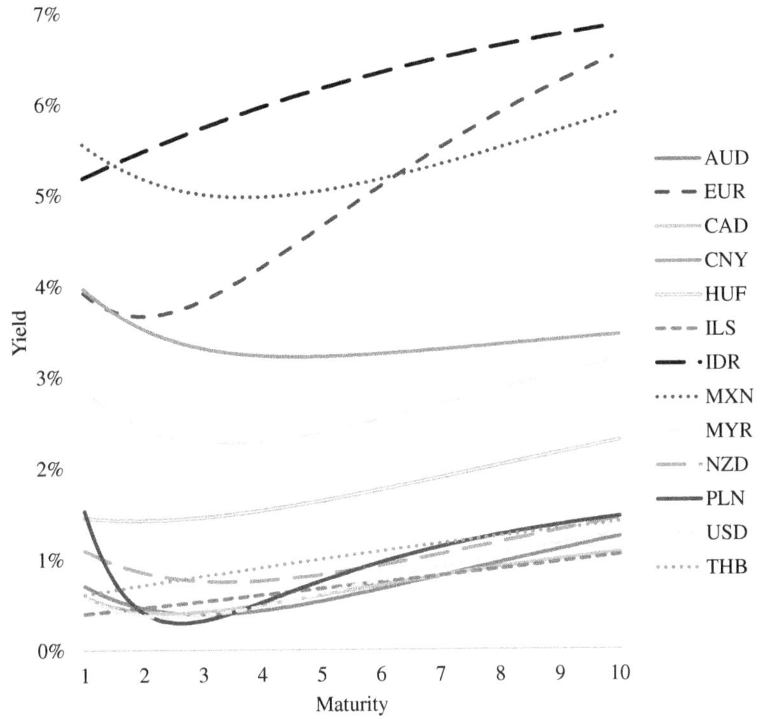

Figure 12.3: Local Currency Spot Curves

Note: Authors' own estimates. Data obtained from Bloomberg, LLC.

on the currency allocation and compare it to a benchmark. In Figure 12.5, we show the currency allocation of the global bond portfolio invested in local currency government bonds. The bond portfolio has different maturity allocations and currency risks compared to its benchmark index, the ICE BofA Global Government Bond Index.[2] Note that this index is a representative benchmark for roughly 30% of global bond funds according to Morningstar.[3]

Visual inspection of the allocation provides useful information about portfolio currency exposure versus the benchmark currency allocation. From Figure 12.5, we see that the global bond portfolio is somewhat

---

[2] Global bond portfolio benchmarks are discussed in Chapter 2.

[3] See Konstantinov (2016).

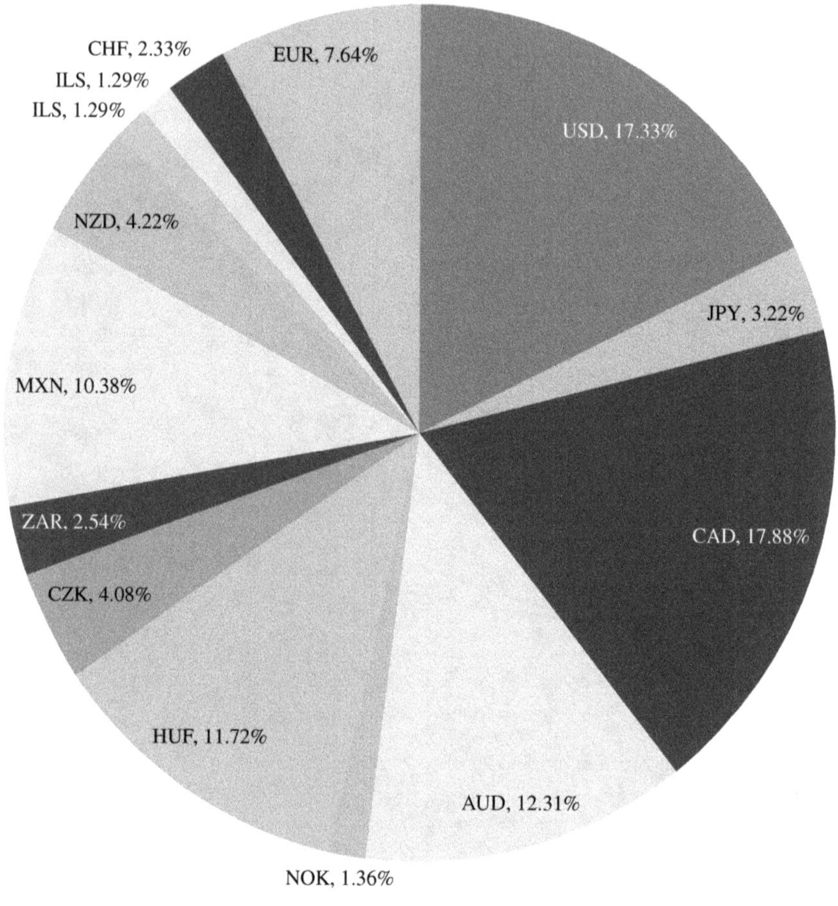

Figure 12.4: Portfolio Currency Allocation

aggressively positioned against the benchmark. The portfolio overweights emerging markets (South Africa, Hungary, and South Korea) and underweights the G3 markets (US, Japan, and Europe). This portfolio strategy is representative of a "risk-on" strategy with significant carry risk, which comes from the different currency and yield curve exposures. Hypothetically, this positioning could be due to the fact that portfolio managers typically overweight risky assets in higher interest-rate regimes in anticipation of falling rates in the future.

In Table.12.1, we show the active maturity allocations and visually illustrate them in Figure 12.6. We use one-year maturity buckets to allow a better overview of the allocation. The short maturity bucket ends with bonds up to 1.5 years of maturity. The second maturity bucket comprises

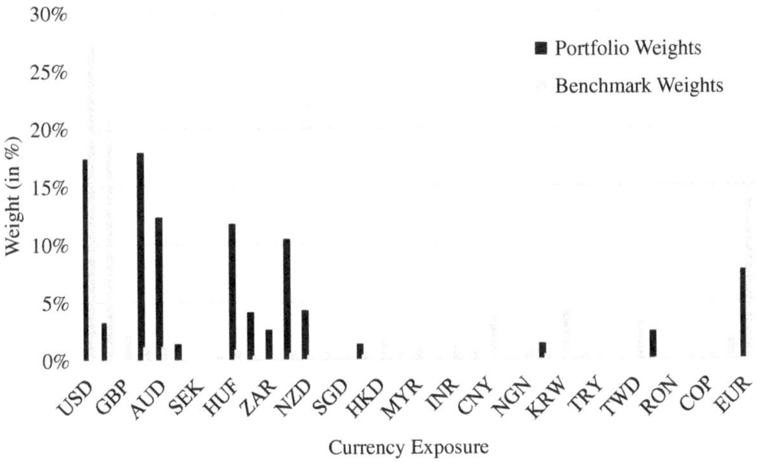

Figure 12.5: Active Currency Allocation of the Global Bond Portfolio vs. Benchmark

Note: Authors' own estimates. Data obtained from Bloomberg, LLC.

Table 12.1: Portfolio and Benchmark Maturity Allocation

	<1.5	**1.5–2.5**	**2.5–3.5**	**3.5–4.5**	**4.5–5.5**	**5.5–6.5**	**6.5–7.5**	**7.5–8.5**	**8.5–9.5**	**9.5<**
Portfolio	0.00	1.42	0.00	18.30	12.14	17.93	16.60	16.72	3.22	9.97
Benchmark	6.73	12.04	10.05	9.30	7.93	6.00	5.59	4.56	4.73	33.05
Active	−6.73	−10.62	−10.05	9.00	4.22	11.93	11.01	12.15	−1.51	−23.08

Note: Authors' own estimates; Data obtained from Bloomberg, LLC.

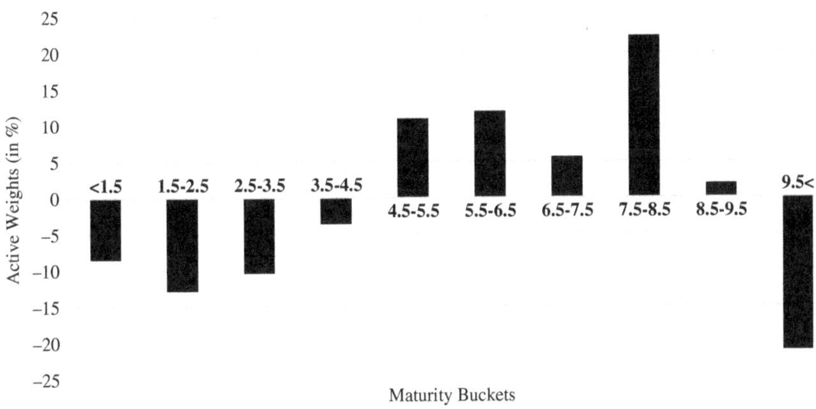

Figure 12.6: Active Maturity Allocation

Note: Authors' own estimates. The data correspond to the third row of Table 12.1. Data obtained from Bloomberg, LLC.

the bonds with a maturity from 1.5 to 2.5 years and so on. The long-term bonds are allocated in the maturity bucket with maturities greater than 9.5 years.

Figure 12.6 provides an overview of the active maturity allocation of the global bond portfolio compared to the benchmark. Note again that the granularity of maturity buckets provides a good overview about the active exposure associated with different maturity risks. For example, the active maturity allocation is concentrated in the buckets between 4-year and 9-year maturity segments.

We show the active maturity allocation of our hypothetical portfolio in Figure 12.6, and we see that the portfolio is allocated to the middle maturity buckets, thus having an active bullet allocation. Recall from Chapter 4 that in a bullet allocation, portfolio exposure is concentrated in the middle maturity buckets. In contrast, in a barbell allocation bonds are allocated in the short-term and long-term maturity buckets.

Because benchmarks and portfolios are usually exposed to several currencies, it is often easier to show exchange rate returns in matrix form. We do this in Table 12.2.

We can now turn our attention to the yield curve effects in the portfolio and benchmark and examine the active yield curve effects of the different local yield curves. First, we provide an overview of the overall effects. The upper row in Table 12.2 indicates the base currency of a portfolio and the elements in the first column indicate the respective currency return against the base currency. For example, the EUR/AUD exchange rate return is 0.34%, and the AUD/EUR return is −0.32%. In

Table 12.2: Portfolio Base Currency Returns in a Matrix Form

	AUD (%)	EUR (%)	CAD (%)	JPY (%)	CHF (%)	USD (%)	GBP (%)
AUD		−0.32	−1.21	0.60	−0.07	−1.19	−1.22
EUR	0.34		−0.88	0.90	0.32	−0.88	−0.93
CAD	1.17	0.89		1.81	1.14	0.0	0.05
JPY	−0.60	−0.90	−1.75		−0.66	−1.78	−1.80
CHF	0.04	−0.27	−1.12	0.66		−1.15	−1.18
USD	1.20	0.88	0.01	1.81	1.15		−0.04
GBP	1.25	0.91	0.04	1.84	1.19	0.04	

Note: Authors' own estimates. Data obtained from Bloomberg, LLC.

other words, in the casé where the portfolio base currency is the EUR, the AUD has depreciated against it by −0.32%. This is a negative impact for a EUR-based portfolio. Alternatively, the EUR exposure of an AUD-based portfolio has appreciated by 0.34%. The EUR/CAD return is −0.88%, but the CAD/EUR is 0.89%. In other words, a portfolio with base currency in EUR has gained 0.89% by investing in CAD. Similarly, a USD-based portfolio experienced a loss against the EUR, because the USD/EUR return is −0.88%, but the EUR-based global bond portfolio gained 0.88% in USD exposure.

In summary, we see in Table 12.3 that the portfolio lost 57 bps in local currency terms while the benchmark lost 45 bps, resulting in a net active bond return of 12bps. Both the twist and butterfly effects show negative contributions of −79 bps and −8 bps, respectively, which sums up to the structure effect of −87 bps. A positive parallel contribution of 7 bps mitigates the significant negative yield curve impact of −80 bps. In an active context, this portfolio underperformed the benchmark which has much less twist exposure than our hypothetical portfolio. Both positive spread and parallel effects were not large enough to compensate for the negative impact of the twist and butterfly effects.

The benchmark experienced negative effects from structure changes of −0.46%, but the positive contribution of the spread effects was only 0.04%. Parallel changes of the yield curve result in a marginally positive effect of 0.02%.

The results show that the portfolio loss relative to the benchmark is 0.12%. The main drivers of this loss were the negative structure effects. Summing up the yield curve effects (parallel, twist, and butterfly), we see that the portfolio loss was clearly attributable to the changes in the yield curve profile. In Figure 12.7, we show a visual illustration of the local

Table 12.3: Local Currency Spot Curve-based Bond Effects

Yield Curve Impact (%)		**Roll Down (%)**	**Parallel (%)**	**Structure (%)**	**Twist (%)**	**Butterfly (%)**	**Spread (%)**	**Total (%)**
−0.80	Portfolio	−0.03	0.07	−0.87	−0.79	−0.08	0.26	−0.57
−0.44	Benchmark	−0.04	0.02	−0.46	−0.44	−0.02	0.04	−0.45
−0.36	Active	0.01	0.05	−0.41	−0.35	−0.06	0.22	−0.12

Note: Authors' own estimates. Data obtained from Bloomberg, LLC.

Figure 12.7: Yield Curve Effects for the Portfolio, Benchmark, and Active Allocation
Note: Authors' own estimates. Data obtained from Bloomberg, LLC.

yield curve attribution in local currency. Again, the structure effect is the sum of the twist and butterfly effects. Both for the portfolio and against the benchmark, the structure effect (the twist in particular) is responsible for the underperformance of the portfolio against the benchmark.

The local currency returns are the same for all investors in this portfolio regardless of the portfolio base currency. However, the base currency of the portfolio, and the net asset value reported, has a significant impact on the return effects in the corresponding currency. With this in mind, we now turn our attention to currency effects.

To show how the different base currencies reflect the bond portfolio and currency allocation, in Table 12.4 we show the same local currency bond exposure in seven base currency regimes. The *total* column summarizes the foreign exchange and bond price effects in each currency. The *resid* column shows the unexplained difference between the attribution bond return and market price return. The *Total Attribution* (*Basis*) column shows our yield curve-based attribution model decomposition, and the *FX Contribution* represents the foreign exchange price impact. Again, we show the different between the returns of the global bond portfolio in the seven different base currencies and the benchmark to derive the active returns.

The local currency bond return of −0.57% is identical for all portfolios. The total portfolio return for the U.S. dollar portfolio of −0.77% is the sum of the local currency bond returns. The total return of the benchmark is −0.47% which is equal for all investors because it is in local currency. Similarly, the US dollar total return which includes the bond and currency returns is −1.07%. We highlight the fact that different segments of the portfolio react differently to the currency impact. For example, the −0.56% of pure bond portfolio return is improved to 0.03% due to the FX contribution of 0.60% for a euro-based (EUR) portfolio, but the weighted currency impact of the invested currencies against the CAD results in a degradation of return from −0.21% to −0.78%. The local currency bond portfolio has a portfolio return of −0.56%, but portfolios denominated in different base currencies show completely different total returns. A global bond portfolio denominated in JPY has the highest positive return of 1.51% due to favorable currency movements. Our case study once again highlights the importance of precisely calibrating the portfolio's FX exposure.

Local currency effects are independent of the base currency. The base currency nevertheless determines the final portfolio return to a large

Table 12.4: Attribution and the Role of the Base Currency in Global Bond Portfolios

	Total (%)	Attribution Bond Returns (%)	Market Price Returns (%)	Total Attribution (Basis) (%)	FX Contribution (%)	Resid (%)
Portfolio						
USD	–0.77	–0.57	–0.56	–0.77	–0.21	0.00
EUR	0.03	–0.57	–0.56	0.03	0.60	0.00
JPY	0.94	–0.57	–0.56	0.93	1.51	0.00
CAD	–0.77	–0.57	–0.56	–0.78	–0.21	0.00
GBP	–0.81	–0.57	–0.56	–0.81	–0.25	0.00
CHF	0.33	–0.57	–0.56	0.33	0.90	0.00
AUD	0.34	–0.57	–0.56	0.33	0.90	0.00
Benchmark						
USD	–1.07	–0.47	–0.48	–1.07	–0.61	0.00
EUR	–0.21	–0.47	–0.48	–0.21	0.26	0.00
JPY	0.69	–0.47	–0.48	0.70	1.17	0.00
CAD	–1.00	–0.47	–0.48	–0.99	–0.52	0.00
GBP	–1.11	–0.47	–0.48	–1.11	–0.64	0.00
CHF	0.12	–0.47	–0.48	0.12	0.60	0.00
AUD	0.07	–0.47	–0.48	0.07	0.55	0.00
Active						
USD	0.30	–0.09	–0.09	0.30	0.40	–0.01
EUR	0.25	–0.09	–0.09	0.24	0.34	–0.01
JPY	0.24	–0.09	–0.09	0.23	0.34	–0.01
CAD	0.22	–0.09	–0.09	0.22	0.31	–0.01
GBP	0.30	–0.09	–0.09	0.30	0.40	–0.01
CHF	0.21	–0.09	–0.09	0.20	0.30	–0.01
AUD	0.26	–0.09	–0.09	0.26	0.36	–0.01

Note: Authors' own estimates. Data obtained from Bloomberg, LLC.

extent. This is because exchange rates express a relation, not an absolute value. According to Strange (1998), base currency depreciation against all currencies in a portfolio has a positive effect on portfolio performance. Similarly, Konstantinov (2022) observed that base currency appreciation in hard currency bond portfolios has negative effects and base portfolio currency depreciation has positive effects on the portfolio.

Table 12.5 provides information about currency attribution effects — carry, value and momentum — and the impact of the portfolio's base currency.

Table 12.5: Currency Return Decomposition in Global Bond Portfolios

	FX Contribution (%)	FX Carry (%)	FX Momentum (%)	FX Value (%)	FX Resid (%)
Portfolio					
USD	–0.21	–0.28	–0.68	0.82	–0.07
EUR	0.60	–0.47	–0.67	1.74	0.00
JPY	1.51	–1.09	–0.16	2.75	0.00
CAD	–0.21	–0.09	–1.53	1.41	0.00
GBP	–0.25	–0.04	0.12	–0.25	–0.07
CHF	0.90	–0.76	–2.39	4.03	0.02
AUD	0.90	–0.24	0.62	0.50	0.03
Benchmark					
USD	–0.61	0.27	–0.43	–0.23	–0.21
EUR	0.26	0.18	–0.42	0.53	–0.03
JPY	1.17	0.10	0.11	0.81	0.15
CAD	–0.52	0.26	–1.32	0.67	–0.13
GBP	–0.64	0.26	0.34	–1.02	–0.23
CHF	0.60	0.17	–2.13	2.47	0.09
AUD	0.55	0.16	0.82	–0.47	0.03
Active					
USD	0.40	–0.54	–0.25	1.05	0.15
EUR	0.34	–0.65	–0.25	1.21	0.03
JPY	0.34	–1.19	–0.27	1.94	–0.15
CAD	0.31	–0.34	–0.21	0.74	0.13
GBP	0.40	–0.30	–0.22	0.76	0.16
CHF	0.30	–0.93	–0.26	1.56	–0.06
AUD	0.36	–0.40	–0.20	0.97	0.00

Note: Authors' own estimates. Data obtained from Bloomberg, LLC.

For example, if we look at Table 12.5, we can clearly see that the impact (size) and direction of the specific currency return factor — carry, momentum, and value — depend on the base currency. For example, the USD-based portfolio lost a total of 21 bps due to FX movements. The drivers of the loss are FX momentum with a loss of 68 bps and carry with a loss of 28 bps. In contrast, FX value compensated the drag of the latter two factors with 82 bps of positive return.

A further investigation of Table 12.5 shows that the euro-based portfolio gain in currencies was 0.6%. Notably, FX momentum lost 0.67%, carry produced a loss of −0.47%, while the gain from FX value is 1.74%. The currency total return of 90 bps for the AUD-based portfolio reveals that there is a negative contribution from the carry returns of −24 bps, but positive gain of 62 bps resulting from momentum and 62 bps from the value factor. For the USD- and EUR-based portfolios, the active returns against the benchmark are 40 bps and 34 bps, respectively. We note however, that in absolute terms the difference in performance between the portfolios depends on the base currencies that they are denominated in.

It is worth noting the large FX residual impacts for the benchmark. These are the residuals or unexplained movements in the benchmark portfolio that might result from changes in currency volatility — which is not captured in this model — and the large number of securities in the benchmark. Indeed, the impact of currency volatility results in −7 bps of unexplained returns for both USD and GBP.

12.2.2 *Emerging markets hard currency bond portfolio case study*

We now investigate the portfolio return attribution of an emerging market bond portfolio, separating yield curve-based effects and showing the currency effects. For this purpose, an example portfolio comprising US dollar-denominated bonds is investigated. We use an emerging market hard currency bond portfolio comprising 14 countries and 60 individual US-dollar-denominated bonds. To provide insights as to how emerging market hard currency portfolios work, we use different portfolio base currencies — U.S. dollar, euro, Canadian dollar, Australian dollar, Japanese yen, Swiss franc, and British pound.

Note the first major difference between the local currency portfolio and the emerging market hard currency portfolio, which lies in the currency exposure. Compared to the global bond portfolio in the local currency case study, in which the currency risk exposure is heterogeneous (AUD, GBP, ZAR, KRW, JPY, USD, and EUR among others), the emerging market portfolio exposure has only one currency exposure (USD). However, the base currency of the portfolio is different, which results in different currency risks — AUD, GBP, USD, EUR, CHF, JPY, and GBP. For emerging market bonds, a currency curve represents a country spot curve in a hard currency. Thus, all yield curves are country specific, but the bond currency denomination is the US dollar instead of the local currency.

In Table 12.6, several Nelson-Siegel parameters are shown and in Figure 12.8 we plot the corresponding spot curves.

Table 12.6: Nelson-Siegel Spot Curve Parameters for Selected Countries from the J.P. Morgan EMBI + Index

Curve *t*=0	**Beta 0**	**Beta 1**	**Beta 2**	**Tau**	**Curve *t*=1**	**Beta 0**	**Beta 1**	**Beta 2**	**Tau**
CHILE	0.043	0.009	−0.097	1.946	CHILE	0.042	0.005	−0.096	1.942
CHINA	0.034	0.015	−0.091	1.594	CHINA	0.031	0.039	−0.125	1.131
HUNGARY	0.043	−0.018	−0.075	3.060	HUNGARY	0.045	−0.024	−0.071	3.061
INDONESIA	0.048	0.007	−0.130	1.468	INDONESIA	0.045	0.001	−0.116	1.548
MALAYSIA	0.059	−0.053	−0.007	16.469	MALAYSIA	0.056	−0.051	−0.007	16.287
MEXICO	0.063	−0.053	−0.010	5.329	MEXICO	0.073	−0.032	−0.048	3.893
PARAGUAY	0.054	−0.010	−0.106	2.106	PARAGUAY	0.054	0.001	−0.128	1.968
PERU	0.045	0.056	−0.189	1.527	PERU	0.047	0.011	−0.130	1.940
QATAR	0.038	0.003	−0.103	1.647	QATAR	0.036	0.003	−0.097	1.622
ROMANIA	0.054	−0.017	−0.110	2.240	ROMANIA	0.049	0.000	−0.119	2.075
RUSSIA	0.032	−0.003	0.034	0.336	RUSSIA	0.032	−0.003	0.034	0.336
SAUDI ARABIA	0.045	−0.034	−0.053	2.793	SAUDI ARABIA	0.042	−0.028	−0.060	2.174
SOUTH AFRICA	0.066	−0.043	0.066	9.509	SOUTH AFRICA	0.078	−0.078	0.000	3.728
UNITED ARAB EMIRATES	0.042	0.110	−0.224	1.220	UNITED ARAB EMIRATES	0.041	0.092	−0.208	1.257

Note: Authors' own estimates. Data obtained from Bloomberg, LLC.

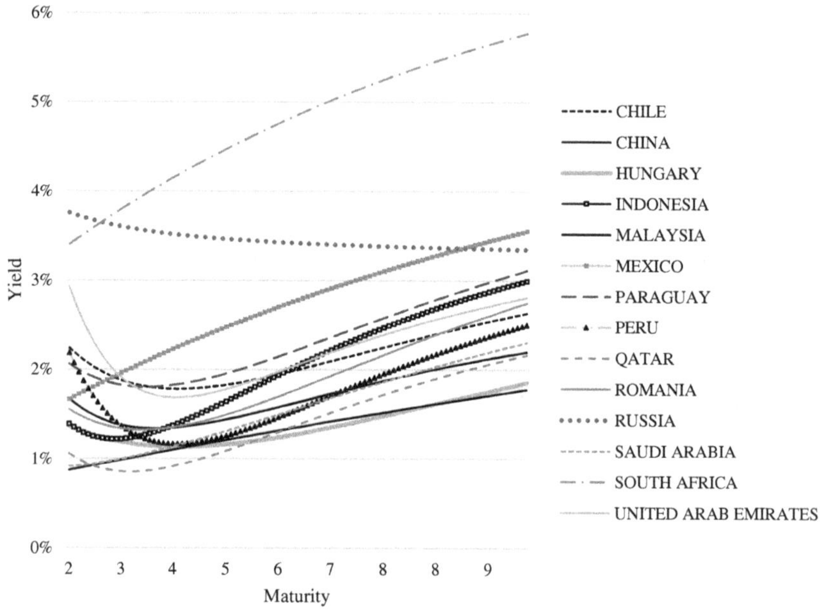

Figure 12.8: Selected Hard Currency (USD) Spot Curves

Note: Authors' own estimates. Data obtained from Bloomberg, LLC.

Because we are illustrating an actively managed portfolio, we also show attribution results for the portfolio and benchmark.[4] The portfolio has an overall neutral duration to the benchmark, which is 7.5. The portfolio also has a neutral maturity bucket allocation relative to the benchmark index. While the results are not shown here, the deviations between portfolio and benchmark are based on the country allocations and rating allocation. Figure 12.9 captures the portfolio country weights.

Splitting the separate attribution effects shows us the different return components for each portfolio. Specifically, it provides information regarding how the bond manager utilized yield curve management relative to the benchmark. Visual inspection of Figure 12.10 shows that the

[4] We note that there is generally a contrast between managed portfolios and benchmarks in terms of the number of holdings in each. Thus, while the J.P. Morgan EMBI+ Index comprises 800+ bonds, our hypothetical portfolio comprises 60 bonds.

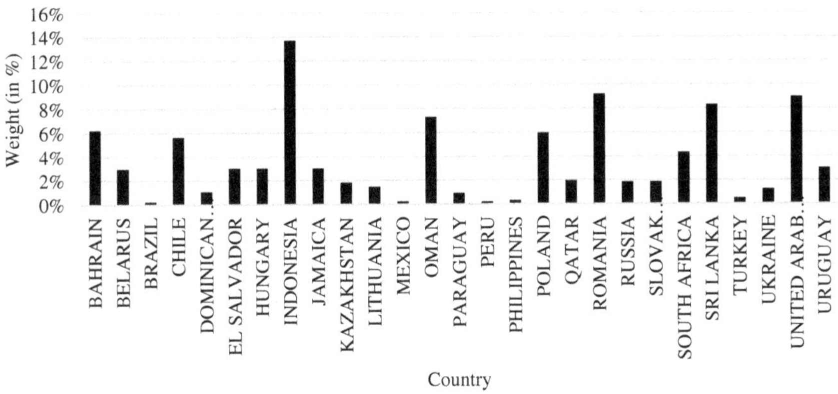

Figure 12.9: Emerging Markets Hard Currency Portfolio Country Allocation

portfolio manager achieved roll down returns of 26 bps compared to the benchmark, which produced 9 bps of roll return. The parallel shift was also advantageous for our hypothetical portfolio, compared to the negative effect in the benchmark, which resulted in 5 bps of outperformance for the portfolio. In fact, the entire yield curve impact generated 206 bps of outperformance. The portfolio manager lost alpha due to spread effects in the amount of 129 bps. In sum, the manager outperformed the benchmark by 107 bps. The bond returns in this example are hard currency returns. Specifically, the denomination in US dollar is equal for the portfolio and for the benchmark.

The results in the "Attribution in Base Currency" column in Table 12.7 show that the portfolio return in euro (EUR) drops to 2.07% due to a negative currency effect of −2.03%. In our Australian portfolio, the benchmark is denominated in US dollars and its return is 2.99%, but if the portfolio is unhedged in AUD, the performance in hard currency terms of 4.06% shrinks to −0.10% and in this case with a negative currency exposure of 4.30%. Similar cases of negative currency results occur in all other examples for the base currency. To better understand the results, we also compute the benchmark returns in the corresponding base currencies.

The most important point here is that in absolute terms, the fund performance differences are primarily due to unhedged currency effects. And the practical takeaway is that currency hedging may be more important when managing hard currency debt versus debt denominated in local currencies.

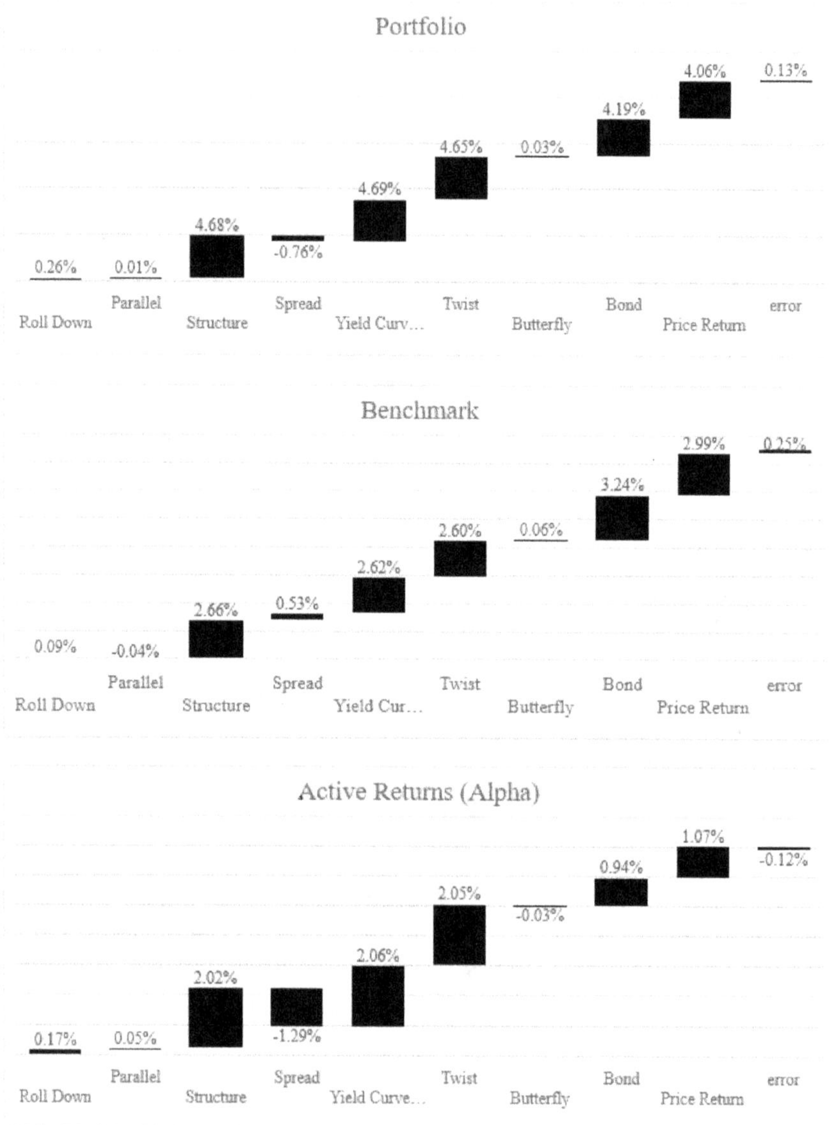

	Roll Down (%)	Parallel (%)	Structure (%)	Spread (%)	Yield Curve Impact (%)	Twist (%)	Butterfly (%)	Bond (%)	Price Return (%)	Error (%)
Portfolio	0.26	0.01	4.68	−0.76	4.69	4.65	0.03	4.19	4.06	0.13
Benchmark	0.09	−0.04	2.66	0.53	2.62	2.60	0.06	3.24	2.99	0.25
Active	0.17	0.05	2.02	−1.29	2.06	2.05	−0.03	0.94	1.07	−0.12

Figure 12.10: Yield Curve Attribution: Portfolio, Benchmark, and Active Management

Notes: Authors' own estimates. Data obtained by the authors from Bloomberg, LLC.

Table 12.7: Effects of Currency Hedging

Base	Total (%)	Attribution Returns (%)	Market Returns (%)	Attribution in Base Currency (%)	FX Effect (%)	Resid (%)
Portfolio						
USD	4.06	4.19	4.06	4.19	0.00	0.13
EUR	1.95	4.19	4.06	2.07	–2.03	0.13
JPY	3.78	4.19	4.06	3.90	–0.27	0.13
CAD	1.64	4.19	4.06	1.77	–2.32	0.13
GBP	1.12	4.19	4.06	1.24	–2.83	0.13
CHF	3.38	4.19	4.06	3.50	–0.66	0.13
AUD	–0.22	4.19	4.06	–0.10	–4.11	0.13
Benchmark						
USD	3.03	3.28	3.03	3.28	0.00	0.25
EUR	0.84	3.28	3.03	1.08	–2.12	0.25
JPY	2.73	3.28	3.03	2.98	–0.29	0.25
CAD	0.52	3.28	3.03	0.77	–2.43	0.25
GBP	–0.02	3.28	3.03	0.22	–2.96	0.25
CHF	2.32	3.28	3.03	2.57	–0.69	0.25
AUD	–1.40	3.28	3.03	–1.16	–4.30	0.25
Active						
USD	1.03	0.91	1.03	0.91	0.00	–0.12
EUR	1.11	0.91	1.03	0.99	0.10	–0.12
JPY	1.04	0.91	1.03	0.92	0.01	–0.12
CAD	1.12	0.91	1.03	1.00	0.11	–0.12
GBP	1.14	0.91	1.03	1.02	0.13	–0.12
CHF	1.06	0.91	1.03	0.94	0.03	–0.12
AUD	1.19	0.91	1.03	1.07	0.19	–0.12

Notes: Authors' own estimates. Data obtained from Bloomberg, LLC.

12.3 Key Takeaways

- Performance attribution is critical for every type of investment management style — both discretionary and systematic — and is important for both portfolio managers and investors. A yield curve-based attribution model allows information to be gained regarding different yield curve dynamics in the underlying currency exposures and different interest-rate regimes.
- The yield curve-based approach to return attribution helps reveal one of the most important dimensions of managing global multi-currency or hard currency bond portfolios, which is the consideration of currency and interest-rate effects together. The yield curve-based return factors include roll down, parallel, structure, spread, and coupon factors. The structure factor can be further decomposed into twist and butterfly factors. Specifically, the return decomposition shows that local currency bond effects are equal for all investors holding the same portfolio, but the base currency of the funds causes the differentiation in their returns.
- The currency factors are decomposed into currency carry, value, and momentum factors. To show the separate currency effects as a total sum, it is necessary to determine the single bond currency impact using bond price effects and multiplying them by the portfolio weights. Measuring the effects in local currency in every sector, country, or asset class allows identification of the sources of return which result from a portfolio's positioning in different yield curves.

References

Baek, S., K. Y. Lee, and M. Glambosky. 2019. "Dynamic Risk Factors in Carry Trades". *Journal of Fixed Income* 29(1): 55–75.

Brinson, G. P., L. R. Hood, and G. L. Beebower. 1986. "Determinants of Portfolio Performance". *Financial Analysts Journal* 42(4): 39–44.

Brinson, G. P., B. D. Singer, and G. L. Beebower. 1991. "Determinants of Portfolio Performance II: An Update". *Financial Analysts Journal* 47(3): 40–48.

Campisi, S. 2000. "Primer on Fixed Income Performance Attribution". *Journal of Performance Measurement* 4(4): 14–25.

Colin, A. M. 2005. *Fixed Income Attribution*. Hoboken, NJ: John Wiley & Sons.

Colin, A. M., M. Cubilie, and F. Bardoux. 2006. "A New Approach to the Decomposition of Yield Curve Movements for Fixed Income Attribution". *Journal of Performance Measurement* 10(4): 18–28.

Dai, T. and M. Elliot. 2014/2015. "Fixed Income Attribution with Carry Effect". *Journal of Performance Measurement* 19(2): 7–18.

Fischer, B. and R. Wermers. 2013. *Performance Evaluation and Attribution of Security Portfolios*. Oxford, UK: AP Elsevier.

Kazemi, H., Black, K. H., and R. D. Chambers. 2016. *Alternative Investments: CAIA Level II*. 3rd Edition, Hoboken New Jersey: John Wiley & Sons.

Litterman, R. and J. Scheinkman. 1991. "Common Factors Affecting Bond Returns". *Journal of Fixed Income* 1(1): 54–61.

Lord, T. J. 1997. "The Attribution of Portfolio and Index Returns in Fixed Income". *Journal of Performance Measurement* 2(1): 45–57.

Konstantinov, G. S. 2016. "Capturing Short-term and Long-term Alpha of Global Bond Portfolios: Evidence from EUR-Investors' Perspective". *Financial Markets and Portfolio Management* 30(3): 337–365.

Konstantinov, G. S. 2022. "Emerging Market Bonds: Expected Returns and Currency Impact". *Journal of Portfolio Management* 48(8): 139–158.

McLaren, A. 2001. "A Geometric Methodology for Performance Attribution". *Journal of Performance Measurement* 6(4): 59–79.

McLaren, A. 2002. "A Framework for Multiple Currency Fixed Income Attribution". *Journal of Performance Measurement* 6(4): 59–79.

Menchero, J. G. and B. Davis. 2009. "Multi-Currency Performance Attribution". *Journal of Performance Measurement* 14(1): 45–55.

Strange, B. 1998. "Currency Overlay Managers Show Consistency: In the Long Run Count on Them for Adding Value". *Pensions & Investments* 26(12): 26–31.

Van Breukelen, G. 2000. "Fixed Income Attribution". *Journal of Performance Measurement* 4(4): 61–68.

Index

Q

R

www.ingramcontent.com/pod-product-compliance
Lightning Source LLC
LaVergne TN
LVHW011700200926
848484LV00004B/1007
* 9 7 8 9 8 1 1 2 7 2 5 6 1 *